The Jesuits

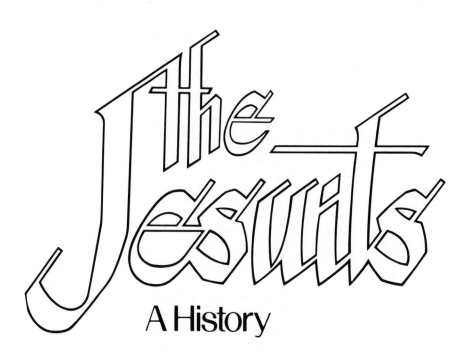

The Jesuits

A History

by David Mitchell

FRANKLIN WATTS
New York/London/Toronto/Sydney
1981

ILLUSTRATIONS
We acknowledge the permission to reproduce
the following pictures: 1, 2, 3, 5, 9, 10, 11, 12,
32: Radio Times Hulton Picture Library; 6, 8,
13, 16, 18: Mary Evans Picture Library; 7, 17,
19, 24, 25, 26, 27, 30, 33: Mansell Collection;
4: British Museum; 31: Popperfoto; 14: from
Description de l'Empire de la Chine (1736) by
J. B. du Halde, SJ; 15: from *China Illustrata*
(1667) by Athanasius Kircher, SJ; 20, 21, 22,
23: from *Societas Jesu Militans* (1675) by
Matthias Tanner, SJ; 28, 29: Philip Caraman,
SJ; 34, 35, 36, 37, 38: Jesuit Yearbook

First published 1980
by Macdonald Futura Publishers
Paulton House
8 Shepherdess Walk
London N1 7LW

For information address the publisher:
Franklin Watts, Inc.
730 Fifth Avenue
New York, New York 10019

Library of Congress Cataloging in Publication Data
Mitchell, David J
The Jesuits, a history.
Bibliography: p.
Includes index.
1. Jesuits—History.   I.   Title.
BX3706.2.M57   1981   271'.53   80-25316

Contents

Acknowledgements

Special thanks are due to Mr Hugh Kay, Jesuit Information Officer at Mount Street, London; Fr C. Byrne, Librarian at Mount Street; Professor Anthony Levi, University of St Andrews, who read and criticized the text; the staffs of the London Library, the Forest Hill Public Library, the Catholic Central Library and the Evangelical Library; Fr Gerald R. Sheahan, USA Regional Assistant to General Pedro Arrupe; Fr Jean-Claude Dietsch of the Jesuit Press and Information Office, Rome; Fr Gino K. Piovesana, Rector of the Pontificium Collegium Russicum; Fr Hans Grünewald, SJ; Fr Henri Chambre, SJ; Fr Florent E. van Ommeslaeghe SJ (Bollandist); Fr Philip Caraman SJ; Fr Robert McCown SJ (Dallas, Texas); Fr Michael Kyne, Vice-Provincial for Formation in the English Province; and Fr Hilary Lawton, Socius to the Provincial Superior in Ireland.

I should also like to thank Desmond Seward; Marina Warner; Peter Hebblethwaite; Professor J. S. Cummins; Professor H. R. Trevor-Roper; George Robinson; Gerald Brenan; Macdonald Hastings; Fr Michael MacGreil SJ; Fr Charles E. O'Neill of the Instituto Storico della Compagnia di Gesù; Fr Robert A. Graham (*Civiltà Cattolica*); Fr Pedro A. Suarez SJ, Santo Domingo, Dominican Republic; Fr Justin M'Loughlin, OFM; Fr Peter Edgar, OP; and Eric Simmons, Father Superior of the Community of Resurrection, Mirfield. All have been patient and helpful in answering queries.

David Mitchell

Introduction

LIKE THE CATHOLIC CHURCH itself, the Society of Jesus is in a state of painful transition. From a peak of 36,038 in 1965 its membership sank to 27,031 in 1978. For long regarded as the pope's janissaries and credited with a monolithic solidarity, Jesuits have in the past twenty years gained a reputation for insubordination and disunity. Pope Paul VI professed to be shocked by this contrast. Yet ever since its foundation in 1540 the Society has been accused, not least by various popes, of arrogance and disobedience. For much of that time it has acted as a kind of loyal opposition within the Church. The graph of its fortunes follows the rise and dip of papal prestige and its history vividly illustrates the Church's crises of authority.

For many people – Catholics among them – Ignatius Loyola, the founder of the Society of Jesus, is one of the least attractive of the major Christian saints. They can admire the courage of Jesuit missionaries, but are repelled by the political or 'court' Jesuits of Europe. Accommodation to 'noble' savages or to cultured Chinese seems acceptable, accommodation to 'dirty' European power politics does not.

After more than four centuries there is still a tendency to regard the Jesuits as upstarts compared with more ancient orders, perhaps a tribute to Benedictine, Franciscan and Dominican propaganda. Yet all four orders have survived only by strenuous compromise and repeated adaptation. Though the baroque style was not a Jesuit invention, the Society's thorough exploitation of its possibilities laid it open to a charge of bad taste. 'Those mass-producers of spirituality, the Jesuits, perfected a simple technique for the fabrication of orthodox ecstasies,' wrote Aldous Huxley in an essay, *Meditation on El Greco* (1931). 'They had cheapened an experience hitherto accessible only to the spiritually wealthy . . . "St Teresa for All", "A St John of the Cross in Every Home", might have been their slogans. Was it to be wondered at if their sublimities were a trifle theatrical, their tendernesses treacly, their spiritual intuitions rather commonplace and vulgar?'

Just as Jesuit adaptability and Catholic art irritate the puritan and the

[7]

purist, so Jesuit concentration on administrative detail, including a system of 'internal espionage', rouses suspicion in a generation heavily alerted to techniques of dehumanization. But Ignatius (SPN or Sanctus Pater Noster to his subjects) realized that in an age of sharpening nationalism and centralizing government the survival of the Church – by the time his Company got into its stride very much the *Roman* Catholic Church thanks to the inroads of Luther and Calvin – required a disciplined, tightly-knit *corps d'élite* to match the political machines controlled by such Machiavellian operators as Thomas Cromwell and the Cecils. He knew that the Jesuits would meet jealous opposition and misrepresentation on both sides of the politico-theological divide. He also sensed that turbulence was their element and *raison d'être*, warning his disciples that 'no storm is so insidious as a perfect calm, no enemy so dangerous as the absence of all enemies.'

Launched in a state of siege, the Society has thrived upon tension and political turmoil. In the 1950s Peter Lippert, a German Jesuit, wrote that 'round it there was always a loneliness, the loneliness of a gathering storm'. The excitement of playing a lone hand even within the Catholic world helps to account for the cloak-and-dagger attraction of this most controversial and mythologized of Christian orders. In its heyday in the late sixteenth century it had a fascination for brilliant, idealistic adventurers like Robert Parsons, Edmund Campion, Robert Southwell, John Gerard, similar to that of the Communist Party in the 1930s. In 1614 the Annual Letter of the English Jesuits (the Society's insistence upon frequent, detailed reports has made it the most densely documented religious congregation) reported with pride on 'the slanders and abuse by which the heretics seek to make the very name Jesuit a bug-bear . . . We are called the Pope's janissaries; the favourite brood of anti-Christ . . . They say that hell has sent us forth fully equipped with learning and other gifts in order to prop up the Papacy, now tottering to its fall.'

In fact for nearly two and a half centuries, from 1540 to their suppression by Pope Clement XIV in 1773, there was hardly a section of society, lay or ecclesiastical, which was not at one time or another after the blood of the Jesuits. The 'Black Popes' (Jesuit generals) had been accused of arranging the assassination or attempted assassination of William of Orange in 1584, Henry III and Henry IV of France in 1589 and 1610, and Elizabeth I of England, and of hastening the deaths of a number of refractory 'White' popes. They were also accused of implication in the Gunpowder Plot of 5 November 1605, and most European governments had at some point decreed their expulsion.

Such a record argues unusual resilience and a perennial utility, often attributed to an unscrupulous adjustment to the ways of the world. In one of Walter Savage Landor's *Imaginary Conversations* (written over the period 1824 to 1853) Fr Lachaise, Louis XIV's Jesuit confessor, exonerates the King for condoning atrocities in the war against Dutch heretics, but reproves him for taking the sacrament after eating a mince-pie. Penance is prescribed in the form of scattering a handful of ashes on the royal peruke and curtailing the royal menu ('Six dishes alone shall come upon the table; and although fasting does not extend to wines or liqueurs, I order that three kinds of wine only be presented and three of liqueur. Oysters? Those come in barrels . . . Your Majesty must either eat them raw from the barrel or dressed in scallop, or both; but beware, I say, of dishing this article, as your soul shall answer for it at the last day').

Thomas Carlyle considered the 'Gospel of Loyola', with its alleged equivocations and mental reservations, 'the most fatal of all time'. In *Britons, Guard Your Own* (1852), a denunciation of the alliance between Napoleon III and the papacy, Alfred Lord Tennyson wrote:

Rome's dearest daughter now is captive France
The Jesuit laughs and reckoning on his chance
Would unrelenting
Kill all dissenting
Till we were left to fight for truth alone . . .

In *Westward Ho!* Charles Kingsley calls the Society of Jesus 'the Upas-shadow which has blighted the whole Romish Church', and when Eustace Leigh, having betrayed his countrymen to the Inquisition in New Spain, enters the Society he is 'a man no longer . . . a thing, a tool, a Jesuit.'

One of the most remarkable attacks came from Goldsworthy Lowes Dickinson, a usually mild and peaceable academic who was a harbinger of the Bloomsbury Group. For him ecclesiasticism was the main enemy of intellectual progress, striving as it did 'not merely to create an atmosphere but to paralyse beforehand the agency by which that atmosphere might be disturbed'. Its aim was petrifaction and its most perfect expression 'the discipline devised for the propagation of his Order by one who was, perhaps, the greatest ecclesiastical genius the world has ever known: I mean the founder of the Society of Jesus.' Loyola's *Spiritual Exercises,* probably the most famous and effective of all

Christian training manuals, was, thought Lowes Dickinson, cleverly designed to hallucinate the personality into submission. After that the Jesuit could 'develop' within rigidly defined limits, could 'devise means but not consider ends'. A Jesuit should be up-to-date in his knowledge of the arts and sciences, but only 'in order to meet the enemy on his own ground . . . Once for all he has been cured of the possibility of asking "Why?" His reason has not been killed. No! It has been chained to the car of Faith; and in the car rides theology triumphant, surrounded by the Saints of the Order, and crushing under the wheels the heretic, the speculator, and the unbeliever.'

In his vehemence, Lowes Dickinson came close to the wilder fantasies of the Protestant Evangelicals whom he found equally abhorrent. *A Glimpse of the Great Secret Society* (1872), for instance, had pictured Jesuitism as 'the very masterpiece of Popery . . . priestcraft so artfully regulated as to hide its work, caring for nothing but success'; suggested that 'Jesuit influence' was 'behind the discontinuation of the service for the 5th of November attached to the Book of Common Prayer'; and alleged that the Franco-German War of 1870 had been engineered by Jesuits 'to excite the idea that Providence had interposed in favour of the new dogma' (Papal Infallibility), thus 'distracting the minds of men from a critical consideration of their proceedings and overpowering the noble freedom of German thought.'*

Quite as fantastic is the theory, first advanced early in the seventeenth century, that the real inspiration for the Society of Jesus was Muslim. In 1849 Isaac Taylor compared the technique and imagery of the *Spiritual Exercises* with those of the Koran, rather as other writers have surmised that St John of the Cross – a Jesuit pupil – was influenced by the manuals of Muslim mystics. 'Loyola endeavours to work upon the five senses, or upon the mind's power of repeating their impressions,' observed Taylor, 'but Mahomet has done this in a far more effectual style.' In *The Jesuits* (1938) F. A. Ridley argued that Ignatius, born in a country which had been fighting Islam for eight centuries, would have known of the fanatical sect of the Assassins, celebrated for its cult of absolute obedience; and that the Society of Jesus was in essence 'an order of Christian dervishes . . . St Peter allied with Mohammed to defeat Luther and Calvin'. He also suggests that 'with the entry of the Jesuits upon the stage of history a new science was born: the science of counter-

---

*In *The Foundations of Christianity* the German Marxist Karl Kautsky described Jesuit culture as 'humanism at a lower mental level, robbed of its spiritual independence, rigidly organised, and pressed into the service of the Church'. Rather like Marxist humanism?

revolution . . . It was not until our own century that Lenin adopted the essential Jesuit principles of super-centralization and the corps of professional revolutionaries. And no revolutionary movement has ever remotely approached, let alone equalled, the marvellous Jesuit organization.'

In *The Decline of the West* (1918) Oswald Spengler selects Ignatius as the chief architect of 'Faustian-Baroque Christianity' and asserts that the style of the Counter-Reformation was 'definitely fixed by the Spaniard Loyola and the Council of Trent which he spiritually dominated'. Nor have liberal progressives always felt hostile towards the Society. Aldous Huxley considered that on balance it was a good thing that the 'lax' Jesuits, with their belief in human perfectibility, defeated the high-puritan Jansenists with their bleak insistence on the total depravity of man. In his *Short History of the World* (1933) H. G. Wells praised the Society's 'attempt to bring the generous and chivalrous traditions of military discipline into the service of religion . . . It became one of the greatest teaching and missionary societies the world has ever seen. It carried Christianity to India, China, and America. It raised the standard of education throughout the Catholic world . . . and quickened the Catholic conscience everywhere. It stimulated Protestant Europe to competitive educational efforts. The vigorous Roman Catholic Church we know today is largely the product of this Jesuit revival.'

Writing in 1840 the Whig historian Lord Macaulay, though insisting that 'the North owes its great civilisation and prosperity chiefly to the moral effects of the Protestant Reformation' and that 'the decay of the southern countries of Europe is to be mainly ascribed to the Catholic revival', did not hide his romantic admiration for Jesuit enterprise. 'The history of the Order of Jesus,' he wrote, 'is the history of the Catholic reaction. That order possessed itself at once of the strongholds which command the public mind, of the pulpit, of the confessional, of the academies . . . Literature and science, lately associated with infidelity or heresy, now became the allies of orthodoxy . . . The truly devout listened to the high and saintly morality of the Jesuit. The gay cavalier who had run his rival through the body, the frail beauty who had forgotten her marriage vow, found in the Jesuit an easy well-bred man of the world who knew how to make allowances for the little irregularities of people of fashion. The confessor was strict or lax according to the temper of the penitent. The first object was to drive no person out of the pale of the Church . . . If a person was so unfortunate as to be a bravo, a libertine, or a gambler, that was no reason to make him a heretic too.'

Then how spectacularly successful the Jesuit-led counter-attack had been. 'Fifty years after the Lutheran separation,' says Macaulay, 'Catholicism could scarcely maintain itself on the shores of the Mediterranean. A hundred years after the separation, Protestantism could scarcely maintain itself on the shores of the Baltic.' Jesuit exploits outside Europe were equally astonishing. 'They were to be found in the depths of the Peruvian mines, at the marts of the African slave-caravans, on the shores of the Spice Islands, in the observatories of China. They made converts in regions which neither avarice nor curiosity had tempted any of their countrymen to enter; and preached and disputed in tongues of which no other native of the West understood a word.'

Despite rhetorical exaggeration, Macaulay's summary of the heroic period of the Society (approximately from 1540 to 1640) contains more than a grain of truth, as does the recent verdict of a Benedictine historian, Dom David Knowles – 'perhaps the greatest single religious impulse since the preaching of the apostles.' The long-odds gamble, comparable perhaps with that of the handful of Bolshevik revolutionists in 1917, had come off. The story is one of history's more exciting ideological thrillers. Unfurling it, one begins to understand why the Jesuits were credited with demonic powers such as were attributed to the Jews in the *Protocols of the Elders of Zion*, an anti-Semitic tract published in Russia in 1905, purporting to describe a conspiracy by the Jewish 'secret government' to achieve world domination.

CHAPTER ONE

Roman Revivals

LENNY BRUCE, the Jewish-American satirist of the 1960s, used to refer to the Catholic Church as 'the only *the* Church'. He knew what he was talking about, having once taken advantage of its renown by posing as a Catholic priest and collecting over $8,000 for a leper colony in British Guiana, half of which he kept for his own pressing needs. Behind that renown stretched centuries of politico-theological conflict during which the shape of the orthodox faith and the limits of papal power had been defined.

From the first century A.D. onwards egalitarian zealots had been bitterly opposed to centralization and the growth of a hierarchy which, in H.L. Mencken's words, affected and exploited 'a rank superior to that attained by Christ'. For this reason among others Ignatius Loyola insisted that no member of the Society (or Company) of Jesus should, unless forced by the pope, accept preferment. Jesuits were to be content with their own internal hierarchy, servants of the man who styled himself 'servant of the servants of God'. Despite formal disclaimers this did not mean that the Society, any more than the various Roman *corps d'élite* which had preceded it, could keep clear of politics. It simply meant that political influence was to be acquired and used as discreetly as possible. This was the grey eminence technique employed *Ad Majorem Dei Gloriam* (to the greater glory of God), a phrase which, by dint of sheer repetition, Ignatius made his, and his Company's, own.

Whether as a sometimes tolerated, sometimes persecuted sect or, from early in the fourth century (at the Emperor Constantine's decree) as the official religion of the Roman Empire, Christianity had been heavily involved in politics. Eusebius, a Christian chronicler of the time, was so excited by this momentous change that he wrote as if the Kingdom of God had come on earth. Armed with authority, the Church prepared to smite its enemies, and as the Roman Empire crumbled in the West Christian leaders looked to achieve quasi-imperial status. Eleven centuries before Ignatius Loyola, in his 'Rules for Thinking with the Church', insisted that 'we should put away completely our own opinion . . . To arrive at complete certainty I will believe that the white object that I see is black if that should be the decision of the hierarchical Church', St Augustine, Bishop of Hippo, declared: 'I would not even believe the Gospel if the Catholic Church did not urge me to do so.' The greater the ambition and the responsibility, the greater the need for dogma and discipline.

The gap between clergy and laity, once non-existent, widened inexorably with the expansion, professionalization and politicization of the Church. St Augustine had placed the foundations of the City of God firmly in this world, and since the Emperor had made Constantinople his capital and personal monument, the bishops of Rome, escaping the servile destiny of the Byzantine patriarchs, proceeded to enlarge their powers by a mixture of courage, cunning and fraud. The glorification of St Peter as the Prince of the Apostles and of the bishops of Rome as his only true successors was the first shot in a rivalry which led to the ecclesiastical split forbidden by Constantine. Division deepened as missionaries from the two main Christian centres clashed over the boundaries of their jurisdiction: Byzantine evangelists took the Greek 'Orthodox' (according to Rome the 'Greek schismatic') faith to Russia and penetrated westward into the Slav lands. Theological differences over the doctrine of the Trinity and the manhood/divinity of Christ soon developed; any lingering hope of unification was destroyed by the sack of Constantinople during the fourth Crusade (1204) and by the sack of Alexandria in 1365.

These murderous forays were largely responsible for the final collapse of the eastern Empire and the fall of Constantinople to the Turks in 1453. They also fixed a gulf between the Catholic and Orthodox Churches almost as wide as that between Christians and Muslims. The loss of such a huge fragment of Christendom never ceased to rankle. For several decades from the middle of the thirteenth century the papacy negotiated with Genghiz Khan and his successors at the Mongol court, hoping to convert the rulers and so strike a blow both at Islam and the Orthodox Church. Franciscan and Dominican envoys found the Khans tolerant of all sects, Buddhist, Taoist, Muslim, Jewish or Christian, fond of presiding over theological debates, but disinclined to commit themselves to any single creed. After the collapse of the Mongol empire it was left to the Jesuits, at the courts of Mogul and Ming emperors, Japanese shoguns, Russian tsars, and later Bolshevik commissars, to revive Christian missionary enterprise in Asia and renew the attempt to oust the Orthodox Church.

Palace politics, not least the favour or conversion of empresses, had helped Christianity on its way to political influence. The rapid sophistication of the faith and the manoeuvres of courtier-bureaucrat priests angered rigorist Christians; but by the eighth century, after forging the so-called 'Donation of Constantine', the papacy claimed to have been given control of all the western provinces of the empire. Thus the idea of the Holy Roman Empire was conceived; and the rulers of the Catholicized Franks, first Pepin then Charlemagne (who in 800 was crowned Holy Roman Emperor by Leo III), gave it a certain political reality. Charlemagne not only protected the papacy from Italian enemies, but forcibly settled the boundary dispute with Byzantium and launched the popes on their long, stormy and devious course as king- and emperor-makers, notwithstanding the violence and intrigue inseparable from the election of the pontiffs and the brevity and insecurity of their tenure. By the end of the eighth century there had been ten anti-popes or rival pontiffs. By the end of the fifteenth century there had been twenty-three more.

Papal pretensions reached a climax with Innocent III (1198-1216), a lawyer-pope who asserted the jurisdiction of the Vicar of Christ over all temporal rulers ('by me kings reign and princes decree justice'), placed England and France under interdict, bullied the kings of England, Aragon and Portugal into 'surrendering' their realms as fiefs held of the Holy See, organized the terrible crusades against the Albigensian heresy in southern France, and used every political and spiritual weapon at his command in a deadly struggle with the Emperor Frederick II. But the limitations of papal sovereignty were dramatically demonstrated when Edward I of England and Philip IV of France called the bluff of Pope Boniface VIII. In two celebrated bulls, *Clericos laicos* (1296) and *Unam Sanctam* (1300) he renewed the assault on what he called 'the spirit of hostility shown by laymen towards the clergy'. The first forbade clerics (men in holy orders) to pay taxes to the state and threatened tax collectors with excommunication. The second asserted the pope's divine right to judge and use the temporal authority and stated that 'it is altogether necessary to salvation for every human creature to be subject to the Roman pontiff'. Edward I ordered the seizure of Church property, Philip publicly burned the bulls and banned the export of currency. When Boniface uttered further threats Philip, with the backing of the Estates-General, accused him of illegal election, immorality, heresy and simony. Arrested and imprisoned by a gang of Roman malcontents led by a French agent, the Pope died soon after his release

[15]

in 1303. Two years later the papal curia moved from the tumult of Rome to Avignon, under French protection. After the 'Babylonian captivity' of 1305-77, when there were seven French puppet-popes, came the 'Great Schism' of 1378-1417 during which a sequence of four popes and anti-popes, backed by Italian or French factions, disputed the tiara. This was followed by the conciliar movement of the fifteenth century. Launched from France in the hope of reforming the Church, it proposed to subject the popes to a permanent system of international control.

The fantasy of papal overlordship (identified with the concept of Christendom), though not abandoned in theory until 1870, when it was replaced by the vague dogma of papal 'infallibility', had been exposed for what it was; and the dissolution in 1312, by papal decree under French royal pressure, of the Order of Knights Templars – a *cause célèbre* often compared with the suppression of the Society of Jesus in 1773 – underlined the weakness of the papacy and its inability to protect its servants, especially when they had become plunder-worthy. Founded in the twelfth century for military service in the Holy Land the Templars, like the Jesuits, grew into an international organization with enormous property holdings, its own diplomatic network and an efficient banking system. As with the Jesuits, their papal privileges, including exemption from episcopal control, angered the secular clergy and their independence was seen as a threat to Church and State. Like the Jesuits they were accused of every heresy and perversion their opponents could think of. There were tales of secret rituals at which candidates had to make a triple denial of Christ and spit on a crucifix in token of absolute obedience to their superiors; and the order was said to be a crypto-Islamic state-within-the-state, corrupted by its dealings with the infidels.

The ever-mounting expenses of the papal court and of the great bishoprics made fund-raising a prime consideration, and the laity was unmercifully and cynically milked, the concept of purgatory being exploited to the hilt. Soul masses, chantry priests, the endowment of abbeys and priories, indulgences plenary or limited, all could shorten a sinner's term. Sin became a profitable business as casuistry of the sort widely believed to have been invented by the Jesuits found reasons for commuting penances into payments in cash or in kind. Churches and chapels were sometimes little more than repositories for relics, most of them fakes. Auricular confession, made compulsory by the Lateran Council of 1215, was another useful lever; and all these developments favoured the rich. As a Spanish proverb put it: 'Don Dinero es muy Catolico.' (Money is very Catholic.)

Inevitably the popes were involved in a struggle for survival not only with rebellious royal clients but with the great mass of the poor, including hordes of ignorant parish priests barely distinguishable from their peasant flocks. The papal intelligence network, however, was the best available, and lay authorities, whatever their quarrel with Rome, were willing enough to act as the 'secular arm' when 'heresy' seemed to threaten social revolution. Waldensians, Lollards, Humiliati and the Gnostic Cathars (or Albigenses) were part of a vast movement of unofficial reform. Confident that their revivalist or variant Christianity would triumph they went cheerfully to their deaths. The first batch was burned at Orleans in 1022. In the Albigensian crusades of the early thirteenth century they were slaughtered in tens of thousands and papal victory was followed by the establishment of the Holy Roman Inquisition. 'Action,' said Innocent III, 'ranks higher than contemplation.' This sentiment, though without the slaughterhouse implications, was to become Loyola's battle cry.

The mendicant orders, Franciscans and Dominicans (known as friars), were, apart from a continual effort to pack people off on 'crusades' where they could turn their fury against Jews or Muslims rather than against the Church, the papacy's main weapons in the struggle with these counter-Churches. From the second century onward Christian hermits had fled to the desert as much from the worldliness and corruption of the Church as from Roman persecution. But by the sixth century St Benedict had completed the gradual process of collectivizing the monastic urge, giving it a detailed Rule and harnessing it to the Church. As agriculturists, scholars, scribes and medical practitioners the Benedictines, whose monasteries spread all over western Europe, performed prodigies of civilization: but they, and the monks of the Cluniac and Cistercian reforms of the eleventh and twelfth centuries, gradually drifted away from the original spirit of strict separation from the world. Only the Carthusians, founded by St Bruno in 1086, remained faithful to this tradition.

Individual sanctification remained the objective, poverty, obedience and chastity the triple tie. But as landlords and farmers the old orders became very much part of the lay scene, with retinues of servants and illiterate lay brothers to do the manual chores. The monks, who looked down upon the secular clergy with increasingly aristocratic scorn, spent their time at study or in choir, where chant and ritual became almost a full-time occupation. Though a St Bernard of Clairvaux might preach inflammatory crusade sermons there was in general little sense of mission. Monasteries tended to be in the remoter countryside far from the expanding and turbulent towns which were the new centres of intellectual and commercial vitality. Innocent III's recognition of the friars' movement was, like Paul III's approval of the Society of Jesus more than three centuries later, a last resort in a Reformation crisis. The hope was that the Franciscans would outvie the heretics in apostolic poverty and Christian idealism and that the Dominicans, fiercely orthodox but eager to take their message to the vulnerable, benighted masses, would find the popular touch.

Francis of Assisi regarded poverty as the root of true Christianity: no houses, no cloister, no books (he loathed theologians), no possessions (including holy orders and papal privileges), no power but that of the Holy Spirit. He accepted the need for papal recognition and for a Rule, if only to protect his followers from confusion with the 'heretics' – many of whom flocked to join his movement for that very reason. In his own lifetime Francis who, with his closest disciples, was suspected of heresy, saw the movement turned into an Order which laid minimal stress on poverty and itinerant preaching. By the end of the thirteenth century there were more than 1,500 Franciscan houses and a bitter duel had developed between 'Conventuals' and 'Spirituals'. As the Jesuits were to discover, rapid expansion and institutionalization brought problems while the many demands made upon these new champions of the faith caused a specialization far removed from the purposes of the founder. Like the great Dominicans Albertus Magnus and Thomas Aquinas, Franciscan intellectuals such as Roger Bacon and Arnold of Villanova settled in universities surrounded by books, seeking to reconcile faith and reason, Catholicizing the pagan philosophers.

The friars, but particularly the Dominicans, were soon part of the ecclesiastical machine: as prelates – in England, for instance, there were about fifty Dominican bishops between 1350 and 1535 – and as inquisitors. Unlike Francis, the Castilian Dominic had been trained for the Church and was a cathedral dignitary. Sent in 1206 to Provence as a missionary to the Albigensians, he realized that no impact would be made unless the intelligence and austerity of the heretic priests could be matched. To meet this emergency he trained a body of intellectual shock-troops and in so doing provided what, with a carefully controlled element of Franciscan ecstasy, became virtually a blueprint for the Society of Jesus. The Order of Preachers was the Catholic Truth Society of its time, a hit squad ready to go wherever the need seemed most urgent. Each Dominican community contained a professor of theology, study was paramount, choir duty cut to a minimum, manual labour eschewed, tactics fitted to circumstances. The Cathars believed that Satan ruled the world, that the Cross was the symbol of his victory over Christ, and that the Church of Rome was the Synagogue of Satan. Deeply embedded in Dominican-Inquisitional psychology, this Manichean dualism was at the core of siege Catholicism. So was its corollary that the end justifies the means: a deduction commonly attributed to the Jesuits, who in fact only multiplied the means.

Not without misgivings the Franciscans and Dominicans undertook the direction of nuns, while 'Third Orders' designed to encourage and channel lay fervour organized large numbers of 'tertiaries' of both sexes who sought to live the monastic ideal in the world. The Church had acquired a formidable missionary force, but at the expense of loosing upon Europe an army of wandering monks, often of dubious credentials. Before long, as the tales of Boccaccio, Chaucer, Aretino, Massuccio and Bandello (himself a Dominican) amply demonstrate, the word 'monk' became synonymous with greed, trickery and lechery. In popular estimation almost all priests were corrupt, but decadent friars were specially despised and feared, being not only hypocrites but very likely agents of the hated Inquisition. Deservedly or not the Jesuits were to acquire a similar reputation.

The Renaissance popes, notably Leo X whose court buffoons included two monks, privately ridiculed the mendicant orders as peddlers of bogus miracles and relics. Girolamo Savonarola, a reformed and reforming Dominican who seemed to threaten the Borgia Pope Alexander VI, was burned at the stake in 1498. For five years he ruled Florence as Calvin later ruled Geneva. The dramatic processions and public holocausts of objects of vanity – dice, cards, song-books, manuals of magic, novels, false hair, cosmetics – which temporarily restored the Dominicans to popular favour – were the models for Jesuit revivalist campaigns; and his educational programme foreshadowed that of Ignatius Loyola. Science was to be patrolled by a monastic élite. Classical texts were to be carefully selected and edited. All cultural activity was to be directed by pious pedagogues who would indoctrinate rulers with a spirit of militant righteousness.

If more than a small minority of friars had behaved like Savonarola their orders would probably have been disbanded. But for every mendicant firebrand there was a crowd of ingenious fund-raisers, men like the Dominican John Tetzel, who assured their 'customers' that 'so soon as the coin rings in the chest, the soul will go straight to heaven'.

[19]

For some years Luther's revolt was written off as the passing extravagance of an ex-Augustinian monk. Enthusiasm, save for the patronage of the arts and the advancement of family interests, was laughed at in Rome. *Sacro egoismo* was the fashionable cult. Machiavelli hoped that Cesare Borgia, a ruthless Spaniard, might secularize the papal states (something which the Emperor Charles V seriously considered) and even abolish the papacy – the two main causes of foreign intervention and Italian disunity.

Northern Europe, and Germany in particular, was treated like a backward colony whose privilege it was to foot the bill for a higher civilization in which Christianity was hardly more than an allegorical ingredient, a theme for Raphael or Michelangelo to play with. In Italy the Inquisition was dormant. Machiavelli regarded conventional religion as something suitable only for the masses, while popes and princes preferred neo-Platonic allegories to the vulgar asperities of the Bible. Printing presses multiplied editions of the Greek classics; Erasmus's sparkling satires on mechanical religion and monks were best-sellers; occultism was rampant and astrologers much in demand. Rare indeed was the prelate without a mistress, and despite the stern decrees of medieval pontiffs every parish priest felt entitled to a concubine (housekeeper). Clerical celibacy, or rather the lack of it, was perhaps the most important grievance against the Church. Erasmus, the son of a washerwoman and a priest, was one of thousands of clerical bastards for whom the Church offered the only hope of a career. Thus the scandal of hypocrisy and forced vocations was perpetuated and the concept of the priesthood as sacramentally valid whatever the failings of the man was in itself a confession of defeat. Small wonder that Ignatius prescribed a long period of 'formation' during which a Jesuit could be released if he proved unsuitable.

Though Machiavelli looked to Cesare Borgia as a potential saviour, many Italians hated the Borgias as blatant examples of a new and increasing menace – Spanish domination. By 1540, when Pope Paul III approved the Society of Jesus (a decision widely believed to be the result of Spanish pressure), this process was almost complete. More than sixty years of Franco-Spanish rivalry ended with the papal states sandwiched between two areas of Spanish rule, the Kingdom of the Two Sicilies in the south, the Duchy of Milan in the north. And in May 1527 the most drastic of the many sacks of Rome was carried out by the forces of Charles V, Holy Roman Emperor, King of Spain, and Most Catholic Monarch, as punishment for the futile political intrigues of Pope Clement VII.

Churches and convents were rifled, priests slaughtered, nuns beaten and raped, St Peter's and the Vatican Palace used as stables, an aged cardinal paraded through the streets in a coffin, and other prelates, surrounded by drunken troops in priestly vestments, dragged about like slaves. The warnings of Savonarola and other prophets of doom were recalled, the catastrophe seen as divine chastisement for the sins of the Eternal City. The Spanish fury was the most effective spur to long-delayed reform, but no one loves those who pitchfork them into repentance. Ten years later the fierce zeal of the small band of itinerant followers of Loyola, known as *Iñiguistas*, appeared to some Italians as part of an odious sequel, dictated by Spaniards, which included an Index of Prohibited Books, a revival of the Inquisition along Spanish lines, and a general crushing of the spirit of fun, tolerance and religious indifference.

Though said to have regularized his life after ordination to the priesthood in 1519 Paul III, the first 'reformed' pope, was hardly a puritan. Nicknamed 'the petticoat cardinal', Alessandro Farnese owed his rapid advancement to the fact that his sister Giulia was Pope Alexander VI's mistress. His own mistress bore him a daughter and three sons, one of whom, Pierluigi, was accused of raping the Bishop of Fano. A munificent patron of the arts and protector of the scoundrelly Benvenuto Cellini ('a true artist,' he explained, 'is above the laws of morality'), he was, after his election in 1534, still famed for uninhibited parties featuring dancing girls, female singers and capering buffoons. No enemy of nepotism, he raised two teenage grandsons, euphemistically described as nephews, to the Sacred College of Cardinals. A seasoned diplomat who went gingerly about the business of reform, he was not inclined to make war on fashionable superstition and never held a consistory until his astrologers had fixed the hour when the omens were favourable.

Such was the pontiff with whom Ignatius Loyola had to negotiate for the survival of his Company. Such, in the 1540s, was the condition of the Catholic Church, of which Hilaire Belloc remarked that 'no merely human institution conducted with such knavish imbecility would have lasted a fortnight'.

CHAPTER TWO

Holy Fool

ONLY IN THE WRITINGS OF some Jesuit historians does Ignatius Loyola emerge as a more or less human being rather than as a personification of the Church Militant; the man who resolved to make the Church morally and intellectually respectable, a glacial figure who inspires respect rather than affection. In Protestant legend he is the ogre who master-minded the Counter-Reformation. But even hostile writers show a grudging admiration: if only, they seem to imply, he had applied his energies to a better cause. A famous passage in Francis Parkman's *The Jesuits in North America*, published in 1899, illustrates this ambivalence. 'It was an evil day for new-born Protestantism when a French artilleryman fired the shot that struck down Ignatius Loyola . . . The soldier gave himself to a new warfare. In the forge of his great intellect, heated but not disturbed by the intense fires of zeal, was wrought the prodigious enginery whose power has been felt to the uttermost confines of the world . . . the Church to rule the world; the Pope to rule the Church; the Jesuits to rule the Pope; such was and is the programme of the Order of Jesus.'

In *A History of Christianity*, published in 1976, Paul Johnson, himself educated at Stonyhurst, the Jesuit public school in Lancashire, describes Ignatius as 'an ascetic and a puritan', an astute operator who 'turned the reforming process on its head by translating the Lutheran doctrine of justification by faith into the principle of absolute obedience to the Church'. Francis Thompson ended his biography in a blaze of romantic imagery, picturing Ignatius as 'the man who might have ruled provinces in the greatest empire of the sixteenth century; but chose rather to rule, from the altars of the Church, an army which has outlasted the armies of Spain and made conquests more perdurable than the vast empire which drifted to its fall in the wake of the broken galleons of the Armada.' But he stresses the 'hand of steel' beneath the 'benevolent patience and forbearance' with which Ignatius ruled the Society. Juan Polanco, his secretary – his 'hands and feet' – declared that until Ignatius lay dying 'the Saint had not for years spoken to him with any sign of friendship' and remarked that though Ignatius often wrote or dictated thirty letters a day, there was not one that he did not read twice over. As Thompson says, 'any human business directed with wisdom so consummate must have succeeded'.

Even more than SS Benedict, Francis, Dominic and Teresa Ignatius imposed his own carefully codified experience as a pattern on the Society he created, endeavouring with monomaniac industry to avoid the mistakes which had exposed previous Orders to scandal and corruption: multiplying rules, beginning a process of strangulation by solicitude. A task force originally intended to have a maximum of sixty members with the 'interior law of charity' as the only rule acquired Constitutions as elaborate as those compiled by the ultra-legalistic Calvin, whose organization closely paralleled the Society of Jesus.

The *Spiritual Exercises*, themselves elaborated by a string of after-thoughts and later supplemented by a *Directory*, set the tone for Jesuit piety. Jesuit training – and even now it is almost twice as long as that of a medical doctor – faithfully reflects the founder's long and weary struggle towards maturity and ordination. The two years of probation, with the performance of the *Exercises* in full and six 'trials' or 'experiments', are designed to reproduce the first rapturous but rugged stage of Ignatius' pilgrim's progress. The long years of study in the scholasticate represent his ten-year grind towards academic respectability. The third and final year of proving, a period of rededication known as the Tertianship, corresponds with the testing time through which Ignatius and his first disciples passed in Italy before papal backing was secured. From his desk in Rome and then from the grave he has ordered the lives of hundreds of thousands of Jesuits to the climax of ordination – a moment which, as some wit observed, 'seems the reward of a well-spent life rather than the beginning of a priestly career'.

Throughout his life this accomplished leader shunned personal publicity, with the paradoxical result that he and his society, shrouded in apparent mystery, became doubly notorious. He refused to have his portrait painted, frustrated would-be biographers, and gave only a few sentences to his unregenerate years in his dictated *Autobiography*. Most of what is known about his earlier life is based on the recollections, heavily tinged with pious awe, of aged people who gave evidence of his sanctity during the process of beatification which began not long after his death. There is some uncertainty about the year of his birth and the number of his brothers and sisters. Iñigo Lopez de Loyola (he did not use 'Ignatius' until he was a forty-year-old student in Paris) was born in the castle of Loyola in the Basque province of Guipuzcoa, probably in 1491, the last

[23]

of perhaps thirteen children of Don Beltrán de Loyola and Doña Maria Saenz de Licona. The Loyolas were prominent in a feudal and robustly feuding collection of border chieftains, proud that while crusaders to the south were still struggling to drive the last Moors from Spain, their own wet, densely forested and hilly terrain had long been freed from the taint of Saracen blood and occupation. Doña Maria, daughter of the Crown lawyer, was a useful match at a time when the Loyolas' exuberance had been chastened by the centralizing policies of a monarchy newly-united by the marriage of Ferdinand of Aragon and Isabella of Castile. The castle was gloomy and graceless, not unlike the temperament and the religion of the Basques. They built churches like barns, their Catholicism had a Calvinistic dourness, and they considered themselves descendants of the original Iberians. Their obstinacy was proverbial, their sense of community and isolation enhanced by a language of impenetrable complexity.

The Basques were famed seafarers, and in 1493 Ignatius' eldest brother equipped a vessel which joined the fleet of Columbus on his second expedition to the Indies. He was killed three years later fighting in the expeditionary force which conquered the Kingdom of Naples for Spain. Another brother died in Mexico in 1510, a third fighting the Turks in Hungary. Don Beltrán and most of his sons, perhaps even Ignatius, left illegitimate children. Pero Lopez, who became priest of the neighbouring parish of Azpeitia and was Iñigo's favourite crony, fathered at least four bastards. Iñigo himself, at first destined for a career in the Church, received the tonsure and is said to have claimed clerical immunity when brought to justice for brawling and other youthful escapades. Worn out by incessant pregnancies, his mother died soon after his birth, and his sister-in-law Magdalena de Araoz, who in 1498 married Martin Garcia de Loyola, the heir to the estate, was the 'mother' of his boyhood years. Well-born, richly endowed, a protégée of Queen Isabella, she was noted for her piety, and brought to the castle the books of devotion which were to play a vital part in redirecting Iñigo's ambition.

The first change of direction came in 1506 when, humouring Iñigo's desire to enter the royal service, Don Beltrán arranged for him to go to the court at Arevalo under the guardianship of the Chief Treasurer, a friend of the family. The contemporary Jesuit historian Pedro de Ribadeneira states that the budding courtier Iñigo – short (barely 5' 2") and slight – was 'a gay and elegant fellow'. As a page to the young and lively Queen (Germaine de Foix, King Ferdinand's second wife) he was much concerned with his personal appearance, read *Amadis de Gaul* and other such fashionable romances of knight-errantry, worshipped the Infanta Catherine from afar, and, fired by his brother's exploits, resolved on a military career. He is also reported to have been 'assailed and overcome by temptations of the flesh . . . reckless at games, in adventures with women, in brawls'. It has been suggested that since Arevalo was a centre of Franciscan revivalism Iñigo must have been aware of this aspect of the royal court and may have read such works as *The Way of the Cross* and *The Triumph of the Apostles,* so that his later conversion was not so sudden or surprising. But visiting Azpeitia in 1515 at carnival time, he and his clergyman brother indulged in 'nightly excesses, serious and grave misdemeanours' from the penalties of which they were rescued by his guardian's influence with the episcopal court at Pamplona.

Shortly afterwards Iñigo entered the service of the Duke of Najera, viceroy of Navarre, a relative of the Loyolas who held a key command on the Spanish frontier. He may have taken part in a punitive chore – the destruction of the towers and battlements of the castle of Xavier (a fate which fifty years earlier had befallen the castle of Loyola) – after a Navarrese rebellion against the Crown. Less well-to-do than the Loyolas and even more turbulent, the Xaviers were ardent Navarrese separatists. Francis, whose partnership with Iñigo was, in the phrase of James Brodrick, the great twentieth-century Jesuit historian, to 'make the early history of the Society of Jesus very largely the history of two Basque gentlemen', was ten years old at the time.

Spain was in an extraordinary ferment. After a marathon reconquest that had lasted eight centuries, ending with the capture of Granada from the Moors in 1492, the crusade mentality had become almost engrained in the Spanish temperament. Under the fanatically pious Ferdinand and Isabella a long process of reforming the Church and welding it to the Crown had been completed at a time when the papacy was deep in its pagan-Renaissance gambols; and in Spanish eyes the result was a jewel of Catholic orthodoxy. Nowhere in Europe was royal domination of the Church so total. The knightly crusading orders of Calatrava and Santiago had been disbanded or 'regalized'. The Spanish Inquisition was a powerful and popular instrument of a monarchy which expected it to shield Spain from contamination by foreign influences, including the popes of Rome.

Charles I, born and bred in Flanders and speaking no Spanish when he came to the throne in 1516, was not a popular king. His election in

1519 to the imperial throne of the Habsburgs as Charles V did not please Spaniards. It had cost a fortune in bribes and after 1520 he spent most of his time in Germany. Spanish pride was affronted by the King's foreign entourage and by the introduction of a different brand of Catholicism: the earnest piety of the Brethren of the Common Life as represented by Thomas à Kempis's *Imitation of Christ* and, more controversially, the anti-clerical satires of Erasmus. It was a measure of the Inquisition's subservience to the Crown that until Charles V began to see things the Dominicans' way it defended Erasmus against papal condemnation, the Grand Inquisitor actually declaring that to attack the morals of the pope and the clergy was not heretical. But as the persecution of Jews and Moors continued and the German Reformation gathered impetus, Erasmian humanism was firmly identified with Lutheranism and the universities were purged. The harshly intolerant Catholicism of Spain was ready to make common cause with Savonarolan zeal in Italy.

Life in the Duke of Najera's service was by no means entirely a matter of hunting, jousts, and courtly trifling. Charles V's departure for Germany in 1520 was followed by a widespread revolt against the rule of his Flemish nominees. The town of Najera rose against the Duke, and Iñigo, who was present at its storming, distinguished himself by refusing to take any booty. Navarre, which had been wrested from the French only a few years earlier, was hostile to the royal garrisons. Affrays were frequent and Iñigo had to fight his way out of an ambush in one of Pamplona's narrow streets. When his home province of Guipuzcoa grew restless the viceroy sent him on his first diplomatic mission, and he proved himself 'ingenious and skilful in affairs of this world and very clever in the handling of men.'

But if Guipuzcoa yielded to Iñigo's persuasion, Navarre remained explosive. A series of rebellions stripped Pamplona of troops and officers, including Iñigo, hurried hither and thither. In May 1521 the French king sent an army to besiege the city. Its numbers were swollen by eager Navarrese patriots, including Francis Xavier's brothers. Iñigo and his brother Martin Garcia, now Lord of Loyola, hastened back with their troops; and the former, rejecting the advice of the Duke's deputy, prepared for a death-or-glory stand in the citadel. On May 20th, during the bombardment provoked by this gesture, a cannon-shot shattered Iñigo's right leg and damaged the other. Roughly set by a French surgeon, the mangled limb was jolted in a fortnight's gruelling stretcher journey over the hills to Loyola. There Iñigo endured the torture of twice having the bone re-broken and re-set in the hope of straightening the leg, and the further agony of having a protruding lump of bone sawn off. A rack was used to stretch the leg to its normal length, but without success. Iñigo, who was left with a permanent limp, almost died during this ordeal: and in the long convalescence that followed he read his sister-in-law's books of devotion – a monkish *Life of Christ* and *The Golden Legend* (lives of the saints), writings so laden with myth and miracle that the transition from the fantasy heroics of Amadis de Gaul was an easy one.

His slight deformity would not have been a bar to soldiering, but he now chose to interpret it as a sign that God had a different purpose for his life. What if he were called to follow the example of St Francis (himself once destined for a military career) and St Dominic, to be a Christian warrior in a different sense? Military metaphors abounded in the *Golden Legend:* and the *Life of Christ* by the German Carthusian Ludolph not only made him think of applying to enter the strictly enclosed Carthusian monastery near Seville but provided him with a rough basis for the *Spiritual Exercises.* Christ, he read, was the Liege Lord who wanted His followers to conduct themselves as 'holy knights' in the battle against Satan, Prince of Darkness. Iñigo was being displaced by Ignatius, a name which he later adopted in memory of an early Christian martyr, St Ignatius of Antioch.

In a receptive state of mind after his fearful surgical handling, Ignatius – the new man – suffered agonies of remorse over the sins of a not unduly lurid past; and when, after yet another sleepless night, he beheld a vision of the Virgin and Child, he made a vow of perpetual loyalty and chastity. In the *Autobiography* he claims that from that moment onward he was miraculously protected from the torments of sexual lust. Towards the end of his life St Benedict had made a similar claim, though in his case sublimation had been achieved by jumping naked into a nettlebed at a moment of fierce temptation.

Like St Benedict, who required that 'the life of the monk should at all times be Lenten in its character', Ignatius resolved to obliterate all traces of his previous personality. His one ambition now was to go on pilgrimage to the Holy Land; and early in March 1522, despite the protests of his brother, he set out on muleback for the Benedictine abbey of Montserrat in Catalonia, intending to take ship in Barcelona. At Montserrat he confessed his sins at enormous length and, after a knightly vigil before the shrine of Our Lady, donned rough pilgrim's garb. Then in the neighbouring town of Manresa he divided his time between a cave on a river-bank and a cell in the Dominican priory;

permanently undermined his health by savage austerities worthy of the Desert Fathers; was favoured with 'mystic graces'; and scribbled the first draft of his *Exercises.* Finally he spent time in and around Jerusalem.

Three main points emerge from this two-year period – the considerable, though on occasion intensely frustrating, influence of Benedictines, Dominicans and Franciscans; Ignatius' inability, despite his disguise (gaunt, ragged appearance, with matted hair, wild eyes and begging bowl), to hide his noble birth and courtly background; and his useful rapport with women. In the scholarly cloisters of Montserrat the impetuous hidalgo received his first check: a dawning realization that perhaps he had a lot to learn about the religious life. The decision to postpone the pilgrimage and stay in Manresa was probably a result of this. He talked with his confessor and visited the hermit monks who lived in caves above the abbey. Probably he read, or was given, a copy of Abbot Cisneros' *Spiritual Exercises,* and some recent Benedictine writers have conveyed the impression that the mature Ignatius and his celebrated book of the same title were virtually Benedictine creations.

In Manresa the prudent counsel of his Dominican confessor weaned him from his wild asceticism, soothed his doubts about salvation, and indeed saved his life when he was in the depths of a suicidal despair largely caused by his mentors' emphasis on the subtlety and complexity of a fully-comprehended vocation. After all, they had implied, this is not the twelfth century; times have changed, you must wait on God, decide which order you should join, abandon your freelance whims, have patience. When Ignatius reached the Holy Land (his papal safe-conduct described him as 'Enecus de Loyola, a cleric from Pamplona') after a series of endurance tests stringent enough to satisfy, and sharpen, his appetite for self-mortification, his romantic ardour was again doused: this time by Franciscans. Custodians of the Holy Places which were then under Turkish rule, they warned the pilgrim that if he persisted in his silly plan to evangelize the infidels he would be forcibly deported and perhaps excommunicated. After three weeks of pious tourism including two visits to the Mount of Olives to see 'the stone from which our Lord went up to heaven . . . wherein His footprints may yet be discerned' (he wanted to make sure which way they pointed), he began the return journey.

Prudence, adaptation to circumstances, suiting means to ends – these were to be the keynotes of the *Spiritual Exercises* and of the Jesuit Constitutions. In 1524 they were lessons that Ignatius was learning painfully. There was a sense of defeat in the return to Spain, but there

was comfort in the knowledge that his failure adequately to camouflage his antecedents had resulted in a network of well-placed friends
and disciples. The matrons of Manresa had fed and nursed him (there
had been a good deal of malicious gossip about the *Iñigas,* as these
women were called). Two Barcelona bourgeoises, Inez Pascual and
Isabel Roser, were particularly devoted to him. Penniless and starving in
Venice, he had been befriended by a senator who sensed that he was no
ordinary pilgrim. On his hazardous way through an Italy infested with
plague, bandit-mercenaries and marauding Spanish soldiers he had
been protected by a Countess in the castle of Fondi. These were not the
missionary heroics he had hoped for, but they were all he had to work
with. Now began the slow stain of compromise, the grievous discipline of
humility: the transformation of a dashing spiritual freelance into the
most relentless institutionalizer of his Church and age.

Already Ignatius felt that he must heed and acquire his mentors' kind
of reason and curb his own, the voices and visions, the mystic graces.
Treated as an end in themselves they were self-indulgences and
savoured of pride. It is difficult to say whether a potentially great master
of the spiritual life nipped himself in the bud, content to remain a 'mere'
mystic of action, but the eventual result of this change of spiritual
direction was the Society of Jesus. Through it, and through his often-
revised little manuscript, Ignatius made perhaps the mightiest contribution to the strenuous piety of the Catholic Revival. More than any other
single text, the *Spiritual Exercises* read like stage directions for the florid
religiosity of the Counter-Reformation.

CHAPTER THREE

Mature Student

IGNATIUS WAS NOW CONVINCED that he lacked a vital piece of equipment: formal learning. Above all, he had no Latin. So, as the St Francis mood cooled, St Dominic edged to the foreground. At thirty-three he plunged into the hardest and longest phase of his bizarre apprenticeship, a decade of classrooms. Inez Pascual gave him a room, Isabel Roser paid for his keep, a teacher in the High School at Barcelona provided elementary tuition gratis. Having learned by heart some rhymed syntax rules and a basic vocabulary, Ignatius spent about eighteen months in the school itself with pupils from the age of ten upwards. No doubt this was a considerable test of humility; but in the huge classes of those days – two hundred pupils were not uncommon – old and young were mingled and it was thought quite natural for adults to sit in. Throughout his student period his extra-curricular activities were intense; in fact they represented the 'end', the winning of souls, to which he was laboriously assembling a variety of means. In Barcelona he begged for alms and gave what he collected to the vagrant poor. He also walked about in winter in shoes from which he had cut the soles, and got himself beaten up by a gang of young bloods who resented his efforts to reform the morals of the nuns in a convent which they were in the habit of visiting. He was uncertain whether to wait for a clear revelation of specific purpose or to 'enter some religious congregation that was in decline in order to accept as much suffering as he could'. The deciding factor was the success of his first experiment as a spiritual director. Three young men to whom he had given the *Exercises* responded eagerly to the call for total dedication, thus encouraging a desire 'to bring together in a fraternity men who might be, as it were, the trumpeters of Jesus Christ.'

At the university of Alcala, near Madrid, to which Ignatius and his three disciples moved in 1526, his activities disturbed the authorities. In his zeal for souls and his longing to shorten the academic process, he not only rushed from one lecture hall to another trying to cram philosophy, logic and theology, but, dressed in a monkish robe of coarse grey wool, continued his mission among the poor. The glamour of the pilgrimage to the Holy Land and of his aristocratic birth heightened the appeal of this mysterious stranger and the impact of his *Exercises*. It was reported that members of the group that had formed around the 'Greycoats' had been seen grovelling in convulsions of repentance, fainting away in ecstasy, howling as evil spirits were exorcised. Rumour burgeoned when two female devotees vanished on pilgrimage to a distant shrine without telling anyone. Inquisitors from the Supreme Tribunal of the Faith came from Toledo to investigate the Greycoat scandal.

Was this another manifestation of the illuminist heresy which the Dominicans had been trying to extinguish for three centuries? Ignatius, six weeks in prison and closely questioned, was ordered not to wear his distinctive 'uniform' or to go barefoot and told to stop teaching, in public or in private, on pain of excommunication. The fate of the Greycoats was typical of the harassment which the apparently unorthodox fervour of amateur Catholic reformers faced all over Europe. But Ignatius was not to know this. Angered by the stupidity of a sentence which failed to distinguish novelty of approach from sincere orthodoxy of aim he removed to the ancient university of Salamanca. There, as it happened, the campaign against Erasmian humanism and foreign religious foibles was at its height. Very shortly after their arrival, Ignatius and a companion were once more in prison, chained together, while the text of the *Exercises* was minutely examined for heresy. The chief suspect is said to have awaited the verdict with calm confidence, defiantly remarking that 'in the whole of Salamanca there are not so many footchains and handcuffs that I would not ask for more the love of God'. The verdict was, to a degree, favourable. The doctrine of the *Exercises* was pronounced to be orthodox, but Ignatius was forbidden to act as a director of conscience, pretending to make fine distinctions between mortal and venial sins. At least four years' further study of moral theology was needed for that.

It must have seemed an absurd quibble, since thousands of priests with no or minimal training (seminaries did not exist) were making 'fine distinctions'; and it effectively sabotaged his ministry. Ignatius left Salamanca. But he was not beaten yet. In the university of Paris, with its four thousand or more students of many nationalities and its comparative freedom from inquisitional snooping, he could surely lead the double life that he craved and have the pick of European students to recruit from. Travelling first to Barcelona to collect funds, he set out, driving a donkey laden with his possessions, and arrived in Paris early in February 1528. His Spanish disciples did not follow him this time.

[31]

Under Dominican and Franciscan professors purveying a stale scholasticism, the Sorbonne was no longer a place of much intellectual vitality. But what Paris had lost in liveliness it had gained in discipline and routine, something which greatly impressed Ignatius, now determined to see his academic penance through to the bitter end. During the fifteenth century a system of colleges had been established and some attempt made to separate scholars of different ages. No longer, or less often, did students lodge and work in houses where prostitutes plied their trade, so that 'under the same roof there was a school of learning together with a school of whoring'. A chaotic community of masters and pupils had been replaced by an autocratic government of pupils by masters, a change which reflected the drift towards political absolutism. His Paris experience deeply influenced Ignatius in the drafting of the Jesuit Constitutions.

He spent eighteen months over Latin grammar in the Collège de Montaigu, which Jean Calvin had just left. It was so damp and squalid that Parisians called it 'the cleft in the buttocks of Mother Theology'. Erasmus had loathed the place, Rabelais hoped that someone would set fire to it. Calvin welcomed such tribulations as character-forming: so did Loyola, though he deplored the underfeeding and the merciless bullying of young children. The day began at 4 am, continuing through lessons and two Masses until 6 pm, and a similar routine was in force at the Collège Sainte-Barbe where Ignatius spent four years studying philosophy. In the 1550s a young Jesuit reported that during the midday meal 'in order to make the most of every minute . . . they recite from memory the lessons of the morning', and at the evening meal 'students of Rhetoric take turns in giving declamations and students of philosophy or theology in preaching either in Latin or French . . . then there is private study until 9 o'clock. The day ends with an examination of conscience and prayer.' But the change of college was significant, since while Montaigu was notoriously a bastion of reaction, Sainte-Barbe was the liveliest and most progressive of the four theological establishments.

Having been robbed of the money he brought from Barcelona, Ignatius was forced to beg for his keep, several times applying to Spanish businessmen in Flanders and once – in 1530 – venturing to London where 'he received more alms than in all the former years'. Since he kept in touch with his Barcelona disciples and was helped by them, those forays were not strictly necessary for his own frugal needs. Most of the money was used as a relief fund for poverty-stricken fellow students; and in some cases, notably that of Francis Xavier who, with

Pierre Favre, shared a room at Sainte-Barbe with Ignatius, it was a persuasive supplement to the middle-aged Basque's apostolic fervour.

At Sainte-Barbe he narrowly escaped a public flogging for his allegedly disruptive zeal. His first three Parisian catches slipped through the net. But by 1534 when he graduated as Master of Arts he had six firm recruits, all much younger than himself. It was a cosmopolitan and socially varied group – the Basque Francisco Xavier (twenty-six); three Castilians – Diego Lainez (twenty-one, of Jewish descent on his father's side), Alonso Salmeron (eighteen: like Lainez he had known Ignatius at Alcala), and Nicolas Bobadilla (twenty-four, of humble origin); Simon Rodrigues (twenty-one), a wellborn Portuguese; and Pierre Favre (twenty-six), from Savoy, the son of a peasant. On 15 August 1534, the Feast of Our Lady's Assumption, the seven comrades met in the chapel of the Martyrs on the slopes of Montmartre. Favre, recently ordained, said Mass and they made a curious vow of poverty, chastity, and a pilgrimage to Jerusalem. Master Ignatius, as he was usually known from now on, had evidently infected his company with the idea of a mission to the Muslims: a remarkable achievement, since the great Lutheran debate was raging in Paris and Calvin was on his way to Geneva. It was further decided that if, when all had completed their studies in 1537, it proved impossible to reach the Holy Land or to establish themselves permanently there (perhaps as hospital porters), they would as a last resort travel to Rome and put themselves at the pope's disposal 'that Christ might deign to show them through the indication of His Vicar upon earth what was the way of His greater service'. Such, though the title had not yet been revealed, was the origin of the Society of Jesus.

In the months before this act of hopeful dedication Ignatius, knowing that he was to leave Paris and that the company would not be reunited for about two years, took each disciple through the *Exercises*. This was the real bonding. The flexible formula must have been peculiarly effective in the hands of its author: but it proved hardly less compelling when used later by Jesuit missionaries, whether to secure vocations for the Society or to raise the level of piety – and financial commitment – of lay Catholics. Brief, positive and practical, it was in its very crudity, urgency, and evident optimism about getting results, a revolutionary document. In a time of ideological turmoil it offered a tabloid-orthodox version of the Faith complete with medieval trimmings.

At the Collège de Montaigu the piety *(devotio moderna)* of the Brethren of the Common Life – who themselves had been charged with heresy by the Dominicans – was much in vogue and the *Imitation of Christ* left an obvious mark on the *Exercises*. The author or authors of the *Imitation* had tamed the intellectual exuberance of the medieval mystics, dispensing with extravagant penances, fantastic metaphors, and the kind of fiery contemplative rapture which threatened to play havoc with ecclesiastical formulas. This variety of mysticism was a matter of heightened commonsense for the average bourgeois. If the *Imitation* is a bowdlerized précis of advanced medieval spirituality, the *Exercises,* which summarize, vitalize, and schematize the *Imitation,* are a popularization of a popularization. Their carefully graded pressure is aimed at bringing the retreatant to a definite commitment. 'Man,' declares the Fundamental Principle, 'has been created to praise, reverence and serve our Lord God, thereby saving his soul. Everything else on earth has been created for man's sake to help him achieve this purpose . . . So it follows that man has to use these things as far as they help and abstain from them where they hinder his purpose.' The five senses are not to be despised or transcended but used as tools of sanctification (as in the famous passage on hearing, seeing, feeling, smelling and tasting the torments of hell) to experience the penalties of sin, the life, Passion and triumph of Christ, the reality of His warfare with the hosts of Satan and the delights of salvation. Imagery, though terse and hackneyed, abounds, and is aided by directions that, by keeping the subject in a darkened room for the first, gloomier stages of the retreat and prescribing a sudden burst of illumination at the end, bring the psychodrama to a memorable climax.

Though much is left to the discretion of the director, who is to adapt the outline to differing temperaments, ages and physical conditions, little or nothing is left to chance. Abbot Garcia de Cisneros' *Exercises* envisaged a twenty-one-day course. Loyola expanded this to approximately thirty days divided into four equal periods. Themes are kept to a minimum, with meditations, prayers and examinations of conscience clustered about them. Presumably writing from personal experience, Loyola suggests that prayer-posture should be varied – standing, sitting, kneeling or lying (on front or back) – and he recommends a rhythmic-mesmeric approach ('Every time I breathe in I should pray mentally, saying one word . . . in the space between one word and the next I dwell particularly on the meaning of the word, or on the magnificence of the person addressed, or on my own worthlessness'). Means are to be proportioned to ends (glorifying God and saving one's soul). Penances, therefore, are not to be such as to weaken mental or bodily vigour. 'The safest form . . . seems to be that which causes pain in the flesh but does not penetrate to the bones, that is, which causes suffering but not sickness . . . best to scourge oneself with thin cords which hurt superficially rather than to use means which might produce serious internal injury.' The ideal of poverty should not be pursued in a spirit of singularity or to the point of apostolic inefficiency; nor should excessive religious scruples (perhaps Satan-induced) be allowed to paralyze the will to act ('for example, after treading on two crossed bits of straw, a man may conclude that he has sinned . . . the Enemy is like a woman, weak in face of opposition, strong when not opposed').

Yet there is to the modern mind a pervading sense of minute scrupulosity, together with a steady push towards conformity. The Daily Particular Examination of Conscience sketches a technique for the control of besetting sins ('every time one falls into that particular sin or fault the hand is laid on the breast in token of sorrow for the fall. This can be done even in company without it being noticed'); and to it is appended a diagram for comparing progress from one week to the next, each daily dotted line being drawn slightly shorter. 'By my will,' writes Ignatius, 'I try to evoke the proper sentiments . . . If I am contemplating the Resurrection I will pray for a share in Christ's joy; if the Passion I will ask for suffering, grief and agony.' After a battering which clearly persuaded him that if he could not defy the system indefinitely he must work within it, he had become an almost fanatical Churchman. By the early 1540s, when he put the *Exercises* into final shape, this development, or protective colouring, had become explicit. 'The following rules are to be observed in order that we may hold the opinions we should hold in the Church Militant. We should put away completely our own opinion and give our entire obedience to our holy Mother the hierarchical Church, Christ our Lord's undoubted Spouse . . . should openly approve of the frequent hearing of Mass . . . speak with particular approval of religious orders and the states of virginity and celibacy, not rating matrimony as high as any of these . . . approve of relics of the saints, pilgrimages, indulgences, the lighting of candles . . . church decoration and statues.' Criticism of superiors, even when justified, should not be made public, since this might 'arouse popular hostility towards authority' and scandal must be avoided.

In the final version reference is at last made to the great controversy over faith and works, predestination and free will. Care, Ignatius suggests, should be taken, while admitting that 'no man can be saved without being predestined and without faith and grace', not to over-emphasize predestination, thus giving 'ordinary people' the impression that their future actions will be irrelevant to their eternal destiny: 'Our way of speaking should not be such that the value of our activities and the reality of human freedom might be in any way impaired or disregarded, especially in times like these which are full of dangers.' Again, means are fitted to ends and a temperate, unhectoring approach recommended. This did not, however, indicate tolerance but a desire that Jesuits should appear more reasonable than the often hysterically aggressive Protestants. For Ignatius, as for any true Catholic, there was no salvation outside the Church and he would have endorsed the sentiments of Walter Hilton, a late fourteenth-century Augustinian monk who in *The Ladder of Perfection* remarked that 'hypocrites and heretics do not possess humility . . . A heretic sins mortally through pride because he takes a delight in clinging to his own opinion . . . but he deceives himself, for God and Holy Church are in such accord that whoever opposes one opposes the other.'

The *Exercises* have been violently attacked and as violently defended. Somerset Maugham described them as 'the most wonderful method that has ever been devised to gain control over that unstable and wilful thing, the soul of man . . . four hundred commentaries have been written on it. Leo XIII said of it: "Here is the sustenance that I need for my soul."' In *The Origins of the Jesuits* James Brodrick points out that a volume which is as 'unemotional almost as a treatise of geometry' has nevertheless 'set so many loving hearts on fire and filled the history of the Church with heroes'. Thomas Corbishley SJ, the translator of a recent edition, admits that a mere reading of the text will leave the impression of 'a collection of familiar theological ideas and hackneyed scriptural texts, side by side with naïve medieval imagery, a rather unsubtle psychology and a regrettably reactionary attitude to authority.' In *The Anatomy of Melancholy* Robert Burton, a sceptical seventeenth-century Anglican divine, observed that 'the Jesuits right well perceiving of what force this fasting and solitary meditation is to alter men's minds, when they would make a man mad, ravish him, improve him beyond himself to undertake some great business of moment, to kill a king and the like, they bring him into a melancholy dark chamber . . . no company, little meat, ghastly pictures of Devils all about him, and leave him to lie on the bare floor of this chamber of meditation, as they call it, on his back, side, belly, till by this strange usage they make him quite mad and beside himself.' Nineteenth-century French liberal intellectuals sneered at the plan 'to create ecstatic automata in thirty days'; and William James wrote of 'monoideistic hysteria'.

The old orders, especially the Dominicans, loudly condemned the *Exercises*, a spiritual crash-course with memory, reason and will as its Trinity. Designed for the laity as much as for the priest and the postulant, they brought an element of hustle into religion – Benedictines complained of a coercive, parade-ground attitude to prayer. The impact was sharp and there is no reason to quarrel with Maugham's conclusion that this is a book to be read with awe, 'for it was the efficacious instrument that enabled the Society of Jesus for centuries to maintain its ascendancy.'

The fast-spreading reputation of the *Exercises* was boosted by three main factors: first, the claim that, like the Koran, they were literally inspired; second, Paul III's brief of 1548 which exhorted 'each of Christ's faithful of both sexes to use these so pious instructions and exercises and by them be taught'; third, an element of mystery or mystification. The Jesuits 'gave' the *Exercises*, they did not distribute them willy-nilly. A first edition was printed in 1548, but only for members. The 1548 brief stipulated that they should not be printed 'without the consent of the same Ignatius or his successors, under pain of excommunication and of 500 ducats fine to be applied to works of piety.' Though some more or less garbled versions by retreatants might have been circulating Ignatius had been granted a virtual monopoly of his invention. The prestige of the Jesuits as a spiritual élite was considerably enhanced. Edward Boyd Barrett, who left the Society in 1925, surmised that 'Ignatius saw, with remarkable foresight, the advantage to be gained by holding back the book and arousing a keen hunger for it . . . Had the *Spiritual Exercises* been published at once and made available for all as the Pope evidently intended, the Jesuit Order would not have survived the century.'

CHAPTER FOUR

The Way to Rome

IGNATIUS' HEALTH was frail and he constantly overtaxed it. Perhaps only a Stoic fortitude held the man together. The Stoic ideal of self-control and indifference to wealth and poverty, pleasure and pain, health and sickness, had reached him in a Christianized form in the *Imitation*, which often resembles in tone the *Meditations* of the Stoic Emperor Marcus Aurelius. Both books prescribe a perpetual purging of the passions, incessant self-examination and contempt for worldly values. A life, as Aurelius puts it, 'unspotted by pleasure, undaunted by pain', a strenuous cooperation with God, a sense of man's insignificance except as part of a providential whole, a view of death as a necessary, and longed-for, change.

Prudence and histrionic repentance for the sins of his youth, involving a stern display of indifference to family ties, were typically mingled in Ignatius' first and last revisiting of Spain. In spring 1535, on doctor's orders, he abandoned his theological studies with the Dominicans and travelled on muleback to Spain to take his native air. It was anything but a restful sojourn. He startled the inhabitants of Azpeitia by refusing to stay with his kin and lodging in the local poorhouse ('I have not come to live in a castle,' he told his angry, embarrassed brother, 'but to sow the word of God and to make the people realize how terrible a thing is mortal sin'). He conducted a three-month revivalist campaign, preaching against gambling, brawling and fornication (with particular reference to the clergy), catechizing the children, organizing a system of poor relief, and mounting a night watch on the castle of Loyola to warn off 'loose women'. Then he walked, begging his way, to Pamplona, Almazan and Toledo to deliver letters to the families of Xavier, Lainez and Salmeron and to tell them about the Company. It has been suggested that he undertook this business to make doubly certain that his comrades would hold to the vow of Montmartre.

It had been arranged that the group should meet in Venice when the six disciples had taken their degrees. Ignatius arrived there in December 1535 after walking from Genoa. A vertiginous crawl on hands and knees along a precipitous ledge in the Apennines during a storm had been followed by a humiliating accident at Bologna, where he fell from a footbridge into the slimy moat, was 'so begrimed with mud that the onlookers made him a laughing-stock', and spent two weeks in hospital with high fever. In Venice, with his basic needs met by funds from admirers in Spain, he mixed further studies in theology with street preaching, hospital visiting and giving the *Exercises*. In this way he made some useful contacts and allies, including the Spanish Consul and a cousin of the influential Cardinal Contarini. One Andalusian priest called Diego Hoces joined the company; and Ignatius was already writing letters of spiritual advice to Spanish correspondents, including a Benedictine nun in Barcelona ('Disregard impure or sensual thoughts . . . and spiritual weariness, when these are against your wish, since neither St Peter nor St Paul procured complete immunity from the intrusion of such thoughts . . . Poor in goodness, Iñigo').

In Paris the company had gathered three more recruits, Claude Le Jay, a Savoyard, and two Frenchmen, Paschase Broet and Jean Codure. In the year before his companions made their long trudge to Venice Ignatius, though still hoping to get to Jerusalem, was able to assess the situation in Italy: the urgent need for revival, the various attempts to achieve it, fears in the Vatican that the reform movement might get out of hand. In Spain, as Ignatius well knew, the Church was far from being a model of godliness, but Italy was infinitely worse. Cardinal Contarini openly declared that many convents were in effect brothels, where so-called nuns put on lubricious plays to stimulate the lust of their clients. Absentee bishops and greedy and illiterate priests had created an almost universal contempt for ecclesiastical authority. Large areas were in a state of godless anarchy. In the 1550s Jesuit missionaries were to complain at the folly of sending men overseas when 'the Italian Indies' were in such desperate need of attention. One, working around Bologna and Modena, reported that murders in the mountainous districts reached massacre proportions, and were 'done in ignorance by men who do not know that it is wrong to murder'.

In the towns, churches were used mainly as social centres, even as commercial exchanges or law courts – it was not uncommon for cases to be heard while Mass was in progress. Rome did not set a shining example. In St Peter's canons arriving to sing the office left their swords and fashionable clothes in the atrium while performing their priestly stint. On 1 May there was a tradition of loosing birds into the Santissimi Apostoli church, and a pig which, plunging and squealing, was fought for by the mob. One of the few reforms pushed through with any vigour was a rephrasing of the breviary in classical terms. The Trinity became *Numen Triforme Olympi,* God *Deus deorum maxime,* the Blessed Virgin *felix dea* or *nympha candidissima.*

Lutheranism and, in more fastidious circles where intellectual rigour, elegant Latin prose and vast learning were appreciated, Calvinism, which claimed to restore the ancient simplicity of the Church, had an attraction more powerful than the uncoordinated, anti-intellectual, and fiercely competing groups which in the 1530s had begun the thankless task of kindling a Catholic renaissance. Camaldolesi, Theatines, Barnabites, Somaschi and Capuchins were jostling for attention at a time when enlightened, though often dubiously Christian, prelates were debating whether to suppress religious orders altogether or at least to ensure their extinction by forbidding them to receive novices. The entire monastic-mendicant complex was seen as an obstacle to rationalization, a gift to Protestant propaganda, and (above all) a threat to the survival of the papacy. Savonarola's crusade had not been forgotten; and the perils of rabble-rousing religious enthusiasm had been frighteningly illustrated in Germany by the Anabaptists who drove Luther into close alliance with the princes and produced his bitter counter-revolutionary tract *Against the Murdering Thieving Horde of Peasants.*

But 'families' of zealots gathered around a 'father' in the Ignatian manner continued their efforts. Partly to overcome the objections of the hierarchy to monasticism they called themselves 'clerks regular' – a category soon to be adopted and adapted by Ignatius. In essence this was a revival of the mobile task force mentality of the early Franciscans and Dominicans. Clerks regular were to live in community under a Rule and take the triple monastic vow. Their main object was to act as models of priestly virtue to the secular clergy. They were not to wear a distinctive uniform and mobility was to be ensured by cutting choir duties. A period of training – rigorous self-examination and rededication – was to precede missionary activity.

The first media of revival were the Oratories or Fraternities of Divine Love in Rome, Venice, Brescia and Verona. A dominant figure was Giovanni Pietro Carafa, a choleric Neapolitan who in 1524 got permission to found an order of clerks regular, the Theatines, directly responsible to the Holy See (the relative independence of the old orders was a main reason for their unpopularity at Rome). Boosted by Carafa's election as Pope Paul IV, the Theatines spread to Spain, Poland, Austria and Germany in the next thirty years. Many became reforming bishops and in this way, as Ignatius realized, their missionary edge was blunted. But they had set new standards of forthright popular preaching, house-to-house evangelism, and sacrificial relief work among the poor, the sick, orphans and prostitutes.

Among women the Ursulines were the most important of several groups edging towards official recognition. Founded by St Angela Merici, their girls' schools were to parallel the educational achievement of the Jesuits. The Camaldolesi, a reformed offshoot of an eleventh-century order, tended to live with ostentatious austerity in hermit shacks. But the most significant renaissance of the religious old guard took place among the Franciscans. They were already noted for an almost chronic tendency to split and reform. The quarrel between Spirituals and Conventuals had been followed by an Observant-Strict Observant sequence which spawned Celestines in Italy, Colettines in France, Brethren of the Cowl in Spain. Leo X's attempt to sweep all Franciscans into the category of 'Friars Minor' had failed: there were Friars Minor (Grey Friars) and Friars Minor Conventual (Black Franciscans).

A sixteenth-century revival led by the grimly ascetic Spaniard St Peter of Alcantara produced yet another surge of Strict Observance. Its members were known in France as Recollects, and in Italy as Capucini or Capuchins because of the long-pointed cowl (*capuche*) which they wore, together with beards, as outer signs of a return to the style and spirit of St Francis. Not without stiff opposition from 'unreformed' Observants, the new-wave Franciscans won through to papal recognition in 1529. But by the late 1530s the feeling in Rome was that, as in the thirteenth century, Catholic revivalism was spinning out of control and more likely to cause than to solve problems. This suspicion seemed justified when in 1542 Bernardino Ochino, Vicar-General of the Capuchins, turned Protestant and fled to Geneva.

Ignatius got more than a whiff of all this in Venice, a republic noted for its independence and very critical of inflated Roman pretensions. His own zeal brought him once more under suspicion. Charged with heresy, he was fortunate enough to be brought before a judge who had just performed the *Exercises* under his guidance. But his activities exasperated the bitterly anti-Spanish Carafa, who felt that his Theatines needed no help from a subject of the king-emperor whose troops had sacked Rome and who bullied the papacy. Carafa was apt to give the impression that as the first clerks regular the Theatines were entitled to absorb and control late-comers to the scene. When, later, Ignatius refused to unite, he knew he had made a formidable enemy.

With the arrival of the nine disciples from Paris in January 1537 the *Iñiguistas*, as they were soon called, numbered eleven. For almost three months, as there were no pilgrim ships sailing at that time of year and papal permission had still to be sought, the company entered into direct competition with the Theatines in Venice. In the hospice at Manresa Ignatius had mortified his natural inclinations by embracing the most repellently ulcerous inmates; and in Paris, when his hand began to pain him after touching the sores of a plague victim, he had overcome his panic fear by 'thrusting his fingers into his mouth, saying: "If you have the plague in your hand, then get it in your mouth also!"' He now determined – since hospital service might prove to be their best chance for long-term missionary work in the Holy Land – to prove the mettle of his men. Since the heroic age of the Desert Fathers, tempting Providence had been regarded as a virtue that offered a reward whatever happened. If one survived one had extorted a sign, a miracle. If not, one was a stage nearer to Christ. Ignatius wanted his disciples to be ready and eager to gamble on this certainty.

The rites of passage, gruesome as they may seem (William James described them as 'a sort of revelling in hospital purulence which makes us admire and shudder at the same time'), followed activities that had become traditional. Straight to the hospitals, there to make beds, sweep, scrub, dispose of excreta, dig graves, carry coffins, bury the dead. Asked to scratch the pus-laden back of a leper – possibly a syphilitic – Francis Xavier obliged, and licked and sucked his fingers when nausea threatened to unman him. Simon Rodrigues shared his bed with a leper who had been refused admission for lack of space. Until October 1537, when naval war between Venice and the Turks killed any hope of sailing to the Holy Land, the *Iñiguistas* stuck to their self-abasing style of living: sleeping in hovels, caverns or ruins, begging their bread, glorying in the jeers of villagers who mocked their mangled Italian. Rodrigues acquired such a taste for the holy hermit's life that he nearly dropped out of the ranks.

In March 1538 everyone save Ignatius who, politic in such matters, feared that his presence might antagonize Cardinal Carafa, went to Rome. At the instance of Dr Pedro Ortiz, Charles V's special envoy, Paul III received the bedraggled company, gave his permission for the pilgrimage that was not to be, and made the *Iñiguistas* entertain him with a theological debate while he ate his meal. He was sufficiently impressed with their learning to grant a faculty to receive holy orders from any bishop available.

After being ordained Ignatius postponed his first Mass, which he had intended to celebrate at the altar of the Nativity in Jerusalem, until his dream had utterly faded. Then, sending the rest to Ferrara, Bologna and Padua to work among the university students, he, with Favre and Lainez, set out for Rome to put the contingency plan into practice. Whatever the future held, it was clearly vital to multiply contacts and gain some influence at the centre of ecclesiastical power.

Before going their different ways the eleven comrades had discussed what title they should take. It is said that humility prompted their leader to object to the name *Iñiguistas* (Ignatians), partly because he was not yet in the legal sense a founder or a chief with defined authority. Hitherto they had called themselves simply pilgrim priests. Now Ignatius proposed that 'since they had no head except Jesus Christ' they should consider themselves as 'of the Compañia de Jesus or Societatis Jesu'. The designation of Christ as King and Commander-in-Chief in the *Exercises* made a Christian-soldiers interpretation of the word 'Company' possible and even inevitable; but military metaphors had been common ever since St Paul preached and wrote about spiritual warfare. The *Iñiguistas* saw themselves primarily as companions close in affection – though even at this stage Ignatius was chary of 'particular friendships' as undermining 'holy indifference' – who were also subjects of Christ the King.

There has been much learned argument over the exact or predominant meaning of 'Company'. But the real trouble was to come over the words 'of Jesus'. In Italy, Spain, France and England the title was soon attacked as implying arrogance. A Spanish critic complained that it was 'haughty and schismatic, since the whole Christian people is the Society of Jesus'. In 1553 the Jesuit Polanco explained that the title was used 'in the customary way whereby a society or company takes its name from its leader'. But in 1590 Pope Sixtus V ordered the style to be changed to 'Society of the Name of Jesus', and so, for a time, it was. Perhaps the most effective defence of the much-disputed title came from King Henry IV of France. When pressed by the University and Parlement of Paris to forbid its use, he replied: 'Some of my officials are Knights of the Holy Ghost; there is an Order of the Holy Trinity; and in Paris we have a congregation of nuns who call themselves God's Daughters. Why then should we object to a Company of Jesus?'

A few miles from Rome, the three pilgrim priests entered a chapel in the village of La Storta. There, spirits were raised and the choice of title apparently blessed when Ignatius had the vision and heard the voices which have passed into Jesuit legend. 'He told me,' Lainez recorded, 'that it was as if God the Father had impressed these words on his heart: "I shall be favourable to you in Rome." Since our Father did not understand what these words would signify, he added, "Perhaps we shall be crucified . . ." Then he said it seemed to him as if he beheld Christ with the cross on His shoulder and by His side the Eternal Father who thus spoke to His Son: "I desire you to take this man for Your servant." Jesus accepted him with the words "It is My will that you serve Us." '*

Influential Venetians had seen to it that the pilgrim priests did not arrive unheralded in Rome, where two wealthy patricians provided accommodation. The alliance between Ignatius and Dr Ortiz was cemented when they spent a forty-day retreat together in the Benedictine monastery at Monte Cassino. Dr Ortiz took the *Exercises* and Cardinal Contarini was also torpedoed by this secret weapon. Favre and Lainez lectured on theology at the Pope's invitation. When the seven missioners were recalled from the north (Diego Hoces had died, exhausted, in the poorhouse at Padua) Roman churches where sermons were a rarity resounded to passionate salvationist oratory; and during the ferocious winter of 1538 the *Iñiguistas,* as they were still known, distinguished themselves by relief work. They even dared to challenge the orthodoxy of Fra Agostino Mainardi, a well-known Augustinian preacher whom they accused of Lutheran tendencies. After some nasty moments – Fra Agostino suggested that these impertinent foreigners were fugitives from the Inquisition and ought to be burned at the stake or sent to the gallows – they won an eight-month battle of denunciations. Some years later Fra Agostino's flight to Switzerland, where he became a Lutheran minister, seemed to vindicate the Jesuits' acumen.

Theoretically the Ignatians' presence in Rome was temporary. But with the Turkish war continuing and Paul III himself hinting that 'Italy is a good and true Jerusalem for you', it was finally decided that this was the leading of Providence. In November 1538 the Pope accepted their offer to put themselves entirely at his disposal. This was a powerful inducement, outbidding in papalist fervour the Capuchins and Theatines. Within little more than a year the Ignatians were scattered all over Italy. Demand missions – Broet to Siena, Bobadilla to Ischia, Lainez to Parma, Favre with Dr Ortiz to the Diet of Worms as official theologian – followed in swift succession. They set the pattern of the Jesuits' role, and brought prestige and recruits. They also brought problems.

* The word 'Jesuit' was a nickname, at first perhaps derisive, which passed into common usage. Curiously, it was used by Ludolph the Carthusian in his *Life of Christ* ('just as we are called Christians when we are baptized, so we shall be called Jesuits when we enter into glory').

Aware of the hostility of Carafa and other cardinals, the Pope seemed willing, even anxious, to avoid trouble by using the Ignatians as a pool of skilled technicians without the provocation of approving them as a new order. For Ignatius this ambiguity was distressing. It was clearly time to clarify the terms of his quasi-voluntary organization. Urgent debates produced the resolve to add a vow of obedience to one of the group as 'general', and to press hard for papal recognition as an order. By June 1539 Ignatius had drafted a 'Formula of the Institute' repeating the special vow of total availability and adding clauses on individual poverty, prompt obedience to a Father-General when elected, and – taking the concept of mobility much further than the Theatines – the 'sacrifice' of the chanting of Divine Office to leave greater freedom for action. ('All priests of our Society are bound to recite the office, but not in choir lest they be withdrawn from those works of charity to which we have wholly dedicated ourselves').

The language of the Formula was militant, even military ('Whoever chooses to serve as a soldier of God beneath the banner of the Cross in our Society . . . this militia of Christ. . .'). Contarini commended it to the Pope but, as he had foreseen, there was opposition in the Sacred College. To Cardinal Ghinucci the jettisoning of 'choir' savoured of Lutheranism, while the special vow of obedience to the Pope appeared superfluous, for was it not in effect taken by all true Catholics? Cardinal Guidiccioni, who favoured a single order for male religious (bringing them into line with the general category of secular clergy) or at most four orders (Benedictines, Cistercians, Franciscans and Dominicans) because of what he called 'the abominable dissensions, quarrels and contentions, both among themselves and with the secular clergy', rejected the proposal outright.

Ignatius responded to this seeming impasse by organizing the first of those obstinate rearguard actions which were to become a Jesuit speciality during the Society's fight for survival in Rome. It lasted a year. Not only did he bind himself and his nine comrades to say three thousand Masses with the intention of changing Cardinal Guidiccioni's mind, but he solicited a stream of testimonials from the King of Portugal, the Duke of Ferrara, the senators of the republic of Parma, Cardinal Ferrari, the Archbishop of Siena and other notables. The Pope's relatives, especially his daughter Costanza, Countess of Santa Fiora, were asked to put in a good word. The bombardment was successful. Ghinucci's objections melted; Guidiccioni lifted his ban, though insisting that the Society should be limited to a maximum of sixty members; and on these terms

Pope Paul formally approved the new order in the bull *Regimini militantis ecclesiae* of 27 September 1540. The Society of Jesus had been manoeuvred into existence.

Ignatius was elected General in April 1541 after the second ballot when his Franciscan confessor told him that he would be 'sinning against the Spirit' if he refused. Following a Mass of thanksgiving and dedication he embraced each of the five Jesuits then in Rome and 'gave them the kiss of peace and deep affection and interior emotion, with tears of joy in his eyes'. The tears may have been tinged with sadness, for he had reached the end of his pilgrimage.

CHAPTER FIVE

Black Popery

TURKISH IMPERIALIST AMBITION, which had frustrated Loyola's plans for the Holy Land, also influenced the fate of the Society in Europe. Putting the defence of Hungary before the suppression of Protestantism, Charles V was obliged to appease the heretics. Protestant leaders were given breathing-space and bargaining power. The pace and politics of the Reformation, that explosion of the accumulated grievances of the Middle Ages, and of its counterpart, the Catholic Church's belated attempt to come to terms with the post-medieval world, were, ironically, both governed by the ebb and flow of Turkish aggression.

Ironical also, in view of the frequent assumption that the Society sprang out of the earth as a fully-formed engine of counter-reformation, is the fact that Ignatius and his tiny headquarters staff were forced, by the demands made on their services, to change the whole emphasis of their work by a series of inspired but sometimes almost frantic improvisations. As with other clerks regular, their first priorities were for relief work among the poor and the wretched. This involved fund-raising, which meant cultivating the rich. As commitments increased – schools and colleges especially required heavy financial support – the original priorities were submerged though not abandoned. The alliance with and dependence upon wealthy benefactors, together with the obvious tactical advantage of acting as their spiritual advisers, completed an end-justifies-means process affecting the Capuchins no less than the Jesuits.

Their rivalry, and the open hostility of the Dominicans and Franciscans, forced Ignatius to acquire powerful and wealthy supporters. He did so with a will, remarking that 'he who rejects the opportunity of using worldly patronage for religious ends has clearly not learned to direct all things towards one goal, the greater glory of God'. His success angered those who regarded his Company as upstart and superfluous. But the extension and exploitation of an already considerable network of well-placed contacts was the more vital because of the self-denying ordinance that he himself had insisted upon. Whereas Dominicans and

Franciscans, for instance, readily accepted any preferment from the papacy downwards, Jesuits were forbidden to do so except at the Pope's command. This was partly in the interests of mobility, partly to prevent outstanding Jesuits being creamed off and withdrawn from the General's control, and partly to refute the allegations of the old guard, who accused the newcomers of feigning humility with an eye to grabbing dignities.*

But ostentatious self-denial seemed to be cancelled out by a recruiting policy that stressed the expediency of securing wealthy, well-born novices. The most spectacular instance was that of Francis Borgia, Duke of Gandia, viceroy of Catalonia and great-grandson of Pope Alexander VI. When in 1547 by special papal dispensation he became a 'secret' Jesuit, placing his wealth and influence as a leading Spanish grandee at the disposal of Ignatius, the fraudulence of Jesuit pretensions seemed to many, and not least to the Emperor Charles V, to have been glaringly exposed. Ignatius' nephew, Antonio Araoz, a tireless court Jesuit, was largely responsible for the coup and proved a classic example of the way in which a 'humble' spiritual adviser could be more powerful than any prelate; particularly when armed with papal privileges which, even if used with the discretion urged by Ignatius, removed him from episcopal jurisdiction. The indirect, grey eminence technique was easily construed as a sinister preference for backstairs intrigue; just as Jesuit zeal to extend the range and appeal of a sound Catholic-humanist education by offering it free angered university authorities. In Rome it was whispered that the House of Martha for Reformed Prostitutes was 'the seraglio of the priests of the Society of Jesus'. To a Spanish Franciscan who sneered at such puritanical meddling and said that all the Jesuits in Spain should be sent to the stake Ignatius replied with barbed piety: 'Tell Fray Barbaran I wish that he and all his friends and acquaintances may be consumed by the fire of the Holy Ghost.'

The Company's wholehearted adoption of St Thomas Aquinas, the great scholastic theologian of the thirteenth century, as the grand arbiter of Catholic orthodoxy might have been expected to mollify the Dominicans. But, threatened by Jesuit competition in the universities, they saw

---

*Ignatius not only refused preferment for himself but managed to avert it for Francis Borgia, who in 1565 became the third Jesuit General, Bobadilla, Le Jay, Lainez and Peter Canisius. Lainez, the second General, was in peril of becoming Pope and went into hiding to thwart those who wished to nominate him as a candidate. There have been exceptions to the rule, mainly for bishoprics in mission territory, where, it was argued, careerist ambition and material gain were not involved.

it as an impertinent strutting in stolen plumage, not least because Dominican Thomists began to be outshone by brilliant Jesuit neo-scholastics like Francisco Suarez and Francisco de Toledo. The celebrated clash between Jesuits and Jansenists over the relative importance of divine grace and human free will in the work of salvation was anticipated in a bitter wrangle between Jesuit and Dominican theologians which was temporarily quieted by papal decree. And though one aim of the special vow of obedience to the pope was to combat the spirit of nationalism that had fragmented Catholic Christendom, French, German, Italian, Portuguese and above all Spanish Jesuits soon displayed chauvinist prejudice.

Often it seemed that the Society of Jesus was far more trouble than it was worth. The pioneer Jesuits experienced many of the reactions listed in the early 1970s by Fr Enrique Maza SJ in Mexico: 'If the Jesuits follow this line, they are opportunists. If they don't, they are reactionaries. If they are critical of their own work – hypocrites. If they are not – snobs. If they close a college – irresponsible. If they don't – corrupters of youth. If they educate the rich – exploiters. If they educate the poor – Communists. If they accept an unjust socio-economic system – parasites. If they don't – subversives. In any hypothesis – Machiavellians.' Caught in a web of compromise Ignatius buckled ruefully to the task which every Jesuit General since has undertaken with varying success: that of squaring the Vatican and keeping Catholic enemies at bay. A prime requisite was expertise in the complex world of papal politics. Ignatius made himself an expert: but his *Spiritual Diary,* with its agonized references to a decrease in mystical graces, gives some idea of the cost. More than seven thousand letters written or dictated by him during his generalship survive as the martyr's monument of a reluctant if superhumanly industrious bureaucrat.

A small fraction of these documents, published under the title *St Ignatius Loyola: His Letters to Women,* provide a fascinating sample of his grasp of the importance of gaining the support of the mighty. Like the capture of the Duke of Gandia, they show how thoroughly he exploited his Spanish-Habsburg connections, in close collaboration with Fr Araoz in Madrid. He had not forgotten the scandal of the *Iñigas* at Manresa and Alcala, and cautioned his followers that 'we must keep watch over ourselves and never enter into spiritual converse with women unless they be of noble rank'. There was always a risk, but at least it should be socially and financially worth taking. In his autobiography he recalls some narrow escapes: 'Master Francis [Xavier] heard a woman's confession and visited her several times . . . then it was discovered that the woman was with child. But the Lord ordained that the guilty man should be found. Jean Codure had a similar experience with one of his spiritual daughters, who was caught in the company of a man.'

Yet though Ignatius corresponded with Charles V and later with Philip II, he concentrated mainly on women who belonged to the House of Habsburg or were closely connected with it. Charles V, who regarded both Capuchins and Jesuits as 'sects more productive of scandal than of edification', was hard to win over. He and his formidable sister Maria, ex-Queen of Hungary and Bohemia and Governor of the Netherlands from 1530 to 1535, resisted every blandishment: indeed to her the word Jesuit stood for trouble-stirring fanatic, and until she died the Society's influence in the Netherlands was restricted. Margaret of Austria, her successor as Regent and an illegitimate daughter of Charles V, was very different. Her second husband was Ottavio Farnese, a grandson of Pope Paul III, and she was the first princess to have a Jesuit confessor. Codure was followed by Lainez, and from 1542 Ignatius, who referred to her as 'Nuestra Madonna', acted as her spiritual director. She is said to have urged the Pope to give official recognition to the Society and, together with Doña Leonor de Vega, wife of the Spanish ambassador in Rome, she was a prominent benefactress of the Houses of St Martha. She also helped to persuade the Pope to refuse the Emperor Ferdinand's request for Fr Le Jay to become Bishop of Trieste: and, finally, she opened the Netherlands to full Jesuit activity.

When the Infanta Catherine became Queen of Portugal, she was successfully encouraged to take a Jesuit, Fr Miguel Torres, as confessor, and performed the *Exercises* under his direction. Ignatius went to great lengths to humour her passion for relics, sending Favre from Germany with such items as one of Judas's pieces of silver and mementoes of St Ursula and the virgin-martyrs of Cologne. He also persuaded Pope Julius III to raid a famous collection in Rome for her benefit. Portugal became notorious as the country where Jesuits could do no wrong, and such attentions had helped to make this possible.

With discreet pertinacity Ignatius followed up the good work of his nephew Fr Araoz, who through the royal governess, Doña Leonor Mascarenhas, a staunch ally, had gained influence over Charles V's daughters, the Infantas Maria and Juana. As Regent of Spain from 1548 to 1551 Maria was helpful, and afterwards in Vienna is said to have prevented her *politique* husband, the Emperor Maximilian, from turning Protestant or evolving a mixed religion to satisfy all sides in

Germany. But the most elaborate Ignatian battery was trained on Princess Juana who, in addition to being married to the Portuguese heir-apparent, at the age of nineteen became Regent in the absence of her brother Philip in England after his wedding to Mary Tudor. She seemed to offer a heaven-sent chance to offset Dominican-Franciscan hostility, and no effort was spared to that end. In 1542 her court chaplain had joined the Society and Fr Araoz was in constant attendance. The daughters of the Duke of Gandia were among her ladies-in-waiting, and the Duke, who gave her the *Exercises* when she was seventeen, became her spiritual adviser. Informed of every move, Ignatius commended Borgia's introduction of 'sanctified amusement' in the form of a card-game featuring the virtues and privileges of Our Lady.

During her regency from 1554 to 1559 Princess Juana's palace was reported to be 'more like a convent', which did not prevent rumours that she was the mistress of the Duke and perhaps of Araoz as well. She was a tireless champion of the Society, urging her father to relent, using her influence to thwart his plan to make a cardinal of Borgia, donating money for the Jesuits' Roman College, helping to establish a major college in Valladolid, constantly badgering Charles V to overrule his sister Maria and permit a Jesuit college in Louvain. She intervened to settle several disputes over legacies, notably in Saragossa where the Basque-Castilian alliance of Araoz, Ignatius and the 'Jesuit government' infuriated Aragonese patriots and provoked violent riots during which the Jesuits were denounced as 'messengers of Antichrist'. When Philip II returned to Spain he kept Princess Juana at court as a political consultant and Araoz dominated her entourage as spiritual director. Borgia reported that 'Montoya [her pseudonym in despatches to Rome] grows daily in pious submission to the Society . . . she has in truth a good will for all our affairs.' As a reward for her services Ignatius gave permission for the Princess to become a secret member of the Society. She took the vows of a scholastic, which left the General free to 'release' her should this prove politically desirable: thus becoming the only authenticated Jesuitess or undercover royal Jesuit.*

Ignatius had a brisk correspondence with the Borgia women, and in 1552 the Duke of Gandia's son Juan married Laurencia, heiress of the Loyola estates. He also kept in close touch with the influential Italian noblewomen Vittoria and Joana Colonna, and in one of his very rare

*Though it has been suggested that Maximilian of Bavaria, John III of Portugal, Sigismund of Poland, the Emperors Ferdinand II and III, and Louis XIV came into the latter category.

sorties from Rome travelled to Naples to reconcile Doña Joana and her husband, the Duke of Tagliacozzo. Useful contacts made during Ignatius' two years in Venice were assiduously cultivated. Donna Maria Frassoni del Gesso founded a college in Ferrara. Donna Costanza Pallavicini Cortesi was a generous benefactress in Modena, as was another widow, Donna Marghareta Gigli, in Bologna. Sometimes there were tiresome complications. The case of a female devotee in Naples, who donated her house and all her worldly goods and became a penniless pilgrim who had to be provided for by the Society, developed into a first-class scandal and a series of law suits. Ignatius worked hard to persuade the wayward, Spanish-born Duchess Eleanora of Florence (the wife of Duke Cosimo de Medici) to found a college. Juan Polanco was recalled after criticizing the luxury of the Medici court and the Duchess's mania for gambling, and replaced by Lainez, with instructions to be more tactful. After a visit from the Duke of Gandia in 1550 the Duchess founded a college to the extent of providing premises, but refused to endow it. Her husband was suspicious of the Jesuits ('Surely they have enough money themselves?'), and she had tantrums when Ignatius tried to take Lainez away from her.

The beating which he had received from a gang of bravoes in 1525 had not quenched his interest in the reform of nunneries. For years he had corresponded with a Benedictine nun in Barcelona, Sister Teresa Rejadella ('Your Paternity's most useless slave and servant'), but he was startled when the nuns applied to transfer to Jesuit direction, and alarmed when Fr Araoz, engaged in a reform of convents throughout Catalonia, advocated the formation of a female Society of Jesus. The severest trial came in 1543 when Isabel Roser, now widowed, appeared in Rome and announced her intention of 'placing herself entirely at the disposal of beloved Father Ignatius'. The long-time benefactress was installed as a sort of Mother Superior in the House of St Martha, but that did not satisfy her. She extracted papal permission to take vows and a command that Ignatius should accept them. On Christmas Day 1545 she and her two waiting-women pronounced the vows of the Society in the presence of the reluctant General. News of her achievement spread, bringing applications for similar status from envious benefactresses in Spain and Italy.

When Isabel Roser proposed to return to Barcelona to recruit more Jesuitesses Ignatius petitioned Paul III to reverse his decision and tried to persuade the triumphant widow to withdraw. At a stormy meeting in the Spanish embassy Sister Isabel and her nephew presented a detailed account of all her benefactions, while Ignatius maintained that she owed money to the Society. For months the battle raged, to the delight of Roman scandal mongers. A letter in which the General explained that 'it has seemed to me for God's greater glory that I should separate myself from this care of having you as a spiritual daughter . . . I hand you over to the judgment of the Sovereign Pontiff so that your soul may be tranquil and comforted in all things to God's greater glory' did not disarm the opposition. The nephew replied that 'these Jesuits are all rogues. Ignatius wished to steal all my aunt's fortune; he is a hypocrite and thief.' But judgment went against Sister Isabel. She withdrew her charges, accepted papal dispensation from her vows, and finally took the veil in a Franciscan convent in Barcelona. For Ignatius it was a famous, if distressing, victory.

Paul III responded favourably to his petition that Jesuits 'shall be permanently and forever released from the obligation to undertake the spiritual direction of convents of nuns or female religious who wish to place themselves under the obedience of the said priests; nor finally that of ladies who wish to serve God holily by placing themselves regularly under their direction and following the way of life of the Society.' Even Catherine Wischaven, the sister of a Jesuit who had been acting as housekeeper to the fathers in Louvain, was forced to retire to a convent. Ignatius summarized his attitude in the Constitutions (rules): 'As the men of this Society must be ready at any time to go from one part of the world to another . . . they may not undertake the pastoral care of women, still less that of nuns . . . in the sense that they permanently carry out the duty of confessors and directors of souls; although this does not prevent them hearing the confessions of a community temporarily and for special reasons.'

This formula gave the latitude for which Ignatius constantly strove. With tact and dexterity he kept the esteem of his female followers. Noblewomen had clustered about him in Manresa and Barcelona in the 1520s and in 1556 noblewomen surrounded his corpse in the church of Santa Maria della Strada. Many women, including nuns in Barcelona, gave edifying evidence during the process of beatification and for a long time he was a patron saint of mothers and of women in child-birth, despite the Society's reputation for cradle-snatching. Ignatius' handling of the parents, and especially the mothers, of novices is a fine example of his holy guile. The Church, and the Jesuit Constitutions, took fourteen as the age of decision for the religious life. Ignatius him-self preferred novices to be between eighteen and twenty years old, though the increasing glamour of the counter-reformation 'crusade', as presented in Jesuit classrooms, brought many early applications. He would insist on full consultation with parents while firmly defending a youth's right to follow a genuine vocation even against parental opposition.

Angry mothers made scenes during Mass and deluged cardinals with complaints that 'the Jesuits have only built their colleges to rob us of our children'. But the storm was braved and the Constitutions laid down that if novices were molested by relatives living near their college they should be transferred to a more distant establishment. When the situation had been accepted and a vocation had 'struck' the General himself would write to mothers with news of their sons' progress, allowed occasional home visits, encouraged novices to write to their parents, and instructed Rectors to observe these customs. Particularly cooperative or influential women were rewarded with the honorary title 'Mother of the Society of Jesus': a much-coveted distinction which, like the Masses said for benefactors and other arrangements made to honour their memory, exemplified Loyola's shrewdness and meticulous attention to detail.

In one of his sermons Cardinal Newman described St Ignatius as 'the princely patriarch, the St George of the modern world with his chivalrous lance run through his writhing foe'. That was the militant image beloved of baroque artists. But if the special vow of obedience to the pope and his own rare tropes (if the Society were 'to dissolve like salt in water', he said, a quarter of an hour's recollection would reconcile him to such a fate) reveal a burning and even romantic ambition, the tireless industry with which it was implemented is the most striking feature of his character.

By 1555 Jesuit prestige was so high that Marcellus II, who unfortunately died after a pontificate of only twenty-two days, asked Loyola to appoint two Fathers to live in the papal palace as advisers. In 1544 the sixty-man restriction had been lifted; in 1545 Paul III signed a brief exempting Jesuits from episcopal jurisdiction and empowering them to preach and give the sacraments wherever they might be without asking permission of parish priest or bishop; and in 1546, the year of the tussle with Sister Roser, the brief *Exponi nobis* endorsed the plan, so vital to the Society's expansion, to introduce a system of grades which was an abrupt departure from traditional practice and roused a storm of controversy. Many theologians held that the simple vows taken by unprofessed Jesuits, who were called 'spiritual and temporal coadjutors', meant that they were not genuine religious, a dispute that was not settled until 1584, when Pope Gregory XIII ruled that they were.

To meet the many calls for Jesuit services it was necessary to lower standards of entry while devising a system of training which would raise raw recruits to a competence still lustrous in the general dimness of the clergy. Until 1546 all Jesuits were 'professed of the four vows', the first three being poverty, chastity and obedience. After that, profession would not normally be awarded, if at all, until a seventeen-year 'formation' had been completed (though the fourth vow taken by the professed fathers – of special obedience to the pope – committed all Jesuits). In training, which often involved several years of teaching in one or more colleges, spiritual coadjutors would be bound by simple vows and treated as on approval. They could be used as cheap and dispensable labour in the classroom, or for missions and sacerdotal chores which did not require any great learning. Lay coadjutors – the equivalent of lay brothers – also took simple vows and were classified as religious: but they were 'forbidden to learn more than they knew on entering the Society' and were restricted to such jobs as door-keepers, gardeners or cooks. This did not mean that they were necessarily illiterate or unintelligent. Alphonsus Rodriguez, a Segovian wool merchant, entered the Society as a lay brother at the age of forty and was employed as a door-keeper. Yet his spiritual influence as a person and as a mystical writer was such that he was canonized.

The creation of the spiritual coadjutor grade caused trouble within as well as outside the Society. In 1556, of about fifteen hundred Jesuits only forty-two were professed, including five of the nine founder members. There is evidence that Ignatius intended it to be a temporary expedient, but after his death it was firmly clamped upon the Company. The proportion of professed, though fluctuating, tended to become smaller, an élite within the élite monopolizing the most responsible positions. From 1616 to 1966 extensive theological learning was a prerequisite for profession, and from 1829 to 1964 over sixty per cent of priests pronouncing final or 'solemn' vows were assigned to the grade of spiritual coadjutor. This virtual relegation to second-class Jesuit citizenship has been a source of much resentment, and was already beginning to ferment when in 1550 Julius III, in the bull *Exposcit debitum,* while confirming the privileges of the Society and praising it fulsomely, approved the system by which coadjutors 'would be bound for whatever time the superior general should see fit to employ them'; while the Formula appended to the bull declared that 'none shall be permitted to pronounce his profession unless his life and doctrine have been probed by long and exacting tests.'

Though Ignatius prayed and wept over every clause in the Constitutions, he was not unaided in the awesome task of codifying the information supplied by Jesuit envoys and administrators right across Europe. Codure, who died in 1541, was succeeded as his secretary by the supremely efficient Juan Polanco who, like Lainez, was of Jewish *converso* or 'New Christian' stock. This reflected the General's disregard for racial origins, but helped to precipitate a conflict with the Spanish Inquisition and with racist-minded Jesuits that smouldered on to a fiery climax in the 1590s.

At Alcala in 1527 Ignatius had denied that his seemingly unorthodox fervour was 'tainted' by Judaism, indignantly retorting that he was a noble from a part of Spain that had hardly known Jews. Later, the hounding of Jewish and Moorish *conversos* by 'Old Christian' inquisitors who proclaimed *limpieza de sangre* (purity of blood) as the true test of orthodoxy amused and disgusted him. The first two Grand Inquisitors, Torquemada and Diego Deza, both had Jewish blood, and centuries of intermarriage between Spaniards, Jews and Moors had produced a society in which only 'the people' could boast of pure blood with any degree of confidence. Luther's rabid anti-semitism, based on the medieval belief that the Jews had crucified Christ and stole Christian infants for ritual sacrifice, seemed to make a more charitable attitude not only desirable but useful as propaganda. Ignatius, who had not forgotten his dream of a mission to the Muslims, set up a refuge in Rome for Moors and Jews who wanted to turn Catholic, and declared that he would have considered it a divine favour to be of Jewish descent ('What! To be related to Christ our Lord and to Our Lady the glorious Virgin Mary?').

In 1551 the Archbishop of Toledo insisted on screening priests in the Jesuit college at Alcala. The rector, Francisco de Villanueva, who as a near-illiterate Estremaduran peasant had joined the Society ten years earlier, reported to Rome: 'It is a great pity that nobody seems willing to leave these poor people anywhere to stay on earth, and I would like to have the courage to become their defender, particularly since one encounters among them more virtue than among the Old Christians and the hidalgos.' It made sense that there should be at least one Catholic order open to the talents of *converso* priests, scholars, merchants and artisans driven from Spain. But Fr Araoz, reluctant to challenge an hysterical prejudice for fear of the effect on Jesuit recruiting, did not agree, and warned his uncle of the consequences. Ignatius, who caustically referred to the *limpieza* cult as 'the Spanish humour', stood firm, advising *conversos* to join the Society in Italy rather than in Spain, and one of the first professors in the show-piece Roman College was a Jewish *converso* Jesuit, Fr Eliano. Bearing in mind that (despite Luther's ravings) the Archbishop of Toledo and Philip II alleged that 'the principal heretics of Germany are all descendants of Jews' and that Cardinal Carafa, in his hatred of all things Iberian, was apt to denounce Spaniards as 'the spawn of Moors and Jews, the dregs of the earth', this showed real courage.

Perhaps the legend of the Islamic origins of the Society had its roots in this bitter controversy. The election of Lainez as General in 1558 was fiercely opposed by Philip II and the Spanish Church: but both he and his successor Francis Borgia, an unimpeachably Old Christian, refused to abandon the policy of Ignatius. When questioned about it by Philip II's prime minister, the Prince of Eboli, Borgia replied: 'Why does the King keep in his service people who are *conversos*? If His Majesty disregards this in his household, why should I make an issue about admitting them into the service of that Lord for whom there is no distinction between persons?' But the Dominican-controlled Spanish Inquisition put some of Borgia's writings on the Index; and the gathering revolt of Spanish Jesuits against rule from Rome had been pushed a stage further when in 1554 Ignatius named the now overtly Jesuit Francis Borgia Commissary-General in Spain over the heads of Fr Araoz and the other two provincial superiors.

In his chronicle of the first sixteen years of the Society Polanco states that through all these years of multiple activity and frequent crises his master 'suffered often so severely from stomach pains that he could make no movement and lay simply helpless. He always felt better when some important matter had to be tackled: then he started to labour day and night.' He had not envisaged the Society as primarily a teaching order any more than he had seen it as spearhead of the Counter-Reformation. Yet once Lainez and Favre – who in Germany had noticed the relative efficiency of Protestant schools – had convinced him that a classroom apostolate was crucial not only for the equipment of Jesuit priests but for all comers, lay or clerical, his commitment to yet another huge task of improvisation was total. The lifting of the restriction on membership and approval for the coadjutor system were important moves in a development which by the end of the sixteenth century had grown to the extent that perhaps three-quarters of Jesuit houses in

Europe and overseas were schools and nearly four-fifths of Jesuits –
mostly scholastics – were teaching.

The first Jesuit 'colleges' were residences in university towns where,
under supervision, students attended the existing courses. This arrangement was first made in Paris in 1540, then, during the next four years, at
Coimbra, Padua, Louvain, Cologne and Valencia. Except in Paris the
lack of method and discipline forced Ignatius and his advisers, chiefly
Lainez, Polanco and Jeronimo Nadal, to think in terms of a separate
system that would synthesize what was best or most suitable in contemporary curricula. Ignatius himself had personal experience of Alcala,
Salamanca and Paris: and though Paris remained the great exemplar, he
and his aides also studied the constitutions of the universities of
Valencia, Coimbra, Louvain, Cologne, Bologna and Padua – as well as
the methods of Protestant pioneers at Nîmes and Strasbourg. At first
they were concerned only with the formation of Jesuits, but their
religiously-toned version of classical humanism was soon adapted for the
use of lay pupils and non-Jesuit seminarians (called 'externs') who were
to be distinguished in dress from the Society's scholastics. Objectives
multiplied: priests were to be trained (and used as teachers during their
training); a lay Catholic élite was to be fashioned; new recruits were to be
found; and eventually the children of heretic parents were to be
admitted and perhaps weaned from their heresy.

The first externs, lay and clerical, were admitted in Goa in 1543 on
Xavier's initiative. Three years later the college at Gandia, founded by
Francis Borgia, followed suit; and in 1548, at the invitation of his friend
Don Juan de Vega, the Spanish Viceroy, Ignatius sent a team of ten
crack Jesuits to Messina in Sicily to open the first school primarily
designed for secular pupils. Its curriculum became a model for future
establishments, the first stage in a process of experiment, fact-gathering
and analysis which culminated in the *Ratio Studiorum* (Plan of Studies) of
1599. By 1556 the Jesuits were running thirty-five colleges in Sicily,
Italy, Spain, Portugal, Austria, France, Bohemia and Germany. By 1586
the number had risen to one hundred and sixty-two (of which fifteen
were for Jesuit seminarians only), and by the early seventeenth century,
a mere sixty years after the initial gropings, there were nearly three
hundred Jesuit schools of various types. There were those mainly for lay
externs but with some Jesuit scholastics; board residences for seminarians who went elsewhere for lectures; and a few boarding colleges for
fee-paying lay students such as the one opened in Vienna in 1553.
Boarding was a rarity because of the extra staff needed and disciplinary

problems with aristocratic pupils, often accompanied by a retinue of servants. In the day schools provision was made 'from time to time and for good reasons, to admit the sons of the rich or of the nobles when they pay their own expenses'. The common charge that the Jesuits concerned themselves mainly with upper-class students does not bear scrutiny. The very opposite is true: so much so that Voltaire and other class-conscious rationalist critics of the eighteenth century were to complain that Jesuit colleges were giving far too many lower-class boys ideas above their station.

The Roman College, opened in 1551 and later to become the Gregorian University, began in a small way with a notice nailed to the door which summed up the Ignatian system: 'School of Grammar, Humanities and Christian Doctrine. Free.' Francis Borgia, who also paid for the first printing of the *Exercises,* was a generous benefactor; but the German College, opened in 1552, ran into financial troubles. Cardinals did not give the money they had promised ('Very well,' Ignatius is said to have commented, 'I shall keep the house going on my own even if I have to sell myself'). Such painful experiences with unreliable patrons caused him to be very precise in these matters. He would not found a college except on his own terms – a good site; a sound building; a populous locality; a foundation without any strings attached and adequate for long-term development. Clauses in that section of the Constitutions devoted to 'the Remembrance of Founders and Benefactors of the Society' insist that gratitude for their generosity does not imply 'any right of patronage or any claim belonging to them or their successors against the college or its temporal goods', and warn that 'the possessions and fixed revenues of the colleges' will be defended 'even in court if this should be expedient and necessary'.

Wherever a Jesuit college opened it was likely to be faced with hostility from local grammar-school masters whose livelihood was threatened by a rival offering an education at once free and usually superior. Windows were smashed, accusations of heresy, incompetence and immorality hurled. In Paris and other university cities opposition was stern and prolonged. But after heroic persistence – there were remarkably few closures – the Jesuits took root. The curriculum revolved around five main principles: a solid grounding in Latin grammar; classes arranged according to the capacity of students, each class (though still very large) having a distinct grade and separate teacher; a planned progression or 'ascent' of studies from the lowest class of grammar to humanities and rhetoric, then through the arts courses (philosophy, mathematics etc.)

[59]

and theology (mainly for star pupils); punctual and constant attendance; related exercises and homework – repetitions, disputations, memory tests, compositions. Three hours of classes in the morning and three in the afternoon was the norm. There were few Jesuit universities as such. A school like the Roman College became a university by the addition of the higher faculties of arts and theology, but some colleges extended their range to include logic, physics, and theology, thus providing a secondary education for five years up to rhetoric class, and a higher education of sorts for a further three years. As a general rule pupils were expected to have learned to read and write before admission. Peter Canisius, the renowned theologian Robert Bellarmine, the dramatists Corneille and Calderon, all, after elementary teaching by private tutors, entered Jesuit colleges at the age of about nine, studied languages (Latin and Greek with some vernacular work) from ten to thirteen, arts from fourteen to sixteen, and theology from seventeen to twenty-one.

In Jesuit as in other schools the size of classes and lack of textbooks made a system of 'emulation' inevitable. Pupils were sorted into groups with a 'leader' ('it would be wise,' say the Constitutions, 'to place together some of equal ability who with holy rivalry may spur one another on'). The recommendation of Fr Nadal, first rector of the college at Messina, that 'the Rector will have in each class censors from whom he may learn what takes place in the school. . . . If there are students of the Society in the classes they should be chosen' has been represented as a shocking example of Jesuit espionage. Yet the censor or monitor system was used everywhere at that time: in Sturm's school at Strasbourg, in the University of Paris, in England at Winchester and St Paul's. The office of censor soon became an honour, which, in many schools, it still is.

Discipline was strict, but less harsh than at Paris, and rectors were exhorted to 'mingle severity with kindness'. Floggings were at first administered by a 'corrector', a non-Jesuit employee. The arrangement was abandoned when correctors were assaulted in the streets by resentful students. More important and pervasive was moral pressure. Boys attended Mass and made an examination of conscience daily, were catechized every week, listened to a sermon every Sunday, went monthly to confession, and strove to belong to the élite Marian congregation. Scholastics (Jesuit students) were expected to set a good example ('their conversation with students from outside the Society should be only about matters pertaining to learning and spirituality'). Every minute of the day was filled with prescribed activity and as far as possible children were never left alone; for the acceptance of sexual curiosity so general in medieval society was now being replaced by the ideal of respectability which the Jesuits did much to foster. Confessors' manuals warned that masturbation was a fruit of original sin and urged grown-ups to avoid lewd language and behaviour before children.

Expurgation of the classics was not new, though it was carried out with characteristic thoroughness. The Constitutions required that 'in the books of humane letters by pagan authors nothing immoral should be lectured on; and what remains can be used by the Society like the spoils of Egypt. In the case of Christian authors, even though a work may be good it should not be lectured on when the author is bad, lest attachment to him be acquired.' Terence was altogether banned, though the ingenious Fr André des Freux, who had already prepared suitable editions of Horace and Martial, suggested that his more licentious passages could be rewritten as scenes of pure conjugal love. In due course the Jesuits incorporated regular, organized games in the curriculum, publishing Latin treatises on gymnastics and tabulating the rules of recommended pastimes. Here was a wholesome outlet for youthful energy that, like the plays and ballets with edifying themes which soon became a feature of Jesuit schools, combined social advantages with team and competitive spirit.

The entire system, the first in Europe on such an ambitious scale, was carefully articulated towards an end: the catholicization of thought and personality. But then what educational system with any vitality has not been a means to an end that its pioneers have considered desirable? The Jesuit scheme was far from universally perfect in execution, as witness the report of one of the Society's commissioners in Germany appointed to help prepare the *Ratio Studiorum*: 'Inadequately instructed scholastics become incapable teachers,' he wrote in 1586. 'They produce unlearned Superiors ignorant of all humanistic knowledge, not a few of whom cannot even write a grammatical letter . . . The Rector and Prefect of Studies are not greatly concerned about the manner of teaching . . . Before the masters have learned to teach they receive orders to stop. What respect, and what experience, can they have? There is no city that changes its executioner or hangman once a year, and yet we believe that this constant fluctuation is good for study!'

Local opposition, varying from riots to concerted legal obstruction, religious wars and political upheavals, periodical expulsions, growing pains, and a sense of urgency which increased the temptation to spread resources thin, were the main reasons for such shortcomings. The wonder is not that Jesuit schools were often more impressive on paper than in practice, but that they survived at all and reached a level of relative efficiency, not least as propagators of Counter-Reformation ideology. Obedience to Catholic authority in Church and State was so firmly proclaimed that in 1580 the Prince of Parma, Governor of the Netherlands, wrote to Philip II: 'Your Majesty desired me to build a citadel at Maastricht. I thought a college of the Jesuits would be a fortress more likely to protect the inhabitants against the enemies of the Altar and the Throne. I have built it.' Ignatius could not have wished for a better testimonial.

In 1553 Jeronimo Nadal, who had also studied at Alcala and Paris, was appointed Vicar-General of the Society and began a fifteen-year tour of Europe to promulgate the Constitutions and supervise the educational programme. It took him through Italy, Spain and Portugal (twice), Belgium and Germany (twice), Austria and Bohemia. He stayed in thirty-five cities, organizing, persuading, listening, adapting rules to local or national conditions, collecting funds for the Roman College.

The section on education, though the longest, is one of ten into which the Constitutions were divided. With Polanco and Nadal taking much of the strain of day-to-day government, Ignatius was freed to apply himself to the task of fleshing out the sketch provided by the Formula; and from 1547, in close partnership with Polanco, this was his chief preoccupation. It is a manic attempt to institutionalize a way of life, a spirituality, which had grown naturally among the founder members. A company is transformed into a legalistic, hierarchical Society, a pilgrim priest into a mass-produced, conformist Jesuit, who is bade to resemble in his purity the chastity of the angels, with the help of thirteen Rules of Modesty which reflect the founder's courtly training: 'As regards the conversation of Ours let it be said in general that in all outward actions there should appear modesty and humility joined with religious maturity . . . For the most part let the eyes be downcast . . . When speaking, especially with men of authority, let not the gaze be fixed full upon the face but rather a little between the eyes . . . Wrinkles on the forehead and much more on the nose are to be avoided so that outward serenity may appear as a testimony to inner serenity . . . The hands, if not engaged in holding one's cloak, should be kept decently quiet . . . The gait should be moderate without notable haste unless necessity requires it; in which case care of decorum should be had . . . All gestures and movements should be such as to give edification to all.'

The collection and collating of data from the field continued until the moment of Ignatius' death, though by 1550, when foundation members were summoned to Rome to consider and criticize the text, it was virtually complete. Advice was taken from a group of physicians when it was learned that novices were 'wasting away and dying because of the austerities they practised'. The physicians' recommendations – seven hours' sleep, mental prayer not to exceed an hour, adequate rest after meals, a maximum of two hours' intensive study at a time, plenty of exercise – were written into the Rules, as were earlier cautions against excessive penance. A sound mind in a sound body was the ideal if a Jesuit was to be an effective instrument 'to the greater glory of God' – a phrase that recurs in the Constitutions about once to each manuscript page.

A note of regimental pride sounds throughout the document and there is more than a hint that Ours are the Lord's elect. There is something almost sinister in Ignatius' curiosity about every detail of his Jesuits' lives. Fr da Camara records that he 'used to have letters read, especially those from India, two or three times, and wanted to know what his brethren ate, how they slept etc., and once he broke out, "Oh, I should like to know how many fleas bite my Fathers at night."' Though ill health forced Ignatius to delegate authority, paternalism, the longing to permeate every nook and cranny of a 'family' which even in his lifetime was turning into an international organization, was the ideal behind the Society's command structure: every superior to be seen as in the place of Christ, but the General, elected for life, having the power to appoint the other superiors who when their term of office expired could be, and sometimes in a frenzy of humility scrambled to be, demoted to menial tasks. At regular intervals a subject was to make manifestation of conscience to a superior, 'that is to say, he must reveal the whole of his interior life, his temptations, difficulties and progress.' That this vigilance might be all-embracing, an admonitor was attached to the staffs of the General and the Provincial Superiors (Provincials), specially concerned with sanctification and for this purpose having access to the records of all 'manifestations'.

Add to this the obligation of detailed reports to Rome (Italian superiors had to report once a month, superiors elsewhere in Europe every four months, those in oversea missions annually) and one begins to see why Isaac Taylor, a nineteenth-century historian of religion, described the system as 'the panopticon of soul-despotism'. True, each Jesuit had the right to communicate directly with the General, the Constitutions declare that they aim not at uniformity but at unity, provision is made for regional or local adaptation, and Ignatius rebuked and sometimes removed over-tyrannical superiors. On paper, recognition of the need for latitude is so impressive that a recent authority has suggested that Ignatius aimed at 'a dialectic of obedience and initiative. Few religious superiors can have told members of their order so firmly to forget the rules and do what they thought best.'

Constant physical pain sometimes eroded the General's serenity and drove him to exasperation, but in major crises he showed a sense of politic proportion. When in 1548 Bobadilla bluntly criticized Charles V's attempts to reach a compromise religious settlement in Germany, he was switched to Naples and kept out of harm's way as superintendent of a Jesuit school. Simon Rodrigues, who had gone his own way in Portugal to the extent of running a separate Society, received a letter on obedience stuffed with clichés about corpse-like submission, statue-like indifference, and stick-like humility: but as a firm favourite with the Portuguese court he was treated with great lenience. For, as Ignatius put it in one of the very last clauses of the Constitutions: 'First of all an effort should be made to retain the benevolence of the Holy See . . . and then that of the temporal rulers and noble and powerful persons whose favour or disfavour does much toward opening or closing the gate to the service of God and the good of souls.' This example of selective punishment was to speak louder than written counsels of perfection in the ears of many superiors and successive generals, as the age of heroic improvisation and almost unlimited scope passed and the letter of the law tended to stifle its spirit. In 1609 the best-selling *Practice of Christian Perfection* by Alfonso Rodriguez SJ reasoned that 'one of the great consolations of the religious life is the assurance we have that in obeying we can commit no fault . . . The moment what you did was done obediently, God wipes it out of your account and charges it to the Superior. So that St Jerome well exclaimed, in celebrating the advantages of obedience, "Oh sovereign liberty! Oh holy and blessed security by which one becomes almost impeccable!"'

Though a tireless fund-raiser, Ignatius laid heavy stress on the ideal of poverty. But though no fees might be accepted for preaching, teaching, Masses or the giving of the *Exercises*, this very abnegation was liable to attract gifts far larger than the fattest of fees; and in profane eyes the distinction between corporate wealth and individual poverty became blurred to the point of invisibility.

Exhausted and keenly conscious of all the pitfalls, Ignatius tried to resign in 1551. His request was refused and his activity actually increased. His one relaxation or relief was the 'gift' of tears. The

1. (*Above left*) St Ignatius Loyola (1491-1556), founder of the Society of Jesus.

2. (*Above right*) Paul III, the pope who approved the Society's foundation in 1540.

3. (*Below*) Ignatius flanked by some eminent early Jesuits.

EGO VOBIS ROMÆ PROPITIVS ERO.

4.   The vision of Ignatius on the road to Rome in 1537.

5.   St Peter Canisius (1521-1597),
the revered Dutch Jesuit who led the
16th-century Catholic revival
in Germany.

6.   Claudio Aquaviva, the Society's first
Italian general from 1581 to 1615:
said to have introduced 'jesuitical
techniques'.

7. (*Above*) The Council of Trent in session, c. 1545.

8. (*Below*) 'I leave you the world!' An apocryphal version of Ignatius on his deathbed in 1556.

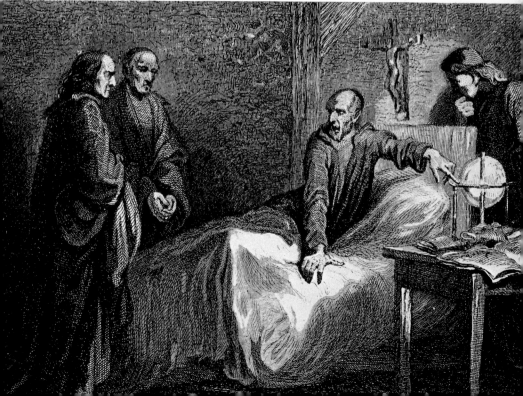

9. *(Above left)*   Paul IV, a Jesuit-hating pope who tried to limit the
Society's autonomy.
10. *(Above right)*   The death of St Francis Xavier (1552), in sight of the China coast.
11. *(Below left)*   St Robert Bellarmine (1542-1621), Italian theologian and
controversialist, appointed cardinal in 1599.
12. *(Below right)*   St Francis Borgia (1510-1572) the third Jesuit general.

Spiritual Diary is full of entries on the subject and da Camara relates that 'when he did not weep three times at Mass he felt deprived of consolation'. His pursuit of this consolation was so orgiastic that his eyesight was damaged and from 1544 he had to confine his celebration of Mass to Sundays and feast days. Yet when a doctor ordered him to cease this indulgence he did so, noting that his consolations were increased and writing to Francis Borgia to warn him that exterior as opposed to interior lachrymosity was a dangerous gift, 'because these tears do not serve to increase charity . . . being harmful to the body and head.' He continued, however, to set an example of obsessive spiritual hygiene. A Jesuit who, when asked at mid-day how often he had examined his conscience, replied 'Seven times,' received the implied rebuke: 'So few?' On the hour, every hour, day and, so far as possible, night, was Ignatius' routine; he frequently astounded his confessor with a discharge of finicky scruples. For anyone else such scrupulosity would have been as engrossing as full choir. But he continued to frown on 'depth' mysticism. For Jesuits with a stubbornly contemplative streak a transfer to the Carthusians was the answer.

Slowly crushed by the burden of acting out the role of Jesuit paragon, he could reflect that a company which had started with ten apostles and the loan of a tiny house in Rome had in fifteen years grown to possess a hundred houses and more than fifteen hundred members, distributed in the eleven provinces of Italy, Sicily, Portugal, Aragon, Castile, Andalusia, Upper and Lower Germany, France, India and Brazil. Ignatius had been desperately ill so often that little notice was taken when he collapsed on 30 July 1556. He told the physician to give priority to other sick Jesuits, instructed Polanco, who had a press of correspondence, not to interrupt his labours, and died without the Last Sacraments. William James conceded that 'his mysticism made him assuredly one of the most powerfully practical human engines that ever lived' and one can well believe the story that when Paul III died in 1549 Ignatius had some backing as his successor. The codification of his experience in the *Spiritual Exercises* and the Constitutions had fashioned a commando religion, a kind of Catholic Methodism.

His most hyperbolical flights of fancy had been used to romanticize the concept of loyalty to the pope. He was reported as saying that 'if the Holy Father were to order me to abandon myself to the sea without a mast, without sails, oars or rudder . . . I would obey not only with alacrity but without anxiety or repugnance, and even with great internal satisfaction.' He may even, in his longing for solitude, have meant what he said. But when, in his last days, Cardinal Carafa became Pope Paul IV, his loyalty was put to a severer test. He confided that the news 'made him shake in every bone of his body'. Paul IV was known to be intent on restoring choir and limiting the Jesuit general's term of office to three years. Lainez had to accept these conditions, and in 1558, when the Constitutions were first printed, an addendum slip was inserted to this effect. But Paul IV died in 1559 and his instructions were cancelled by his successor: a coincidence which gave a certain plausibility to the rumour that the Jesuits were either very lucky or had their own methods of disposing of refractory popes to the greater glory of God and of His Society.

CHAPTER SIX

Trent

IGNATIUS HAD NEVER DOUBTED that he who wills the end must will the means. By the time he reached Venice in 1535 he was painfully aware that the Church was a highly political organization, which may have been one reason why he wanted to escape to the Holy Land. When this escape was blocked he set himself, with characteristic application, to master the intricacies of ecclesiastical politics in the incessant power-scramble of Rome. Machiavelli had proclaimed that idealism without power was impotent fantasy, and in *The Rise of European Liberalism* Harold Laski argues that Machiavelli's ruthless-only-to-be-effective Prince is 'not a caricature of the century which followed, but an index to it. We find him in all its typical men, in Cromwell and Walsingham in England, and even, under their special protective colouring, in Luther and Calvin and popes like Paul III. He is in religious zealots like Loyola not less than in splendid pirates like Hawkins and Drake. A new enterprise, a new efficiency, serves a new ideal.'

The bargain which Ignatius struck with Paul III resembled a 'no prey, no pay' buccaneering commission, and the Jesuits were expected to show quick results. Nowhere was this more vital than in Germany, the heartland of the Reformation, and in the closely-linked tournament known as the Council of Trent, where Jesuit champions were expected to defend papal sovereignty against the Habsburg lobby, dissident bishops, and schemes for conciliar government of the Church with the pope as a figurehead president. When Paul III sent Favre to Germany in 1541 it is doubtful whether he expected this to be more than a gesture or perhaps a humouring of the importunate Basque. Chafing at Spanish dictation, he reached the point, after the assassination of his disreputable son Pierluigi, of preparing a Holy League against the Emperor; and while Frs Bobadilla, Le Jay and Canisius were laying the foundations of Jesuit influence as spiritual advisers to the court at Vienna, he was proposing a Turkish invasion of Austria.

The German problem, a mass of conflicting, overlapping interests, had stuck fast in a quagmire of insincere and inconclusive 'dialogue' in which religion played no more than a terminological part. The Turkish threat removed any possibility of a Catholic counter-crusade. The Valois-Habsburg balance of power duel made this even more impracticable, since French policy was to keep Germany disunited and troublesome: no difficult task when the chaotic Holy Roman Empire consisted of hundreds of electorates, principalities, duchies and prince-bishoprics. The fear and bloody suppression of Anabaptist revolt had brought Lutheran rulers and the Catholic Emperor closer together. A spirit of co-existence and religious indifference succeeded the pugnacious bravado of Luther's early broadsides. Catholic-Protestant marriages became quite common and despite papal protests Catholic princes appointed Protestant officials and political advisers. Wealthy, worldly prelates had no wish to be reformed. Most people favoured a settlement based on the realities of the situation, which meant accepting the fact that large areas were lost to the Roman Church. Semi-official religious conferences at Worms and Regensburg in 1540 to 1541 achieved little. Angered by the Pope's prevarication, Charles V, desperate for some kind of solution, signed the Interim of Augsburg in 1548 which authorized married priests to continue their ministry and permitted the laity to take communion in both kinds. Seven years later the Peace of Augsburg, intended as a temporary arrangement, recognized the *cujus regio, ejus religio* principle that each ruler should choose between Catholicism and Lutheranism. Subjects were expected to follow their ruler's choice.

It was no longer possible to pretend that the religious debate was between representatives of parties within the Catholic Church. The spirit of co-existence was driven underground, religion firmly welded to court politics, Calvinists antagonized by their exclusion from the deal. Yet the Emperor had persisted with plans for an ecumenical gathering. Paul III reluctantly consented to a council under threat – the more ominous because of Henry VIII's recent break with Rome – that if he did not German affairs would be settled by a national assembly in which Rome would have no say. Since Lutheran representatives refused to attend a council held in Italy, the Tyrolean town of Trent was selected as a compromise venue, being within the boundaries of the Empire and therefore acceptable to the Germans, but Italian-speaking and near enough to Italy to placate the papacy. The opening session, scheduled for 1542, had to be postponed until 1545 because of war between France and the Emperor. Most Catholics and Lutherans viewed it with boredom or contempt. When, under duress, some Lutheran delegates attended in 1551, their demand for conciliar government and the annulment of all previous dogmatic decisions caused deadlock. When the imperial armies were defeated in Germany and Charles V fled, the Lutherans departed and in 1552 the Council once more disbanded, not to meet again for ten years.

At this moment, thanks to the urgent begging of Ignatius and Nadal, the German College was opened to prepare selected candidates for the uphill task of re-catholicizing the Empire. With this, the Roman College, and a network of seminaries and 'mixed' schools the Society had begun the clerical reformation which was not officially decreed until the 1560s. By then, wrote the historian Leopold von Ranke, the Josuits had 'occupied Bavaria, Tyrol, Franconia, much of the Rhine Province and Austria, and had penetrated into Hungary and Moravia. It was the first durable anti-Protestant check that Germany had received.'

In 1541, when this remarkable surge began, the just-recognized Society had nothing to lose and everything to gain. The courage, intelligence and sheer stamina of Favre, Le Jay, Bobadilla and Canisius were tremendous assets; but Loyola's instructions to them were a model of prudence. Now was not the time for bold polemics. 'Your defence of the Apostolic See,' he wrote, 'should never go so far that you lose control of yourselves and get decried as Papists . . . Try to make friends with the leaders of the opposition and with those who have most influence among heretics and wavering Catholics and loose them from their error through wisdom and love.' Favre, who had already been active in Italy, Spain and Germany, was, like Le Jay and Canisius after him, a peacemaker by temperament. Like them he also stressed that the advance of Protestantism owed more to the incompetence and corruption of the Catholic clergy than to 'the apparent righteousness of Lutheran teaching'.

These three men, and the combative Bobadilla, appeared like angels of light in a dingy and demoralized scene. Care for the sick, alms for the poor, prison visiting, threadbare cassocks, sermons of fiery yet charitable zeal, all this seemed nothing short of sensational; and reports assured Ignatius that the *Exercises* were working their customary magic on lapsed believers in places of power. In this respect Favre's most important catch was Peter Kanis (Canisius), a Dutchman from Nijmegen who was to become the most tireless Jesuit apostle in Central Europe. Writer, preacher, teacher, founder of colleges, prodigious traveller, he was a whirlwind of energy and versatility. His correspondence alone, collected from more than two hundred and fifty libraries in eleven countries, runs to nearly eight thousand octavo pages.

Papal privileges did not prevent rough handling from bands of mercenaries, Lutheran and Catholic mobs, and local authorities who saw the Jesuits as troublemakers. When Favre died in 1546, Le Jay and Canisius continued his irenic approach. Both, at the invitation of Duke William of Bavaria, lectured at the University of Ingolstadt, and pressed hard for the establishment of Jesuit schools. The first two were set up at Ingolstadt and Vienna. Nadal noted that German pupils disliked being flogged by an outsider, preferring to take their punishment from a teacher, so the rule was altered. He also approved elementary reading and writing classes in German colleges because, as he wrote to Ignatius, 'we could not allow that at such a tender age the boys should be taught by heretics or men suspected of heresy; for this is the condition of practically all the teachers even in areas which are predominantly Catholic.'

Ignatius replied with detailed suggestions: 'Since Canisius will be at Ingolstadt and because of his experience he should be allowed to legislate as he sees fit. It will be well to consider whether a Latin oration should be delivered to the people at the opening of the college to explain the Society's aims and purpose in education, and another oration might be delivered in German to the same end, setting forth among other things that the college will provide not only theological lectures but also a classical course in Latin, Greek and Hebrew ... Theodore Van Pelt will teach rhetoric and Greek ... He could also give a lesson in Hebrew. If this should prove too arduous, let Gerard Warden assist him ... Let the masters show great diligence in class-exercises, repetitions, disputations, written compositions; and let them use every means to inculcate in their pupils, even in the youngest, the Catholic teaching, remembering that they are instructors in virtuous habits no less than in letters. The labours of all should be tempered with discretion. Thus the class periods ought to be of moderate length and once a week let there be a day or half-day of recreation.'

One of Nadal's first priorities in Germany, where a sectarian pamphlet war had raged for three decades with no effective Catholic rejoinder, was to set up a printing press in Vienna. There Canisius produced his *Survey of Christian Doctrine*, a catechism which proved such a success that the author was publicly denounced at Wittenberg, the Lutheran stronghold, as 'the impudent and odious fellow whose name is derived from the Latin for a dog'; while in Johann Wigand's *Scriptural Refutation of the Jesuit Catechism* he was referred to as 'a dog of a monk, idolater, wolf, ass of the Pope, swindling trickster, shameless and miserable devil'.

Canisius, who in the next thirty years was constantly on the move in Germany, Austria, Bohemia, Switzerland and Italy, was far too busy to reply to such crude attacks. At Vienna, under the leadership of Claude Le Jay, he was part of an all-action Jesuit community that included Frenchmen, Flemings, Spaniards, Germans, Austrians, Dutchmen and Hungarians. They lived in makeshift quarters, stirred up the stagnant university, evangelized Italian engineers brought in to fortify the city against a Turkish siege, and tried to plug the yawning gaps in a Church which was in an advanced stage of decay. For twenty years, they learned, not a single priest had been ordained in Vienna, and in the adjoining diocese of Passau some two hundred and fifty parishes were priestless. Canisius, who had been summoned to one of the sessions at Trent (and thereafter deluged the Council with specimens of Protestant literature), was prominent in all these undertakings and also appointed himself prison chaplain. In 1556 he was made Superior of the new province of Upper Germany, covering Austria, Bohemia, Bavaria and Tyrol. Asked for a report on his personality and achievements, another Jesuit replied: 'I think his match is not to be found on earth . . . Day and night he sweats and toils to promote true religion. Among Catholics he is universally venerated. This is what I have to report about our Father Canisius.'

As an army chaplain Nicolas Bobadilla had followed the Catholic forces on a mule. Now at the zenith of his influence, he was a formidable controversialist and much in demand as a spiritual adviser. Unlike Favre, Le Jay and Canisius he was much inclined to sing his own praises and temperamentally incapable of toeing a diplomatic line. Charles V's brother, King Ferdinand, was very fond of him, perhaps because of his brashness. 'As far as I can see,' Bobadilla informed Ignatius, 'I am having better fruit in these parts than any of our men in Germany. All and sundry, King, Court and Nuncio, are pleased with me, though I tell them plainly that I am not so with them . . . I am on intimate terms with the Venetian ambassador . . . There is not much business transacted by the King to which he does not make me privy. He carries out every good work which I recommend. The esteem and authority which I have with him would appear to be the doing of God.' Bobadilla also charmed and amused the harassed Emperor until he overstepped the mark by circulating angry criticisms of the Interim of Augsburg, and was removed from his position. No longer were the literary labours of Ignatius and Polanco lightened by such examples of Bobadilla's touch as a letter that ended by requesting prayers for his apostolic labours in Germany, 'which are very different from those of your garden and kitchen in Rome'.

Jesuit bulletins from Trent had few fireworks to report. Though Lainez was, in his way, quite as pugnacious as Bobadilla, neither he, Salmeron nor Le Jay, the chief representatives of the Society, were noted for exuberance. All three had been chosen as special theologians of the Holy See, arriving at Trent in May 1546. Lainez, with Canisius to assist him as translator, was commissioned by Cardinal Cervini to compile 'a list of all the dogmatic errors of the heretics which are to be condemned by the Council'. The youth of this Jesuit quartet was striking: Canisius twenty-six, Salmeron and Le Jay thirty-one, Lainez thirty-four – and their zeal impressive, though not such as to please the Emperor in his pursuit of appeasement. Their brief extended to a close watch on dangerous tendencies detectable in the many sessions devoted to defining the doctrine of justification. The somewhat over-ecumenical suggestions of one cardinal were attacked by Lainez in a three-hour refutation so admired that it was included in the official record. Pale, thin, hook-nosed and sharp-eyed, he led the group in their role as watch-dogs. This did not endear them to the Spanish Dominicans, headed by the irascible Melchior Cano. But, as some typically exacting 'suggestions' from Rome made clear, this was by no means their only duty. Ignatius reminded them that 'the greater glory of God is the purpose of our Fathers at Trent, and this will be furthered by preaching, hearing confessions, lecturing, teaching children, visiting the poor in hospitals . . . In preaching I would not touch at all on the differences between Protestants and Catholics, but simply exhort to good habits and devotion . . . I would constantly mention the Council in sermons and end each of them with prayers for it.'

During a four-year break in the Council's deliberations from 1547 to 1551, caused by political bickering and an outbreak of plague, Salmeron made a revivalist preaching tour of Italy and, having at the General's insistence collected a degree in theology at Bologna, journeyed to Ingolstadt with Canisius and Le Jay to teach there. Lainez preached, lectured and catechized in Italian towns from Palermo to Bologna and accompanied a punitive expedition to Tunis as chaplain. The resumption of the Council was marked by a sharp exchange between the new Pope, Julius III, and the French king, who forbade any of 'his' bishops to attend. The arrival of the shabbily-dressed Lainez and Salmeron, who were lodged in what the former described as 'a small, smoky oven of a room', is said to have caused a ripple of excitement among the few Fathers in town.

Sure enough some Jesuit-Dominican sparks flew. Hoping to persuade

Cano, then at the height of an anti-Jesuit crusade in Spain, that the Society was not composed of monsters or deliberate stealers of Dominican thunder – in fact that they should cooperate for the greater glory of God – Lainez and Salmeron called upon the great man in his rather more spacious lodging. The meeting was a disaster. After much wrangling, Lainez exclaimed: 'Why do you take upon yourself the office of the Bishops and the Supreme Pastor, to condemn those whom they approve?' Cano's reply: 'Would you not have the dogs bark when the shepherds sleep?' drew the retort: 'Yes, but at the wolves and not at other dogs.' A furious row ensued, and Lainez's swift and humble apology did not pacify the irate Dominican.*

Far worse than Melchior Cano's hostility was the frigid reception which awaited Lainez in Rome for this and other misdemeanours. 'Our Father,' he was informed in a letter dictated to Polanco, 'is not a little vexed with your Reverence, and so much the more in proportion as the faults of those who are greatly loved weigh more heavily on those who love them.' Told to decide what penance he deserved, the culprit replied: 'I accept lovingly all that you say to me lovingly, and feel as if my hungry soul was waxing fat on a dainty feast . . . If I were to be treated as I deserve, namely as dung and nothingness, it would help me to live interiorly with my God . . . I choose that your Reverence should deprive me of the charge of others which I hold, stop my preaching and studying, and leaving me only my Breviary, order me to beg my way to Rome and there exercise me in the kitchen or in the garden . . . If, however, I am found no good for such tasks, then in the lowest class of grammar in the school. All this to be until death, without any more external care of me than if I were the remains of an old broom.'

Such was Jesuit democracy in full flush. Even founder members and future generals played the worm and affected to love the plough that cut them.

---

* According to Fr T. J. Campbell's history of the Society, Cano's hatred pursued the Jesuits even from the grave. 'God grant,' he is alleged to have written in a sort of last testament, 'that I may not be a Cassandra, who was believed only after the sack of Troy. If the religious of this Society continue as they have begun, there may come a time, which I hope God will avert, when the kings of Europe would wish to resist them but will be unable to do so.'

CHAPTER SEVEN

Star in the East

OUTSIDE EUROPE, too, eager Jesuits met with suspicion and obstruction: this time entirely from Catholic rivals, since not until the nineteenth century did Protestantism develop any substantial overseas missionary drive. In Luther's opinion 'the faith of Jews, Turks, and Papists is all one thing' – a view that caused the Jesuit controversialist Robert Bellarmine to retort that 'heretics are never said to have converted Jews or pagans, but only to have persecuted Christians'.

Not until they reached Japan, China and the remoter regions of South America did Jesuit missionaries have the field to themselves for a while. Everywhere else Franciscans, Dominicans, Augustinians and Mercedarians had preceded them, and often resented their intrusion. Jesuit missionaries' reports were used to bring funds, recruits and prestige: Xavier's bulletins from the East Indies not only lured the invaluable Nadal into the Society but persuaded King John III of Portugal to increase his endowment of the college at Coimbra. Failures and shortcomings were, naturally, edited out before publication. All was triumph and heroism – mass baptisms, miracles, savage chieftains or oriental potentates won for the Church, vices forsworn, idols abandoned or smashed. Even the lethal hazards were presented as inducements. A cult of martyrdom as the missionary's crown was sedulously fostered. 'There is no better rest in this restless world,' wrote Francis Xavier to Simon Rodrigues from Cochin in 1549, 'than to face imminent peril of death solely for the love and service of God our Lord.'

Critics supplied the gaps in the *Letters* with equally partisan fervour. According to them conversion statistics were exaggerated, martyrdoms grossly exploited, unscrupulous commercial activities and scandalous concessions to paganism concealed. A familiar pattern soon took shape. The Jesuits' enthusiasm and ingenuity, together with their role as papal mediators, antagonized the old guard. Hostility sharpened Jesuit wits, and the Society's opponents redoubled their accusations, with the advantage that there were many Franciscan and Dominican prelates and a powerful caucus in Rome that became more vigilant with every Jesuit success. Ignoring the fact that the flexible Ignatian approach had many Catholic precedents, an attempt was made to draw a line between Jesuit and 'orthodox' missionary methods as artificial as the Chinese Wall of dogma which the Fathers of Trent laboriously raised against the tide of heresy.

In 1540 all this was in the not-too-distant future, as Ignatius carefully selected four of his ten men for missions abroad. The dizzy vistas opened up by the rapid expansion of the Portuguese and Spanish empires, promising a harvest of souls to offset the losses to heresy in Europe, caused a flurry of activity such as had not been seen since the fourteenth century when Franciscan venturers wearing Mongol costume tried to convert the leaders of the Golden Horde and penetrated the court of Timur, the successor of Kubla Khan, in Peking. The astounding victories of the conquistadores in Mexico and Peru evoked a triumphant sense of racial, cultural, and religious superiority in Europeans; as did the successes of Albuquerque and the Portuguese in India. Cortes and Albuquerque had called for priests to complete and sanctify their conquests, and the embryonic Society strained its resources to meet the challenge.

Its first assignment, a papal request for a reconnaissance of Ireland, was something of a farce, though Ignatius gave it his usual earnest attention. His brief for Frs Salmeron and Broet, papal nuncios whose total ignorance of Ireland matched his own, was typical of the pragmatic philosophy that marked all his instructions. 'Let us follow the method adopted by our enemy, the devil, in his dealings. . . For he goes in by the other's door to come out by his own, not contradicting but approving his habits, taking stock of his soul . . . In like manner we, for our good purpose, may agree with another in regard to some matter in itself innocent, passing over other things of a bad complexion, so as to win his sympathy.' The envoys were to travel and lodge cheaply, begging their way as far as possible (mendicancy was not a fetish in the Society, but a matter of policy or necessity) and taking no unnecessary risks. 'In so far as it is necessary for the glory of God and the common good to risk your lives, you must not refuse to do so, but without rashness . . . you will use all possible dexterity and prudence not to be captured.' Their main task was to report on the fidelity of the Irish clergy.

Pausing in Edinburgh to deliver a papal brief to King James V, they learned something of the turbulent state of Ireland, where nearly all the bishops and the two principal chieftains had recognized the ecclesiastical headship of Henry VIII and 'loyal' Catholics spent much of their time quarrelling among themselves. Leaving Ireland in March 1542 after a cautious five-week probe, the bewildered nuncios, looking so bedraggled that in Lyons they were arrested and jailed as suspicious vagrants, struggled back to Rome to deliver a gloomy report. Yet within twenty years hunted Jesuit missionaries began to play a role as bog-school teachers and spiritual leaders that did more than their mere numbers would suggest to identify the Church of Rome with Irish patriotism.

The Society's African ventures, sponsored by Portugal, were not very successful. In North Africa two Jesuits acted for a time as chaplains and ransom agents among Christian captives in Ceuta and Tetuan. Others went to the Congo, but after a promising start the mission was expelled by the local ruler, affronted by criticism of his polygamy. Their main achievement was, as a Jesuit historian put it, 'personal sanctification through suffering'. And that was to be the mark of a longer but equally abortive enterprise in Ethiopia. It was ruled, in medieval legend, by Prester John, a Christian monarch descended from King Solomon and the Queen of Sheba; but in the 1540s its actual ruler was a crafty Coptic Negus who appealed for Portuguese military aid against Muslim invasion, promising to convert his subjects to Catholicism in return. When the soldiers had done their part, King John III selected Pierre Favre, probably the most likeable and widely popular of the early Jesuits, as Patriarch of Ethiopia to conclude the second half of the bargain. Favre died, and his replacement, the Portuguese Fr João Nunes Barreto, met with procrastination and blunt hostility. So did his successors. A century later Franz Storer, who had smuggled himself into Ethiopia disguised as an Armenian physician, vanished, presumed dead. The mission that had kindled a romantic enthusiasm in Ignatius was finally abandoned. But his instructions, issued only a few months before his death, summarized the hard-won lessons of Jesuits in Africa, Brazil, India and Japan. The Patriarch was advised to adapt himself to the customs of the country and, with the aid of learned books and scientific instruments, to dazzle the monarch with the wonders of European technology.

Jesuit missionaries were reluctantly driven to admit that the idea of wiping the slate clean and writing a new creed upon it was impossible, even in the case of the most primitive savages. They set themselves to learn the languages, observe the customs, and reconstruct the history of their quarries: and a look at the index of Robert Burton's *Anatomy of Melancholy* of 1621 shows what astonishing progress they had made in less than a century. 'One had much better, as Pope Alexander VI long since observed, provoke a great Prince than a begging friar,' wrote Burton. 'A Jesuit, I will add, for they are an irrefragable society, they must and will have the last word.' He quotes at length from the books and reports of 'land-leaping Jesuits' in China, Japan and South America. 'At this day in China the common people live in a manner altogether on roots and herbs, and to the wealthier horse, ass, mule, dogs, cats-flesh, is as delightsome as the rest; so Mat. Riccius [Matteo Ricci] the Jesuit relates, who lived many years amongst them'; or 'What strange sacraments, like ours of Baptism and the Lord's Supper, what goodly Temples, Priests, Sacrifices, they had in America when the Spaniards first landed there, let Acosta the Jesuit [José de Acosta, author of *The Nature of the New World* and *The Natural and Moral History of the Indians*] relate.'

This expertise was won at the cost of dogged perseverance in gruelling conditions. It was not, of course, a Jesuit invention. Nor were Jesuits the first to champion the rights of Amerindians against the greed and contempt of Spanish and Portuguese officials and settlers. In 1511 Antonio de Montesinos, a Dominican missionary, had denounced racism: 'Tell me by what right or justice do you keep these Indians in such cruel and humble servitude and kill them with the desire to extract gold every day? Are these not men? Have they not rational souls? Are you not bound to love them as you love yourselves? Be certain that in such a state you can no more be saved than Moors or Turks.' The tremendous indictments of another Dominican, Bartolomé de las Casas, soon became a chief source for Protestant propagandists of Spanish cruelty. The Franciscan Juan de Zumarraga, first Bishop of Mexico, had established Indian schools, challenged rapacious officials, and encouraged natives to come to him with their grievances.

When Francis Xavier began his ten-year odyssey in India, the Moluccas and Japan, and the equally vigorous Manuel de Nobrega and José de Anchieta opened the Jesuit enterprise in Brazil, the fervour of the first missionary wave had begun to evaporate. Facile optimism had given way to despair or cynicism as the absurdity of early estimates was acknowledged. In 1538 a friar had exulted that 'the idolatry of the masses is blotted out. The Indians have forgotten these idols as completely as if a century had passed.' Priests in remote mission stations resented the luxury of the 'gilded clergy' in the new towns, who in turn despised their uncouth upcountry brethren. Missionaries' scoldings about polygamy and promiscuity grew less shrilll as the example of harem-keeping officials, soldiers and settlers made nonsense of their message. The ecclesiastical hubbub of Europe was soon heard in the colonies. Disputes between the various orders, strife between Spaniards and Creoles in the same order, the familiar clash of religious and secular clergy, filled the courts with litigation. The clergy's immunity from civil action caused friction between viceroys and prelates. The operation of the Patronato (or in the case of the Portuguese, Padroado) Real de las Indias – the royal patronage of the Indies – provoked a bitter feud between crown and papacy, pope's men and regalists.

The royal grip on the Church was even tighter than in Spain and Portugal, involving control of ecclesiastical appointments. Papal bulls and briefs were not to be promulgated or enforced without the approval of royal officials. The colonial Church was in essence a branch of the royal government. Its leaders were very loosely attached to Rome and sternly resisted any poaching on their preserves – as papal legate and roving Portuguese ambassador Xavier was careful not to trespass on Spanish territory in the Philippines. In theory Spanish and Portuguese colonies were closed to all but Spanish or Portuguese missionaries (Xavier caused dismay by expressing a preference for Belgians and Germans). As avowedly cosmopolitan pope's men and late arrivals, the Jesuits had to tread gingerly in minefields of prejudice quite as explosive as those in Europe.

St Francis Xavier was early encrusted with legend. Pedro de Ribadeneira credited him with 'very illustrious miracles . . . he cured infirmities of many kinds, drove many demons from human bodies, restored sight to the blind and raised the dead to life'; and Francisco de Sousa popularized the story of the pious crab which restored to the grateful missionary a crucifix that he had dropped overboard ('the new standard-bearer of Christ crawled towards the Saint with the crucifix held upright in its claws or pincers'). For more than a century his body, which was taken to Goa, remained incorrupt and even today is said to be in a remarkable state of preservation. Protestant missionaries have sung his praises, Pope Benedict XIV made him patron saint of India and all the East in the eighteenth century, and he was later declared patron of all Catholic foreign missions.

Xavier's reputation as the most congenial of the founding fathers is partly due to the fact that he was not sullied by the political intrigue of Europe. In 1539, before the Society had gained recognition, he had been appointed secretary to Ignatius and proved an incompetent one. He was not Ignatius' first choice for the Indian mission, going as substitute for Bobadilla, who had been taken ill; and seems to have been the least intellectual, most old-fashioned and intolerant of the ten apostles. But total devotion to his chief, a blinkered sense of duty, and lack of linguistic ability, combined with a native cunning, an iron constitution, and a rather breezy Christianity kept him going where angels might have feared to tread.

The bull naming him 'Apostolic Nuncio to the islands of the Red Sea, the Persian Gulf, and the Indian Ocean, as well as to the provinces and places of India this side the Ganges and the promontory called the Cape of Good Hope, and beyond' held no terrors for a temperament such as his. Writing from Mozambique on his way to Goa, he cheerfully remarked of himself and his three Jesuit companions: 'One of the things which greatly comforts us and makes us hope increasingly for the mercy of God is the complete conviction we have of lacking every talent necessary for the preaching of the Gospel in pagan lands.' His self-mortification was not confined to the episode in Venice. In Paris, where he had gained some renown as an athlete, he not only, after performing the *Exercises,* 'fasted severely, but roped his upper limbs so tightly that he could no longer move, and thus trussed up made his meditations'; the story goes that he burst a blood vessel while mentally wrestling with lewd thoughts. Just before embarking in Lisbon in April 1541 he refused a nobleman's offer of a personal servant as befitting his ambassadorial status ('It is this dignity of yours which has brought the Church of God to her present plight . . . the best way to acquire true dignity is to wash one's own clout and do one's own cooking'). During the long voyage – it took more than a year, including six months at Mozambique waiting for a favourable wind – he begged alms from rich passengers for the poor and sick, whom he nursed. Many died, but though ill with fever he refused to stop his ministrations.

Xavier was apt to reprove Jesuit missionaries for lack of humility ('this least Company cannot suffer proud, arrogant men . . . this is a Company of love, not of rigour or servile fear'); but his bigotry about non-Christian religions amounted at times to crass arrogance. In Lisbon he had watched approvingly while heretics were burned at the stake. His despatches from India record with relish the smashing of idols. His opinion of the moral and spiritual state of the Indians (and of most Portuguese in India) was so low that he concentrated on baptizing infants, who, such was the mortality rate, were likelier candidates for heaven: 'Few people,' he wrote, 'whether white or black, go from India to Paradise, except such as die in a state of innocence at the age of fourteen or under.' His evangelistic method was to attract the children first, make them learn the Christian elements by heart, then set them to instruct the adults.

Realizing the strength of the opposition, Xavier tried not to offend the secular clergy or the Franciscans. But he often rebuked and finally dismissed Fr Antonio Gomes, Rector of the Jesuit College in Goa, a tactless martinet who proposed to get rid of all non-European students and admit only the sons of Portuguese 'gentlemen'. Like the vast majority of missionaries, Gomes was oblivious of the Asiatic origins of the Christian religion. He saw no future in training a native or half-caste clergy – 'the people of this land are for the most part poor-spirited and without Portuguese priests we will achieve nothing. For Portuguese laymen will not go to confession with an Indian or Eurasian priest, but only with a pure-bred Portuguese.' Yet with the vast expanse of Brazil to colonize and a home population of not more than a million, Portugal could not send many white priests to her African and Indian empires; most of them were stationed in the towns, garrisons and trading posts to minister to Portuguese soldiers and merchants. Some non-European priests were, therefore, reluctantly ordained. But the religious orders – Franciscans, Dominicans, Augustinians and Theatines as well as Jesuits – made no exceptions. Xavier went along with this policy, believing that Indian trainees (whose lack of academic qualifications was largely due to the insistence on Latin as the teaching language for higher studies) could not hope to be more than catechists or, at a pinch, diocesan priests. This attitude did not improve relations with the secular clergy; and the exclusion of Indians, which remained in force until the suppression of the Society in 1773, was the more galling since Japanese, Chinese, Indochinese and Koreans *were* admitted, albeit in small numbers.

Though two of his most valued lieutenants, Fr Henriques and Fr de Castro, were New Christians of Jewish extraction, Xavier was forced to accept a ban on *conversos,* however gifted. He would have ignored the anti-semitic tirades of Gomes, but could not afford to flout the prejudices of the Portuguese King on whose support the Jesuit mission depended. Henriques had been expelled by the Franciscans when his Jewish lineage came to light and Ignatius had arranged a papal dispensation to admit him to the Society. Both he and Xavier resisted pressure from Portuguese Jesuits to debar Henriques from taking his final vows, and the episode rankled. Xavier described Goa as a sink of corruption, denounced the cruelty and greed of Portuguese traders and officials, especially when it affected the pearl-divers of the Coromandel

Coast, who were his own particular flock, and fired off some uncompromising letters to King John III. The Inquisition, he suggested, should be established in Goa primarily to check the morals and religion of the Portuguese ('many nominal Christians live openly as Jews or Mohammedans'). Unscrupulous, ungodly governors should be stripped of property and office and 'put in chains for several years . . . No more effective means exists to make all Indians Christians than for your Highness to punish a governor severely.' Writing to Simon Rodrigues he warned that racketeering was universal: 'All go the same road of "I plunder, thou plunderest" and it terrifies me to see how many moods and tenses of that miserable verb *rapio* those who come to India discover.' Nicolas Lancillotto, one of the second batch of Jesuit missionaries, summed up the situation: 'Those who become Christians do so for temporal advantage . . . Slaves of the Moors or Hindus seek baptism to free themselves, others to get protection from tyrants or for the sake of a turban, a shirt, or to escape being hanged. The man who embraces the faith from honest conviction is regarded as a fool . . . many revert to their former paganism . . . This country is so vast that a hundred thousand priests would not be sufficient to evangelize all its population.'

Such misgivings did not figure in Xavier's letter written in January 1545 and selected for publication with such gratifying results. 'I must tell you,' it said, 'how in Travancore, a kingdom out here . . . in a single month I baptized more than ten thousand men, women and children . . . I could not express to you the consolation it gave me to watch the idols being destroyed . . . I went from village to village making Christians and in each place I left a written copy of doctrine and prayers in their language' (Tamil). He also spoke of bright prospects in the Indonesian archipelago. King John III directed that the letter should be read from every pulpit in the land, and it drew a rush of donations and applications from both Spain and Portugal. From Coimbra, the rector reported that such was the enthusiasm of the students that he would 'have little difficulty in transferring the whole college to India'.

The idea of fancy approaches to the heathen such as those used by some of his Jesuit successors in India never entered Xavier's head. He was a stickler for monogamy and temperance, forbidding his pearl-fishers to drink the palm-sap liquor in which they were accustomed to drown their sorrows. In Japan he brushed aside the subtle speculations of Buddhist bonzes (priests) about the problem of evil as feeble excuses and furiously denounced their pederastic liaisons with young novices. Misled by incompetent interpreters, his Tamil and Japanese versions of basic prayers and doctrines were laughably defective and had to be completely overhauled by more learned missionaries. He struggled unsuccessfully with only two of India's scores of languages and five hundred-odd dialects and his sense of urgency did not allow him to linger and consolidate. But his low-caste converts, gathering at first in makeshift wattle-and-daub churches, stood firm against the persuasions of Dutch and, later, English Protestant missionaries; and he gave shrewd advice to the thirty Jesuits whom he had stationed in India and Indonesia by 1548. 'Not all the poor are deserving,' he said, 'and cadgers are to be found among them sunk in vice and sin . . . Put heart into penitents. Tell them that whatever they have to confess will be no news to you, for you have knowledge of much graver sins. Sometimes, as I know from experience, people are helped by your telling them in general terms about your own lamentable past . . . May our Lord be with you as much as I would like Him to be with myself. Your loving brother, Francis.'

Xavier could not complain of the courage or stamina of most of his subordinates. The Fleming Gaspard Berze, a soldier then a hermit at Montserrat before joining the Society, was his choice as Superior of the Indian province and a man after his own heart who could write persuasively: 'Here you have no table, no bed, no roof over you. . . There is no leave whatever, no time to say Mass, not even liberty to exist. . . . O my Brothers, come!' The Italian Antonio Criminali, speared to death in a native rebellion, was the first of more than a thousand Jesuit martyrs. Fr Juan Beira, striving to win Malayans for the Lord, was so harassed and, finally, tortured by Muslims that he went mad. The outlook, Xavier informed Rodrigues, was satisfactory: 'Let, then, such of our brethren as long to give their lives for Christ be of good cheer, for there is prepared a seminary of martyrdom where they may fulfil their desire.'

By 1549, however, sickened by Portuguese rapacity and contempt for low-caste Christians, by Muslim perfidy, and by what he regarded as the vile injustice of the Indian caste system, Xavier was eager for fresh fields. His frustration burst out in an impassioned letter to John III, in which, after commending a few officials for their honesty, he ended: 'Senhor: It is a sort of martyrdom to watch the destruction of what one has built up so laboriously . . . I have learned that Your Highness has no power to spread the faith of Christ in India, only to seize and enjoy all the country's temporal riches . . . therefore I am, as it were, fleeing to Japan so as not to lose more time.'

Portuguese traders had stimulated his wanderlust with stories of the mysterious, xenophobic Chinese Empire on whose outer fringes they plied a profitable but dangerous contraband trade, and with garbled information about Zipangu, the Land of the Rising Sun, unknown to Europeans until in 1542 a Portuguese ship sighted its shores when blown off course by a storm. Waiting in Malacca for a passage to Goa after more than three years of almost incessant journeying he met Yajiro, a Japanese who had fled westward after murdering a man. Grateful for Xavier's spiritual comfort, Yajiro excited him with visions of a people whose rulers would respond to reason and admired asceticism. At Goa Yajiro was rechristened Paul of the Holy Faith and in May 1549 he and Xavier, accompanied by Fr Cosmas de Torres and Brother Juan Fernandez, were back in Malacca. In August, after a nine-week voyage in a Chinese junk, they landed at Kagoshima.

Though jeered and spat at, baffled by the language ('we are like so many statues among them'), and made to look silly by the mistranslations of Yajiro, Xavier described the Japanese, after two and a half gruelling years among them, as 'the delight of my heart'. Physical hardships did not deter him – he leapt and sang in the snow. Persecution stimulated his zeal. The feudal chaos of Japan was not unfamiliar to an hidalgo from Navarre. But Xavier's hopes of making Japan a Christian country on the *cujus regio* principle by converting an all-powerful Emperor were shattered. The Mikado, a ritual figurehead in a rotting wooden palace, was so poor that he charged a fee for an audience. That discovery was the sole reward for Xavier's three-hundred-mile barefoot slog through the snows of winter. Better informed about the true wielders of power, Xavier and his companions, who were often assumed to be members of some nomadic Buddhist sect, then paid court to the *daimyo* (robber baron) Ouchi Yoshitaka of Yamaguchi. Determined to cut a dash, Xavier used a consignment of fine pepper donated by Pedro da Gama, the Captain of Malacca, to buy clothes of suitable splendour: his first, and last, gesture of 'accommodation'.

It worked. Impressed by the ornately inscribed ambassadorial credentials and delighted with the chiming grandfather clock, musical box, spectacles, musket, crystal vases, barrels of port, and oil paintings (also provided by Pedro da Gama), Yoshitaka reacted generously. The 'Bonzes from the West' were given licence to preach and allowed to stay in a disused Buddhist temple. Still regarded as freaks, they were teased and insulted for the amusement of the *daimyo* and his courtiers; but Xavier's habit was to give as good as he got ('by despising death we shall show ourselves superior to this proud people'). Brother Fernandez, a wealthy Spanish silk merchant until he turned Jesuit, expected 'the stroke of a sabre' to sweep his head from his shoulders after some particularly heated exchanges. But the reputation of the fearless priests soared. Curious crowds pressed round the temple, and several hundred converts were made in the next two months. It was exhausting work, as Xavier explained in a letter to Ignatius: 'Our Fathers going to Japan will be harassed. . . At all hours of the day and night they will be pestered with visits and questions . . . no time for spiritual recollection, to say the office, or to eat and sleep.'*

The Jesuits were now in demand. The *daimyo* of Bungo invited them to his court and welcomed them warmly. But fond as he was of the Japanese and exhilarated by the sudden breakthrough, Xavier's thoughts were again wandering. If, as he had heard, Japan looked to the sages of China for religious and cultural leadership, and if the Chinese Emperor actually wielded power, did this not open a marvellous prospect, the very apotheosis of the *cujus regio* technique? Leaving Torres and Fernandez behind to care for the Japanese Christians, he sailed from Bungo in November 1551 to deal with the Antonio Gomes crisis, redeploy his Indian missionaries, and send reinforcements to Japan. In Malacca he concocted a plan for a merchant friend of his, Diego Pereira, to be accredited Portuguese ambassador to China, with Xavier travelling in his entourage. Returning there after concluding his business in Goa, and persuading the Viceroy to approve his enterprise, he ran into trouble. Don Pedro's brother Alvaro da Gama was now Captain there, and by no means sympathetic to this swashbuckling Spanish priest. Pereira was forbidden to leave Malacca, Xavier's threat of excommunication for obstructing an apostolic nuncio had no effect (he was accused of forging his credentials), and he had to set out alone.

Reaching the island trading post of San Chian in August 1552, he arranged with a Chinese captain to transport him to Canton, only thirty miles away. The vessel did not arrive, and on 2 December Xavier, who could find no other ship to take him on such a foolhardy mission, died of fever and exposure in a cold and wretched hut. He had planned when he reached Canton to produce his letter of episcopal recommendation and declare, quite simply, to the Chinese (whom he imagined to be 'a

---

* These letters, which took up to three years to reach Rome, were sent in triplicate by three different ships, in the hope that at least one might reach its destination after running the gauntlet of pirates and tempests.

white, bearded race') that he had come 'to declare the law of God': a good example of the sublime simplicity that had always been his strength.

His last message contained an uncharacteristic phrase – 'it is a long time since I felt less inclined to go on living'. His hard-driven body had at last accepted defeat, and as his biographer James Brodrick says, 'no saint ever more flagrantly burned the candle at both ends'. But his rather pathetic failure resounded through the Jesuit houses of Europe as not even his most triumphant successes had done; and to redeem it later missionaries evolved methods of an obliquity which would have startled their hero. His lonely death within sight of the mountains of mainland China provided the challenge; but the pomp of his entry to the court of Yoshitaka, bearing gifts that emphasized the technological ingenuity of the West, provided the model for the finesse of Matteo Ricci some thirty years later.

Despite the propaganda value of Xavier's bulletin of 1545 Ignatius had written to warn him of the perils of mass baptism without adequate instruction. But he had honoured the work of Xavier by making India the first of the Jesuit provinces after Spain and Portugal: the few surviving letters between them are full of deep and moving affection. 'My true Father,' Xavier had written early in 1552, 'I received a letter of your holy charity at Malacca on my way back from Japan, and God our Lord knows what a comfort it was to have news of the health and life of one so dear to me. Among many other holy words and consolations . . . I read the concluding ones, "Entirely yours, without power or possibility of ever forgetting you, Ignatio." I read them with tears, and with tears now write them, remembering the past and the great love which you always bore towards me and still bear.'

When, after many months, the news of Xavier's death reached Rome, the last great missionary enterprise begun under Ignatius' auspices was well established. The pioneer Jesuit team of 1549 in Brazil was larger and more carefully balanced than the makeshift trio that had sailed for India in 1541. Manoel de Nobrega, the Superior, was a highly intelligent, cultured aristocrat. Of the three other Fathers, the Basque Juan de Apilcueta was a brilliant linguist, Leonardo Nunes a bustling evangelist, Antonio Pires a skilled architect. One of the two Brothers was a carpenter, the other a schoolmaster. They were soon joined by José de Anchieta, a renowned scholar from Tenerife. Within a year of his arrival he had drafted a grammar of the Tupi-Guarani language and was turning native chants into Christian hymns. The general approach was far more scientific, though in the end hardly more successful, than Xavier's headlong improvisation.

Like Xavier, the Jesuits in Brazil soon discovered that the noble sentiments of distant kings and dedicated missionaries were not shared by colonists. Nobrega reported his disgust at the laxity and cynicism of the clergy but assured John III that 'the conversion of these heathens is an easy matter: they are a blank page on which one can write at will, provided there are enough workers to sustain them by example and continual converse.' This estimate was soon revised.

Cannibalism (caused largely by protein deficiency: it ended when cattle were introduced), persistent sexual promiscuity and the settlers' hypocritical use of these 'sins' as an excuse for punitive slave raids forced a realization that the building of a true Church would be a long, arduous undertaking. The notion of persuading colonists to leave the coastal settlements and travel inland with the missionaries was quickly abandoned. Instead the ideal was to gather the natives into large compounds or 'reductions' where they would be protected from spiritual contamination. 'These heathen, Father,' Ignatius was informed, 'will not be converted by simply reasoning and preaching.' They would have to be subjected to a long, minutely-regulated process of catholicization. Amerinidians were vulnerable to diseases like smallpox, typhoid and yellow fever, brought by the Europeans or off the African slave ships, and the reductions multiplied the risk of epidemics and frightful mortality. But it was a risk from which the Fathers did not flinch. A dead, safely baptized Indian was a trophy of grace.

There were to be tens of thousands of such trophies as the Jesuit missionaries moved fearlessly, even rapturously, among the dying. Their devotion was not always appreciated. Often they were regarded as merchants of death. In 1554 two Jesuits were martyred: and São Paulo, selected by Nobrega as the site for a school and seminary, was to become the base for a series of devastating slave raids on Jesuit reductions.

CHAPTER EIGHT

The Struggle in Europe

IN THE PERIOD OF political and religious tension culminating in the terrible Thirty Years War of 1618 to 1648 Jesuit and Capuchin rivalry reached its height. Both orders continued to expand swiftly; the Jesuits to about sixteen thousand, the Capuchins, recognized as an independent Franciscan organization with their own Superior-General, to about eighteen thousand. The Jesuit grip on education was a decisive factor, and in speculative theology the Society produced two outstanding figures, Francisco Suarez and Francisco de Toledo. In apologetics the formidable Robert Bellarmine led the field and like Toledo became a cardinal. In moral theology Antonio Escobar and other Jesuits set the pace. Lainez and Salmeron were prominent in the final sessions of the Council of Trent: and at the Colloquy of Poissy, called to work out a compromise settlement with the Huguenots, Lainez, who unlike Ignatius spent much of his generalship away from Rome, argued passionately against a pact with the Huguenots.

Argument conducted in theological jargon barely distinguishable from that of the fourth century filled the rare gaps between armed conflicts. The interminable controversy about the primacy of faith or works, the squabbles over what exactly St Augustine had said or meant, the vilification and counter-vilification of Luther, Calvin and Loyola, of the Pope of Rome and the 'Pope of Geneva', closely resembled twentieth-century claims and counter-claims about 'true' democracy.

As the zone of devastation, misery and religious indifference widened, the propaganda barrage intensified. Every book, every pamphlet, evoked an instant reply. On the run in England, the English Jesuit missionaries Campion and Parsons published some stirring manifestos on their secret press, and Campion's 'Brag', with the impact of its message heightened by his martyrdom, remains a classic of guerrilla polemics. Other Jesuit brags were less attractive and even ludicrous, though no more so than many a Protestant effusion. By 1640 the Society boasted thirty-five provinces, three vice-provinces, over five hundred colleges, forty-nine seminaries, forty-four novitiates, twenty-four professed houses, nearly three hundred residences and missions. Centenary self-congratulation seemed to be called for, and in one case at least was not hampered by modesty.

A thousand-page panegyric compiled by the Belgian province, the *Imago primi saeculi* (Portrait of the First Century), asserted that 'the Society is not a new order but a renewal of the first religious community whose one and only founder was Jesus . . . Equipped with wisdom, virtue, intelligence, sagacity and industry, the Jesuits distinguish truth from falsehood . . . All that is flourishing in the humanities, all the intricacies of philosophy, all the hidden things in nature, all the difficulties in mathematics, all the mysteries of Godhead, are proclaimed by their works, which would fill great libraries.' The careful moderation of Favre and Canisius had been exchanged for the blunt weapons of Bobadilla in such passages as that on Luther, 'the infamous apostate who led to battle ignorant persons sprung from foul dens of godless and infamous life, notorious for immorality, harpies of the Holy Scripture . . . As long as there is life in us, we will bark at the wolves for the defence of the Catholic flock.' To complete the fanfare, each page is embellished with baroque engravings. A vast candle glimmering over a town-and-country panorama is captioned 'The spread of the Society of Jesus . . . once lighted it fills the world with its radiance.' A star-filled night sky bears the legend 'In its contempt for honours the Society attains greater distinction . . . In darkness the stars glitter more brightly.'

Severely criticized by Father-General Muzio Vitelleschi for being so boastfully at odds with Ignatius' conception of 'this least society', the *Portrait* offered a tempting quarry for hostile writers. But the tribute of Pope Gregory XIII, addressing the fourth General Congregation assembled in 1581 to elect a new general, had been acceptably heartening: 'You direct kingdoms, provinces, indeed the whole world . . . there is today no single instrument raised up by God against heretics greater than your holy order.'

During the generalship of Claudio Aquaviva from 1581 to 1615, the longest in Jesuit history, the Society had gone from strength to strength. Its reputation as the vanguard of militant Catholicism was boosted as much by Protestant publicists as by its own propaganda or by papal commendation. The anti-Jesuit anthology *Stupenda Jesuitica* pictured it as a network of assassins and sexual perverts. The *Monita Secreta Societatis Jesu,* allegedly written by an embittered Polish ex-Jesuit, revealed techniques by which Jesuits wheedled legacies from rich widows and schemed their way to power at court. Robert Burton, sighing for an end to religious bigotry, lamented the success of 'those praetorian soldiers, his janissary Jesuits . . . the last effort of the Devil and the very excrement of time.' Through them the 'bull-bellowing Pope' achieved more than with garrisons and armies, 'for the rest are but his dromedaries and asses . . . What so powerful an engine as superstition? Which they right well perceiving are of no religion at all themselves. For truly, as Calvin rightly suspects, the first of the secrets of these theologians, by which they rule, is that they hold there is no God.'

To edify their pupils the Jesuits spread the fame of three youthful saints, Aloysius Gonzaga, Stanislaus Kostka and Johannes Berchmans. Aloysius, elder son of the Marquis of Castiglione, was repelled by the violence and licentiousness of Italian high society, ran away from court and camp and entered the Society in defiance of his father's wishes. He became a model novice and died an exemplary death while nursing plague victims in Rome. Stanislaus, a Pole of noble birth, is said to have walked all the way to Rome, where he died aged eighteen in the odour of sanctity. Aloysius was obsessed with the idea of transmuting his flesh into angelic substance by prayer and penance. Both he and Berchmans, a Brabanter, were ultra-diligent noters of imperfections in the Ignation style, eschewers of laughter and enemies of the monstrous indulgence of sleep. All three youths have since been held up to Jesuit pupils as paragons of virtue, sentimentalized myths as useful in their way as St Ignatius or St Francis Xavier, and the Jesuit Sodality of the Blessed Virgin was outstandingly popular. Inaugurated in Rome in 1563, it had by 1576 enrolled some thirty thousand members dedicated to personal sanctification and social service.

The first English Jesuit, Simon Belost, joined the Society in 1559 at the age of fifty-five, and was followed by nineteen-year-old Alexander Belseyr, an Old Etonian. But recruits were of every nationality in Europe. In the 1560s the Roman novitiate housed a polyglot intake – Spanish, Italian, German, French, English, Irish, Flemish, Greek, Scandinavian, Slav – all striving to master the Latin lingua franca. When Francis Borgia died in 1572 the first non-Spanish general, Everard Mercurian from Belgian Luxembourg, was elected. He was of peasant origin, and Nadal, replying to criticisms that the Society's main criteria for membership were wealth and social standing, maintained that 'you will find that scarcely one in fifty of us had possessed anything of this world's goods.' Jesuit schools continued to proliferate, taking pupils mainly from the middle and lower classes; after a twenty-year process of drafting and redrafting the educational system was finally codified in the bulky *Ratio Studiorum,* approved in 1599 and not revised until 1832.

The lure of free education had local authorities clamouring to attract Jesuit attention. Aquaviva rejected many invitations to open a school. But primary as well as secondary education became almost a Jesuit monopoly in Spain, which was also remarkable for its insistence that no foreigners should hold positions of responsibility except in the English and Irish colleges at Salamanca, Valladolid and Seville. Elsewhere an international approach was the rule. In the 1570s two Scotsmen, William Crichton and Edmund Hay, presided over the colleges in Lyons and Paris. Another Scot, John Tyrie, was Rector of Clermont College, and later Assistant for France and Germany and a member of the committee that drafted the *Ratio Studiorum* of 1586. Adam Brook, an Englishman, was Rector of the college at Vilna in Poland. Richard Fleming, an Irishman, became professor of theology at Clermont and first Chancellor of the University of Pont-à-Mousson in Lorraine.

At Clermont College Juan Maldonado's lectures drew such crowds that the dons of the University of Paris did their best to convict him of heresy. The sceptical Montaigne, whom a Jesuit was later to accuse of 'softly, as with a silken cord, strangling the sentiment of religion', found Maldonado very sympathetic, and in his horror of sectarian strife wished the Society well in its catholicizing mission. On a visit to Rome he found Jesuit preachers particularly impressive, writing in 1581 that 'there never was a brotherhood among us that produced such results . . . this is the one limb of the Church that most threatens the heretics.' By that time the Roman College of All Nations was being transformed into the Gregorian University (Fr Clavius, the Bavarian Jesuit mathematician, was mainly responsible for devising the Gregorian calendar). Pope Gregory XIII also entrusted the Hungarian, Greek and English colleges in Rome to the Society, which brought accusations of Jesuit megalomania.

The austerity, sincerity, and industry of Lainez and his successors merely encouraged shafts of envy. Lainez, who as Jesuit General and papal theologian rode to the Colloquy of Poissy on a mule carrying some straw bedding, was obsessed with the needs of the poor and the selfishness of the wealthy. His sermons bristled with appeals for generous giving and he wrote a pamphlet declaring war on the cosmetics, perfumes and elaborate coiffures which wasted the wealth that should have gone to relieve the miseries of the poor. In the summer of 1561 at Poissy he caused something of a sensation by questioning the validity of such a gathering at a time when the Council of Trent was still in session. Though France was on the brink of civil war he saw no future in appeasement.

He reminded the Regent of France, Catherine de Medici, that 'the faith is not national but universal and Catholic. Your Majesty should recognize it to be outside your province and that of any temporal prince to deal with matters of faith . . . This is the business of priests and it belongs to the Supreme Priest and to the General Council to define them.' In a letter to the Huguenot leader, the Prince de Condé, he reasoned that the only hope for lasting peace was to return to a Catholic Church cleansed and reformed, 'the one true Church outside which there is no hope of salvation'; and he invited Theodore Beza and other Huguenot spokesmen to accompany him to Trent.

The closing stages of the Council from January 1562 to December 1563 were precipitated as much by the threat of a French National Assembly as by any genuine desire to complete the work of reform. The division of Charles V's unwieldy empire between Philip II and Charles V's brother, now Emperor Ferdinand I, brought new problems. Ferdinand agreed with Catherine de Medici that the business of the Council should be begun from scratch in the hope that this would induce their Protestant subjects to participate, while Philip II insisted that the new Assembly should be a continuation of the old. Ferdinand not only threatened to withdraw his bishops, but at a meeting with the Cardinal of Lorraine discussed the possibility of ousting the papacy from leadership of the Council. Last-minute negotiation averted the danger. The Emperor was induced to drop his demand, the Cardinal was bribed, and decrees on indulgences, purgatory, celibacy, and veneration of the saints were rushed through while the going was good.

A special pulpit was wheeled in for Lainez to deliver a lengthy disquisition on the Last Supper as the First Mass, and he vigorously opposed the grant of the chalice to the laity which was urged by delegates from Bohemia, Germany and Hungary. Salmeron caused more restlessness by speaking for three hours and more on various theological niceties. But quite as important as the definition of Holy Scripture and tradition as the twin sources of the true faith was the complicated battle over the respective authority of bishop and pope. This was a matter of supreme importance for the Society as well as for its patron and protector. If the demand for clear recognition of the authority of a reformed episcopacy were pushed to 'divine right' lengths – as the Spanish delegation wanted – what would become of the divine right of the pope or of the hard-won papal privileges that had given Jesuits the freedom and mobility they needed to function effectively?

Crippled with arthritis and burdened with the cares of administration though he was, Lainez's treatment of this crucial question was, by common consent, a *tour de force*. While arguing that papal sovereignty was divinely ordained, he maintained that the power of the bishops had been, and should remain, limited by historical and tactical considerations. Bishops, in fact, were useful and venerable instruments, but they were not local popes entitled to obstruct the flow of papally-blessed missionary enterprise. Though tactfully phrased, this thesis was briskly attacked by French and Spanish prelates, who rightly interpreted his defence of papal sovereignty as an attempt to keep the field open for Jesuit activism. No speech, however cogent, could resolve a conflict which faced the Jesuits wherever they went. Nor was the drift of Lainez's reasoning entirely acceptable to the papacy. If, as has been suggested, it left the pope as 'the only plank between a Jesuit and a Presbyterian', the logic of the historical conditioning of the episcopacy could very easily be applied to the Bishop of Rome: a possibility which was not overlooked by the papal legates. The Vatican could not commit itself to Lainez's formula or to that of the extreme episcopalists. The result was an uneasy compromise.

In any case the decrees of Trent, so impressive on paper, were ignored (in France they were not even published until 1615) or, where approved, slow to take effect. So few and inefficient were the episcopal seminaries that in 1620 Vincent de Paul thundered that 'the Church has no worse enemies than priests who live as most priests do today'. A papal legate reported that with the exception of the Carthusians the monastic orders were 'dissolute, ignorant, mean, dirty and lazy'. The Abbess of Maubuisson, Angélique d'Estrées, sister of Henry IV's mistress, bore twelve children; in 1602 the nuns of Port-Royal, later so celebrated for sanctity, spent most of their time staging masquerades and throwing parties. The real lessons of Trent were that nationalism was supreme; that the universal Catholic Church and papal sovereignty were illusions; and that no order was likely to prosper unless it had the ear of the monarchs who in effect controlled national Churches.

The Society's greatest asset was its educational influence, but the shortage of teachers was acute. In the late 1570s some four thousand Jesuits, of whom at least a third were scholastics, were hard pressed to staff more than two hundred colleges and missions. Clermont College tried desperately to find space and teachers for three thousand pupils. Some superiors grudged the money and talent absorbed by the Roman College. 'Many of us,' wrote Fr Pelletier sarcastically to Lainez, 'wonder what becomes of all those whom that great generator of men produces. I believe that one day, like the Trojan horse, it will launch them forth to overcome and conquer the entire world. May our Lord Jesus Christ bring it to pass soon.' Every fully-trained Jesuit jailed or killed was a serious loss, and hazards abounded, especially in war-torn France. Nadal and his two companions were seized, beaten up, and nearly shot by a Huguenot patrol. Three Spanish Jesuits on their way to the General Congregation of 1573 were captured and imprisoned. One died, another was badly crippled. Ransoming such victims was expensive, but they were almost worth their weight in gold.

Schools in Huguenot territory were often at risk. Evacuations were frequent, starvation seldom far away, fuel scarce, walls and roofs broken and patched. In Paris the notable success of Clermont stirred intense and long-lasting enmity, with Dominican professors and the lawyers of the Parliament collaborating in obstruction and denunciation. Ignatius was described as 'no better than Luther, creating confusion in the affairs of God and man', while the Society's privileges made it 'a grave danger to the peace and security of the state'. The Huguenot menace was, after all, a blessing in disguise: without it the Jesuits would not have been accorded even semi-legal status.

While Jesuit evangelists walked hundreds of miles to reach the neglected masses the Company was obliged to change its title to 'La Société du Collège de Clermont' in Paris. Maldonado was driven from the city for alleged unsoundness on the doctrine of purgatory and for refusing to treat the tradition of the Immaculate Conception as an article of faith. And in 1565 the University opened a two-century-long legal attack through the lawyer Étienne Pasquier. His indictment was the first comprehensive statement of anti-Jesuit propaganda, and his pamphlet *A Catechism of the Jesuits* reappeared with embellishments thirty years later in the writings of Antoine Arnauld. The windows of Clermont were smashed, Jesuits stoned in the streets and ridiculed on the stage. In every political crisis they were cast as the villains. Arnauld's fulminations summarized popular legend about Jesuit responsibility for the murderous struggle between the Catholic League headed by the Guises, which favoured all-out war on the Huguenots with military help from Spain, and a Centre Party led by the Regent and her sons, which with some waverings – the Massacre of St Bartholomew being the wildest – preferred negotiation. Despite warnings from Rome to stay out of politics, Jesuits were inevitably involved in both factions. But Arnauld branded them all as 'trumpets of war . . . torches of sedition, roaring tempests disturbing the tranquillity of France . . . authors of all the excesses of the League, whose Bacchanalian orgies were held in the Jesuit college and church . . . The Society is the workshop of Satan, filled with traitors and scoundrels, assassins of kings.'

Lainez had not only deplored appeasement of the Huguenots but, reiterating a doctrine common to most medieval theorists, including Aquinas, declared that a king who betrayed his trust (i.e. undermined the Catholic faith) forfeited his right to the loyalty of 'the sovereign people'. When Jacques Clément, a Dominican monk, assassinated the notorious homosexual and appeaser King Henry III and his act was approved in a treatise written by the Spanish Jesuit Juan Mariana, it was easy to pin the blame on the Society. Though Mariana's comments were disavowed by Aquaviva, the Jesuits were also held responsible for both the attempted and actual assassination of Henry IV. The fact that the would-be assassin had attended philosophy lectures at Clermont was enough to justify the arrest of two professors, one of whom was burned at the stake, and the expulsion of the Jesuits from Paris in 1595.

The difficulty of juggling with two absolute masters, pope and king, was illustrated by the Society's confused reactions to the 'conversion' of the nominally Huguenot Henry of Navarre. Some Jesuits preached resistance to the impostor-king who in 1585 had been excommunicated by Sixtus V as a relapsed heretic. Aquaviva, while forbidding French Jesuits to take the oath of allegiance to Henry IV until the excommunication was lifted, worked hard to get it lifted. In 1595 Pope Clement VIII obliged. Henry IV showed his gratitude by taking Fr Pierre Coton SJ as his confessor. But not until 1603 were the Jesuits readmitted to Paris, and when the king was murdered seven years later they immediately came under suspicion. Bellarmine's defence of the 'indirect' power of the papacy and Suarez's attack on the divine right of kings were cited as evidence of complicity; and ironically, while French Jesuits protested their loyalty to the Crown and the Gallican Church, Bellarmine's doctrine was attacked in Rome as underplaying papal rights.

The Society's theoretical cosmopolitanism was constantly under fire and under revision. Though educated by the Jesuits, Cardinal Richelieu was chary of their papalism and chose a Capuchin, François Leclerc du Tremblay – Father Joseph – as his confidential adviser. In 1625 French Jesuits, already exasperated by the indiscretions of their Spanish and Italian brethren, were embarrassed by the publication of Antonio Santarelli's rehash of the Bellarmine-Suarez teaching. A Parisian lawyer lashed himself into such a rage while denouncing it that he died of apoplexy; Richelieu muttered that 'maxims of this kind can wreck the

Church'; Pope Urban VIII reprimanded General Vitelleschi. After anxious consultations with Richelieu the French Jesuits signed a document which virtually denied the pope's indirect powers, and worked overtime to prove their patriotism: 'Who,' asked the professor of rhetoric at the college of La Flèche, 'can worthily expound the privileges and liberties of the Gallican Church and the realm of the Most Christian King? What Catholic Frenchman will not defend them vigorously?'

Mariana's disquisition had been composed on the instruction of King Philip II as a manual on the art of kingship for his heir; and no doubt he reckoned that the fate of Henry III would teach the boy not to stray from the path of Catholic orthodoxy. But he kept his Jesuits on a very tight rein, forbidding them to go to areas of Protestant 'contamination' in northern Europe and vetoing donations to the Roman College. The Spanish occupation of Portugal from 1580 to 1640 following King Sebastian's catastrophic crusade in Morocco caused patriotic Portuguese Jesuits much distress. Several openly preached against the Spanish usurpation and as openly rejoiced when it ended. In the meantime, relations between Spanish and Portuguese Jesuits were more than usually strained.

The Jesuits were expelled from the republic of Venice, long jealous of papal encroachment and, like the great commercial centres of Lucca and Milan, fearful of the consequences for trade of the Counter-Reformation's 'crusade'. They did not get back for fifty years. Their arch-enemy Paolo Sarpi, a Servite friar, envisaged an alliance of anti-papalists including French Gallicans, some north Italian principalities, and English, Dutch and German Protestants. Italians continued to regard the Society as an agent of the occupying power, particularly in Naples and Milan, the two main centres of Spanish rule. In Milan during the 1570s this tendency, together with the creaming-off of the best recruits to the detriment of his seminaries, provoked the saintly Archbishop Carlo Borromeo to fury despite his admiration for the *Exercises* and his preference for Jesuit confessors. In Sicily a Mafia that had resisted every foreign invasion did not take kindly to Spanish Jesuits and the Rector of the College at Palermo was murdered.

One way and another the running conflict between Spanish and Italian chauvinism, between the autocracies of the Vatican and the Escorial, plagued the Society and almost destroyed it. Antonio Araoz, Provincial of Castile, Francisco Estrada, Provincial of Aragon, and Francis Borgia had all treated Nadal arrogantly. In Spain as in

Portugal the Ignatian recipe for moderation in penance was not always acceptable. Borgia once remarked that it would 'drive him to the Carthusians', and there was a tendency to edge the Society closer to the Carthusian ideal and to deride the *Exercises* as 'perambulator mysticism'. Baltasar Alvarez, who had been chosen as spiritual director of the Carmelite nun Teresa of Avila, was a leader of this movement. Having tried unsuccessfully to apply the straitjacket of the *Exercises* to his ebullient charge, he himself was converted to 'the prayer of quiet and union' while Rector and novice master in the College at Medina del Campo where Juan de Yepes (later canonized as St John of the Cross) was a pupil. Alvarez and Antonio Cordeses were reprimanded by General Mercurian, fearful lest Melchior Cano should seize upon such 'excesses' as evidence of the individualist heresy of which SS Teresa and John of the Cross were accused.

In Rome too there had been a sharp clash of Jesuit factions. The two-year interregnum from 1556 to 1558 between the death of Ignatius and the election of Lainez was partly due to Italo-Spanish hostilities provoked by Paul IV's violent tirades against Spaniards and the dying Emperor Charles V. While the Duke of Alva, Viceroy of Milan, moved to besiege Rome, devastating towns and villages as he went, the Pope's soldier-of-fortune nephew Carlo Carafa prepared to defend the city with a force of German Lutheran mercenaries. Jesuits and other religious were ordered to help with emergency entrenchments, and Francis Borgia suggested that it would be advisable to hold the General Congregation in Spain. Representing this to the easily inflamed Pope as a deliberate affront to his authority, Bobadilla advised that until the Constitutions had been formally ratified the Society should be governed by the five surviving founding fathers as a committee of equals. He also, in a memorandum to the Pope, bitterly criticized the Constitutions: 'Master Ignatius alone had any say in their composition, for he did whatever he liked . . . They are a labyrinth of confusion, so much so that neither subjects nor superiors can understand them, much less observe them . . . The Society has so many Apostolic bulls conferring privileges and exemptions that they have made the name of Jesuit odious . . . After the death of Master Ignatius two or three persons [Lainez, Polanco and Nadal], wishing to ape him in everything, have brought the Society into bad odour . . . No doubt Ignatius was a wise man, but still a man, and as your Holiness knows, wedded to his own ideas. Let us take what was good in them and not obstinately defend the bad.'

After a good deal of cut-and-thrust the assault was repulsed and both

Bobadilla and his seconder, Ponce Cogordan, stayed in the Society. But Paul IV's wrath had not yet cooled. Lainez and Salmeron, kneeling before him as 'sons of obedience', were forced to repeat that the jettisoning of choir was a rebellion against the Church and an encouragement to heretics. Paul IV also hinted that the Society should not presume to trust in its privileges, for 'what one pope has done another can undo', and suggested that, as in other orders, the general's term of office should be limited to three years. Lainez himself seized upon this last point, canvassing the professed fathers as to whether he should resign. They, including Bobadilla, almost unanimously vetoed the idea, not surprisingly at a time when Lainez's reputation and membership of the Society were soaring: in the first three months of 1561 alone there were forty recruits.

The Carafa storm was weathered but papal sniping continued. Pius V, a Dominican and former Inquisitor-General, again raised the question of Divine Office and required scholastics to pronounce solemn vows before ordination, thus dissolving the distinction between professed and coadjutors; but only for five years, since Gregory XIII yielded to Jesuit persuasion. He also, however, listened to complaints, some of them from non-Spanish Jesuits, that too many of the higher posts were monopolized by Spaniards. King Sebastian of Portugal demanded a ban on the election of Juan Polanco, the obvious first choice, on the ground that he had Jewish blood and was sympathetic to New Christians. Mercurian, who took the Italian Antonio Possevino as secretary in place of Polanco, was succeeded by Aquaviva, the first of five successive Italian Generals.

In 1590 Sixtus V, reviving previous objections to the Society's title, formally requested that it be changed to 'Society of the Faith of Jesus', but died before the change had been made official. Some years later Clement VIII broached the matter of a limited term for the General, suggesting that Aquaviva be removed from office by appointment as Archbishop of Naples. Spanish pressure was brought to bear and the Pope was induced to order Aquaviva to accept an invitation to visit King Philip III in Madrid. His convenient, but genuine, illness lasted long enough to avert this danger; and indeed the Spanish fury that surrounded this aristocratic master politician might well have broken the health and will of lesser mortals. Spanish pride had been affronted by the choice of an Italian as General. Philip II had been angered by Aquaviva's refusal to allow a Jesuit to occupy an important post in the Spanish Inquisition – an attempt to draw the two organizations closer together in what might, he felt, have been a fatal embrace. The separatist feeling among Spanish Jesuits, always evident, was now rampant.

Dispatches to the Vatican, approved by the Crown, recommended abolition of the General's right to appoint rectors and provincials, complained of over-centralization in Rome, and demanded a thorough investigation of the grievances of the Spanish Jesuits by a Visitor who would act according to the procedure of the Spanish Inquisition. Hints of heresy were freely sprinkled and only an avalanche of solicited testimonials blocked the plan (Aquaviva also scored by pointing out that the bishop selected as Visitor was the father of three bastards). In a second assault, the Spanish caucus called for a General Congregation to examine the role of the General. This, to the accompaniment of an ominous message from Clement VIII, opened in 1593. After weeks of intensive lobbying Aquaviva was exonerated and a proposal presented by the Spanish ambassador for changes to the Constitutions was rejected.

In a curious postscript to the affair it was revealed, or alleged, that of the twenty-seven leading conspirators no fewer than twenty-five were New Christians of Jewish or Moorish descent. There seems a strong possibility that their eager co-operation with the Inquisition was partly the result of blackmail, but the Congregation, alarmed by a near-boycott of the Society in Spain, decreed the expulsion of those who refused to take an oath of submission and barred men of Jewish or Arabic origins from membership. The veteran Ribadeneira was almost alone in voting against the resolution. Thus the 'Italian' victory was won at the cost of making *limpieza de sangre,* at which Ignatius, Borgia and Nadal had scoffed, a condition of entry. This barrier was not finally removed until 1946, though in 1608 a qualifying clause permitted entry to *conversos* who had been Christians for five generations. Passions continued to run high. In 1622 the second volume of Fr Sacchini's history, mentioning that Lainez was of Jewish lineage, appeared, commenting that this was 'not an ignominy but an ennoblement, for he was not a wild shoot, as each of us is, but a fallen branch of the good vine grafted again sweetly and fitly into the parent stock.' Spanish Jesuits immediately demanded 'the removal of so great a slur on the memory of so great a Father ... We ask that the Father-General should cause the page containing this foul blot which damages the whole Society to be cut out and replaced by one asserting the purity and nobility of the Father's lineage.'

Ignatius had survived eight charges of heresy in three countries and it was perhaps not surprising that, having braved the wrath of the Spanish Inquisition and of Iberian monarchs in the matter of *conversos,* the Jesuits, eager to prove their orthodoxy, should have rivalled even the Dominicans as witch-hunters. Witch-mania reached a height in the first half of the seventeenth century. But sceptical Renaissance popes had encouraged it: a sign not only that witches as scapegoats might serve to deflect attention from the shortcomings of the papacy, but also that the Renaissance revived the cult of pagan mystery religions as well as the study of pagan literature. For a long time the spirit of scientific curiosity was mingled with cabbalistic mumbo-jumbo and cosmological fantasy. The mentality of those who tried Joan of Arc as a witch flourished again in the age of Montaigne, Bacon, Descartes and Pascal. If neo-Platonizing intellectuals could believe in a world of demons and the manipulation of angels, the poverty-stricken masses, particularly in remote mountainous regions where Christianity had scarcely penetrated, could be forgiven for believing in a satanic hierarchy of powers with wonder-working demons or familiars. An ideological slanging match with Luther, Calvin, Loyola and the popes pictured as the spawn of the Devil helped to increase the tension. Each Catholic or Protestant conquest or reconquest was followed by a cleansing holocaust of heretic-witches – clergy, dons and merchants as well as peasants. In the ever more cynical convolutions of the so-called wars of religion, the hysterical 'crusade' against witchcraft became the only real, if perverted, form of spiritual warfare.

Imbued with the simplistic chivalry of the *Exercises,* the Company entered the lists with zeal. The Spanish Jesuits Juan Maldonado and Martin del Rio were acknowledged experts. Del Rio published an encyclopaedia on the subject in 1599 and was the respected, scholarly justifier of the witch-hunt in Spanish Flanders. Maldonado gave many lectures on demonology. William Weston, a Jesuit missionary in England, was obsessed with witches, though powerless to put his fantasies into practice. Pierre de Lancre, the anti-semite who unleashed a reign of terror in Labourd in 1609, boasted of his Jesuit education. According to him, the infestation was a by-product of Jesuit missionary zeal – 'good monks having driven the devils out of India and Japan, these had settled in the Basque country, where they had found persons well disposed to receive them.' He also held that the witches travelled to Newfoundland on the masts of fishing vessels, intent on poisoning the catch. Two Jesuits sent in 1612 to Labourd reported that 'in a cave filled with all sorts of impurities' local priests 'went so far as to simulate the holy sacrifice of the

Mass . . . At these assemblies of sorcerers they concoct a poison boiled in cauldrons to spread disease among the crops.'

Jesuits were prominent in the hunts in Germany, especially during the Thirty Years War. Canisius did not entirely escape the prevailing hysteria, for it was an almost indispensable tool of popular evangelism. The debates and decrees of Trent meant nothing to the vast majority of the taught: but every illiterate understood and relished the world of the sorcerer. Canisius, however, was a model of charity beside such zealots as Georg Scherer, preacher to the imperial court at Vienna; Jerome Drexel, court-preacher to the Duke of Bavaria; Gregory of Valencia, the stern theologian of Ingolstadt; Fr Schorich, preacher to the Duke of Baden; or Peter Thyraeus, adviser to the witch-burning Archbishop of Mainz. In the Rhineland the Archbishop of Trier – 'wonderfully addicted to the Society, for which he built and endowed a fine college' – burned three hundred and sixty-eight witches between 1587 and 1593, including the Rector of the University, who had proved too merciful a magistrate. After 1620 the Catholic terror flared horribly. The Bishop of Wurzburg, for instance, burned nearly a thousand people in eight years, among them nineteen priests and a child of seven. His experience as confessor to the condemned led the Jesuit Friedrich Spee to entertain some radical doubts. Afraid of sharing the fate of another Jesuit, Adam Tanner, whose mild criticisms had infuriated his superiors, Spee circulated his comments anonymously in manuscript. 'Torture,' he wrote, 'fills Germany, and any nation that employs it, with witches. If all of us have not confessed, that is only because we have not all been tortured.'

Spee's manuscript, pirated by Protestant propagandists who in 1631 published it as evidence of Catholic unsoundness in this vital matter, caused alarm on both sides. It is one of the very few sane statements to emerge from that period of terror. But it did not convert many of his brethren, who carried the hunt into Poland and Hungary.

In Germany, Protestant strife helped the Catholic revival, and until his death in 1597 Canisius remained a dynamic example of the Jesuits' role after the Council of Trent. In Augsburg he delivered more than two hundred substantial sermons in eighteen months, apart from hearing confessions, giving retreats, establishing the fifth of his colleges at Innsbruck, teaching children their catechism, and editing a vast edition of St Jerome's letters. The Archbishop of Salzburg told the Duke of Bavaria that 'but for the Jesuits it would be a bad look-out for your Grace's dominions'. By the 1580s twenty colleges had been founded in the Society's three German provinces. By the 1620s Salzburg University, run by the Benedictines, was the only Catholic one in the Empire not founded or partly maintained by the Society.

Protestant pamphleteers increased their abuse as the Jesuits dug in. Accusations of witchcraft, child-murder, sodomy and even bestiality were common. Jesuit teachers were sorcerers who had intercourse with the Devil, smeared pupils with diabolical ointment which ensured lifelong obedience to their evil commands, and instructed children in the arts of poison and death-dealing incantations. Parents were warned not to trust their offspring with 'creatures of the devil whom Hell had vomited forth to destroy the German empire . . . outwardly modest and urbane but in reality fiends and atheists . . . Their purpose is to slay all those who have accepted the Confession of Augsburg . . . They caused the St Bartholomew Massacre . . . in Peru they plunged red-hot irons into the bodies of the Indians to make them reveal their hidden treasures.' Canisius was said to have married an abbess. Bellarmine was 'an Epicurean of the worst type who killed 1,642 victims, 562 of whom were married women. He used magic poison, pitching the corpses into the Tiber . . . He always had in the stable four goats which he used for his pleasure, and died the death of the damned.'

In the 1590s, after half a century of restraint and in spite of Aquaviva's statutory warnings, Jesuit writers began to retaliate with details of Protestant perversions and Luther's swinish habits. The tone, now, was rather that of Mariana, who in his vade-mecum for the future King Philip III had remarked of Protestant rulers: 'It is a glorious thing to exterminate the whole of this pernicious race'; or of the French Provincial Odon Pigenat, a member of the Catholic League's governing committee, who was reckoned by the Huguenots to be 'the cruellest tiger in Paris'. From 1618 on Jesuits and Capuchins accompanying the armies of Tilly and Wallenstein – mercenaries from Switzerland and north Italy who switched sides to the highest bidder and plundered mercilessly – competed in inflammatory sermons. After Tilly's defeat at Breitenfeld by Gustavus Adolphus of Sweden in September 1631 a Jesuit preacher in Strasbourg 'made his prayer to this effect: Lords and ladies, let us pray to God and the Blessed Virgin to cause her Son to defend us against the devil of Sweden and all his helps, the conjurors and witches of Lapland . . . from the adders of England and all their friends, from the beggarly Lutheran princes, that they get not head against us.'

Maximilian of Bavaria and the Emperor Ferdinand II had both been educated in the Jesuit College at Ingolstadt. Tilly and Wallenstein too

[101]

were Jesuit pupils; indeed Tilly, who had nearly become a Jesuit, was notorious for his piety, rededicating the blackened ruins of Magdeburg to the Virgin and naming each of his twelve largest cannon after one of the Apostles. But most of the generals were out to carve principalities for themselves; the Jesuits' success in the scramble for church property restored by the Edict of Restitution of 1629 angered other orders; and with Maximilian wavering and the entry of France and Sweden into the war it became increasingly difficult to maintain a pretence of religious fervour. Pope Urban VIII's remark that the conflict was purely political was borne out by the facts. Catholic France and Protestant Sweden lined up with the Protestant Dutch Republic and Venice against Lutheran Germany, Catholic Austria and Spain, while Savoy wavered from one side to the other. The real issues were whether Sweden should keep Pomerania, France Alsace, Bourbon or Habsburg emerge victorious. To qualify for French funds the Dutch helped to capture La Rochelle, the capital of French Calvinism. Jesuit advisers to Maximilian and Ferdinand were sometimes at daggers drawn, French Jesuits were split between support and condemnation of Richelieu's anti-Habsburg nationalist policy.

Jesuit influence helped to prevent a compromise peace after the victories of Gustavus Adolphus; last-ditch Jesuits worked against 'opportunism' and the 'spirit of surrender' during the negotiations at Münster and Osnabrück which resulted in the Treaties of Westphalia; and Peter Pazmany, freed to become Primate of Hungary by transfer to the Somaschi order (which had no objection to preferment), was a ruthless Catholic hard-liner. But though Jesuit fanaticism gave the Society an unenviable reputation, it paled beside the hatred felt for Cardinal Richelieu, the paymaster of Protestant mercenaries, and in particular for his roving representative, the Capuchin Father Joseph. He, more than any single person, was blamed for prolonging the war. His diplomatic skill helped to ensure that Germany, a patchwork of over three hundred tiny 'states', was politically and economically impotent and the Habsburgs bankrupted. Yet in a moment of despair he had written to nuns of the Calvarian Order, 'I have so little leisure to think of my inward being . . . I know how fatal it is not to be united with God. When I see how I and most creatures live, I come to believe that the world is but a fable . . . for I make no difference, except for a few externals, between ourselves, the pagans and the Turks.'

In Rome fanaticism earned no praise. Jesuit-Habsburg bigotry drove Urban VIII towards Richelieu, Bourbon success inclined his successor

Innocent X towards the Habsburgs. The popes were concerned to defend their heritage as best they might. A bull condemning the peace treaties as 'perpetually null' was published in 1650, but the papacy's political impotence was now so obvious that no one bothered to comment on this refusal to accept that the myth of Catholic Christendom was finally shattered.

Itself increasingly fragmented into nationalist or dynastic factions, the Society was vulnerable to every shift in the balance of power. Its cosmopolitan ambitions were as hollow as those of the papacy. Both were seen as political tools. Wallenstein founded Jesuit colleges on his ill-gotten estates and forced his serfs to send their children as pupils; but he was ready to negotiate with the Swedes to consolidate his personal empire. The bigotry of Catholics and Protestants, the economic catastrophe of a war whose grinding butchery was blessed and perpetuated by the Church, strengthened an anti-clerical mood which presaged ill for a Society identified with a rigid and often vindictive clericalism.

Venetian fears that the Catholic crusade mentality spelt commercial ruin had been fully justified. In the 1540s, when the Jesuits entered the scene, able, ambitious entrepreneurs had fled from Italy to Geneva where their talents were welcomed. Yet during the Thirty Years War nominally Calvinist financiers, refugees from the stifling atmosphere of Geneva and the Netherlands, found more scope in Vienna, Munich and Madrid. The great war of religion was fought and financed by freelances, despisers and exploiters of extremist religious zeal. They were harbingers of a new age.

CHAPTER NINE

Doctors of Dissimulation

NOWHERE DOES THE Counter-Reformation seem so romantically enterprising as in the exploits of Robert Parsons, Edmund Campion, Robert Southwell, John Gerard and Antonio Possevino: two of them martyrs, all of them ready to live on their wits in 'enemy' territory.

Queen Elizabeth was not amused when during a visit to Cambridge University in 1564 she watched a burlesque of the Mass in which a student dressed as a dog capered about the stage with a Host in his mouth. And the insults hurled at the pope, the Roman Church (John Knox called it 'the horrible harlot, the Kirk Malignant'), the Blessed Virgin, the Society of Jesus ('that presumptuous society of our Saviour') and Catholics in general, made these Jesuit gallants quiver with chivalrous devotion.

In the late sixteenth century the business of reclaiming lost sheep and defending the honour of the faith could require patience and cunning as well as a duellist's daring. 'They have been seen in processions of armed men, disguised as courtiers, dressed in silks with gold chains round their necks,' wrote a German pamphleteer in 1575. In *The Foot out of the Snare* (1624) John Gee, a renegade Catholic, warned that 'if about Bloomsbury or Holborn thou meet a good smug fellow in a gold-laced suit, a cloak lined through with velvet . . . rings on his fingers, a stiletto by his side, a man at his heels, willing (upon a small acquaintance) to intrude into thy company, and still desiring further to insinuate with thee, then take heed of a Jesuit.' These missionaries in heretic terrain rivalled the ingenuity of their brethren in India and China. Henry Garnet had eleven aliases, John Gerard nine, Parsons' *noms de guerre* included Ralph, Robert, Stephano, Ottaviano, Inghelberto, Cabel, Rowland, Howlet, Perino and Mr Redman. Jesuit prisoners smuggled out letters written in lemon or orange juice, preferably the latter, for as Gerard explained: 'Lemon juice comes out just as well with water or heat. If the paper is taken out and dried the writing disappears, but it can be read a second time when it is moistened or heated again. Orange juice cannot be read with water . . . Heat brings it out but it stays out. So a letter in orange juice cannot be delivered without the recipient knowing whether or not it has been read.'

In correspondence with Aquaviva, Garnet and Parsons used a 'commercial' code – credit-house for prison, prentice for novice, journeyman or merchant for Jesuit or Ours, workman for seminary priest. Parsons bluffed his way ashore at Dover as an army officer, complete with plumed hat, and later planned to smuggle priests into England posing as repatriated prisoners of war. Other English Jesuits got themselves up as elegant gentlemen, Spanish servants, tailors, and one, operating in Worcestershire, was described in an *Annual Letter* as having a wardrobe full of 'all kinds of dresses . . . appearing one while as a clown upon a packhorse, then, in splendid attire, entering the houses of the nobility, he made himself, like the Apostle Paul, all things to all men, that he might gain all.' Inadequate camouflage was likely to bring painful retribution, as when at Dover a priest was 'sewed up in a bear's skin and exposed in the streets to be torn in pieces by dogs and sported with as a monster'.

On the Continent undercover or semi-official operations seldom entailed such risks: but they were sometimes boldly conceived. By the 1570s Jesuit influence in Poland, begun by Canisius and consolidated under the rule of Sigismund III, a Jesuit pupil, was considerable. From Poland an attempt was launched to reclaim Lutheran Sweden for the Church. King John III of Sweden had married the Polish Catholic Princess Catherine Jagellon, and in 1574 the bizarre ten-year Swedish mission opened with the appearance at court as Polish ambassador of the resourceful Fr Stanislaw Warszewicki. The King was ready to consider the idea of conversion, on the understanding that the realignment of his subjects should be gradual and that clerical celibacy should be optional, Mass in the vernacular, and Communion in two kinds (wine as well as bread).

Warszewicki was succeeded by a Norwegian Jesuit, Laurits Nielssen (Laurentius Norvegus) who, with the King's approval, was appointed president and lecturer in theology at the recently-founded Royal College in Stockholm. His lectures, at first carefully non-controversial, soon attracted a fair number of students, including thirty pastors. In a pre-arranged debate with the King himself, who stoutly defended Lutheran doctrine, he is said to have presented the Catholic case so cogently that many in the audience were shaken, at least to the extent of voting Norvegus the winner. His sapping seemed to have prepared the way for the Society's ace negotiator, Antonio Possevino. With two other Jesuits,

Fr Fournier and an Englishman, William Good, in his retinue he arrived in Stockholm in 1577 as ambassador of the Holy Roman Empire. Possevino, who had spent ten years in France teaching, establishing a college at Avignon, and intervening with some success at a particularly stormy point in the relations between Clermont College and the University of Paris, persuaded King John to take the plunge: but only on the three conditions previously stipulated. Gradual mass conversion under the 'triple dispensation' proved unacceptable in Rome, and in 1579 Possevino returned to Stockholm, this time as Vicar Apostolic to Scandinavia, to announce this decision. The King was both startled and annoyed when, in a dramatic gesture, the Jesuits publicly revealed their identity. Norvegus was banished, but with his help Possevino's two visits had resulted in the placing of about fifty Scandinavians in continental seminaries. There was a belated postscript to the mission when in 1655 Queen Christina, the bluestocking daughter of Gustavus Adolphus, renounced the throne and settled in Rome, a romantic Catholic exile.

Possevino put in a strong plea for a trial of 'dispensational' Catholicism in Sweden, believing that it might spread in Scandinavia and bring the entire region into the Catholic bloc. In 1581 he was on his travels again, this time to the court of Ivan the Terrible, who hoped through papal mediation to get favourable settlement of a frontier dispute with Poland, and offered the bait of a possible opening of his realms to Catholic missionaries. But the Jesuit was again hamstrung by the Vatican's insistence that recognition of the primacy of Rome must precede diplomatic assistance. Taking it upon himself to reverse the order, he negotiated a ten-year truce: but with this in the bag Tsar Ivan ended the discussion about unity by menacing Possevino with a mace-like sceptre recently used to brain his own son. Unfortunately the Russian embassy infuriated the Swedish monarch, who in 1584 expelled the five remaining Jesuits. But victory over the Orthodox Church was a project at least as dear to the papacy as the reclamation of lost Protestant sheep; and in 1603 another attempt, in which Jesuits were again prominent, was made. On the death of Ivan, Boris Godunov seized power and bribed the Patriarch of Constantinople to recognize Moscow as equal with, and independent of, Byzantium in the Orthodox world. Ivan's son had vanished, probably murdered, but a young man who claimed to be the missing Tsarevich Dmitri appeared in Poland, turned Catholic, and assured the papal nuncio that if and when he became Tsar he would enforce union with Rome. The straw was eagerly clutched. The false Dmitri, accompanied by two Polish Jesuit chaplains, advanced into Russia and in June 1605 entered Moscow amid general rejoicing, which evaporated when news spread of the plan for reunion. Within a few months the two Jesuits were warning their protégé of rebellion and in May 1606, soon after Dmitri announced his intention of opening a Jesuit school, he was assassinated.

There was no questioning the skill of Possevino or the audacity of a man who smilingly replied to Tsar Ivan's sneers at the corruption of the papacy that the immorality of some popes did not justify wholesale condemnation any more than did the peculiarities of certain tsars. But Mercurian and Aquaviva saw the danger for the Society of being associated with such obviously hopeless political missions and as the optimism of popes and nuncios faded, the Jesuits seem to have extricated themselves. Like Bobadilla, Possevino was sent back to the classroom, to teach in Padua.

Aquiviva himself volunteered for the English mission in the late 1570s before he was elected General; but Mercurian, though heavily pressed by Parsons and by his friend William (later Cardinal) Allen, did not favour the project. He preferred to station English Jesuits in Europe or overseas according to the needs of the moment rather than to squander valuable men in a risky enterprise. Convinced that the English people would respond to a vigorous lead from Rome, Allen had been instrumental in persuading Pius V to defy the known wishes of Philip II and issue the bull *Regnans in excelsis* of 1570 excommunicating and deposing Queen Elizabeth as a heretic and a bastard and 'freeing' her subjects from allegiance. Parsons and Allen thought in terms of invasion to 'rouse' the slumbering Catholic community, which meant using Spanish military force. Mercurian did not agree with their assessment. He was also sure that missionaries would be classified as political agents, and though papal instructions had forced his hand over the Swedish mission, he deplored clandestinity and disliked the idea of priests living on their own, mingling with people of dubious morals, and being unable to practise their spiritual exercises regularly. All this, he pointed out, was contrary to the Rules.

His misgivings were confirmed by the reaction of some Jesuits to the mission. Having sacrificed careers and taken risks to leave England, not all were keen to go back. Forty years later paintings of Jesuit martyrdoms, including those of Edmund Campion and other heroes of the English mission, hung on the walls of the novitiate in Rome. The novice master would tell his charges, 'My dearly beloved, these are paintings of your brothers who were slain between 1549 and 1606. They are placed

[107]

in this room not only to give honour to their memory but to provide you with examples.'* But from Germany in 1578 Christopher Perkins replied that he would be prepared to return only with papal permission to take the Elizabethan Oath of Allegiance and to attend non-Catholic services. (When, after his dismissal from the Society, Perkins came to England, he converted to Anglicanism, was made Dean of Carlisle, and knighted by James I.) Fr John Gibbons, among others, begged to be excused, admitting that 'he did not find in himself the spiritual strength necessary for such an enterprise'.

Possevino's finesse had paid small dividends, and papally-sponsored Jesuit missions to Scotland and Ireland had been even more unrewarding than the Broet-Salmeron foray of 1541. Salmeron, elected Vicar-General while Lainez and Polanco were in France doing battle with *politiques* (those who believed in a political solution to religious differences) and Huguenots, tried hard to prevent Jesuit involvement in the Scottish mission, pleading shortage of manpower. But Pius IV insisted and after considerable delay an ailing Dutch Father, Nicholas Floris of Gouda (Goudanus), was plucked from semi-retirement and appointed papal envoy. Edmund Hay, returning home to settle his affairs before joining the Society, went on ahead and Goudanus, escorted by Hay's cousin, Fr William Crichton, and Jean Rivat, a French Jesuit, reached Edinburgh in April 1562. Reports from Scotland had been contradictory, and Goudanus was instructed to urge Queen Mary Stuart, a twenty-year-old widow who had only just arrived in Scotland after the unpopular regency of her mother Mary of Guise, to stand firm against heresy.

The timing was unpropitious. Long neglected by the papacy, the Catholic Church in Scotland had sunk into a condition of truly spectacular decay. John Knox, returning from Geneva where he had composed his *First Blast of the Trumpet Against the Monstrous Regiment of Women* (Mary of Guise and Mary Stuart), had swiftly mobilized the people and a land-hungry nobility behind a Calvinist-Presbyterian revolt. Mary Stuart was a prisoner in the Palace of Holyrood. The arrival of the papal embassy was soon known. Goudanus went into hiding, hastily disguised by Crichton in court finery while Presbyterian preachers exhorted their congregations to seize and slaughter 'the ambassador to the Papal Antichrist'.

---

*On 23 October 1970 Pope Paul VI canonized forty martyrs of England and Wales, including nine Jesuit priests and one brother – Campion, Alexander Bryant, Robert Southwell, Henry Walpole, Thomas Garnet, Edmund Arrowsmith, Henry Morse, Philip Evans, David Lewis, and Brother Nicholas Owen (the master hide-maker).

Delivered during a brief, surreptitious audience granted while Protestant courtiers were listening to Knox's thunderings, Goudanus' militant message fell predictably flat. The Queen explained that to save the rump of Catholicism she had been obliged to make sweeping concessions to heresy. Goudanus stressed that his mission was unpolitical, but trembling Scottish prelates could not wait to get him and his associates out of the country, a feeling soon to be shared by harassed Catholic priests and laymen in England. After some hilarious if humiliating adventures Goudanus was finally extricated. He was able to report two small mercies. The Queen had not turned Protestant, Hay and Crichton had won five recruits to the Society. A second visit by Edmund Hay in 1567, when Mary Stuart was on the verge of fleeing to England, was even less productive. Pius V, he told her, was convinced that she must cut down the heretic leaders and set an example of firm, fearless leadership. She replied that even if she had the power to follow such advice she would not be responsible for shedding more blood.

Though farcical, and advantageous to Knox, the Scottish mission had no catastrophic results. The same could not be said of the Irish intervention. David Wolfe, the Society's first Irish recruit, who for some years had been Superior of the Jesuit College in Modena, landed at Cork in 1561. For seven years, as apostolic nuncio, he covered the south consecrating bishops, catechizing, teaching, improvising a 'straggling school' system designed to operate on the run, exhorting upper-class Catholic families to stand firm. Pius IV had high hopes of making Ireland a bastion of Catholic fervour, but Wolfe's modest success brought swift retribution and he was captured and imprisoned in Dublin. Escaping in 1572 he confirmed the English government's worst fears by working in Spain, Portugal and Italy to help raise an expeditionary force. Of Wolfe's two Jesuit companions one, Edmund Daniel, was hanged, drawn and quartered at Cork in October 1572, thus becoming the first Jesuit martyr in Europe; the other, William Good, survived to accompany Possevino to Stockholm in 1577.

In that year Fr Wolfe was ejected from the Society for 'moral delinquencies', a description that could well be applied to the papal mission that forced the English government to retaliate, ended Elizabeth's hopes for a peaceful religious settlement, and helped to create the 'Irish problem'. A native population full of a novel enthusiasm for the Roman faith henceforth identified it with a passionate hatred of the English; and a new breed of colonists identified Protestantism with their own ascendancy, which for lack of adequate military force was defended by a reign of terror. Ireland, over which the popes still claimed feudal sovereignty, was England's Achilles' heel, having, as one writer observed, 'very good timber and convenient havens: and if the Spaniard might be master of them he would in a short space be master of the seas.'

In 1580, while Campion and Parsons were waiting at Rheims to cross the Channel, Pope Gregory XIII had despatched another nuncio, Dr Nicholas Sanders, with a small fleet of troop carriers, to assist rebellion in Ireland. Most of the expeditionaries were massacred, but this and the trickle of Douai seminary priests to England, together with the prospect of a Jesuit 'invasion', caused a further tightening of security. Recusancy fines and penalties for saying or hearing Mass were steeply increased and it was deemed high treason to convert anyone from allegiance to the Church of England. Campion, a patriotic Englishman who while still in Anglican orders had spent two years in Dublin making plans for a university and writing a *History of Ireland,* was disgusted by news of the papal expedition, which made it easier than ever to damn the English mission as politically motivated. To Allen and Parsons, seeing English Catholicism thrust into a ghetto where it might wither away, becoming little more than an obstinate, inbred nonconformist sect, this development heightened the need for some kind of action. Mercurian had finally given way and Aquaviva, who succeeded him, was more committed to the operation, defending it against papal doubts (though by 1586, replying to an appeal for reinforcements, he complained that it would be 'like sending lambs to the slaughter').

Campion, though prepared for martyrdom, was far from enthusiastic. An outstanding student and teacher, he was one of a series of Oxford graduates (Parsons, William Weston, William Holt, Thomas Stephens, John Lane) to join the Society in Rome in the mid-1570s. All had been influenced by the fanatical Allen, who eventually came to feel that the Jesuits, and in particular his old friend Parsons, were taking the pick of the recruits, leaving Douai with the second-raters. Having accepted the arduous conditions demanded of every postulant, Campion had been sent to the Austrian province for his novitiate. A distinguished professor and preacher at the University of Prague, he was also noted for writing and producing Latin plays to be performed by his students. He told Allen on arrival at Rheims: 'Well, Sir, here I am. You have desired my going to England and I came a long journey. . . Do you think that my labours in England will countervail all the travail as well as my absence from Bohemia, where though I did not much, yet was I not idle nor unemployed and that also against heretics?'

Evelyn Waugh and Graham Greene have drawn parallels between the hazards of missionary priests in Elizabethan England and the persecution of Christians in the prison camps of Hitler and Stalin. The hazards were real but the comparison is misleading. The English government, struggling for survival against what for a long time seemed the overwhelming might of Spain, was anxious to make concessions to all but religious extremists, and Jesuits were soon bracketed with strict Puritans in that category. Most people, not least the Catholic clergy and laity, were ready for compromise after a half century of kaleidoscopic religious change. The spirit of compromise and even outright indifference was far more widespread than the heated polemics of professional agitators, including such brilliant journalists as Gerard, Parsons and Weston, were prepared to admit.

General Mercurian's instructions specified that 'as regards dealing with strangers, they should at first be with the upper classes rather than with the common people, both on account of the greater fruit to be gathered and because the former will be able to protect them against violence.' Robert Southwell and John Gerard were of appropriate social grace and background. Both went about as country gentlemen (Southwell carefully learned the correct terminology for hunting and falconry) and only a handful of die-hard aristocratic Catholics who provided funds, recruits, lodgings and hiding-holes really welcomed the Jesuits. The courage and noble bombast of Campion and Southwell tend to obscure the fact that Aquaviva's warning to steer clear of politics and the plea that theirs was a spiritual mission were, in the circumstances, pure charade.

The cunning was mostly on the government's side. It soon realized that the mounting resentment of the Marian secular clergy and of some seminary priests at the Jesuit monopoly of rich patrons, cultural prestige, and plum chaplaincies offered a good chance to split the Catholic community. In Rome, Parsons and Aquaviva had difficulty countering complaints of Jesuit intrigue. Those who appealed to Rome were known as appellants, and the appellant controversy bedevilled the mission for decades.

It is easy to forget, when admiring the extravagant prose of Campion and the baroque poems of Southwell, that these men had been formed by a cultural renaissance that flowered in England at a time when, as the historian G. M. Trevelyan remarked, in Italy it was 'fast withering away under the hands of Spaniards and Jesuits'. The collection of antiquities in the Vatican narrowly escaped destruction by puritanical Counter-

Reformation popes, who ordered the fig-leafing of Michelangelo's nudes and had adulterers publicly flogged.

John Donne, a convert to Anglicanism, knew well the mentality he deplored in his tract *Pseudo-Martyr*, having been brought up in the feverish climate of Jesuit devotion. His mother was what became known as a 'Jesuited Catholic', two of his uncles were Jesuits, and he himself had been impressed by them. But he came to believe that 'the Jesuits exceed all others in all those points which beget or cherish this corrupt desire of false martyrdom': and this view is perfectly illustrated in the *Brag* which Campion, anticipating arrest, had composed for the benefit of 'the Lords of Her Majesty's Privy Council . . . I never had mind, and am strictly forbidden by our Father that sent me, to deal in any respect with matter of State or Policy of this realm. . . And touching our Society, be it known to you that we have made a league – all the Jesuits in the world, whose succession and multitude must overreach all the practices of England – cheerfully to carry the cross you shall lay upon us, and never to despair your recovery, while we have a man left to enjoy your Tyburn or to be racked with your torments, or consumed with your prisons. The expense is reckoned, the enterprise is begun: it is of God, it cannot be withstood. So the faith was planted: so it must be restored.' The same kind of masochistic defiance breathes in a sermon on the Day of Judgment by Peter Wright, a Jesuit executed at Tyburn in 1649: 'Oh what a comfort will it be to those souls that shall be able to say . . . for being a Catholic the sheriff drove away all my cattle, seized upon all my goods . . . pursuivants searching my house and a priest being found therein, all my lands were confiscated . . . yea, for assisting men, and persuading them to embrace your saving faith, I was hanged till I was half dead, had my belly ripped open, my bowels and heart torn out and cast into the fire, my head with an axe cut from my body and every quarter pricked upon a several pole . . . what a joy it will be to those souls that in that day can produce for themselves any of these heroic acts.'

Campion and Southwell are saints in the calendar. Parsons, who died in his bed in Rome in 1610, is not, and is widely regarded as the archetypal scheming Jesuit. Yet it was his planning and pleading which made possible the mission and, together with the mole-like burrowing of Henry Garnet, from 1586 to 1606 Superior in England, preserved it. Their achievement can be gauged from the vilifications of their Protestant and Catholic opponents. Garnet was accused of fornication, drunkenness, and being expelled from Winchester for gross immorality and sneaking. The ex-Balliol College don Parsons, son of a Somerset blacksmith, was said to be a monk's bastard; a rabid homosexual who had smuggled a hermaphrodite into the English College at Rome; an embezzler; a vicious bully who had Cardinal Allen poisoned, and who when the pope threatened to oust the Jesuits from all seminaries controlled by them, menaced him with the wrath of the King of Spain; a coward who fled from England in 1581 leaving poor Campion to his fate. On his deathbed, according to a Jesuit account, Parsons 'asked that the cords with which his dear friend Edmund Campion had been tortured should be wound round his neck. He blessed the cords very reverently . . . and thereat fell a-weeping that since God had not accepted his blood, He had at least accepted the sweat of almost thirty years.'

Parson's bold improvisations were often disapproved by other Jesuits, but his vitality, industry and ingenuity were prodigious. Parsons, who spent ten years in Spain, was welcome at court and made the most of it. But he treated Philip II as a sort of honorary Englishman. Racy controversialist, tireless fund-raiser, and busy politician, he also wrote *The Christian Directory* (a book of devotion so appealing that it was used, in edited form, by Protestants), founded English seminaries at Valladolid and Seville (to help finance which he obtained a royal licence to import and sell English cloth in Spain),* was commissioned by Aquaviva to assess and pacify the Spanish Jesuit revolt, and did what he could to free, or improve the conditions of, English prisoners of war slaving in Spanish galleys. He criticized the strict surveillance of pupils in Continental colleges and tried to mitigate it; organized an efficient intelligence and communication system for the English mission, from which all Catholics entering or leaving the country benefited; and not least in 1593 founded an English school at St Omers in Spanish Flanders, which was the direct ancestor of Stonyhurst College. Visiting it in 1609 a papal nuncio reported that 'these youths might be said to be the flower of English Catholicism; many are noble and some are sons of heretics or at least of such as through worldly policy only exteriorly follow the times. . . At dinner and supper various disputations were held, in Greek and Latin, and with so much ease that I was truly astonished.'

Mercurian's fears about the dangers of long-term undercover work were not unfounded. Loneliness, depression, fear and bribery caused frequent apostasies among missionary priests; some marrying, others

---

*Irish and Scottish seminaries were founded by Thomas White and William Crichton in Spain, Portugal, France and Italy.

becoming informers, some turning Anglican. Comparatively few Jesuits fell by the wayside, though some missionaries broke down and had to be nursed along or sent across the Channel to recuperate. Thomas Wright left the Society and after negotiations with the government toured mission areas seeking support for a plan whereby an oath of loyalty to the Queen (including an explicit rejection of Jesuit Romanism) would be traded for a measure of religious toleration.

The lengthy Ignatian training sequence then in course of elaboration had not been followed by English missioners, who were often rushed into action with a minimum of preparation. At the beginning of the 1590s not one of them had made his final profession. John Gerard and Edward Oldcorne had served only a few months' novitiate in Rome, and the same was true of many of their colleagues. In the case of brothers recruited in England Aquaviva consented to accept their proven loyalty in lieu of formal training.* Garnet was professed while acting as Superior, and it was he who began a tradition of twice-yearly 'conferences', attended by all Jesuits not in prison and by selected seminary priests for discussion of tactics, renewal of vows and spiritual retreat. Garnet placed missioners in pairs, like policemen on a tough beat; and Gerard, describing the terrible torture of the manacles in the Tower, wrote: 'If I had any spirit left in me it was given by God and given to me, although most unworthy, because I shared the fellowship of the Society.'

After the defeat of the Spanish Armada and the executions in 1595 of Southwell and Walpole, Garnet pleaded with Aquaviva to send 'some Scotch or Italian Jesuits that could speak English; for such are not subject to the law and many would deal better with them that leave us.' The suggestion was not taken up and there was a tendency, much promoted by Parsons' incurable optimism, to pin great hopes on the conversion of Mary Stuart's son James VI of Scotland (from 1603 James I of England). 'In the name of Christ, King of Kings,' wrote Cardinal Bellarmine, 'I beg of you, Sir, to remember that when you openly deny yourself to be a Papist, you are denying the religion of all the Scottish kings who reigned before you . . . How would it be if the great Donald [the first Scottish king] were to say: My child, what possessed you to embrace the religion of a fellow called Knox, one truly most noxious both to you and your kingdom? And if your grand-father James V and his daughter Mary, your mother, should surround you and demand a

---

*Some of the most distinguished English Jesuits chose not to be ordained. A Jesuit became a Jesuit after pronouncing the simple vows at the end of his novitiate.

reason for your change of religion (which will certainly happen to you on the Day of Judgment), what answer would you be able to give them?' The bitter disappointment of these hopes culminated in the Gunpowder Plot of 1605 and the arrest , trial and execution of Garnet for complicity. In his speech for the prosecution Sir Edward Coke, the Attorney-General, alleged that treason was 'the Jesuits' proprietary thing . . . since they set foot in this land there never passed four years without a most pestilent and pernicious treason tending to the subversion of the whole State.' Campion and Parsons, he said, had formed a 'pope's party' and Garnet was 'the harbinger of the Armada'.

From Rome, Parsons wrote: 'God hath sent a sore storm upon you. It may be our negligence and over-careless proceeding hath been some cause. God pardon those gentlemen's souls . . . Now, in Claude's [Aquaviva's] opinion and mine also, it is the time for every man to renew all good purposes, make special exercises, attend to mortification . . . edifying all and giving no just offence to any.' By 1625 there were one hundred and fifteen priests and students working in the Low Countries and more than a hundred priests and brothers in England, with a well-defined chain of command radiating from Rome. Conditions had always varied from one part of the country to another depending on the attitude of local magistrates and the strength of the Catholic gentry. Robert Jones spent twenty years on the mission, mostly in Wales. The *Annual Letter* of 1615, the year of his death, reported that 'it often happened to him after having journeyed through deep snow, to find that there were Protestants in the house he came to visit. In order to prevent discovery he would wait outside for hours together in frost and cold; he thereby contracted several ailments, a thing which often happens to our missioners when called to administer the Sacraments at some Catholic house.'

After five years in France, Richard Holtby, a former seminary priest, returned to his native Yorkshire in 1589 and for fifty years led the Jesuit mission in north-east England. In Northumberland, where for a time pursuivants, informers, and Protestant gentry were active in persecution, Catholic families quit their homes and hid in caves dug beneath the roots of trees or in the cellars of ancient ruins. There, reported Garnet, 'for their fellow-occupants they had toads, frogs, adders, lizards and such-like creatures. On one occasion it was necessary to administer drugs to a maid who believed that an adder had slipped down her throat while she was asleep.' Holtby, a capable carpenter and mason, was equal to all emergencies. But perhaps his most remarkable contribution to the

English province was to loose Mary Ward, a Yorkshirewoman and perhaps the most dynamic Jesuit of her time, onto the scene.

Between 1598 and 1650 more than five thousand English men and women, gripped by Counter-Reformation fervour, had entered the religious life abroad: a migration comparable with that of the Puritans to the American colonies. Staying close to the rules laid down by Loyola, the Society directed would-be nuns to Benedictine, Franciscan, Carmelite or Capuchin convents, but there were frequent embarrassments when they demanded Jesuit spiritual directors. Mary Ward, a born leader with a mind of her own and a liveliness equal to that of St Teresa, had a similarly devastating effect on her directors. Sent to St Omers by Fr Holtby, she was given charge of a girls' school. There she gathered a group of disciples and launched out on her own.

The rules of her order – the English Ladies – closely resembled those of the Society of Jesus. Its members, most of them bound by temporary vows, were to be subject to the pope alone, freed from enclosure and choir, and able to move about on pastoral or missionary work as well as to teach. Mary found the *Spiritual Exercises* rather elementary, preferred God as a director, challenged the conservatism of Jesuit spirituality, and, amazingly, received support from many Jesuits. By the 1620s the 'Galloping Girls' had opened houses in London, Rome, Naples, Perugia, Cologne, Vienna, Munich, Augsburg and Prague: a surge which even Canisius might have envied. Its schools, using a slightly adapted Jesuit curriculum, numbered thousands of pupils. But the teaching of dogmatic and moral theology 'so that they may not be taken in by their confessors' shocked the conventional mind. So did Mary Ward's sturdy feminism. 'There is no such difference,' she wrote, 'between men and women that women may not do great things. Heretofore we have been told by men we must believe . . . but let us be wise and know what we are to believe and what not . . . I know a missioner in England who said he would not for a thousand worlds be a woman because he thought a woman could not apprehend God. I answered nothing but only smiled.'

Rome was deluged with denunciations of the 'Jesuitesses'. Richard Blount, the English Provincial, and General Vitelleschi were determined to unload this liability. John Gerard, one of Mary's warmest admirers, was disciplined, her confessor ordered to England from St Omers. Her houses in Flanders, Germany, and Italy were suppressed. In 1631 a papal bull dissolved her order and she herself, arrested as 'a heretic, schismatic, and rebel to the Holy Church', was imprisoned in a Poor Clares convent in Munich.

Eccentricity was increasingly frowned upon. In 1585 Jasper Heywood, Donne's uncle, then the only Jesuit on the English mission, had scandalized old-fashioned Catholics by eating meat on a Friday. This had been authorized on the Continent but was not acceptable in recusant households. Heywood was recalled and severely reprimanded, but his 'foreign' laxity and arrogance were for long quoted by the appellants as typical of the Society. Missioners were now instructed above all to avoid provocation, and for eighty years after the death of Garnet the mission was relatively inactive. Charles I's marriage to the French Catholic Henrietta Maria brought a flutter of hope and some easing of conditions. But the Queen was surrounded by Capuchins and Jesuit influence at court depended on their goodwill. A Catholic Queen was no guarantee of toleration and most Jesuits continued to live and die in hiding, 'sitting alone like sparrows upon the housetop, expecting the happy day and the advent of the glory of the great God.' In Flanders they settled to a routine of teaching or published polemical books and pamphlets at the St Omers Press. John Floyd's *The Overthrow of the Protestants' Pulpit-Babels, Convicting their Preachers of Lying and Railing* was a typical production: but two of the most effective – *A Search made into Matters of Religion* and *The History of the Conversion of a Gentleman* – were written by Francis Walsingham, a near relation of Elizabeth's Secretary of State.

The quarrel between Jesuits and 'Ignatians' (Jesuit-trained seminary priests) and straightforward secular priests actually intensified as numbers, and therefore competition, increased. Wealthy patrons tended to give seculars the dreariest beats, regarding them as second-class clergy only fit for the servants' quarters. Their letters complain bitterly of 'counterfeit brethren' (Ignatians) and of 'the smooth operations of a lying Jesuit's tongue'. The appellants continued to agitate for a Jesuit-damning Oath of Allegiance, and were delighted when Richard Smith, appointed Bishop of Chalcedon and Vicar Apostolic in England in 1625, took their side, though himself trained by the Jesuits in Rome and Valladolid. A protégé of Cardinal Richelieu and a fervent champion of episcopal authority, he blamed Jesuit intransigence for the persecution of the Catholic community, accusing the ageing Gerard of implication in the Gunpowder Plot, and forced Richard Blount to dismiss Fr Thomas Poulton from the Society for making uncomplimentary remarks about himself and Richelieu in a private letter. When Smith died in 1631 Poulton was reinstated, but the much-publicized incident caused so much trouble that Vitelleschi, under papal pressure to end this interminable squabble or dissolve the mission, imposed a ban on Jesuit polemics.

The fate of John Ogilvie, the first Scottish Jesuit to die for the faith, in Glasgow in 1615, could be seen as a good omen. Whole families went into exile and religion at Jesuit prompting. Of the Corby family the father and three sons joined the Society, the mother and two daughters became nuns. A sprinkling of high-born converts provided substantial encouragement. A theological tourney between Archbishop Laud and a Jesuit champion resulted in the capture of the Duchess of Buckingham. The Earl of Worcester was another very useful catch – Worcester House in London became a Jesuit centre and Raglan Castle was the focal point of a mission in Wales. But when in 1632 another convert, George Calvert, Lord Baltimore, obtained a royal commission to found the colony of Maryland, Jesuits eagerly volunteered to escape an atmosphere of vicious Catholic animosity. Andrew White, the Superior of the Maryland contingent, reported that the natives were 'possessed with a wonderful longing for civilized intercourse and for European garments', but the colony did not turn out to be the expected Catholic Utopia. The terms of their charter obliged the Calverts to support an Anglican establishment. Nunneries were vetoed and Catholics enjoyed only a limited toleration. In angry dismay, the Jesuits accused the Calverts, who sent their sons to St Omers and had defended the Society against the attacks of Bishop Smith, of crypto-Protestantism.

After the outbreak of civil war in England in 1642 the Maryland mission was destroyed by Puritan raiders from Virginia. At home the predominance of 'Church Papism' (compromising Catholicism) was heavily underlined. There were examples of last-ditch Catholic royalism, but most tried to stay neutral, some served in the New Model Army, others negotiated with General Fairfax for limited tolerance in return for a rejection of the pope's political authority. Republican gentry often preferred the company of Catholics to that of the wilder sectarian revolutionaries, and William Metham, a Catholic, was Cromwell's unofficial agent in Rome.

Cromwell was no more inclined to execute priests than were Elizabeth, James I or Charles I, preferring banishment and if possible a settlement. Spanish power was waning, memories of the Armada and the Powder Plot seemed to be fading, discretion and respectability marked the Jesuit mission. Its tone had become far less sharply distinct from that of the Church Papists whose prudent tactics ensured the survival of the Catholic community. It could be argued that Jesuit militancy's most valuable service to the small minority of ultra-loyalists had been to sharpen their business sense, so that fines, or bribes to avoid them, could be paid. In some cases they were the most ruthless enclosers of common land and evicters of tenants. If the Society's indirect part in this development was noticed, it was not likely to have increased its popularity. Of a hundred and eighty-two Catholics executed in Elizabeth's reign, eleven at most could be classified as Jesuits, and eight of these were seminary priests admitted to the Society as an honour while awaiting execution; but for all their dogged attempts to prove that they were good, and thoroughly English, citizens the Jesuits were still suspect.

During his examination by Sir Edward Coke Gerard had explained that equivocation was different from lying, since 'the intention was not to deceive but simply to withhold the truth in cases where the questioned party is not bound to reveal it . . . The board examining me now would equivocate if, for example, they were questioned about some secret sin or were attacked by thieves and asked where their money was hidden . . . Our Lord equivocated when He told His apostles that no one knew the day of judgment, not even the Son of man.' But Coke's peroration at the show trial of Henry Garnet was closer to the popular legend, which it was designed to perpetuate. 'A man of many names – Whalley, Darcy, Roberts, Farmer, Phillips . . . he wrote cunningly with the juice of an orange or a lemon . . . a Jesuit and a Superior as indeed he is Superior to all his predecessors in devilish treason, a Doctor of Dissimulation, Deposing of Princes, Disposing of Kingdoms, Daunting and deterring of subjects, and Destruction.'

CHAPTER TEN

Confessional Politics

Equivocation and mental reservation were hardly peculiar to the Jesuits. But such was their success and so tempting a target was the Society in the first flush of its self-righteous zeal that these universally human proclivities came to be associated with the sons of Ignatius. For the word 'Jesuit' most dictionaries give as a secondary definition 'crafty person, intriguer, casuist, sophist'; and the adjective 'jesuitical' is synonymous with 'cunning' or 'deceitful'. Many nineteenth-century Protestant or liberal novelists and historians condemn 'Jesuit morality' as a spiritual sewer and imply that the French wars of religion and the Thirty Years War were largely due to the evil, devious fanaticism of court Jesuits. A nineteenth-century German historian, Theodor Griesinger, suggests that Henry III's choice of Edmond Auger as a confessor was a result of his – and the Jesuits' – degenerate addiction to flagellation and alleges that Jesuit confessors had worked on the German Emperors Rudolf II and Matthias by providing them with brain-washed mistresses.

The effectiveness of the Society's confessional politics, sometimes established in Jesuit classrooms as in the cases of Maximilian of Bavaria and the Emperor Ferdinand II, was often exaggerated. King Gustavus Adolphus is said to have raged that 'there are three Ls I should like to see hanged: the Jesuit Lamormaini, the Jesuit Laymann and the Jesuit Laurentius Forer.' The papal nuncio in Vienna reported in 1626 that 'the Jesuits have the upper hand in everything, even over the leading ministers of state . . . Their influence had always been considerable, but it has reached its zenith since Father Lamormaini became confessor to the Emperor.' Fr Luis Gonçalves da Camara, while tutor to King Sebastian of Portugal, was rumoured to have encouraged a monkish fanaticism and to have promoted a crusade against the Moors in North Africa which ended disastrously and facilitated the Spanish takeover of Portugal and her empire. The French kings' confessors were represented as Machiavellian manipulators. And the whole operation was assumed to have been deliberately planned by the 'black popes'.

The reality was slightly different. The Jesuit stress on frequent communion and confession was, together with their educational surge, part of a definite plan to involve the laity in the Catholic Reformation and to strengthen the Church's grip on the faithful. They and the Theatines are credited with inventing the box-confessional as a means of popularizing a 'duty' which until then had been, for most Catholics, a twice-yearly occurrence at most. Ignatius had accepted the logic of directing the consciences of rulers, though hoping that not too many of his men would be tied up in this way, considering each case on its merits, and accompanying each permission with counsels of prudence.

His successors issued similar cautions. 'The other day,' Mercurian informed Fr Mengin, confessor to Duke William of Bavaria, in 1579, 'a father wrote to me that a man of great distinction had said to him: "Your people would do well if they kept within their pastoral limits."' But as opportunities multiplied and rivalry with the Capuchins increased, the tone of the directions changed. In 1602 Aquaviva recommended that 'if the Society can no longer escape such an office because, for various reasons, the greater glory of God seems to require it, then care should be taken as to the choice of suitable persons and the manner in which they carry out their duties . . . It is fitting that the priest should be allowed to suggest what he considers good for the greater service of God and the sovereign, and not only with regard to such things as he might know from him in the character of penitent, but also with regard to those which he might hear elsewhere requiring a remedy.' By the end of the sixteenth century the General Congregations in Rome, with delegates from all the Jesuit provinces, had taken on the character of political intelligence meetings and there was keen competition for posts that offered prestige and perquisites. Père Lachaise, Louis XIV's long-serving confessor, was given a fine country house on ground later used for the cemetery which bears his name.

In 1598 Fr Viller, confessor to Archduke Charles of Styria, complained to Aquaviva about the malice of his brethren: 'In the early days of our Society we all rejoiced if one of us found favour with a prince. Now there are some who are jealous if anyone is in favour and labours with good result. Under the pretence of virtue they show zeal for the discipline of the Society and are filled with envy.' Aquaviva's reaction was to advise confessors to 'use reserve . . . suggest that in some things princes should apply to other members of our order, or even to persons outside it, according to circumstances, so that it may not appear as though our members directed everything.' Some twenty years later, in an attempt to keep royal confessors under bureaucratic supervision Vitelleschi, whose generalship was almost as long and eventful as Aquaviva's, ruled that 'when sovereigns require a Jesuit's opinion on any subject, the Jesuit in question is to report the matter to his Superior, who is to lay it before several Jesuits for discussion. The resolution formed after this conference is to be supplied to the Jesuit who has been consulted by the sovereign.'

The selection, surveillance and replacing of key confessors proved a constant headache to headquarters. Ignatius had incurred the wrath of King John III of Portugal by withdrawing the wayward Simon Rodrigues, whose transfer provoked a mass exodus of Portuguese Jesuits from the Society. Fr Camara was up against the determination of a scheming Dowager Queen to prevent young King Sebastian from marrying, and did all he could to rid his pupil of the Moorish crusade fantasy which he was subsequently accused of fostering. So did his successor, Gaspar Serpe, who was forced to accompany the Portuguese expeditionary force, captured, and beheaded. Aquaviva's efforts to dislodge refractory Jesuits from their confessional niches were not always successful, especially in Spain, where the tendency was to ignore messages from Rome. Fernando Mendoza, confessor to the Countess of Lemos, sister of the influential Duke of Lerma, not only refused to stand down but persuaded Philip III to invite the General to travel to Spain to 'discuss' the matter. He had to be bribed away with the offer of the bishopric of Cuzco in Peru.

Vitelleschi was distracted by the spectacle of Maximilian of Bavaria's advisers, enmeshed in the complex politics of the Thirty Years War, treating the Jesuit advisers of Ferdinand II as enemies, and vice versa. His own directive, quoted above, came under righteous fire. Nicolas Caussin, Louis XIII's confessor, pointed out that it breached professional etiquette: 'I am reproached for not seeking advice from my Superiors in the matters I discuss with the King . . . But I know from Thomas Aquinas that matters of confession are to be kept secret . . . What law or what constitution of the Society is there that bids the Father Confessor report to his Superiors on the affairs of his penitents? Is the King's conscience to be revealed to as many persons as there are Consultors in our houses?'

James Brodrick described Fr Auger as 'the first of that long line of martyrs, the Jesuit confessors of the Kings of France'. Auger had to come to terms with the superstition and homosexuality of Henry III. Pierre Coton was appointed confessor to Henry IV partly as a token of gratitude for the Society's service in persuading the Pope to cease treating him as a heretic usurper, partly as a hostage for the good behaviour of French Jesuits. The saying was that the King 'had Coton in his ears'; but it is very doubtful if the Jesuit exercised much influence, morally or politically, on Henry IV, and court life must have been a purgatorial experience for a conscientious apostle of reformed, respectable Catholicism. The king and his courtiers wandered the palace singing bawdy songs. The infant Louis XIII, brought up with a flock of royal bastards, was put to bed with his sister or with maidservants and encouraged to sexual exploration for the amusement of his parents. Vitelleschi's directives must have been doubly galling to Jesuits who, apart from being tormented by a licentiousness which they were powerless to check, had to suffer the vigilance of Cardinal Richelieu. After one Jesuit had been dismissed for a show of independence, his successor Jean Suffren accurately forecast that he also would not survive for long. Confessors were ordered not to go near the King unless summoned, and Caussin, who pleaded with Louis XIII to end the misery caused by Richelieu's war policy, was banished.

Jesuit confessors were particularly numerous in what was called the Holy Roman Empire of the German Nation. Not only did Emperor Ferdinand II's brothers, the Archdukes Ernest, Leopold and Charles, each have one, but Wilhelm Lamormaini followed Fr Becan as the Emperor's *éminence grise*. A lanky, austere Luxemburger with a pronounced limp, Lamormaini was a man of exceptional ability. As Ferdinand II's confessor and political adviser, he needed to be. The Emperor, though pedantically pious, was no puppet. He could be as peremptory as Richelieu with offending clergy and it says much for Lamormaini's tact and usefulness that he remained more or less in favour for thirteen years. He was faced with the hostility of his fellow-Jesuits at Munich, since Maximilian's role as protector of German liberties conflicted with Ferdinand's (and Lamormaini's) policy of forcible catholicization. He also had to cope with the tensions between Austrian and Spanish Habsburgs: Ferdinand being mainly concerned with the situation in Germany, Philip IV with the reconquest of the Netherlands and Spanish interests in Italy. Tilly and Wallenstein, both Jesuit pupils and protégés, not only absorbed some sizeable Jesuit loans to keep the heretics at bay but intrigued against each other; while Pope Urban VIII, alarmed by Habsburg threats, intrigued with Richelieu and Maximilian and complained to Vitelleschi about Lamormaini's machinations.

Under pressure from Urban VIII and Vitelleschi, who wanted an all-out anti-Protestant alliance between France and the Emperor, Lamormaini strained every nerve to prevent Ferdinand from patching up a peace with the German Protestant princes and, with their help, waging war more effectively against France and Sweden. He failed, but his efforts angered the Spanish government. The Spanish ambassador in Rome protested vehemently and other critics pointed out that Lamormaini's room resembled the office of a prime minister, with cabinets full of neatly-labelled international correspondence. Vitelleschi sent a somewhat equivocal rebuke: 'There have been complaints about your prolific correspondence; and although I do not consider this in itself blameworthy, it would seem desirable either to remove this evidence altogether or at least to hide it from visitors by a curtain.'

Lamormaini was as indifferent to mass suffering as were the Emperor, Richelieu, Fr Joseph or the soldiers who plundered and massacred and changed sides. Austria and Bohemia were purified of heresy, thanks largely to Lamormaini's stiffening of Ferdinand's will to resist the temptation of a compromise peace. But central Germany was a chaos of refugees who had little choice but to join the armies as troops or camp-followers. Competing with Richelieu's bribes, Maximilian's Jesuits – notably his confessor Adam Contzen, who sat in at meetings of the Privy Council – also worked hard to keep their ambitious penitent on the narrow path of war. Though politically volatile, Maximilian was a model of propriety, decreeing the death penalty for adulterers, prohibiting the 'lust-inciting' dances of his peasants, and insisting that male and female field labourers should sleep in separate shelters. In Hungary the Jesuit-Somaschi Archbishop Pazmany set up a Catholic reign of terror and supported the belligerence of Lamormaini and Contzen. At the final peace conferences Jesuits, lobbying and writing acid pamphlets against the sin of surrender and ignoble opportunism, vainly tried to stop the rot. There seem to have been few if any Canisiuses or Favres among the Jesuit confessor-politicians of central Europe. But then the political scene was very different; and their reward was two-thirds of Germany Catholic and studded with Jesuit colleges.

Yet not even Lamormaini could claim to have approached the Capuchin Fr Joseph's baleful diplomatic efficiency, let alone his versatility as mystic, revivalist preacher, Apostolic Commissary for Home Missions, founder of a congregation of nuns, and chaplain, chief of intelligence, and military adviser at the siege of La Rochelle. One Jesuit however at least equalled Fr Joseph in breadth of achievement and was a more sympathetic character. Antonio Vieira joined the Society in Brazil in 1623 at the age of fifteen and though nearly dismissed on at least one occasion was a Jesuit for seventy-four years. At eighteen he was already famed for his learning, and in 1641 travelled to Portugal, where he was appointed tutor to the Infante Don Pedro, court preacher, and a member of the royal council. In the next eleven years he reorganized the army and navy, overhauled the taxation system, founded a Brazilian trading company, and led diplomatic missions to England, France, Holland and Italy. His sermons and writings rank among the classics of Portuguese oratory and literature. Though a patriot he criticized the Portuguese Inquisition's hounding of New Christians; and in 1649 this, together with the sheer range and independence of his activities, so alarmed General Vincenzo Carafa that Vieira was told to transfer to another order. This was averted by John IV's obstinacy, Carafa's death, and a reversal of the decision by the new General, Francesco Piccolomini. Vieira returned to Brazil, where his attempts to protect the Indians so infuriated the colonists that in 1661 he was deported to Lisbon and put under house arrest by the Inquisition.

At the French court, Richelieu's brow-beaten sequence of Jesuit marionettes ended when Vincent de Paul, founder of the Lazarist missioners and of the 'unenclosed' Sisters of Charity, became confessor to the Regent, Anne of Austria, during the minority of Louis XIV. Francis de Sales, Vincent de Paul, Jean Eudes, Jean-Jacques Olier – France was full of home missioners, sometimes accompanied by bands of lady catechists, taking the faith to remote rural areas, stirring up the local clergy, drawing huge audiences, beating the drum for the Catholic Reformation. This was something that the Jesuits had pioneered in the 1560s, and they were still prominent a century later. François Régis, vowed to the service of the poor, walked barefoot from hamlet to hamlet in the Cévennes. For forty-three years in Brittany Julien Maunoir, who opened one of the first Jesuit retreat houses at Quimper, led a team of evangelists specializing in a pageant of the Passion of Christ which wrought crowds to a pitch of hysterical receptivity for the sermon that followed. In Spain the fiery itinerant preacher Jeronimo Lopez used similar methods, finding the public display of a corpse a useful aid to repentance.

To offset criticisms of court Jesuitry Aquaviva relaxed Mercurian's veto on 'advanced' mysticism. His cautious blessing was seized upon by a group of French Jesuits who gathered round Fr Louis Lallemant, master of novices at Rouen. Maunoir was a disciple, but Lallemant's most celebrated follower was Jean-Joseph Surin, who in 1634 was sent to exorcize an allegedly demon-possessed community of Ursuline nuns at Loudun. His subsequent insanity and reputation for violent austerities caused Vitelleschi to investigate the Lallemant school.

He found little to condemn. Surin, the son of a wealthy merchant who had been a generous benefactor of the Jesuit college in Bordeaux, was apt in his letters of spiritual advice to mingle passages about the soul 'plunging herself into the abyss of faith, wholly lost in the close darkness which God inhabits' with pointed reminders to Catholic landowners of their right and duty to persecute the Huguenots. The Marquis de Jonizac is urged to 'perform a work of great importance for the service of God – to remove the preaching house. The edict of Nantes [which in 1598 had recognized Huguenot zones of influence in France] allows Catholic lords of the manor to overthrow the preaching houses on their lands . . . and it is the means of quietly destroying heresy.' Jesuit correspondents are exhorted to realize the honour and responsibility of belonging to 'a Company which is called to this eminent sanctity' and the vows of the professed are compared with the outpouring of grace on the day of Pentecost.

Lallemant's and Surin's recipe for heroic sanctity is very much what Erasmus had in mind when he wrote, in his *Praise of Folly,* that 'the great Stoic Seneca takes from a wise man all affections whatever, yet in doing so he leaves him not so much a Man, but rather a new kind of God, that was never yet, nor can ever be.' A hyper-Ignatian self-denial was declared the mark of the truly dedicated Jesuit. How otherwise, asked Lallemant, to balance 'a deep love of heavenly things' with the 'scientific studies and other natural occupations' which were a necessary part of a Jesuit's armoury but could easily become all-absorbing? Surin's golden rule was 'to deny ourselves, never to say we like this better than that. The life of grace makes us oppose the propension of nature.' In 1658, more than twenty years after his experience as an exorcist, he wrote to the Ursulines of Loudun: 'After so many favours, must God be meanly served, my dear Sisters? When in the morning the bell rings, we must get up at once as if the bed were on fire . . . wear down the flesh by austerities. . . . A body that is often beaten by penances frightens the Devil. Delicate souls who content themselves with some slight strokes and then rest themselves in their nest, which is slothfulness, cannot be thought fit for the intercourse of Angels.'

Celebrated Jesuits like Lamormaini, who made no pretence of being high contemplatives, were notorious for their Spartan habits. As Cardinal-Archbishop of Padua Robert Bellarmine, though a terror to heretics, refused to kill the fleas about his person; since they would not qualify for Heaven, why deny them such pleasure and nourishment as they could find? He is also said to have pawned his ring and even his mattress to give alms, and, remarking that 'the walls won't catch cold', to have had the splendid hangings in his house removed and made into garments for the poor. Francisco Suarez, probably the most learned theologian and controversialist of his generation, whose immense tome on international law earned him the title of 'progenitor of the League of Nations', always rose before dawn for an hour and a half of prayer before his first lecture. Plagued by rheumatism, gastritis and bronchitis, he never curtailed his penances, fasting three times a week and not eating until noon. Ten hours a day were spent in study, six at his devotions. His literary output was staggering. The *Metaphysics* accounted for two thousand double-columned octavo pages, the *Treatise on Angels* runs to three-quarters of a million words. He admitted that there were times when the labour palled: 'I am always turning my millstone, always grinding out these scholastic aridities,' he groaned in a letter to a Jesuit missionary in Mexico. 'No doubt death will find me thus occupied. But,' he dutifully concluded, 'if I am doing the will of our Lord, I ask nothing more of this life.'

Luis de Molina, another Spanish professor at the University of Coimbra, whose *The Concordance of Free Will with the Gifts of Grace* of 1588 drew the wrath of the watchful Dominicans and was cited as evidence of 'laxism', was as industrious as Suarez and no merely theoretical liberal. He held that missionaries should be careful not to preach war on the heathen or countenance the seizure of their property; and actually visited the docks in Lisbon to interview slave-traders. He concluded that the enterprise was purely commercial and that any talk about converting the slaves to Christianity was sheer hypocrisy. Antonio Escobar y Mendoza, perhaps the most reviled of all Jesuits thanks largely to the Arnaulds and Blaise Pascal, became a symbol of unprincipled sophistry. But he was, it seems, a saintly and industrious man who not only wrote millions of edifying words but was revered as a preacher, missioner, prison and hospital visitor. The playwright Calderon was one of his pupils, he himself composed many dialogues and sketches to be acted by schoolboys, and when he died at the age of eighty there was public mourning in Valladolid. His *Handbook of Moral Theology* went through many editions in every Catholic country and for ten years was praised as a useful and unexceptionable compendium, with the usual quota of examples of sexual transgressions. Then, quite suddenly, it was given a wider fame by anti-Jesuit writers as a turgid classic of pornography and equivocation.

Molina's prolix, erudite attempt to square a theological circle by reconciling the operation of divine grace with freedom of the human will was a logical outcome of Ignatian strategy as outlined in the *Spiritual Exercises* ('we ought not to speak nor insist on the doctrine of grace so strongly as to encourage the poisonous theory that takes away free will'); and of a determination, much in evidence at the Council of Trent, to distinguish Catholic 'humanism' from the crude, 'God-honouring' predestinarian emphasis of Calvin. Like Escobar, Molina was not putting forward any new ideas but laboriously sorting and carefully restating very traditional ones. After thirty years of cogitation he suggested that the God/man equation might be solved by assuming that 'sufficient grace', always available, became 'efficient grace' when the human will cooperated with it, and that God's honour would be saved by the hypothesis of the *scientia media* – the wisdom by which the Almighty foreknows the reaction of the human will.

This solution followed the pattern set by St Augustine in his fight against two heresies, the' rigorism of the Donatists who wanted to exclude 'sinners' from a Church of 'saints', and the pan-salvationism of the Pelagians who stressed the essential goodness of human nature. But in keeping with Jesuit ambition to widen and diversify the Church's appeal it was tipped towards a (Catholic) 'universalism' and therefore vulnerable to a charge of being 'semi-Pelagian'. Led by Domingo Bañez, the Spanish Dominicans were quick to attack Molina's book, and there ensued one of the most acrid theological vendettas in the history of the Church. Many Jesuits felt that Molina had overstated his case and he was censured. But though Bellarmine and Suarez modified the offending thesis with the notion of 'congruism' (*congruous* grace being such as to obtain the free consent of the will as opposed to *incongruous* grace which though 'sufficient' is not 'efficient'), corporate pride encouraged solidarity. Jesuit scholarship and orthodoxy were stoutly defended and the Dominican thesis attacked as savouring of Calvinism. Philip III of Spain and the Empress Maria of Austria expressed support for Molinism, theologians belaboured each other in print, and the Vatican was swamped with documents and deputations.

From 1598 to 1607 a special committee appointed by Clement VIII, the *Congregatio de auxiliis,* tried to reach a conclusion. Twice the verdict

Emperor.	D. *Ambassador.*	G. *Emperor's Life Guard.*
Jesuits.	E. *The chief of his Retinue.*	H. *Russian Interpreter in the Tartar La*
...nba & Algamba, Minister.	F. *Principal Ministers of State.*	I. *Chinese Interpreter in the same.*

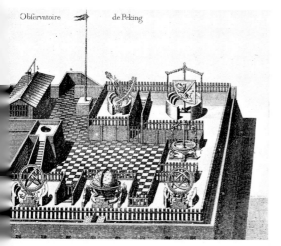

(*Top*) A banquet for Jesuit missionaries held by the Emperor of China.

(*Above left*) Observatory in Peking designed and supervised by Jesuit astronomers and mathematicians.

(*Right*) Matteo Ricci (right) and Adam von Schall holding up map of China; frontispiece to *China Illustrata* published in 1667.

16. (*Above left*) Robert Parsons, who led (1580) and later organized the Jesuit mission to England.

17. (*Above right*) St Edmund Campion: like Parsons an Anglican convert. Executed in 1581.

18. (*Below*) Jesuit 'conspirators' in England, c. 1610.

LE PERE LA CHAISE.

Tres Habile Confesseur.

Dauid pecha, Nathan lui dit :
Mais moi j'absous et ie pardonne,
Par la i'avance ma personne,
Et a ma secte en fin ie donne du credit.

19. Fr Lachaise, long-serving confessor to Louis XIV, was considered a classic example of the 'political' court Jesuit.

Many missionaries met a violent end: 20. (*above left*), Portuguese Jesuits
drowned on the way to Brazil; 21. (*above right*), death of two Jesuits in Japan;
22. (*below left*), torture and decapitation of two Belgians; 23. (*below right*),
Isaac Jogues, killed by Iroquois in Canada in 1646.

went against the Society, but partisanship was so frantic that the decision was not published and Jesuit fervour for the papal cause in Venice helped to persuade Paul V that it would be impolitic to offend such faithful servants. After two decades a compromise was reached. To avoid any further scandal both parties were to stop calling each other names. In Spain the Jesuits celebrated the decision as a triumph for the Society. Firework displays, masked balls, bullfights, and street notices proclaiming MOLINA VICTOR drove home the message to all sections of the population. That it probably was a popular victory was indicated by the success of a Jesuit-inspired play, *El Condenado por Desconfiado* (The Man Damned by Doubt), which contrasted the fate of a bandit who after a career of crime is saved by a confessor on the scaffold (efficient grace) and a saintly hermit who despite his austerities is damned by a nagging (Calvinist-Dominican) suspicion that he is irredeemable.

The English socialist historian R.H.Tawney defined casuistry as 'the application of general principles to particular cases which is involved in any living system of jurisprudence, whether ecclesiastical or secular'; and in the third century AD Tertullian, a Roman lawyer converted to Christianity, had begun the process. At that time a main problem was how far a Christian soldier in the Roman army could take part in pagan ceremonies, and already it was becoming apparent that 'absolute' morality was an illusion which had to be modified according to circumstances, temperaments and ecclesiastical strategy. By the eighth century AD Penitentials were prescribing penances for a wide range of homosexual offences, making careful distinctions between 'kissing, licentious kissing, and kissing with accompanying emission'; while fellatio, sodomy, and the use of an artificial phallus by nuns were discussed in some detail. After the Fourth Lateran Council of 1215, which required all Catholics to go to confession at least once a year, guidebooks for confessors multiplied. Dominicans produced the first systematically arranged manual, with many examples of the sins of the flesh. The Jesuits were to be accused of corrupting Catholic simplicity and muddying the limpid morality of the Bible with 'subtle Talmudic for-mulas'. But the inevitable business of interpreting and re-interpret-ing the Ten Commandments and the ambiguous teachings of the New Testament was already well advanced before they took a hand. Murder, theft, fraud, sexual activity in all its permutations, abortion, the setting of a just price, the problem of usury, the degrees of fasting, the use of cos-metics, chastity and unchastity in dress, dancing or reading matter, the rights and duties of officials – all had been scrutinized and categorized.

[129]

Cases of 'natural law' (the light of reason) were distinguished from those of 'positive law' (divine or human, revealed or decreed), cases of 'anterior conscience', concerned with future actions, from those of 'posterior conscience' dealing with the past. Schools of casuistry had acquired their own nuances and labels. 'Absolute tutiorists' demanded observance of the letter of the law; 'moderate tutiorists' were less exacting; 'probabiliorists' reckoned non-observance of a law to be justified if arguments for this were weightier than those against; 'equiprobabilists' allowed non-observance of a law whenever the arguments for and against were equally powerful. Still keeping their lead as moral theologians, the Dominicans were the acknowledged architects of probabilism in its final form. 'If an educated man considers two opinions to be probable,' wrote the Dominican theologian Vitoria in 1539, 'then no matter which of the two he follows he does not sin.' Melchior Cano, the hammer of the Jesuits, added that a confessor would often be justified in following a probable opinion even if it was contrary to what he himself believed; and in 1577 Bartolomeo de Medina assured his readers that 'if an opinion is probable it is lawful to follow it even though the opposite opinion be more probable.'

Thus, although the Jesuits rapidly established themselves as casuists-in-chief, they hardly deserve either the praise or the blame which has been so freely lavished upon them as pioneers in this line. In an essay of 1902 entitled *The Velvet Path* Rémy de Gourmont saw them as 'representing the sanest portion of Christianity . . . they hardly believed in the responsibility of the sinner; no more than the philosopher of today believes in the responsibility of the criminal.' To have demonstrated that 'there are cases of conscience but no absolute morality, diseases and a few remedies', was, he thought, clear moral gain, 'an act of intellectual boldness and scientific probity'. In proof that the Jesuits, as men of action, 'showed little esteem for the inactive virtues such as chastity', he quotes the verdict of the Jesuit moral theologian Cornelius à Lapide on the biblical episode of Susanna and the Elders: 'The chaste Susanna acted like an heroic woman; but in such a peril of infamy and death she could have limited herself to enduring everything from the two old men without consenting or cooperating inwardly, because existence and reputation are more valuable than chastity . . . Young virgins think themselves guilty if they do not struggle and scream, whereas it is sufficient to execrate the act to which they are forced.' De Gourmont also cites the opinion of Fr Airault, one of Pascal's butts, on the morality of abortion: 'I reply (1) That if the fruit is not animated and if pregnancy is dangerous to her, she may procure abortion, either directly or indirectly; (2) If the fruit is already animated and she would die with the child, she may before delivery take such remedies as indirectly harm the child and directly aid her; (3) If a chaste girl has been corrupted against her will she may, before the fruit is animated, get rid of it as she chooses, for fear of losing her honour, which is far more precious to her than life itself.'

De Gourmont is enthusiastic about this reasoning. ('The Jesuits were Christians to such a slight extent! The boldest of our politicians would not dare to sign that obscure Jesuit's proposition!') But most of the daring permissiveness attributed to the casuists of the Society had been anticipated by their predecessors; and, in some respects, especially in the early years, they were stern enemies of laxity. In *Aspects of the Rise of Economic Individualism* Professor H.M.Roberton, rejecting the theory that capitalism is primarily a Protestant phenomenon, suggested that the Jesuits, 'always informed about commercial needs and always willing to take them into account when giving opinions in cases of conscience . . . contrasted violently with the less adaptable Calvinists. The argument that Calvinism relaxed the discipline of the Christian in his conduct of commercial affairs is untrue. Jesuitry relaxed this discipline more than any other branch of religion.' But this statement is contradicted by the recorded opinions of Lainez and Canisius. Canisius in particular had a very traditional attitude to usury, being flatly opposed to the taking of interest on loans. His sermons to the merchants and bankers of Augsburg were uncompromising on this point: 'This city,' he said, 'is full of those who grind the faces of the poor . . . who seek only gain, oppressing their neighbour in buying and selling, taking six or ten per cent per annum on loans . . . And now come the new preachers to increase their licence, so that merchants sin without any conscience, nobody makes restitution and whole families are on the way to damnation owing to the unjust riches acquired through usury.' Hostility to his old-fashioned ideas was so pronounced that the Jesuits were forced to leave the city for a while. Yet the banking family, the Fuggers, were close friends of Canisius and the businessmen he berated were potential benefactors of the colleges he was so desperately keen to found.

Escobar's definition of probabilism was conservative and showed a similar bias towards mercy for the poor: 'I give greater approval to the opinion which is more favourable to religion, piety and justice . . . In the matter of vows, oaths and wills, my approval goes to the opinion which tends more to the protection of orphans, widows, strangers from foreign

[131]

parts, and other persons called in law *miserabiles.'* He considered tax-evasion a venial offence and commended officials who showed indulgence, 'particularly towards the poor and those who normally pay promptly'. Debtors should be allowed to keep enough of their possessions to live frugally according to their station. Jesuit casuists studied the class structure of the time, and Canisius' simple rich/poor scheme was gradually replaced by a minutely-graded scale. The manner of restitution or apology prescribed began to vary according to the social status of offender and victim. Much allowance was made for a lethal sense of honour as manifested in homicide or duelling, and an addiction to gambling. Scrupulously-minded servants were absolved from guilt in saddling the horses or holding the ladders which they knew were to take their masters to impure assignations. Less scrupulous servants were excused if they stole a little, the amount being calculated according to the wealth of the employer.

Escobar's condoning of the use of false weights and measures was not intended to encourage the cheating of customers but to help dealers who might be ruined if they observed the official price when, according to general agreement, it had been set unfairly low. The law could not be openly flouted, but guile was permissible, local authorities were guiltless if they connived at it, and dealers, if questioned in court, could deny a charge of dishonesty. An analogy is offered: 'For instance, if Titus kills Caius in reasonable and blameless self-defence, he can deny having killed him before the judge, because what the judge means by his question is whether Titus has *murdered* Caius, and that Titus has not done.' Such casuistry can be seen as an example of the attempt to balance the scales of justice (and gain support from grateful clients) by minimizing what had to be rendered unto Caesar. But by the mid-seventeenth century Dominican laxity, which had come under Jesuit fire in the 1570s, was being extended rather than criticized. Hermann Busenbaum of Cologne – the Jesuit who is said to have taught that the end justifies the means – wrote that 'the father-confessor or any other learned authority may advise one who comes for advice in accordance with the probable opinion of others, if this opinion is more favourable to the person concerned; in such a case the father-confessor must disregard his own more probable and certain opinion.' Other casuists held that 'those should not be condemned who flit from one authority to another until they find one whose opinion is favourable, provided that the authority seems learned, pious, and not entirely alone in his opinion.'

That comprehensively 'understanding' casuistry had its dangers is indicated by the indiscreet exultation of the *Imago primi saeculi* of 1640: 'Now, thanks to the Society of Jesus, sins are atoned more speedily and eagerly than they were formerly committed; nothing is more common than monthly or even weekly confession; most people have scarcely committed a sin before they confess it.' Some Catholics were shocked by this development. It seemed to be dragging the anchor of personal responsibility, opening the floodgates to ethical anarchy. Jesuit confessional politicians derided Armand de Rancé, the rigorist Abbot of La Trappe, and he in turn blasted the Molinists (as he called them): 'Unless God takes pity on the world and subverts the zeal which is applied to destroying right principles and replacing them by wrong ones, the evil will continue to increase and we shall soon see an almost universal devastation.'

Pascal and the Jansenists were to be the instruments of providence in this respect. But the Jesuit formula of detailed and constantly revised guidance, though open to criticism for its unwieldiness and monumental pedantry, was imitated as well as reviled, even by Protestants. Jeremy Taylor's *Holy Living* of 1650, a highly schematic Anglican equivalent of the *Spiritual Exercises,* was followed in 1660 by his *Ductor Dubitantium,* a full-scale essay in moral theology. Bishop Taylor shudders at the 'impure curiosity' of such Jesuit experts as Manuel de Sa and Diana, groans at their prolixity, and frowns on their perversion of 'simple' Gospel truths. Yet his own definition of probabilism ('that is more probable which hath fairer reasons, that is more safe and farther distant from sin') is not very different from Escobar's. Nor are his sources – 'scriptural or universal tradition, right reason discernible by every disinterested person, the laws of wise commonwealths, the sayings of wise men, the proverbs of the ancients, the great examples of saints.' Taylor's 'handbook' runs to four volumes and he stoops to consider such problems as whether 'public stews' (brothels) are justifiable in the interests of public order, concluding that they may be the lesser of two evils.

The Protestant challenge had made sacramentalist, confessional religion more than ever the mark of Catholic identity. But the fact remained that while the Society's missioners and mystics strove for spiritual revival, its casuists seemed to be encouraging and exploiting an over-mechanical religion of the type which the Catholic Reform had aimed at least to modify. Fervent Catholics whose misgivings were voiced by de Rancé and Pascal, as well as by professionally jealous rivals, branded the Jesuits as cynical salesmen of a flexible faith, reckless impresarios of a baroque religiosity.

CHAPTER ELEVEN

The Baroque Style

IN 1633 A PORTRAIT OF Peter Canisius in a Jesuit house in Quito was reported to have broken into beads of sweat as a sign that the Counter-Reformation was going badly in Germany: a curiously apt phenomenon focused on the man who had been a strong advocate of lavish imagery in Catholic churches. 'The innovators,' he wrote in a treatise on the Blessed Virgin, 'accuse us of prodigality in ornamentation. They resemble Judas reproaching Mary Magdalen for pouring the precious ointment on the head of Christ.'

There was much speculation within the Society about the founder's wishes in the matter. Would he have felt that grandiose structures contradicted the image of apostolic poverty which he regarded as so vital? Would he have approved the expansion of theatrical perform-ances in Jesuit schools – let alone plays, however 'sacred', given in Jesuit churches? What would he have thought of *Constantine,* a two-day spectacular staged at Munich in 1574, with a thousand participants, students and townsmen? Or of the German College as one of the most fashionable centres of baroque music in Rome, with a *maestro di capella,* boy sopranos, *castrati,* hired instrumentalists, and students singing or reciting the entire office on fifty-two feast days? Or, finally, of his own apotheosis and that of Francis Xavier in St Peter's on 12 March 1622 when, in company with Teresa of Avila, Philip Neri and Isidore of Madrid, they were canonized in a ceremony of unprecedented splen-dour?

The nave of the newly-completed basilica was crammed with people, silver trumpets sounded a fanfare, the Sistine choir sang, tapestries covered the walls, and from the ceiling hung enormous banners painted with images of the saints of the moment: swooning Teresa, penetrated by the angel's fiery lance; Philip Neri gazing at a vision of the Virgin and Child; Ignatius presenting the Constitutions of the Society; Xavier baring his breast in token of consuming evangelic love; Isidore, a farmworker of the twelfth century, tilling the soil from which (as his legend related) a spring of living water gushed. It was significant that four of these saints were Spanish, gratifying to the Society that two were Jesuits. The choice was not only politic in the uneasy state of papal-Habsburg relations, but just in recognizing Spain's overwhelming contribution to the impetus and character of the Catholic renaissance.

'The Virgin Triumphing over Luther and Calvin', the theme of a canvas commissioned by the Dominicans, typified an atmosphere of edgy braggadocio which resembled 'pagan' Renaissance hyperbole. Self-conscious, artificial and apprehensive, the triumphalism had much in common with the inflated pretensions of Pope Boniface VIII, whose tremendous anathemas had been rapidly followed by his own arrest and death, the Avignonese captivity, and the Great Schism.

The baroque style perfectly expressed this truculent mood, and the Jesuit mystique, though it did not create that style, fitted it like a glove. The Catholic retort to Protestant iconoclasm was to multiply paintings, frescoes, statues, gilt, marble, lapis lazuli, precious metals, emotional themes. They were designed, among other things, to astound and instruct a largely illiterate populace. The *Spiritual Exercises* were a vital ingredient, together with the stories of Ignatius' gift of tears. How he besought the Virgin to plead for him and felt himself 'raised up to God the Father . . . my hair bristled on my head and my whole body was penetrated by great heat, then followed a stream of tears accompanied by great sweetness'; how he 'discoursed with the Holy Ghost, weeping the while, and saw and felt it as brightness and flame'; how according to Ribadeneira his eyes were so damaged that he could no longer read the Breviary, and 'the number of his tears was so great that he collected them in a large vessel'.

When Francis Borgia, Duke of Gandia, resolved to become a Jesuit Ignatius had rejoiced in 'the great mercy with which God has refreshed the Society' and described his decision as 'ringing like a cannon shot across Europe'. The Duke's fiercely ascetic ambitions had a certain comic-baroque quality – he was so corpulent that a half-moon was cut in the table to accommodate his belly. And it was he who, shocked to find Ignatius living in squalor and Jesuits preaching in a small chapel inadequate for the crowds they attracted, used his influence to get permission to build a large and impressive church in the Piazza Venezia. Michelangelo, then seventy-nine, was approached to design it, but fourteen years passed before the foundation stone of the Gesù was laid. Urgently occupied with other matters, Ignatius raised no objections to the plan. Nor was he put out by the news that the Collegio Mamertino at Messina had produced a play or dialogue in 1551. And he was not in principle opposed to the use of music – actually regretting the loss of a sung Office – and enjoyed listening to Fr André des Freux playing the the clavichord.

The Council of Trent had decreed that Catholic iconography should be controlled and standardized. Bishops were supposed to ensure that images were 'not inspired by erroneous dogma which might lead the simple astray' or tainted with 'impurity and suggestive charm'; and a few prelates, notably Borromeo, took this seriously. Apocryphal or pagan themes, paganized Christian themes and nudity were banned. Daniel of Volterra ('The Trouserer') was called in to clothe Michelangelo's figures in the Sistine Chapel; as late as 1650 Innocent X had an Infant Jesus by Guercino covered with a shirt; Paolo Veronese was rebuked by the Inquisition for sullying a Last Supper with figures unworthy of the subject's solemnity; and Bellarmine bragged of having persuaded a well-known artist never again to paint a nude. But as Gianlorenzo Bernini proved, draperies however ample did not exlude eroticism.

There was no question of economy. Work in St Peter's went ahead regardless of cost. Rome had to match the mood of a revived if only superficially reformed papacy. Elsewhere new churches were built and old ones restored. Far more money and effort went into all this than into the episcopal seminaries that were supposed to provide competent, conscientious priests. The scope was greater than ever, but artists were expected to make propaganda, concentrating on such themes as the cult of the Virgin, the primacy of St Peter, the mystery of the sacraments, veneration of images and relics. With Bernini, in effect cultural commissar of Rome for half a century from 1624, Catholic art, using architecture, painting, sculpture, lighting effects, and the full-throated baroque organ to make a grand theatrical assault on the senses, acquired something of the oppressiveness of Fascist art under Mussolini. A close friend of Giovanni Oliva, Vicar and then General of the Society of Jesus from 1661 to 1681, Bernini was the creator of High Baroque, a master of projecting religious emotion, and so prodigally productive against a background of mass poverty and near-famine that in 1670 the municipal authorities censured him for 'instigating the Popes to wasteful expenditure in calamitous times'.

His favourite books were the *Imitation of Christ* and the *Spiritual Exercises*; he went to Mass every morning, prayed in the Gesù every evening, communicated twice a week, had hanging over his bed a picture of Christ on the Cross hovering above a sea of redeeming blood (said to have been inspired by one of Oliva's sermons), and made an annual retreat under Jesuit direction. The Society could, therefore, claim that he was their man. Michelangelo too is said to have been influenced by Jesuit piety in his rejection of 'the passionate illusion that made me look upon art as a sovereign idol'. Other artists came under the Jesuit spell, vowing like Carlo Dolci never to paint a figure which could not lead souls to devotion. In 1572 the Florentine sculptor Bartolommeo Ammanati defaced some of his earlier work, advised fellow-artists to cease producing 'lascivious objects', paid for the building of a Jesuit college, and willed all his possessions to it. Pietro da Cortona, a baroque painter and architect who received some Jesuit commissions, was one of many artists who paid lip service to a treatise by Fr Ottonnelli, published in 1652, which put the Society's official view on such matters as the use of mistresses as models, whether one could work on feast days ('Yes, but you must not prepare colours or prime canvases'), and whether all unregenerate productions should be destroyed ('one should not burn all indecent works . . . painters and sculptors often represent the nude body so that one may admire its wonderful composition').

The architect Borromini, also patronized by the Jesuits, bequeathed a large sum to embellish the altar dedicated to St Ignatius. And as a sign that earlier austerity had been relaxed the irrepressibly luscious Rubens, assisted by Van Dyck and other pupils, executed thirty-nine ceiling-paintings and two large altarpieces, depicting the miracles of SS Ignatius and Xavier, for the Jesuit church in Antwerp. According to some accounts he had made the *Exercises* and was a prefect in his local Marian Congregation, and the Antwerp assignment, the most grandiose of all his ecclesiastical commissions, kept his workshop busy for several years. When the church, a new one designed by Brother Pieter Huyssens on the model of the Gesù, was consecrated, visitors were amazed by the splendour of Rubens' 'brave paintings' and by a dazzling wealth of gold and marble. General Vitelleschi, informed of the enormous cost, forbade the church to be opened, put Huyssens under house arrest, and ordered him to cease work as an architect. But his commands were overruled by the Infanta Isabella, widow of the Archduke Albert; she insisted on Huyssens' release, commissioned him to design a chapel for her, sent him to Italy to select the finest marble, and encouraged him in the building of his next ambitious venture, St Peter's at Ghent, for which Rubens painted *The Martyrdom of St Lieven.*

Undoubtedly Ignatius would have applauded this sanctification of the studio. He might even have approved the process which, under the direction of General Oliva, turned the interior of the Gesù and of the

[137]

church of San Ignazio (begun in 1626) into a riot of coloured marble, stucco and gold; thus, as in most baroque interiors, banishing the Gothic sense of mystery. Yet until 1658, when the close partnership of Oliva and Bernini began and the latter started work in the church of Sant' Andrea, the Jesuit part in the baroque movement was haphazard and often reluctant.

In 1558 the first General Congregation had specified that Jesuit buildings should not be lavish or over-decorated and that all projects should be approved by the General. Standard designs were used, with local variation, by run-of-the-mill Jesuit architects but mostly ignored by outsiders, who were allotted Jesuit theological advisers and supplied with craftsmen from a pool of excellent carpenters, carvers, and cabinet-makers. Like the Jesuit architects and artists, they kept down expenses. A few achieved real eminence: for instance Brother Andrea Pozzo, a talented illusionist painter whose treatise on perspective was translated into English and is supposed to have decided Joshua Reynolds to become an artist; and Brother Wilhelm Hermans, a Fleming who pioneered the development of the baroque organ.

The exterior of the Gesù, the Society's mother church, designed by Giacomo da Vignola to the taste of the patron, Cardinal Alessandro Farnese, was sufficiently sober to please the puritans. The interior answered the demand for a spacious, uncluttered nave which accommodated a large congregation, gave a clear view of the high altar and the Mass ritual, and was bordered by side chapels and box-confessionals: stripped, in fact, for action. But there were disputes between the Jesuits, who wanted a flat roof, and Farnese, who insisted on a dome. When the Cardinal died funds were cut off and decorations by some undistinguished Jesuit artists made a hideous jumble of the interior. Aquaviva protested that Ammanati's design for the Florentine College was too ostentatious, but since Ammanati was paying for the work he got his way. Austere plans for the Roman College were overruled by Gregory XIII and there were more problems over money when Cardinal Ludovico Ludovisi, who had agreed to finance the San Ignazio church, died in disgrace and his relatives declined to contribute.

Some Jesuits welcomed these mishaps, and there was a continuous undertow of resistance to baroque extravagance. In his *Spiritual Painting* of 1611 Louis Richeôme, a French Jesuit whose ideal of didactic art was a lifelike rendering of a gory martyrdom, pleaded for architectural simplicity, deploring 'Ionic columns crowned with scroll-like ornaments, pilasters, pedestals, paintings and reliefs'. The Spanish General

Vincenzo Carafa, a near-iconoclast, removed all paintings from his quarters and refused a donation to decorate the chapel of St Ignatius, saying that he would prefer the money to be spent on the poor. As late as the early eighteenth century many Jesuits were offended by the theatrical paraphernalia of Sant' Andrea and the bedizening of San Ignazio. They complained that insofar as there was a florid Jesuit style it had been imposed on the Society by non-Jesuit artists in league with General Oliva, a keen connoisseur who, after his friend Prince Pamphili donated the first of many large sums to rebuild Sant' Andrea, promoted every artistic enterprise undertaken by the Society. Oliva, a Genoese of noble birth, argued that high baroque was perfectly compatible with the 'reformed' concept of 'art for edification not admiration', and made a careful distinction between Jesuit residences, which should reflect holy poverty, and Jesuit churches, which should 'try to reach up to the sublimity of God's eternal omnipotence with such appurtenances of glory as we can achieve.'

Not without some moments of anxiety, the guardians of Jesuit orthodoxy fought off another 'baroque' challenge. The fashion for Christian, or Christianized, occultism seems to have originated in Spain, where two Jesuit architects, Juan Villalpando and Jeronimo del Prado, delved deep into esoteric lore, attempting to prove that the five orders of classical architecture were derived from the divine plan of Solomon's Temple. Villalpando's book on the subject, drawing on a number of ancient sources and analyzing the mystical properties of colours and precious stones, was widely read. But what threatened to develop into a minor movement was driven underground by a violent attack. Led by Bellarmine and the demonologist Martin del Rio, this campaign resulted in a purge of occult literature and errant Jesuits; and when Baltasar Gracian, an Aragonese schoolteacher and one of the most talented baroque writers of the period, was judged to have shown symptoms of occultism (he also criticized the fossilization of the Jesuit educational system), he was brutally disciplined. Forbidden to publish and refused permission to leave the Society, he died in solitary confinement in 1658.

Villalpando and Gracian were unlucky. Both, in their way, had been trying to extend the limits of the pagan-Christian synthesis, to widen the range of Jesuit humanism. The official blessing that was withheld from them was, eventually, given to puritan-baroque drama. Successive revisions of the *Ratio Studiorum* in 1586, 1591 and 1599, based on a sampling of opinion throughout Europe and, as far as possible, overseas, show how opposition from rigorists was overcome by the logic of success

[139]

and expediency. As long as the plays were in Latin – or mostly, then partly, in Latin – as long as the subject matter was edifying, they were acceptable: so, in due course and as adjuncts, were singing, dancing, orchestras, and all the technical ingenuity that could be mustered in the way of stagecraft.

To the dismay of conservatives, concessions were made to demands for freer use of the vernacular, for female roles (but not actresses), for women to attend performances, for performances to be more frequent, for comic interludes, for the use of churches as theatres. In Vienna, Paris and Madrid Jesuit school productions offered virtually an alternative court theatre, patronized by fashionable society. It was argued that the growth of a flourishing secular drama had to be challenged; and in Germany Protestant propaganda plays, in which Jesuits were coarsely handled, called for a reply. In the 1560s a dialogue for use in grammar classes listed reasons for encouraging theatricals: '(1) The clever acting of poor students often moves the wealthy to help them; (2) the plays bring renown to the masters and to the school; (3) they are an excellent way of exercizing the memory; (4) they are a great help to students in learning Latin; (5) they inculcate lessons of virtue.'

The spirit of emulation was increased by rivalry between schools proud of contributing to a theatrical counter-reformation. The musical programme at the German College, at first heavily criticized, was gradually accepted for its cultural prestige value. In 1579 Claudio Aquaviva, then Superior of the Roman province, noted that 'some Bishops from Germany, and Prince Electors of the Empire, have requested young men from this college to be masters of ceremonies in their churches and chapels . . . it is so famous in Germany that its graduates are called to care for many churches there.' Such was the fame of the Germanicum that in 1629 Giacomo Carissimi turned down the chance to take Monteverdi's place in Venice to become *maestro di capella,* later combining this with a similar post in ex-Queen Christina's court-in-exile.

The growth of musical activities to such ambitious proportions was paralleled by a burst of technical inventiveness, despite much disapproval of the time and expense involved. Play themes remained relentlessly edifying, as indicated by such titles as *Philoprutus, or the Sorry Outcome of Avarice, Euripus, or the Emptiness of All Things,* and *Philothea, or the Wonderful Love of God for the Soul of Man, Drawn from Holy Scripture and Set to Delightful Melody.* These were little more than baroque mystery plays, stuffed with personifications of vice and virtue and garnished with crowd-pulling gimmicks. The magic lantern, perfected by Fr Athanasius Kircher, was used for realistic dream or fire sequences. Plays became longer, varying from two to seven hours, and effects more spectacular. Audience participation was heightened by the device of placing actors, who suddenly took part in the action or dialogue, among the spectators. Music and dancing were featured in Spain as early as 1558, and by 1643 a performance of *Theophilus* in Munich required thirty-two musicians and forty singers. In the finale of a play celebrating the canonization of the founder, staged at Pont-à-Mousson in 1623, St Ignatius appeared above a roof and, descending by a mechanical device, set fire to a castle representing Protestant heresy and filled with fireworks. At Graz in 1640 a giant puppet figure of Jezebel was torn to pieces by dogs.

Often a stage was erected in the courtyard of a school, but by the mid-seventeenth century the larger colleges were elaborately equipped. Clermont (later Collège Louis-le-Grand) had three theatres of varying size for different productions with opulent scenery and scene-shifting apparatus, flying machines, trapdoors, wind-and-thunder-making contraptions. This battery of effects could simulate such dramatic episodes as the crossing of the Red Sea by the Israelites. In Rome the Germanicum provided singers and expertise to compete with profane opera, and the Jesuits learned much from Bernini, who created richly illusionist scenic effects not only for his own plays but for ecclesiastical occasions – in 1628, for instance, dramatizing the Quarantore or 'Forty Hours' Devotion* in the Pauline Chapel of the Vatican by filling the vault with artificial clouds upon which hidden lamps cast a 'heavenly' light. A five-act drama put on at the Roman College to mark the canonization of Ignatius and Xavier included scenes set in the monastery of Montserrat, Hell, and the cave of Manresa, and a pageant of Jesuit triumphs. A figure representing the Church Militant descended from the clouds, and during a temptation scene the painted heavens opened to reveal the Archangel Michael offering the armour of God to Ignatius. From 1640 onwards the Gesù was used for spectacular biblical pageants designed to compete with the attractions of the Roman carnival. In a typical extravaganza the vast backdrop filled the whole choir. The Host appeared in a cloud, surrounded by angels, while beneath the theme of the Old and New Dispensations was enacted, with Moses and the Ark of the Covenant at the Red Sea in the foreground, Jesus

---

*An exposition of the Blessed Sacrament arranged to commemorate the time that our Lord spent in the tomb.

and his disciples in the Garden of Gethsemane behind. Thousands of lights with adjustable flames provided a flood of shadow-free, trembling radiance which seemed to enclose actors and audience in a visionary spell.

This hallucinatory technique, bringing saints and Gospel characters so close as to be almost tangibly real, was based on the magic-lantern methods of the *Spiritual Exercises*. It is not surprising that the great baroque playwrights Calderon, Lope de Vega and Corneille were educated by the Jesuits. Will-power and self-control, energy and stoicism – the Jesuit virtues – characterize the heroes and heroines of Corneille: but though his plays have classical settings the fatalism of Greek tragedy, too Calvinist, is replaced by the idea of co-operation, as in *Oedipus* ('The heavens, fair in reward and punishment/To give to deeds their penalty or mead/Must offer us their aid, then let us act'). Calderon was more explicit. In *The Great Theatre of the World* the producer is God, the Prompter the Law of Efficacious Grace; *Belshazzar's Feast* sets forth the dogma of the Redemption; in *The Great Prince of Fez* the hero, a convert to Catholicism, joins the Society of Jesus chanting a hymn of praise to Ignatius. Such devotion might have been expected to please his old masters, who, however, deplored his scenes of human passion and were envious of the super-lavish productions which his plays were given. One, taking place on a lake lit by three thousand lanterns, with the court watching from gondolas, offered a shipwreck, a triumphal chariot pulled by dolphins, and the destruction of Circe's palace to the crash and flare of artillery and fireworks.

Molière, once a pupil at Clermont, grieved the Jesuits by his gaiety and anti-clerical cynicism, and they were prominent in the constant attacks made on the prolific and popular Lope de Vega. He was described as a wolf feeding on lost souls, a monster who had done more damage to Spain by the worldliness of his plays than had Luther to Germany by his heresy. Yet Jesuit drama did not escape sporadic Inquisitorial attention, and the authorities of Paris University frequently denounced the Society's excessive cult of the theatre.

Nowhere did the baroque style manifest itself more spectacularly than in the case of Urbain Grandier, in which the Society was deeply involved. Grandier, the learned, lecherous parish priest of Loudun who in 1634 was burned at the stake for alleged diabolism, was another Jesuit-educated embarrassment. But at least he departed this world in a blaze before thirty thousand spectators: while the hysterical nuns' writhing and mouthing, first of satanic obscenities then of chaste devotional clichés, under the exorcism of Fr Surin, afforded a dénouement which not even Calderon or Lope de Vega would have dared to contrive.

France provided two more heavily-exploited examples of real-life baroque theatre. The mystical effusions of Marie de l'Incarnation, an Ursuline recruited by the Society for the Canadian mission field, seemed to Francis Parkman evidence of 'the tendency of the erotic principle to ally itself with high religious excitement': but to her contemporaries they seemed the height of the sublime. So, in its gorier way, did the heroism of Isaac Jogues. A pupil of Fr Lallemant, he returned to France in 1644 after being horribly mutilated by the Mohawk Indians he was trying to convert. Paraded at court as an object of veneration – the Queen publicly kissed his crippled hands – he sailed for New France (Canada) again and this time was butchered to death. Shortly before that he had written in a letter: 'May the little blood that I shed in that land be a pledge of what I am willing to give from all the veins of my body.' When the noble-Roman antics of the Jesuit drama began to pall, the curtain rose or fell upon a series of bizarre episodes in the distant missions.

CHAPTER TWELVE

Chameleons of God

THE COMPANY'S ACHIEVEMENTS in Europe, though remarkable, were for many Jesuits a secondary consideration, a next best. Ignatius himself had hoped to lead the mission to Ethiopia. Lainez was bombarded with letters from Spanish and Portuguese Jesuits volunteering to go overseas. 'I beg you, Father, prostrate at your feet, to send me of your charity and by the blood of Jesus Christ to China,' wrote one. 'I am no good as a preacher, because I stammer and have very little learning,' wrote another, 'but I have good health, glory be to God, and find it no great hardship to spend the entire day in the confessional, often for days on end. In fact, I practically live in it.' A third appeal, from a young professor of theology, included the almost obligatory avowal that 'I feel drawn to the East Indies or China for no other reason than that I imagine there will be more hardship and suffering in those countries ... If I heard of a country which provided a still larger share of the cross, I would transfer my affections to it immediately.'

Not until the eighteenth century was the ban on non-Iberian missionaries in Latin America finally breached, though an Englishman, John Yate, and an Irishman, Thomas Fields, were smuggled into Brazil in 1575; and a little later missionaries from Flanders, France and Germany, going under assumed Spanish names, were assigned to Mexico and Paraguay. From 1632 Canada was the preserve of French Jesuits. But whatever their country of origin, the desire for hardship and martyrdom was abundantly satisfied. Of fifty-six missionaries sent to Ethiopia between 1554 and 1639, twenty were captured by Barbary corsairs or executed by Coptic Christians. In Japan, during the massacres that all but obliterated the Catholic Church, eighty-seven Jesuits (half of them Japanese) were killed: some at the stake, some by water torture, some hanging head downwards over pits filled with excrement. Many volunteers never reached their destination. It has been estimated that five hundred of the six hundred sent to China between 1580 and 1680 perished on the way from disease, shipwreck or piracy. In 1570, fifty-two Jesuits bound for Brazil were slaughtered and thrown overboard by Huguenot privateers from La Rochelle.

The fickleness of rulers was not the only political hazard. Almost everywhere the Jesuits roused episcopal resentment, and opposition from other missionary orders increased as competition grew stronger. The Jesuit monopoly in Japan and China was broken. French, Dutch and English ambition pressed hard on the Iberian empires. Spanish and Portuguese colonists continued to resist the Indian-protecting policies of the Society in South America.

An attempt to enlist papal aid in overcoming these difficulties promised well, but at best was a paper victory. General Borgia suggested to Pius V that all missionary activity should be controlled by a central authority in Rome; in 1568 a committee of four cardinals looked into the matter and in 1622 the Congregation for the Propagation of the Faith ('Propaganda' for short) came into existence. It was hoped that a system of roving Vicars Apostolic would tidy up a chaotic scene and help the Society in its struggle with Catholic enemies. Grateful for Jesuit support, Propaganda warmly commended the 'adaptive' approach so bitterly attacked by the Dominicans, asserting that 'there is no stronger cause for alienation than an attack on local customs, especially when these go back to a venerable antiquity. Do not draw invidious contrasts between the customs of these peoples and those of Europe; do your utmost to adapt yourselves to them.'

Iberian pride was affronted by the scheme, which took a long time to come into operation and, as the event proved, could just as easily be made to work against as for the Jesuits. The Molinist controversy, which merged into the Jansenist uproar over Jesuit 'laxism', was used to blacken Jesuit adaptation in China, India and Japan, and the onslaughts were made more effective by a lack of unity within the Society. Aquaviva and Bellarmine deplored the tactics of some evangelists in India, as did more conventional missionaries. National rivalries simmered between Spanish, Portuguese and Italian Jesuits, and France's entry into the mission field increased the possibilities of disruption. When the Neapolitan Alessandro Valignano, a consummate missionary statesman who was appointed Vicar-General in the Orient, visited Japan in 1579 his plans to give Jesuit priests the appearance and status of Zen *bonzes* and to admit Japanese to the Company were obstinately opposed by the Portuguese Superior, Francisco Cabral, who also objected to the choice of silk for Jesuit robes (he thought cotton more in keeping with evangelical poverty). Cabral was removed from office, but the dispute rumbled on, flaring up with the arrival of Spanish friars from Manila. Franciscans accused the Jesuits of fawning on the *daimyos* and neglecting the poor. Jesuit élitists sneered at the Franciscans' cult of squalor and refusal to face political realities. In China Dominicans made similar accusations, and it was rumoured that the Jesuits rid themselves of some uncouth friars by persuading the authorities to execute them.

When dealing with less sophisticated societies, and in a position of comparative power, Jesuit adaptation was strictly limited. In Canada for instance, though requesting images and paintings of Christ without a beard (since the Indians were beardless), the Black Robes made few other concessions. With the full backing of Governors Samuel de Champlain and Charles de Montmagny they fought successfully to exclude not only Huguenot but Capuchin missionaries, and in the vicinity of their church of Notre Dame des Anges at Quebec ruled over an enclave at least as suffocatingly puritanical as any in New England. Paul le Jeune, the first Superior of the mission, persisted in trying to teach Indian children to pray in Latin. Colonists chafed under a régime half military, half monastic. Traders and trappers, tied to a post with collar and chain like a dog for failure to attend Mass, sent a deputation to France to complain of the theocratic 'hell' they were forced to endure.

In Canada the authority of the Jesuits was as closely allied with the royal power as in Vienna or Munich during the Thirty Years War. But they were also explorers, diplomats, pioneer linguists, interpreters, cartographers, anthropologists and natural historians. Trappers frustrated in their unscrupulous search for furs – the Jesuits also tried to end the liquor trade and the exploitation of tribal feuds – saw the missionaries' zeal as a cloak for commercial ambition, an accusation repeated by angry settlers in South America and India. The Society's determination to make missions pay their own way, a necessary precaution when royal subsidies from Spain and Portugal began to dwindle, soon gave rise to a legend of financial imperialism. Money-lending in China (at considerably below the official rate), involvement in the Macao silk trade and as bullion-brokers in Nagasaki; a profitable trade in hides, grain, tobacco, sugar, cotton and yerba maté ('Jesuit tea') from Jesuit estates in South America; alleged profits from the fur trade – all were represented as a sinister, unseemly preoccupation with worldly goods. And it was pointed out that a worldwide banking system and a chain of apothecary shops seemed to be in flat contradiction to the Society's Constitutions, which forbade trading.

All this seemed to imply enormous wealth, and non-Jesuit merchants, alarmed by the efficiency of the Fathers, spread stories about a network of 'secret Jesuit' agents, including Indians, Turks, Armenians and suborned officials. Jesuit envoys to Lisbon, Madrid and Rome worked desperately to counteract such accusations, repeated as they were in long bulletins from colonial bishops which were main sources of anti-Jesuit propaganda for years to come. In 1644 Bernardino de Cárdenas, the Franciscan Bishop of Asunción, charged the Jesuits in Paraguay with disobedience amounting to rebellion, concealing profits made with Indian slave labour, evading royal and episcopal taxes, and monopolizing the output of silver and gold mines whose whereabouts they refused to reveal. The equally imperious and excitable Juan de Palafox y Mendoza, Bishop of Puebla de los Angeles in Mexico, declared war on *all* the religious orders, but after a long tussle with the Jesuits concluded that they were the chief villains. His massive letter to Pope Innocent X, composed in 1649, alleged that power-hungry Jesuits had forced him to go into hiding for fear of assassination, that they controlled the wealth of Mexico, paid no taxes, used the secrets of the confessional for their own ends, and made their schoolboys indulge in lewd, blasphemous dances on the feast of St Ignatius. They were, he said, the most insidious foes of the papacy, the episcopacy, and the Catholic faith. Their wings might be clipped by radically changing their Constitutions, but the only safe course was to suppress them altogether.

Such was the penalty paid for the self-denying ordinance which deprived Jesuit missionaries of the protection of Jesuit bishops. The popes, knowing that the Franciscan operation in Spanish America was more extensive and quite as open to charges of self-interest, did not take the complaints of Cárdenas and Palafox too seriously. Yet the accusations were constantly reiterated as a consequence not only of the Jesuits' efficiency as farmers, traders and administrators, but of their role as Indian-protectors, trying to enforce the concept of trusteeship expressed in royal decrees but seldom observed either by colonists or by friars wearied by the unequal struggle. Again it was their latecomers' zeal that was their glory and their downfall.

The first Jesuits to reach New Spain (Mexico) provided the Society's first martyr in North America: Fr Pedro Martinez, clubbed to death on the mosquito-infested shore of Florida on the way to the garrison town of Fort Augustine, abut a hundred miles north of Cape Canaveral. They had been sent at the request of the conquistador Pedro Menendez de Aviles, who, commissioned in 1565 to end French Huguenot occupation, did so by massacring every male over the age of fifteen. In 1570, disgusted by the cruelty and licentiousness of Menendez and his soldiers, Fr Segura and seven companions followed the example of their brethren in Brazil and struck inland, hoping for greater success among the natives well away from the pollution of Christian colonists. All were killed, having reached a point near what is now the James River in Virginia, and in 1572 the few Jesuits who had remained at Fort Augustine moved to Mexico City. In Mexico too, though establishing schools in or near the towns (in the teeth of opposition from the friars), the Jesuits pushed into the wilderness, sometimes in the wake of punitive expeditions, pacifying the Indians and settling some fifty thousand of them in a chain of villages. Such was their dominance that the region was named Jesuit Land. In Chile Luis de Valdivia, who after denouncing the corruption of officials and merchants was appointed Royal Visitor, followed a similar policy of pacification and reduction.

In Brazil the Jesuits vigorously took over the role of imperial avant-garde pioneered by the friars. The reduction system had been in force since early in the sixteenth century: the ideal being that when a group of Indians had been sufficiently domesticated, Spanish or Portuguese settlers would move in to manage the land and the workshops, with a priest and a European *corregidor* – superintendent – in charge of the settlement. The process was often skimped, with disastrous results, and the Jesuits began to think in terms of a much longer spell of spiritual and social engineering. They did not invent, though they developed, the use of music, singing, dancing, pageantry and simple mystery plays. But they did inaugurate a hierarchy of splendidly costumed Indian officials, brought agricultural and industrial techniques to a higher pitch of efficiency, and set up a communal economy with surplus goods being sold for the benefit of the mission, the Jesuit province, or the Society in general. And they determined to keep visits from European outsiders to the barest minimum.

By the 1560s, in the villages around Bahia (Salvador), the routine and the objectives had been firmly laid down. Cannibalism was to be stamped out and monogamy enforced, clothing was obligatory, shamans had to be discredited (by ridicule or public flogging), and the Indians were not to move unless to another reduction. Youthful converts were encouraged to knock their elders into shape. 'The boys,' said one report, 'are daily increasing in love and zeal for our law. One came and denounced his own father who was secretly practising witchcraft. When the father found out he beat him terribly, but the boy suffered it patiently for the love of God.' The community was run by two black-robed Jesuits.

Promiscuity was abolished, boys and girls married soon after puberty (in the case of adults previous 'marriages' were annulled and a 'real' marriage arranged), and each couple occupied a mud-and-wattle hut.* In the schools boys and girls were strictly segregated. The rectangular huts were set on a symmetrical grid of streets radiating from a large square dominated by the church.

Labour was lightened and sanctified by turning the walk to the fields into a religious procession with banners, images and hymn-singing. Fun was provided by song and dance at religious festivals to the music of flutes, oboes, viols and tambourines, performers being allowed to paint their bodies and deck themselves with bird plumes. Indian craftsmen were taught to carve and gild statues of the Holy Family and the Jesuit saints. Sometimes a mock battle, with fireworks, might be arranged to let off some martial steam; and a taste for flagellation was (apart from public beatings for sexual immorality and other misdemeanours) satisfied during the Holy Week processions. But between festivals the spirits of these Indians tended to droop as they went about their duties in long cotton robes chanting hymns composed by the all-powerful Fathers, whose quarters were markedly more spacious and handsomely constructed than theirs. The church bell sounded reveille an hour before sunrise. There was an early morning Mass, then a distribution of rations and tasks for the day.

The Fathers in São Paulo supplied contingents of Indian soldiers for the siege of Guanabana (Rio de Janeiro), from which Huguenot colonists were driven in 1565, and were rewarded with the gift of a large site for a college; and in 1615, when the Catholic French settlement of St Louis was destroyed, Jesuits took over the missions from the Capuchins. Jesuit-trained Indian troops also played an important part in campaigns against the Dutch who had occupied Pernambuco (Recife). But their commander Manoel de Moraes, a Creole Jesuit, caused dismay by apostasizing after his capture in 1635. 'Moraes,' it was reported, 'left our Holy Faith and turned Calvinist, let his beard grow and changed his dress, assembled his Indians and made them join the enemy's side.'

This misfortune did not prevent the Jesuits, largely through the

---

*Jesuits were particularly shocked by the sexual peculiarities of the nomadic Guaycuru Indians in the Gran Chaco. The women performed abortions to such an extent that children were stolen from other tribes to make up the deficiency. Male transvestites were common. 'These nefarious demons,' reported one missionary, 'dress like women, speak like them, do the same work, urinate squatting, have a "husband" who looks after them, and once a month pretend that they are menstruating.'

influence of Antonio Vieira, from gaining the right to supervise all Indian mission villages on the Amazon. This in itself was a guarantee of hostility from other orders; and Vieira, trying to police punitive raids (nominally to ransom captives taken during inter-tribal wars), was driven into a compromising co-operation with the very authorities whom he lashed unsparingly in his sermons ('That Indian will be your slave for the few days that he lives; but your soul will be enslaved for eternity . . . all of you are going directly to Hell!'). He advocated importing African slaves as the best way of protecting the Indians. Mortality in the crowded reductions, often caused by smallpox brought by Negroes shipped from Angola with the co-operation of Jesuit missionaries there, remained terrifying; and ever-alert Jesuit baptizers were thought to be dispensing 'death-water'. As soon as the compounds were emptied they were replenished. But exasperation at continued Indian resistance to Catholic truth increased as the first fine rapture faded quite away. It was, Vieira admitted, a severe trial for cultured Jesuits to 'adapt themselves to the most unintelligent, inarticulate people that nature ever created or aborted'.

The boundary between Portuguese Brazil and Spanish territory was ill-defined, particularly since from 1580 to 1640 Spain was nominally in control of both. Formed early in the seventeenth century, the enormous Spanish Jesuit province of Paraguay, with headquarters at Asunción, included parts of Bolivia, the entire Chaco, all present-day Argentina, Uruguay and Paraguay, and the Brazilian provinces of Rio Grande do Sul and Guaira. The missionaries based their methods on the pioneering work of Luis de Bolanos, a Franciscan who by 1593 had established eighteen Indian reductions and compiled the first Guarani grammar, vocabulary and prayer book. Pushing west and east, the Jesuits had little success among the Guaycuru tribes in the Chaco, but between 1622 and 1628, under the leadership of Ruiz de Montoya, eleven townships were planted in the mountainous terrain of Guaira, the last in the chain being less than a hundred miles from São Paulo and the Atlantic coast.

These reductions, numbering thousands of docile Guarani, proved an irresistible temptation to the *bandeirantes* of São Paulo, brigand mercenaries who sometimes acted as a frontier force but more often as slave-raiders. Led by an assortment of European adventurers and half-breeds known as *mamelucos,* the expeditions were joined by hundreds of Tupi Indians from the coastal belt. Thanks to their prodigious but bloody feats of exploration, the slave stockades of São Paulo were constantly replenished beneath the eyes of helpless priests: and Jesuit missionaries, no strangers to hardship, expressed the same reluctant admiration for the courage and endurance of these bandits as did Livingstone for that of Arab slavers in East Africa. Sometimes they even took along a bogus Jesuit chaplain, and after several devastating raids between 1627 and 1631 had wrecked nine reductions and made off with some sixty thousand Indians, the story was put about that the Jesuits and the *bandeirantes* were in league.

Having appealed in vain for Spanish military aid, Montoya assembled the survivors for a mass migration, in hundreds of canoes, down the River Paraná to Paraguay. The refugees settled in two areas, some towards the Atlantic coast in what is now the southern Matto Grosso, most in what is now the province of Rio Grande do Sul. Several Jesuits had been killed in the raids and more perished when these were renewed in 1635. *Bandeirantes,* who laughed at their excommunication by the Bishop of Buenos Aires, actually attended Mass in mission churches and listened to fiery Jesuit sermons while their able-bodied captives (the old, the infirm, and the very young having been massacred) were roped together for the long trek to São Paulo. By the end of the 1630s the coastward missions had been wiped out or evacuated, by 1650 only twenty-two of the original forty-eight reductions were functioning. But they had a total population of some fifty thousand, and in 1639 and again in 1641 the Christian Indian militia at last defeated the *bandeirantes* in the inner bastion of Paraguay. The battle of Mbororé on the River Acaragua involved a tremendous clash between canoe flotillas. 'One of our musketeers fired and St Francis Xavier guided the ball, so that it hit a Portuguese on the thigh and broke it,' wrote one of the Fathers. They had mustered three thousand warriors, set up a field hospital, and spent three days confessing their troops before the fighting began.

Jesuit propaganda, notably *The Spiritual Conquest Made by the Missionaries of the Society of Jesus* by Montoya, persuaded King Philip IV to authorize the arming of the Indians. This had been done unofficially for twenty years, though often the muskets were made of thick bamboo canes bound with oxhide. Spanish garrisons being sparse and doubtfully loyal, the Jesuit militia provided the main defence, used to repel Indian raiders from the Chaco, *bandeirantes,* French attacks on Buenos Aires – and to repress a rebellion of Spanish colonists. Madrid encouraged the growth of the Jesuit 'empire' in the hope that the tens of thousands of industrious converts would yield a substantial return in taxes, from which Indians who undertook military service were exempted. It was a cheap way of acquiring a highly efficient frontier force. But as Jesuit power and prosperity grew, so did the envy and resentment of Spanish colonists and officials, pointedly excluded from the Paraná reductions.

Arriving at the height of the Society's renown in South America, China and Japan, the Jesuits in Canada were expected to work wonders. Le Jeune expressed his ambition to create 'a second Paraguay', but nomadic Huron hunters intent on trading furs for guns, brandy, rum, and tobacco supplied by French *coureurs du bois* (pioneer traders) or Dutch and English colonists, were less docile than the Guarani. The Iroquois, armed by the Dutch, were poised to annihilate the Hurons and seize their hunting territory. The Hurons, under very nominal French protection, looked to the 'Black Robes' for magical help, the Iroquois regarded them as agents of French political and commercial interests; an impression confirmed when in 1647 the Jesuit mission Superior became a member of the all-powerful Council of New France. In 1648 Iroquois attacks were intensified. Two years later the Huron mission, in which seven out of twenty-nine Jesuits lost their lives, was abandoned and Fr Gabriel Druilletes, braving a law that barred Jesuits from a colony which prided itself on being 'a bulwark against the kingdom of Antichrist which the Jesuits labour to rear up in all places of the world', visited Boston in a vain attempt to forge an Anglo-French alliance.

Edited versions of missionary bulletins – the *Relations* – and the despatch to France of some Huron converts, who were treated like fashionable pets, brought funds and volunteers. But the reality was grim. The contests between priests and shamans were treated as a camp-fire diversion by Indians who, though willing to accept the notion of a Big Chief in the Sky, were first puzzled then frightened by the religious paraphernalia of the Black Robes. Every disaster was attributed to the witches from the West. The Mass ritual seemed an infernal incantation. The doctrine that the body and blood of Christ were truly present in the bread and wine led to a rumour that the Jesuits were hiding a corpse which spread the plague. Lurid paintings of souls in hell, displayed in forest chapels, inspired terror. Talk of sanctification through suffering was incomprehensible, and when in 1649 Fr Jean Brébeuf was tortured to death by the Iroquois scalding water was poured over his head in mock baptism while spectators jeered: 'You told us that the more one suffers on earth, the happier he is in Heaven . . . We torment you because we love you, and you ought to thank us for it.'

Brébeuf's *Instructions for the Fathers of Our Society Who Shall Be Sent to the Hurons*, written in 1637, warned, rather in the tone of Vieira, that 'leaving a highly civilized community, you will find yourselves among a barbarous people who care but little for your philosophy and theology. All the fine qualities which might make you respected in France are like pearls trampled under the feet of swine, or rather mules, which utterly despise you when they see you are not such good pack animals as they are.' It was no use standing on dignity – 'to conciliate the savages you must be careful never to make them wait for you in embarking . . . Provide yourself with a tinder box or a burning mirror or both, to furnish them with fire in the daytime and to light their pipes and in the evening when they encamp; these little services win their hearts . . . Be careful not to annoy anyone in the canoe with your hat. It would be better to take your night cap. There is no impropriety among the savages.' Sixty years later François de Crepieul, a missionary on the Lower St Lawrence, had the same message: 'The life is a long and slow martyrdom, truly penitential and humiliating, especially in the cabins and on journeys with the savages.' Hardships included snow-blindness ('so that you cannot read the Breviary'), smoke-filled tents or cabins, half-cooked meat, dishes 'wiped with a greasy piece of skin or licked clean by the dogs', sweating by day and freezing by night.

For historians, geographers and ethnologists the *Relations,* published in a series of seventy-three volumes together with private letters and journals, amply justify the ordeals of these explorer-evangelists. Fr Anne de Noë, an elderly priest who often wept over imagined lapses in obedience, was the first martyr, dying of exposure in 1646. His body was found 'leaning slightly forward, resting on a bank of snow and frozen to the hardness of marble'. Many reports were scribbled in camp amid a distracting hubbub, often furtively since the sight of a Black Robe writing was enough to arouse suspicion of sorcery. The Jesuit journalists' fame in France was hard-earned, but the published *Relations* came to an abrupt end in 1673. Jesuit 'accommodation' in India and China had caused such a furore that Pope Clement X forbade the publication of any mission literature without the approval of Propaganda. French Jesuits dared not seek this since Louis XIV and the Gallican Church did not recognize the jurisdiction of Rome. They and the *Relations* were silenced by a double gag.

Silence was what Alessandro Valignano, as certain as Xavier that Japan offered the best hope for a quick breakthrough in Asia, laboured but failed to maintain: so that at the same time as the Iroquois were massacring the Hurons in Canada a rapidly expanding Church in Japan, with a membership of several hundred thousand in 1600, was all but annihilated. Valignano persuaded the Pope to endorse his view that the friars should be excluded from Japan in the interests of unity, which had given the Jesuits an edge over their Buddhist rivals, split as they were into quarrelling sects. But the papal decree of 1585 was ignored by Spanish missionaries coming from the Philippines, all busily brandishing the Cross which, because the Japanese associated it with a shameful criminality, the Jesuits had kept out of sight. Valignano's plans for a Japanese priesthood were vetoed in Rome, and Aquaviva reluctantly permitted some Japanese to enter the Society as brothers. Buddhist assertions that the Jesuits were agents of Portuguese imperialism were made credible by the behaviour of Fathers who taught converts to pray for the King of Portugal as their potential protector. The Shogun Hideyoshi's suspicions were aroused when the Jesuit Vice-Provincial, Gaspar Coelho, offered to supply Catholic Japanese troops for a projected expedition against China; and matters were made worse when in 1587, after Hideyoshi had ordered the expulsion of Christian missionaries, Coelho appealed for Spanish and Portuguese military aid and tried to raise a rebellion.

Valignano's diplomacy, helped by a threat that the lucrative Portuguese trade might be cut off and by Hideyoshi's fondness for European culture, which the Jesuits had done much to commend, prevented a more than nominal enforcement of the order. But ten years later a threat from the Governor of Manila was answered by the crucifixion of six Franciscans, three Jesuit brothers, and nineteen Japanese Christians. When Dutch and English ships broke the Hispano-Portuguese blockade and ended the trading monopoly the Jesuits' most valuable bargaining counter had gone. Protestant tales of Spanish aggression and Jesuit plotting helped convince Hideyoshi's successors that the time had come to rid Japan of foreign intruders. In 1614 all but a few Jesuit missionaries, who went underground, were sent packing and Japanese Christians were ordered to adopt one form or another of Buddhism.

From their base at Macao the Jesuits smuggled in funds, supplies, and sometimes missionaries to Japan. So did the friars from Manila. Priest-holes were dug in the earth and covered with mats, and a Dutch merchant reported that lepers' huts were used as hiding places, 'for the lepers, who are numerous, are greatly abhorred and no one will easily be persuaded to enter their hovels.' At first usually disguised as Spanish or Portuguese merchants, missionaries were later forced to masquerade as samurai, peasants, pedlars, and even women. Thirty thousand Japanese

Christians perished in the savage repression of the Shimabara Rebellion of 1637 to 1638; four thousand others were executed in various pogroms. Jesuits and friars argued with each other, and among themselves, about the tactics and ethics of survival. Jesuit manuals exhorted candidates for martyrdom 'never to cherish an evil thought towards judge or executioner . . . under torture try to visualize the Passion of Jesus.' Apostasies were rare, but by the 1630s, when Portuguese ships were forbidden to dock, Portuguese businessmen were expelled, and relations with Manila severed, the only forlorn hope was to smuggle in supplies and priests on Chinese junks. The last surviving members of the original Jesuit mission, two Japanese and an Italian, were captured in 1639, and in 1640 the superiors of all the religious orders, meeting in Manila, at last recognized that the operation was hopeless.

Xavier had convinced himself that the conversion of China was the key to the catholicization of Asia, a mirage which continued to shimmer tantalizingly on the Jesuit horizon. The Chinese invasion plan had been hatched by Spanish Jesuits in 1586 and approved by the Governor and Council of Manila. The idea was that a ten-thousand-strong expeditionary force should be sent from Europe to join a similar number of troops recruited in Japan and the Philippines. The Portuguese were to support the armada from Macao and Canton, and the Bishop of Manila urged Philip II – then fully occupied organizing the invasion of England – to realize that 'not even Alexander the Great had such a golden opportunity. Spiritually speaking, no greater project has been conceived since the time of the Apostles.'

But under Valignano's direction the quest took a very different form, requiring an oblique approach, immense patience, deep scholarship, shrewd psychology, and a thorough familiarity not only with Chinese culture but with European technology. In the thirty years after Xavier's death more than twenty Jesuits had tried to gain admission to the Celestial Empire. But the founders of the missionary-scientist tradition were two Italians. Michele Ruggieri, assigned to study Chinese at Macao in 1578, was joined four years later by Matteo Ricci. The son of a pharmacist in Macerata, where he went to the Jesuit school, Ricci read law before meeting Valignano and entering the Society. Seven years in Rome, during which he studied mathematics, cosmography and astronomy, were followed by a year in the missionary seminary at Coimbra. Then came two years' teaching in Goa, where he was ordained in 1580, and finally a year's intensive course with Ruggieri in Macao, attuning ear and voice to a five-tone scale which conveyed subtle nuances of meaning. They shaved their heads and beards and wore hooded grey cloaks similar to those of Buddhist monks. Invited to Chao-ch'ing near Canton in 1583 by a mandarin official because of his reputation as a skilled mathematician, Ricci, who described himself as a worshipper of the King of Heaven, spent seventeen years edging his way north to Peking. During that time he had grown his hair and beard; been accepted as a member of the élite mandarin class (adopting its plum-coloured silk robes and tall black hat); made a profound study of Chinese customs and literature; created a stir with his collection of clocks, prisms, astrolabes, oil paintings, and maps of the world; and become known as 'Li-Ma-tou', the Chinese phonetic equivalent of his name.

Aware that the Chinese regarded their civilization as the finest in a world of which China, the Middle Kingdom, was the cultural and geographical centre, Ricci humbly declared his homage to the Son of Heaven: 'Li-Ma-tou, your Majesty's servant, comes from the Far West which has never exchanged gifts with the Middle Kingdom . . . Fame told me of the remarkable teaching and fine institutions with which the imperial court has endowed its pupils. I desired to share these advantages and to live out my life as one of your Majesty's subjects, hoping in return to be of some small use.' The chiming clocks gave him an entrée, together with his map-making expertise. In the next ten years, while some Jesuit missionaries began to establish themselves in the provinces, Ricci laboured to catholicize Confucianism ('Confucius' is his transliteration of K'ung Fu-tsu). He had learned to make a distinction between Taoism (an amalgam of polytheistic superstitions), Buddhism (agnostic and corrupt), and Confucianism, the ethical code of the scholar-bureaucrats.

Since he was aiming at conversion from the top downwards, he concentrated on the 'pure' mandarin version of the code, which became less pure and more encrusted with superstition further down the social scale. Ricci defined it as a moral philosophy rather than a revealed religion, taught that the veneration of ancestors was essentially a civil ceremony and need not be abandoned by Christian converts, and used the Chinese word for ancestor-worship as an equivalent for the Mass. As in Japan, the sacrifice of the Cross was played down, for Ricci believed that conversion would have to be a long, gradual process, requiring, among other major adjustments, a radical revision of the Old Testament, and that much would have to be left to the discretion and initiative of Chinese Christians. He also allowed that the word *Sheng* (holy or venerable) could properly be used of Confucius, thus, in the eyes of the Society's critics, blasphemously adding the Chinese sage to the Christian pantheon as 'St Confucius'.

These feats of intellectual juggling, much admired by Ricci's Chinese friends, got a cold reception from orthodox theologians in Europe. But though he set off many controversies he did settle one query by establishing that the Christian kingdom of Great Cathay mentioned in Marco Polo's *Travels* was in fact China. This conclusion was painfully confirmed by the Portuguese Jesuit Brother Bento de Goes who, disguised as a Persian merchant, made his way over the Himalayas and across the wastes of Asia in search of the mysterious land. He reached the town of Suchow in February 1606, four years after leaving India, and died exhausted after sending a message to Ricci with the information, superfluous as it turned out, that central Asians referred to China as 'Khitai' or 'Cathay'.

A cult figure in the intellectual circles of Peking, Ricci, with two convert collaborators, translated Euclid and Christian philosophers into Chinese and revised his celebrated *Mappa Mundi*. When he died in 1610 he and his Jesuit colleagues had created a Catholic Church with about two and a half thousand members, many of them mandarins. The Emperor Wan-Li granted the Jesuits an estate near Peking large enough to build a chapel, cemetery and residence. But as in Japan the Jesuit presence, and the lives of converts, depended on the fickle winds of imperial favour and the absence of cavilling friars. There were outbursts of persecution in 1616 and 1622, the first Dominicans and Franciscans arrived soon afterwards, and in 1644 the Ming dynasty was replaced by Manchu (Ch'ing) Emperors. A new batch of priests, who brought with them the latest scientific equipment and a library of seven thousand volumes, kept a foothold at court as mathematicians, engineers, ingenious toymakers and, on occasion, cannon-founders. Most important of all in a society where the annual compilation of the imperial calendar – a mixture of astronomical exactitude and astrological lore – was an essential tool of government, the brilliant, resourceful Fr Adam Schall von Bell outsmarted his Muslim rivals and was promoted President of the Mathematical Tribunal, Mandarin First Class, and director of the Peking Observatory, the refitting of which he supervised.

In a sense all this was encouraging. But in what sense? To the court in Peking the Jesuit creed was not Christianity but 'the religion of the great Schall'. And the polyglot band of Fathers was far from united. Nicolo Longobardi, Ricci's successor as mission Superior, though accepting the need to press the scientific advantage, was doubtful about the Confucian rites. Some Jesuits accused Schall of pandering to gross astrological superstition, and there was a disposition to agree with many of the criticisms made by the Spanish Dominican Domingo Navarrete – though not with his opinion that the Devil, who had kept Xavier out of China, was now using the Jesuits as his agents. To Navarrete's assertion that, together with Plato, Socrates and Aristotle, Confucius was irretrievably damned, a Portuguese Father retorted that on the contrary Confucius was probably saved, which was more than could be said of the degenerate King Philip IV of Spain.

With Dominican strictures already reaching Rome and eliciting in 1645 a papal censure of Ricci's accommodations, the Jesuits were forced to send their own spokesman, Fr Martino Martini, who managed to persuade Alexander VII and the Holy Office to approve the Confucian rites as 'a purely civil and political cult'. But there were other problems. Hampered by the papal condemnation thirteen years earlier of the 'hypothesis' of Copernicus and Galileo, Schall and his colleagues were stuck with the outmoded Ptolemaic system. Propaganda cancelled Paul V's permission for a Chinese liturgy. The insistence on Latin was an insulting and ludicrous obstacle to the training of Chinese priests: a Jesuit later reported of a Mass said by one who had been recently ordained that 'he sweated, was in an agony of mind, and those present were equally anxious and irritated. God knows how many mistakes he made, all hot and bothered as he was and reciting parrot-like what he could not understand.' Though Fr Schall's prestige brought a rush of conversions, including one of the emperor's wives, he himself was rumoured to be keeping concubines and at the age of seventy-three was condemned to death with five of his assistants on the familiar charge of being an agent of European imperialism. He was reprieved, but it was clear that the Catholic Church, which in 1650 numbered about a hundred and fifty thousand out of a total population of nearly one hundred million, was precariously balanced and unlikely to amount to much more than a tiny sect.

In India, where caste presented a challenge far more complex than that encountered in Japan or China, the inflexibility of many Jesuits combined with harassment by friars, secular clergy, and settlers to ensure that Catholicism made no significant headway. The conquistador mentality was too deeply engrained, and the Dutch Calvinist threat, which by the 1660s had ousted the Portuguese from southern India, was looming. Valignano himself shared the common prejudice against

Indians, who in his estimation were unfit to be Jesuits because 'like all the dusky races they are stupid and vicious, and also because the Portuguese treat them with the greatest contempt.'

In this inauspicious setting the only sustained attempt at adaptation was made by an Italian Jesuit, Roberto de Nobili, grand-nephew of Pope Julius III, nephew of Cardinal de Nobili (and of Cardinal Bellarmine, who frowned on his experiment), and son of the Lord of Montepulciano in Tuscany. In 1610, after four years in Madurai inland from the south-eastern coast, he set out his conclusions: 'One great mistake made by the Portuguese was to accept the name *parangi* [applied to them by the Hindus] and even to describe Christianity as the religion of the *parangi* . . . Hence the presumption that the crucifix was their peculiar sign. Such mistakes make it impossible to preach the gospel.' He was thinking in particular of the total failure of his fellow missionary in Madurai, Fr Fernandes, who made his few converts dress and eat like Europeans and take Portuguese surnames, thus making them *parangi* outcastes.

Inspired by Ricci's example, de Nobili resolved to disentangle himself from the blunders of Fernandes. After careful study of Brahman tradition, with its horror of ritual pollution, and with the backing of Alberto Laerzio, the Italian Provincial Superior, he sank himself into the role of a *sannyasi guru*: a teacher who has broken every form of attachment to the world. Dressed in an ochre robe, with a triangular mark on his forehead and wooden sandals on his feet, he lived in a hermit's hut and ate only rice, fruit and herbs. Knowing that other missionaries had been despised for linguistic incompetence (the first Tamil dictionary equated 'Mass' with a word which signified 'moustache') and cultural ignorance, he made himself fluent not only in Tamil but, so that he could read the *Vedas*, in Sanskrit. His one concession to ecclesiastical convention was the crucifix that hung from the sacred Brahman cord stretching from the left shoulder to the right thigh. He published a manifesto denying that he was a *parangi* ('I come from Rome, where my family held the same rank as a Rajah'), his *sannyasi* status allowed him to move more freely along the caste-scale, and Laerzio endorsed his opinion that Brahmin converts could keep their caste-marks, notably the white cord and the tuft of hair at the back of a shaven head, since these were not idolatrous but symbols of social status.

By 1611 de Nobili had made a hundred and fifty converts. In the teeth of violent opposition he secured a cautiously favourable verdict from Aquaviva and, through him, a somewhat tepid papal blessing. As lower-caste Indians were drawn towards the Church he organized a two-tier mission, with *Pandaraswamis* ministering to this much larger group while he and a few carefully chosen assistants – the *Brahmanasannyasis* – continued their patient, exacting siege of the spiritual aristocracy. Like Ricci, de Nobili pleaded for time. He also wanted to see Hindus trained for the priesthood and Sanskrit used as the liturgical language. This proposal, together with reports that he handed the eucharist on the end of a stick to pariah converts and accepted the logic of separate caste-congregations, brought howls of outrage from priests who refused to serve under an Indian bishop and treated half-caste Catholic priests like dirt.* The de Nobili system was soon well on the way to becoming as turbulent an issue as the Chinese rites. Though scarcely harsher than some of Xavier's strictures, his affronts to Portuguese pride and a wild, almost Faustian, streak of intellectual arrogance made him a liability to the Society. In 1645 he was withdrawn from the Madurai mission. His last years were spent in disgrace and almost total blindness at Mylapore, near Madras, the traditional site of the martyrdom of St Thomas.

More acceptable to the authorities was an English Jesuit, Thomas Stephens, a friend of Campion. For nearly forty years from 1579 to 1619 Padre Estevan, as the Portuguese called him, worked tirelessly but more conventionally among the people of the Salsette peninsula, near Bombay; and his Christian *purana* (semi-historical, semi-legendary epic poem), written in the Marathi language and idiom, is still considered a classic of its kind. There were high hopes of converting the Emperor Akbar. Persian in origin, tolerantly Muslim in faith, the Mogul régime, almost as contemptuous as the Portuguese of its Indian subjects, seemed to offer a splendid target for a royal coup in the Possevino manner. But Akbar had already decided to proclaim his own composite religion with himself as its prophet, when the first Jesuits came to Agra in 1580 at his invitation for public debates with Mullahs, Sufis and Brahmins in a huge pink hall of worship. Polite but cynical, the Emperor told the leader of the mission – Rodolfo Aquaviva, a nephew of the Jesuit General – that the doctrines of the Trinity and the Incarnation did not suit the eclectic creed with which he hoped to banish religious strife from his realms. He

---

*De Nobili was accused (1) of omitting the use of saliva and breathing on the convert in baptism, (2) advising converts not to call themselves Christians but 'followers of the true God', (3) blessing cow-dung ashes, (4) allowing married girls to wear the *taly*, described as 'a gross image representing a Hindu divinity equivalent to the Roman Priapus', (5) declaring that this was a civil custom and that a 'direction of intention' made it harmless, and (6) inventing a *taly* with the Cross on one side and the objectionable emblem on the other.

did, however, propose to include baptism as a feature of the new faith, which would combine Hindu, Islamic, Zoroastrian and Christian elements.

Rodolfo Aquaviva, an engagingly dotty eccentric troubled with knee-tumours from overmuch kneeling in penance on damp stone floors, was not, despite several applications, allowed to leave Agra until 1583. Jeronimo Xavier, grand-nephew of St Francis, lingered on for thirty years with Akbar and his successor, reduced to such stratagems as finding a Neapolitan juggler to compete with the attraction of a star cornet player who accompanied an English Protestant deputation in 1608. The Mogul quest was pursued fitfully until the dissolution of the Society in 1773.

In all climes and vicissitudes, Jesuit pens were busy scribbling reports of unique value. Antonio de Monserrate's journal of the first Mogul mission shows Aquaviva shabbily dressed, sleeping in his clothes, mislaying his hat and glasses, persisting with his hair shirt and self-flagellation, wandering about Agra singing improvised songs about the Blessed Virgin, grieved by Akbar's voracious curiosity, fundamental indifference, and refusal to disperse his harem. João Rodrigues compiled the first Japanese grammar and began a history of the Japanese mission, with commentaries on architecture, painting, astronomy, costume and etiquette (including a full account of the tea ceremony), which make it a minor classic. Nicholas Trigault wrote a narrative of Bento de Goes' journey. Antonio de Andrade, the first European to enter Tibet, described the strange religious communities he found there. Pedro Chirino's detailed *Account of the Philippine Islands* (1604) listed the customs and culture of that great archipelago.

Jesuit explorers investigated the possibility of an overland route to Peking which might speed up communications. It was common for seven years to elapse between writing and receiving an answer and one letter sent from Macao by Valignano in 1589 did not reach Rome until 1606. In the guise of Armenian merchants two Fathers travelled with a caravan from Smyrna to the Persian Gulf and from there by ship to Goa. Leaving Peking in 1661, Johann Grueber took nearly three years to get to Rome via Suchow, Lhasa, Agra and Smyrna. This was not encouraging: but the decision to stick to the sea-route was influenced by a strong protest from Portugal, insisting that the port of Lisbon always had been, and must remain, the point of departure for the Far East.

The Archbishop of Goa had accused de Nobili and his Italian allies of crypto-paganism and of plotting to seize the Portuguese empire in India.

In Latin America Jesuits were accused of conspiring to 'seize the entire sub-continent with their armies'. The affair of the Chinese rites was coming to the boil and more problems were created by the independent manoeuvres of Alexandre de Rhodes, an outstanding missionary in Indo-china. Born in Avignon of Spanish-Jewish descent, de Rhodes made a real advance in what is now Vietnam, founding a 'company of catechists' living in community and under rule. This celibate lay brotherhood, carefully trained and given elementary instruction in medicine, was intended to fill the gap left by the absence of a native clergy. Expelled from Vietnam in 1645, de Rhodes, who was convinced that the survival of the Churches in Asia depended on the creation of a large number of native priests, pressed Propaganda to send bishops of its own choice to supervise their instruction and ordination. He also suggested the device of Vicars Apostolic responsible directly to the Holy See and helped to found a Foreign Missionary Society in Paris, composed of secular priests whose sole allegiance would be to the Congregation of Propaganda.

After ten years lobbying and negotiation de Rhodes' machinery began to turn. Asia was divided into Vicariates Apostolic and two Frenchmen, François Pallu and Pierre Lambert de la Motte, left for Indo-china in 1659. They sailed into a veritable hornets' nest of hostility. Though some missionaries saw the whole scheme as a Jesuit manoeuvre, many Jesuits were equally opposed to it. Mgr Pallu, titular Bishop of Heliopolis, was shipwrecked in Spanish territory and clapped into jail. Mgr de la Motte, titular Bishop of Berytus (Beirut), escaped arrest by the Portuguese in Siam by taking refuge with a Dutch merchant, and was excommunicated by the Archbishop of Goa. Jesuits united with the friars in resisting this Franco-Roman interference. The prospect of being buffeted between pope and king in Asia as well as in Europe seemed intolerable, especially when a Jesuit hero had done so much to force the dilemma.

CHAPTER THIRTEEN

Wasting Assets

HINDSIGHT SUGGESTS that Jesuit and anti-Jesuit propaganda both exaggerated the power and efficiency of the Society. This was not so obvious in the second half of the seventeenth century. The triumphalism of St Peter's, with its huge colonnaded piazza, was echoed in Giovanni Gaulli's decorations in the Gesù glorifying the Holy Name of Jesus and Jesuit missionary vigour. The vault is one of the most staggering examples of baroque illusionism. In San Ignazio Brother Andrea Pozzo created the likeness of a dome by the use of linear perspective and filled the massive ceiling with a tremendous celebration of the Society. A beam of light travels from God through Christ to Ignatius, who transmits it to Europe, Africa, Asia and the Americas.

Paolo Segneri, Francesco Geronimo and Antonio Baldinucci brought a dramatic energy to the work of revivalism in Italy. For twenty-seven years Segneri strode barefoot through the countryside drawing thousands to hear his sermons. During forty years Geronimo, the apostle of Naples, preached at street corners, attracted more than ten thousand people to a General Communion each month at the Gesù Nuovo Church, evangelized in prisons and brothels, opened rescue homes for children, launched a Jesuit pawnshop, and organized an association of workingmen to help him in his war on vice. Just as newsworthy was the Florentine Baldinucci who, much in the style of Savonarola, scourged himself till he bled in public and climaxed his missions with pyres of cards, dice, novels, musical instruments, and other objects of vanity.

By 1740 the Society was running more than six hundred urban secondary schools, many with nearly two thousand day pupils, in the six main regional groups of Italy, France, Germany, Spain, Portugal and the Americas. This meant that Jesuits were educating one-sixth of the European 'classical' intake from the age of ten to seventeen. Marian sodalities and congregations continued to flourish. Membership of the Society increased to about twenty-three thousand by 1770 during a period when recruitment to the diocesan clergy and to other religious orders drastically declined.

At the Collège Louis-le-Grand the Sun King was glorified in spectacular ballets. In Vienna the Emperor Leopold I attended six or seven performances during the school year and, like Louis XIV, often footed the very considerable bill. In Italy the pseudo-classical plays of Jesuit authors were produced on the secular stage and rivalled the vogue of opera. In Germany Jesuit cantatas, music-dramas and oratorios were forerunners of the cult of opera in court circles. Indeed in the seventeenth and eighteenth centuries Jesuit college productions formed a link between opera and drama, advancing technical expertise in both. Voltaire recalled the plays at Louis-le-Grand as the best aspect of his education there, and apart from Voltaire, Calderon, Lope de Vega, Corneille and Molière, Jesuit-educated playwrights included Maffei, Goldoni, the elder Crébillon and Le Sage. Also in the roll of Jesuit alumni were Popes Gregory XIII and Urban VIII, Bossuet, Cardinal de Bérulle, Montesquieu, Condorcet and Diderot.

Though still keeping clear of permanent responsibility for female religious, Jesuits were much in demand as spiritual directors and reaped a useful reward when Margaret Mary Alacoque, a French nun, claimed to have been favoured with a vision of Christ pointing to His heart and pleading that mankind should at last accept and radiate His divine charity. She also claimed that the Jesuit Claude de la Colombière had been indicated as her associate and that the Society had been chosen to propagate the cult of the Sacred Heart of Jesus – perhaps the most popular of all baroque devotions.

Jesuit casuistry survived the ridicule of Pascal to become the basis of Catholic moral theology as defined by St Alphonsus Liguori, founder of the Redemptorists, in the 1750s ('the opinions of the Jesuits are neither excessively free nor excessively rigid, but maintain a correct balance'). For some time Jesuit confessors had a near-monopoly of royal consciences in Portugal, Spain, France, Austria, Poland and even, though briefly, in England. The Austrian Johann Eberhard Nidhard, confessor to Philip IV's widow, was from 1666 to 1669 a member of the Spanish Council of State, then virtual Prime Minister, and finally Inquisitor-General. Fathers Lachaise and Le Tellier took care of Louis XIV. Philip V of Spain had a string of Jesuit confessors. Two Jesuits – John Warner, his confessor, and Edward Petre, a close friend who was appointed to the Privy Council – were popularly supposed to have been the evil geniuses of James II and, in their way, precipitators of the Glorious Protestant Revolution of 1688. Jan Kasimierz, King of Poland for twenty years, not only had Jesuit confessors but had himself been a Jesuit novice. Fr Carlo

Vota, sent by Pope Innocent X to exhort King Jan Sobieski to join the 'crusade' against the Turkish armies besieging Vienna, acted as the royal confessor during and after the victorious campaign. Forced out of Brazil in 1661, Antonio Vieira was for the next twenty years once more a dominant political figure in Lisbon.

But more than ever this superficially impressive status was a liability rather than an asset. Petre, like Nidhard, seems to have been reluctantly thrust into a role for which he was ill-equipped; Nidhard's triple eminence brought Spain to the verge of civil war (he hurriedly resigned and was made a cardinal).

Benedictines predominated at the court of Charles II and his Portuguese consort, Catherine of Braganza. But the caution shown by Jesuits of the English province, which counted over a hundred missionaries with a novitiate in London, did not prevent Powder Plot memories being revived by any catastrophe, real or imagined. It was rumoured that Jesuits had started the Great Plague and the Great Fire of London. Wildly inflated estimates of Jesuit political activity helped to make plausible the fabrications of Titus Oates, whose Popish Plot scare of 1678 resulted in the execution of eleven Jesuits, including Thomas Whitebread, the provincial Superior. Forty were arrested, eighteen died in prison, some fled abroad. For a while Jesuit missionary activity all but ceased and there was a tendency among secular priests and the Catholic laity to blame the disaster on the Society and even to rejoice in its comeuppance.

According to Oates, a former Anglican parson and naval chaplain who professed conversion to Catholicism, the Jesuits were to mastermind a programme that included the assassination of Charles II, the coronation of his brother (who was to be assassinated when he had served his turn by approving a massacre of Protestants), a French military occupation, and the raising of the Jesuit Provincial to the Archbishopric of Canterbury as a reward for his services. Prudent Catholics as well as bristling Protestants deplored the allegedly Jesuit-inspired reaction under James II, when two Jesuit schools were opened in London at his command. Broadsheets accused Edward Petre of practising black magic and of being the real father – by a nun – of the heir to the throne, supposed to have been smuggled into the Queen's bed in a warming-pan. In the preface to his poem *Religio Laici* (A Layman's Faith) John Dryden, on the verge of becoming a Catholic, warned that sober Romanists should publicly disown 'Jesuited Papists' and 'Jesuitical principles'. Almost a century later the Gordon Riots, provoked by the passing of a Catholic Relief Act, were preceded by lurid tales of an army of Jesuits hidden in underground tunnels waiting for an order from Rome to blow up the banks of the Thames and flood London.

Jesuit confessors could do little about Louis XIV's morals. He rivalled Philip IV of Spain in the number of his mistresses and legitimized bastards, though he liked to take part in such carefully staged pieces of religious theatre as washing and kissing the feet of thirteen poor children on Maundy Thursday, and allowed the famous Jesuit preacher Louis Bourdaloue to chide him from the pulpit. The pious, ambitious Madame de Maintenon, who secretly married the King in 1682 and turned him into a ferociously reformed rake, probably did more than Lachaise and Le Tellier put together to spur on the persecution of the Huguenots.

Though attendance at chapel was compulsory for courtiers, royal bigotry did not imply respect for the Holy See. After the election of Charles de Noyelle as Jesuit General, Lachaise was forced to badger him mercilessly to pay his first diplomatic visit to the French ambassador in Rome. As a result, communication between Madrid and de Noyelle was cut off. The Duc de Saint-Simon, an embittered aristocrat, felt contempt and revulsion for the bigoted Le Tellier, a Norman peasant's son and a close ally of Madame de Maintenon: 'A foe to all frivolity and social pleasures . . . he was a terrible man. If met in a forest he would have inspired terror; his face was sombre and false, his eyes wicked, penetrating and crooked . . . He had no other God but the Society.'

Le Tellier was indeed a devoted Jesuit. According to Saint-Simon he had left Rome under a cloud after a vehement defence of the Chinese rites. In France he helped to launch a 'liberal' publication, the *Journal de Trévoux*, which was a kind of Jesuit forerunner of the eighteenth-century rationalist *Encyclopaedia*, and he drafted or helped to draft the revocation of the Edict of Nantes that in 1685 completed a process begun in the 1660s. Lachaise and Le Tellier, following Madame de Maintenon's example, had helped to accelerate it by telling the King that most of the Huguenots who had not left the country had been converted or were on the point of conversion; while another Jesuit, Fr Meynier, had suggested interpreting the Edict of Nantes in the narrowest possible sense so as to make the heretics realize where their best interests lay. About half a million Huguenots fled to Holland, England, Protestant Germany, Sweden, northern Ireland and Cape Colony: an economic disaster and a spiritual horror. In Holland feeling ran so high that the

Society's forty-five houses were first heavily taxed and later closed. Lachaise and Le Tellier were swimming with the tide. There was no word of condemnation from Pope Innocent XI.

Pope Alexander VII had, at the Spanish Queen Mother's request, over-ruled Nidhard's refusal, prompted by General Oliva, to accept the offices of Grand Inquisitor and Councillor of State: but Oliva did manage to prevent a Fr Fernandes from becoming a councillor of state in Portugal. The fracas over Fr Petre, and James II's repeated requests that he should be made a cardinal, were seized on by enemies of the Society in Rome as evidence of overweening political ambition, and there were the first none-too-faint rumours that the Society might be suppressed. Innocent XI was put under pressure to discipline the French Jesuits by closing their schools and forbidding them to hear confessions, and Oliva commented that 'a plot is in the making against us'. A few years later the Congregation of Propaganda, inundated with complaints of Jesuit obstinacy over the Chinese rites, suggested that recruiting to the Society should cease until its missionaries submitted to decrees condemning the practice of 'accommodation'. Relations with the papacy were not improved by such incidents as that of 1721, when Guillaume Daubenton, Jesuit confessor to Philip V of Spain, persuaded the King to send a royal veto on the election of Cardinal Conti as Pope. The veto did not reach Rome in time and Conti emerged as Innocent XIII.

The nationalist or dynastic pressures which had begun to fragment the Society during the Thirty Years War grew stronger. By the 1650s France had ousted Spain as Europe's leading cultural, religious and military power. Francis de Sales, Vincent de Paul, Jean Eudes, Jean-Jacques Olier, with a group of new orders – the Lazarists, the Sulpicians, the Oratorians – now set the tone and pace of Catholic reform. Living in community but moving about at need, they had the advantage of being pledged to episcopal, not papal, obedience, thus avoiding many of the wrangles that plagued older organizations, particularly the Jesuits. Though the Oratorian leader, Cardinal de Bérulle, was a Jesuit pupil, the two orders were soon rivals. Oratorian schools tended to stress science more than Latin and Greek, and to advocate a milder discipline, while Oratorian piety inclined to the 'quietism' which by a natural recoil succeeded the relentless 'activism' and bloodshed of the wars of religion.

Oratorian and Sulpician seminaries challenged the Jesuit establishments. The University of Paris did not relax its hostility, though in 1719 it followed the Jesuit example by waiving tuition fees. Jean-Baptiste de la

Salle launched his Brothers of the Christian Schools with a fresh approach to primary education, which was given in French. His pioneering of Sunday schools and teacher training colleges caused the kind of stir which had surrounded the early stages of the Jesuit venture. The schools of Port-Royal, catering for limited numbers, also broke new ground by teaching French as a subject worthy of detailed attention and by a highly idealized conception of childhood that with its talk of 'little souls' and 'little angels' was in startling contrast to the harsher view of the Middle Ages and of the Jesuits.

Jesuit teachers, like those at Winchester, Westminster and Eton, could not afford to indulge in little-angel sentiment. The *Ratio Studiorum* provided for the disarming of pupils on entering school. At La Flèche, teachers and college servants armed with muskets and halberds fought a student mob wielding swords, staves and black-jacks during carnival time. And every effort was made to abolish the type of libertine student Montaigne had in mind when he wrote that 'a hundred scholars have caught the pox before getting to their Aristotle lessons'. Apart from mothers, female visitors were confined to the chapel or a special parlour. Vice patrols operated in La Flèche and other towns with large colleges, and attempts were made to end or control prostitution and to enforce a nine o'clock curfew on pupil-lodgers.

Reacting to the innovations of their rivals, the Jesuits made some changes in their curriculum: not teaching French as a distinct subject but allowing its use to translate Latin or Greek passages into 'an elegant vernacular version'; relaxing the rule that pupils not speaking in Latin during school hours should be punished; allowing use of the vernacular in plays, public disputations, and, sometimes, in textbooks. Jesuit historians point out that there was a psychologically sound progression from an exclusively classical stage from the ages of ten to fifteen when memory is keenest and imagination expanding to the exact sciences and philosophy 'when reason began to reign'. This, after all, was the system that equipped René Descartes, educated at La Flèche, with such keen powers of analytical reasoning.

In countries where there was little or no competition and no desire for novelties Jesuit education, not surprisingly, stagnated. In Spain and Portugal a neo-medieval torpor was seldom disturbed. In Austria the story was much the same; and in Poland not until the 1750s did the Jesuits attempt much more than a low-grade parrot-learning, together with a stifling clericalism which made their schools hated as centres of reactionary bigotry.

[168]

In France Jesuit schooling came under fire for different reasons. Between 1618 and 1736, at the large College of Châlons-sur-Marne, it was estimated that sixty per cent of pupils came from the lower or lower middle classes, most of the others from bourgeois homes (lawyers, businessmen, minor officials), and a mere two per cent from the gentry. The same was broadly true of most of the Society's day schools. Richelieu and later Colbert, Louis XIV's Minister for Industry and Commerce, were alarmed by this stampede towards a classical education which favoured the 'liberal professions' or a bureaucratic career at the expense of trade and agriculture. Both drafted plans, which came to nothing for lack of alternative schools and teachers, to cut the number of Jesuit schools and so reduce the manufacture of a surplus of 'gentlemen' which was, in their view, creating a social imbalance. Voltaire, himself a lawyer's son educated at a Jesuit college, also deplored this process. ('I, who farm the land, need agricultural workers and not tonsured clerics... The lower classes should be guided, not educated.') When in 1762 the Jesuits were expelled from Paris the Collège Louis-le-Grand was turned into a model progressive establishment. 'Informing' and corporal punishment ('it degrades but does not correct') were abolished, pupil representatives discussed questions of discipline with the masters. But this seems to have been a belated gesture. An alternative system did not take shape. It was enough to have got rid of the Jesuits.

One of the liveliest Jesuit enterprises – measured by the ecclesiastical commotion it caused – was the *Acta Sanctorum* of the Bollandists. Conceived in 1607 by Fr Rosweyde, a Belgian Jesuit, and begun in earnest by his successor, Fr Bolland, this scientific hagiology aimed to give a full, critical and meticulously researched account of the lives of all the saints. In doing so it angered other orders which found some of their prize legends exposed *as* legends and collected a condemnation from the Spanish Inquisition.* But this fluttering of monastic dovecotes was no real exception to what by the early seventeenth century had become the Society's main characteristic: an ingenious but stultifying counter-reformation sophistry.

Far away from Europe such men as Ricci, de Nobili, Schall and Valignano cut their own patterns and benefited from an *esprit de corps*

---

*Now running to over sixty volumes, this remarkable labour of co-operative scholarship, with headquarters in Brussels, contains extracts in Greek, Syriac, Arabic, Coptic, Ethiopian, Armenian, Georgian, Slavonic and Celtic, with Latin translations. Overmatter research fills eighty-eight volumes of the Analecta Bollandiana. All this has been compiled by a mere seventy Bollandists living and working in community in groups of five or six.

that habitually closed ranks in face of outside criticism, and the writings of Jesuit missionaries were publicized because they brought prestige to the Society. But where in Europe was there a Jesuit to compare with Campanella or Bruno for free-wheeling speculation? Athanasius Kircher, a German who developed the Gnostic-occultist ideas of Villalpando, was probably the nearest equivalent. A renowned mathematician whose writings were much esteemed by Leibnitz, he was not only a prolific inventor of such aids to Jesuit stagecraft as the magic lantern, but devised a scientific reconstruction of Noah's Ark (including a method of sanitation for its human and animal occupants) and discovered in it many hidden meanings – Noah, the first architect, symbolizes Christ, the gopher wood of the Ark prefigures the Cross. He also, in a huge volume on the Tower of Babel, dated the confusion of tongues precisely to the year 1984 after the creation of the world, and indicated Hebrew as the root of all subsequent languages. Fr Kircher measured the craters of Etna and Stromboli and was an oceanographer of some ability. But as a devoted and slightly credulous student of occult writings he rejected any suggestion that the earth revolved about the sun.

English Benedictines like William Gifford, who questioned the pope's right to issue political directions binding in conscience, and kept open the possibility of reunion with the Anglican Church, or John Barnes, who argued that reunion on a large scale would be brought closer if 'mere theological accretions' on both sides were cut away, were denounced as traitors by Jesuits. In Spain a Benedictine monk, Benito Jeronimo Feijoo, professor of philosophy at Oviedo and an open disciple of Newton, Descartes and Francis Bacon, almost single-handedly set going a process of enlightenment which by 1750 had begun to make an impact – 'thanks to the immortal Feijoo,' wrote a contemporary, 'spirits no longer trouble our houses; witches have fled our towns, the evil eye does not plague the tender child, and an eclipse does not dismay us.'

Fr Horazio Grassi, an astronomer of some renown, won the sort of niggling victory that now passed for a Jesuit achievement when, by reopening the question of Galileo's 'orthodoxy', he provoked a belligerently dogmatic vindication that resulted in a second trial and condemnation. Descartes' epoch-making *Discourse on Method*, published in French in 1637, was at first welcomed by the Jesuits; and Descartes, though critical of some shortcomings in his education, hoped that his *Principles of Philosophy* would be used as a textbook in Jesuit colleges. But when the sceptical implications of his reasoning became apparent the

Society had second thoughts about a philosopher who, as Pascal put it, 'would like to dispense with God, but could not help allowing Him a flick of the fingers to set the world in motion', and who, like Montaigne, recommended conformity with the social and religious code of the country in which one happened to have been born. Belgian Jesuits banned the teaching of Cartesian doctrines in their schools and in 1663, with Jesuit connivance, the *Discourse* was placed on the Index. The appearance of a new breed of philosophers, thinking for themselves and encouraging their readers to do likewise – Descartes, Hobbes, Spinoza, Locke, Hume, Voltaire, Diderot, Rousseau – menaced the twin pillars of authority and tradition which the Jesuits, so often accused of heterodoxy, were doubly determined to be seen to uphold.

A passion for clear and distinct ideas also lay behind the plea for a return to Catholic first principles launched in 1640 with the publication of the *Augustinus* by Cornelis Jansen, Bishop of Ypres, whose message was driven home by the redoubtable Antoine Arnauld and magnificently seconded by Blaise Pascal. Realizing that the Jansenist movement, which had powerful allies at court, was primarily aimed at them, the Jesuits managed to secure some pages of the *Augustinus* from the printers and tried to prevent its publication. When that failed, they destroyed as many copies as they could lay hands on. As in the Molinist controversy, the argument centred on 'grace'. 'From the moment of its origin,' wrote Jansen, 'the human race bears the full burden of its condemnation, and its life, if it can be called such, is totally bad . . . Love of vanity . . . gnawing care, unhealthy joys, lusts, adulteries, incests, sacrileges, heresies, swindles . . . Who can describe the yoke that weighs on the sons of Adam?'

His followers, including the reformed worldling Pascal, were also remarkable for an inspissated puritanical gloom. Antoine Arnauld, one of the secular monks who lived in hermitages in the grounds of Port-Royal, attacked the blasphemously mechanical use of the sacrament and recommended abstention as a form of penance. This drew protests from the Society and in 1653 Innocent X was induced to condemn five heretical propositions allegedly found in the *Augustinus*. The Dominican doctors of the Sorbonne, hitherto, as Pascal remarked, hardly favourable to the Jesuit position, upheld the verdict. But his *Provincial Letters*, ridiculing the devious subtleties of Jesuit 'accommodation', lit the dreary conflict with a flash of genius and exposed the plodding hack-work of Jesuit pamphleteers to public derision.

The battle continued with many an ironical twist and turn. Port-Royal

[171]

became a centre of fashionable devotion. The Jesuits accused even the grimly orthodox Bossuet of 'Jansenism', a term which they now tended to apply to any opponent. The Paris Parlement, still seeking allies against the Society, sided with the 'Jansenists', who included some bishops and many of the lower clergy attracted by Jansen's opinion that they were as important as any prelate or religious. Jansenists were supposedly ultra-Gallican by contrast with Jesuit papalism. But during a tussle with Louis XIV over his right to control ecclesiastical appointments some Jansenist bishops criticized the King's tyranny, thus gaining favour in Rome.

In 1679 Innocent XI actually condemned sixty-five 'lax' propositions culled from Jesuit manuals of moral theology. But Louis XIV's fury at the Vatican-Jansenist alliance made it easy for Lachaise and Le Tellier to organize a counter-attack. Port-Royal was forbidden to accept novices, its schools were closed (a persecution obliquely commemorated in Racine's *Esther*). Fresh from his triumph over the Huguenots Le Tellier urged Louis XIV to crush the 'defiance' of the twenty-seven ageing nuns of Port-Royal. In 1709 they were removed to other convents. When the deserted cloisters became a place of pilgrimage they were demolished, and when people continued to flock to the cemetery that too was destroyed. Le Tellier's vindictiveness moved the Bishop of Paris to deprive Jesuits of the right to preach or hear confessions in his diocese and he urged Madame de Maintenon to use her influence to get rid of the madman. Le Tellier struck back by persuading the King to extort from Pope Clement XI the bull *Unigenitus* of 1713 condemning the doctrine of *Moral Reflections on the New Testament* by Pasquier Quesnel. Although when first published in 1671 it had been warmly commended by Lachaise and Bossuet, the author was now described as 'a ravening wolf, false prophet, teacher of lies, knave, hypocrite and poisoner of souls'.

But Jansenism rumbled on. The Paris Parlement refused to recognize the bull, and though several thousand Jansenists were arrested (Louis XIV saw them as republican conspirators) the movement was not checked. Parish priests took Arnauld's teaching about communion so seriously that some were said to have boasted that 'there was not a single sacrilegious communion last year, because no one came to Communion.' Perhaps that was a Jesuit canard: but anti-Jesuit jokes were circulating briskly, often making fun of the cult of the Sacred Heart (Mary Alacoque became 'Marie à la coque').

Meanwhile the Society had become involved in another Molinist controversy, but this time the enemy was 'Molinism' as interpreted by

Miguel de Molinos, a Spanish priest who had studied under the Jesuits in Valencia and Coimbra. His brand of mystical quietism, with its emphasis on the experience of divine love in total contemplative abandonment, threatened to undermine ecclesiasticism at its very centre. In Rome in the 1760s his *Spiritual Guide*, promising liberation from the shackles of formal religion, was infinitely more popular than the *Spiritual Exercises*. Thousands, including Innocent XI, were under the spell. For ten years Miguel de Molinos was the most celebrated spiritual adviser in Italy and anti-Molinist tracts by Fr Segneri and other prominent Jesuits were placed on the Index. But Molinos was arrested in 1685, accused of encouraging antinomian orgies and of a 'Jansenist' view of grace. Segneri's book was removed from the Index and the Society acclaimed as the saviour of orthodoxy and guardian of morality. This useful victory helped to offset the very different image of pedantic but unscrupulous hypocrisy that Pascal had popularized.

The element of anti-clericalism in the *Provincial Letters*, together with their sophisticated elegance, made them sell like hot cakes to a rapidly growing intelligentsia bored with theological hair-splitting and alarmed by the economic madness of militant Catholicism. When Louis XIV died in 1715 Le Tellier was dismissed, more bishops banned Jesuits from preaching and hearing confessions, *Unigenitus* was ignored, and the attempts of Jesuit confessors to discipline Louis XV and his mistresses by withholding absolution were treated as a joke. The subdued laughter that had greeted Pascal's sallies became louder as Voltaire and his allies opened a more explicit anti-clerical campaign. 'I'm tired,' said Voltaire, whose Jansenist father had sent him to a Jesuit school as the best available, 'of being told that twelve men sufficed to establish Christianity, and I long to prove that only one is needed to destroy it.' The Jesuit-Jansenist vendetta seemed to offer a splendid opportunity. 'We must fire on them,' he wrote, 'while they are biting each other. Would it not be fair to suggest that by strangling the last Jesuit in the intestines of the last Jansenist the whole matter would have been brought to a satisfactory conclusion?' Salon wits got a ready laugh with stories such as that of the military tactician who reckoned that soldiers might do better with longer bayonets and shorter rifles, like Jesuits who lengthened the creed and shortened the commandments. By the 1740s Voltaire's letters were being circulated among anti-clerical progressives and free-thinking scoffers.

Yet Voltaire's stilted neo-classical plays owed much to 'improving' Jesuit drama, and he acknowledged the Society's services in providing

[173]

anthropological dynamite for rationalist saboteurs, defended it against charges of moral corruption (his teachers, he insisted, had 'led austere and laborious lives' and had given him 'a taste for letters and virtue'), and went to the trouble of saving an ex-Jesuit accused of pederasty from the stake.

The Society of Jesus, in fact, was a paradoxical institution, half-modern, half-medieval. Its astronomers designed splendid telescopes and sighted new planets, yet obeyed the Church's ruling on Copernicus and Galileo. Some Jesuit scientists were official correspondents of the Royal Society, yet the General Congregations of 1730 and 1751 insisted that Aristotelian physics must rule supreme in Jesuit classrooms. Roger Boscovich, as many-faceted as Kircher but untrammelled by occultist lore, is now regarded as a pioneer of nuclear physics; but his recommendation that such phony relics as an alleged rib of the prophet Isaiah should be thrown away scandalized old-fashioned Jesuit Rectors. The Society's casuists, in Pascal's phrase, 'put cushions under the elbows of sinners'; its missionaries helped to create the myth of the noble savage and the fashionable cult of the civilized Chinese, yet Le Tellier hounded Huguenots and Jansenists. In 1758 José Francisco de Isla SJ, whose favourite reading was Molière, published what is perhaps the only readable Spanish novel of the eighteenth century – *The History of the Famous Preacher Fray Gerundio de Campazas*, a satire on ignorant, idle friars, outdated schooling, and baroque pulpit oratory. Yet at the once-eminent University of Salamanca, where Jesuit influence was paramount, the offer of a department of mathematics was in 1761 rejected as 'fraught with dishonour', Descartes, Gassendi and Newton were banned, theology students debated what language the angels spoke, and Fr Rivera SJ declared post-Aristotelian science the work of the Devil.

The Society resisted Pope Benedict XIV's order to modernize the breviary, but the French Jesuits Jean Hardouin and Isaac Berruyer rewrote the Bible to make the scriptures more palatable and Jacques Berthier, editor of the *Journal de Trévoux*, a monthly review of the arts and sciences, extended an olive branch to Diderot when the first volume of his *Encyclopaedia* appeared in 1751. Berthier stressed his admiration for Descartes, Gassendi, Newton and Leibnitz as 'enemies of ignorance, heresy and enthusiasm' and hinted at common interests: a shared belief in the perfectibility of human nature and in the importance of keeping abreast of the whole range of contemporary scholarship. But the Encyclopaedists' sharply hostile treatment of priestcraft, revealed religion, and the mysteries of the Catholic faith soon killed any hope of a rapprochement. Though claiming that large portions of the first volume of its rival had been plagiarized from the works of Jesuit savants, the *Journal de Trévoux* could not match the verve and bite of Voltaire, Montesquieu, Rousseau and Buffon any more than Jesuit mediocrities had been able to compete with the brilliance of Pascal. Its subscribers fell away and it ceased publication in 1762 after more than fifty years of endeavour.

Leibnitz, who dreamed of a universal science and a United Christian Europe, hoped that the religious orders, particularly the Jesuits, would co-operate in compiling a comprehensive encyclopaedia of human knowledge. But his addiction to the occult and his belief that the truth in all religious and philosophical systems could be distilled into a single essence did not commend him to the clerical mentality. Similar to Leibnitz's projected religion of humanity was the cult of Freemasonry, based on the guild ritual of journeymen builders in the Middle Ages. Reaching the Continent from England, it called for a brotherhood of men retaining their various creeds but linked by an overarching 'natural religion'. It spread rapidly and was soon condemned by the papacy as an insidious deistic foe. In France especially 'liberal' priests joined the movement in large numbers, and the Society of Jesus, alarmed by the threat of a quasi-religious but anti-clerical organization with a missionary drive and a mysterious glamour not unlike its own, was the first order to forbid its members to mix Masonry and Catholicism. The struggle between the two lasted until well into the twentieth century, and Jesuit scare propaganda was paralleled by allegations that Jesuit spies had infiltrated lodges, bemusing honest masons and corrupting their rituals. The Comte de Mirabeau actually suggested that an 'intimate association' of resolute freethinkers should be organized along the lines of the Society of Jesus. 'We have,' he wrote, 'quite contrary views, those of enlightening men, of making them free and happy. But what should prevent us from doing for good what the Jesuits have done for evil?'

The papacy and the Society, united in opposition to the Freemasons, also shared a tendency towards bureaucratic elaboration. The papal curia had swollen to a total of fifteen Congregations, the Jesuit curia grew with every expansion of membership and commitments. Codification and a legalistic mentality, already apparent in the time of Ignatius, had become more marked from the time of Aquaviva onwards. Provincial Superiors groaned at the bulk of the *Ratio Studiorum* and the endless glosses on the Constitutions. The Generals who succeeded Oliva, though beset with problems that might have defeated Aquaviva in his prime, were not of high calibre. The papacy, much reorganized but little reformed, was politically impotent, even if it had been inclined to defend its so-called janissaries. And there were many reasons for not wishing to do so.

The Jesuits' increasingly nationalist or regalist loyalties made them very dubious allies – an expanded system of resident papal nuncios served the purpose better. Innocent XI, having manipulated the election of Tirso Gonzalez, the thirteenth General, with a brief to enforce the slightly less permissive form of casuistry known as 'probabiliorism', saw his frantic efforts to obey frustrated by his lieutenants. Spain, Austria and France were sucked into the probabiliorist vortex, which, to the accompaniment of rumours that French cardinals planned to pack a Jesuit procurators' congregation with probabilists who would vote to depose Gonzalez, whirled away from 1691 to 1705. The capricious refusal of the French Jesuits to modernize the breviary was countered by papal instructions to delay the canonization of Bellarmine.

In Austria the government was, by the 1760s, clearly determined to loosen the Jesuit grip on education. The Habsburg hegemony had been replaced by a Bourbon alliance which threatened the papacy and the Society. Outside Europe the Seven Years War of 1756 to 1763, from which England and Holland, heretic powers, came out victorious, had altered the imperial picture. Spain and Portugal were desperate to exploit their remaining colonial resources more thoroughly and the Jesuit 'empire' in Latin America came under greedy scrutiny. The triumphalist mood was in tatters. Jesuits who in 1640 had acquired and destroyed copies of the *Augustinus* now sought to locate and destroy copies of the *Imago primi saeculi*, published in the same year. Failing that, they tried to pass it off as the work of over-zealous young scholastics.

CHAPTER FOURTEEN

Who needs Jesuits?

'HANG A JESUIT,' says a Spanish proverb, 'and he'll make off with the rope.' In 1723 the Society seemed doomed. Propaganda, arguing that missionary methods in Asia were causing scandal and that Michelangelo Tamburini, the Jesuit General, was 'acting like the Pope of China', was out for blood. Innocent XIII, antagonized by Fr Daubenton's efforts to prevent his election, approved a brief in which Tamburini was accused of failing to enforce the fourth vow and given three years in which to prove his and the Society's loyalty. In the meantime, no more missionaries were to be sent to the Far East, no more novices to be admitted. This was a sentence of slow death. But Innocent XIII died soon after pronouncing it and Tamburini persuaded Benedict XIII to lift the vetoes.

This, however, was no more than a reprieve. Propaganda's hostility did not abate and it was backed by the Paris Foreign Missionary Society. Anti-Jesuit tirades from settlers and officials in South America piled up in Lisbon and Madrid. In Portugal, France and Spain secular clergy and secularizing politicians – the Marquis of Pombal, the Duc de Choiseul, the Conde de Aranda – intensified their attacks. Caught in a crossfire, the popes could at best plead and prevaricate. When in 1758 Lorenzo Ricci was elected General, Clement XIII, friendly but powerless, advised him to rely on prayer and penance for survival, and in the next few years Ricci circulated several letters on this theme. To no avail, for in 1759 it was decreed that all Jesuits in Portuguese territory, over two thousand of them, should be expelled. In 1764 a similar sentence was passed on more than three thousand French Jesuits. Three years later it was the turn of some five thousand Spanish Jesuits. And finally, in 1773, the entire Society was dissolved 'forever' by a papal brief.

Though the writing had been on the wall for at least half a century, the prelude to the last act was complex and confused. Giulio Cordara, the Society's official historian, considered that Ricci had been too yielding and saw that the political onslaught had found ready helpers among 'Jansenist' prelates in Rome. Saddened as he was by the event, the celebrated moral theologian Alphonsus Liguori, founder of the Redemptorist order, cautioned his followers 'lest pride ruin us as it has the Jesuits'; and after searching his heart ('I have perhaps spoken too freely, but none will deny that I have spoken the truth') Cordara endorsed this opinion in his memoirs. 'It was the Divine will rather than any human intrigues that caused the dissolution . . . The sin of pride is secret. It creeps into good actions so as to be hardly distinguishable from virtue. Nothing is more hateful to God . . . Our churches were splendid and their adornment costly. The festivals of the Saints were celebrated with pomp. But was it solely for the sake of religion or rather to show off our power?' Megalomania was so pervasive that Jesuits of all ages deluded themselves that 'all the good in the world was done under the auspices of our Society'. In Italy there was much boasting about the noble birth of many members but all Jesuits, including lay brothers, regarded themselves as aristocrats compared with other religious. They 'looked with something approaching contempt on all other Orders', were 'continually bragging of their Bellarmine and Suarez, having little or no knowledge of other writers', particularly rejoiced in any little victory over the Dominicans, preened themselves on their superior chastity, and seemed to have no idea that lack of humility was 'the special stain which excited the wrath of God against us'.

Cordara was describing symptoms which, in view of the extreme hostility and heady flattery surrounding the Jesuits for two centuries, were hardly surprising. The Dominicans were no more remarkable for genuine humility. The main difference was that they and the Franciscans were protected by an array of popes and prelates from their own ranks who regarded the Society of Jesus as a temporary phenomenon to be tolerated only as long as it seemed to serve a useful purpose; and they could quote Ignatius in support of this attitude. In 1603, announcing to the Parlement his decision to recall the Jesuits from exile, Henry IV had remarked: 'You say they pick out the best for their Society. I commend them for it. The King of Spain employs Jesuits, and I am resolved to do likewise. Why should France fare worse than Spain?' This view of the Society as an élite task force inevitably angered all those whose assumed incompetence was the cause of Jesuit intervention. It also conflicted with the over-centralized, increasingly bureaucratic style of the Society. Philip II and Louis XIV had tried to formalize what had virtually happened anyway – the emergence of separate Spanish and French Societies. The fourth vow was a constant embarrassment. Sporadic efforts to observe it annoyed royal masters. The ensuing retreat or compromise could be used by the papacy as evidence of disloyalty and by nationalists as evidence of actual or potential treason.

Pombal's tactics had all been used or suggested before. He simply pressed them to the point of fully exposing Jesuit vulnerability. A protégé of the Society in the early stages of his diplomatic career, he had lived in London for a time and like Voltaire regarded the English model of a tightly-controlled Church as an ideal arrangement, to be combined with economic and educational reform along rationalist lines. As quasi-dictator of Portugal after the catastrophic Lisbon earthquake of 1755 he had plenty of scope to put his theories into practice; and in a country where Jesuit influence had for two centuries been so dominant, this, together with the Inquisition, was high on his list of enemies of progress. Pombal was confirmed in his anti-Jesuit resolve by three incidents: a surprisingly effective Indian military resistance to a boundary-settling treaty with Spain which involved handing over seven of the Guarani reductions to Portugal; the discovery that unfavourable reports about officials in Brazil had been supplied by Jesuits at the request of the Queen Mother; and a sermon-cum-pamphlet campaign by Gabriele Malagrida, an Italian Jesuit famed as a missionary in Brazil, representing the Lisbon earthquake as God's judgement on a wicked, atheistic tyrant. Pretext enough for a charge of conspiracy, and a strong suspicion that the Jesuits were allied with some sections of the aristocracy in resisting the low-born adventurer Pombal and his new-fangled schemes.

In 1757 Jesuits were banished from the court in Lisbon and in 1758 Benedict XIV was bullied into sending the Portuguese Cardinal Francisco Saldanha to Brazil. Without producing any evidence, Saldanha announced that Jesuit residences and missions in America, Asia, Africa and Europe were part of a huge commercial network. At almost the same time ten Jesuits were arrested in Lisbon accused of conspiring with the Tavora family to murder King Joseph I. In April 1759 the King ordered the expulsion of the Society throughout his realms. A few months later the machinery of eviction began to grind into action and in 1761, with a final touch of ferocity, the aged Malagrida was publicly garrotted and burned at the stake for heresy.

Pombal's pounce was trumpeted and justified by a strenuous propaganda campaign and for the most part Ricci, knowing that the charges had been repeated and refuted a dozen times and warned by the counter-productive effect of Jesuit attacks on the *Provincial Letters*, relied on a dignified silence. Pombal had the field to himself, and plenty of ammunition. Antoine Arnauld had co-ordinated a team which compiled at least three bulky anti-Jesuit anthologies. Paulo da Silva Nunes, a settler in Brazil, had assembled a dossier in which the Jesuits were accused of usurping royal authority, excluding whites from their missions and sometimes imprisoning them, issuing firearms to their converts, encouraging plantation slaves to escape, dealing treasonably with the Spanish, the Dutch and the French, and trading on such a scale that their missions 'looked more like warehouses than centres of religion'. Fr Norbert, an ex-Capuchin missionary in India, who in 1744 had published a further indictment, continued his literary sapping at Lisbon in Pombal's pay. So did an ex-Jesuit, Ibañez de Echevarri, whose *Jesuit Kingdom in Paraguay* appeared in 1770.

The *Brief Account* of the Paraguayan missions and the Indian rebellion which appeared under Pombal's name was translated into French, Spanish, Italian and German, reaching and startling a wide readership which was not already familiar with the subject. In it the Jesuits were charged with every imaginable crime: 'seditious machinations against every government in Europe; scandals in their missions so horrible that they cannot be related without indecency; rebellion against the Sovereign Pontiff; accumulation of vast wealth and the wielding of immense political power . . . teaching the Indians to hate all white men who are not Jesuits . . . taking advantage of the earthquake to attain their detestable ends; surpassing Machiavelli in their diabolical plots . . . calumniating the venerable Palafox; committing crimes worse than those of the Knights Templars . . .' Was it not, he asked, a strange coincidence that Portugal, so powerful and flourishing in 1540 when the first Jesuits arrived in the country, should now have been reduced to beggarly impotence?

In Spain there was no need for a full-scale propaganda barrage. Pombal had said it all, and Arnauld's material had been circulating since the 1650s in a collection entitled *El Teatro Jesuitico*. But in a country where the Inquisition and the Jesuits, now closely allied in the struggle against 'Jansenism' (a blanket term indicating French ideas and godless anti-clericalism), were popularly regarded as bastions of the Spanish tradition, foreign or Francophile ministers had to move more cautiously. Bourbon planners' innovations met with more obstruction than enthusiasm. Roads, canals, street lighting, a clearance of bandits from the Sierra Morena, attempts at agricultural reform and the encouragement of industry were all received with apathy or hostility; and the colonies of German farmers established to bring more land under efficient cultivation were hated with a xenophobic passion which the

Jesuits were able to exploit. They were applauded by many Spaniards for their part in the universities' resistance to curricular changes and in 1766 their suspiciously masterful calming of an angry mob in Madrid was seen as a show of rabble-rousing strength.

Reforming ministers longed to refute the reputation summed up in the contemptuous remark of an English wit that 'a Spaniard without a Jesuit at his elbow is like beef without mustard'. The demagogic-cum-regicidal theories of Mariana and Suarez were disinterred and brandished. The royal minister Campomanes accused the Society of 'papalism' and of trying to organize a state-within-the-state in Spain as in Spanish America. In 1767 he told an emergency meeting of the Royal Council that 'any faction within the state is incompatible with the security of the state . . . either the civil government must perish or the deadly society must be expelled as a political disease of the most acute kind.' The reformers held a trump card. They knew that many of the secular clergy, however reactionary themselves, would rejoice in the downfall of the Jesuits, and that the friars, stung by the satirical barbs of Fr Isla, would be delighted. Learning from the delays caused in Portugal by clumsily improvised arrest and deportation arrangements, the Council laid plans well in advance. Between 31 March and 3 April 1767 detachments of soldiers with sealed instructions surrounded Jesuit houses throughout Spain. The royal decree of exile was read, and within days nearly three thousand Jesuits were on the march to ports of embarkation.

In a belated gesture of appeasement Pope Clement XIII offered to hurry the canonization of Bishop Palafox (already a saint to anti-Jesuits) – a process that the Jesuits were said to have delayed, claiming that his much-used letter from Mexico had been forged. But with barely-veiled sarcasm King Charles III of Spain informed the Pope that 'your Holiness well knows that the first duty of a sovereign ruler consists in watching over the security of his realm and the peace of his subjects. In the fulfilment of this task I have found it necessary to expel all the Jesuits that were in my kingdom and to have them transported to the Papal States under the direct, wise rule of your Holiness . . .' The Bourbon states of Naples and Parma, from which the Jesuits were also expelled, merely observed that the King was answerable to God alone for his decisions. Forty-six of the sixty Spanish bishops had voted in favour of expulsion, and Francisco Vasquez, Superior-General of the Augustinians, exulted in it. Spain, he said, had been purified at last of the Jesuit vermin. The Conde de Campomanes looked forward to clearing the cobwebs of the 'doctrina jesuitica' from colleges and universities. The

[181]

Spanish ambassador in Rome was told to expect 'a handsome gift of several thousand Jesuits'.

In France the dissolution had been spread over a period of two years, involving a clash between the Royal Council and the lawyers of the regional Parlements. Disgusted by Pombal's butchery the anti-clerical lobby, with friends in the Parlements, proposed to conduct the affair in a more leisurely, civilized manner. Voltaire warmly defended Jesuit morality, describing the *Provincial Letters* as an example of 'the art of raillery pressed into service to make indifferent things appear criminal and to clothe insults in elegant language'. But a common estimate of besetting ecclesiastical sins was reflected in the saying: 'Keep your wife from the friars and your money from the Jesuits' – and the tendency to boast of superhuman chastity had almost succeeded in bracketing Jesuits with friars in popular scatology. The case of Jean-Baptiste Girard SJ, accused of debauching Catherine Cadière, a young penitent, but acquitted in 1731 after a sensational trial, had received heavy publicity. However, though the fate of Catherine Cadière was useful ammunition, the main immediate pretext for a serious attack was not sexual but financial.

Like their counterparts in South America, French officials and businessmen in India had long complained of the efficiency and volume of Jesuit commerce. In 1697 the manager of the Trading Company at Pondicherry reported that 'it is an established fact that next to the Dutch the Jesuits carry on the greatest and most successful trade in the East Indies . . . The bales assigned to these fathers, the smallest of which is twice as large as those of the Trading Company, were distributed among all the ships of the squadron and were not filled with rosaries or such other weapons as one might expect in an apostolic consignment. They import as much as they can get on the ships at every outward sailing to sell in this country.' Saint-Simon, in his memoirs, relates that 'when a fleet from the Indies was unloading at Cadiz, eight large cases came to hand labelled "Chocolate for the Father-General of the Society of Jesus". The cases were so exceedingly heavy as to cause curiosity about their contents. They proved to be large balls of chocolate . . . A ball was split open and gold was found inside. The Jesuits were informed, but these cunning politicians were very careful not to claim this valuable "chocolate". They preferred losing it to confessing.'

Their enemies longed for a resounding Jesuit failure; and it happened in the Caribbean to a tycoon-missionary who had been described as 'the most able man in business that the world has beheld for many ages'. Fr Antoine Lavalette, Superior of the mission based on Martinique, devoted himself to improving its shaky finances. Developing sugar, coffee and indigo plantations and shipping the produce to Europe, he borrowed heavily to expand the business, despite warnings from Rome. In 1755, thanks to the activities of English privateers, only one of about twenty cargoes got through. More desperate speculation worsened the situation, as during the Seven Years War the sea-lanes were virtually closed. Lavalette was expelled from the Society, but a large trading house in Marseilles had been bankrupted and others were hard hit.

Creditors held the French Jesuits as a body responsible for the debts. In 1761, appealing against this attitude, the Jesuits took the case to the High Court of the Paris Parlement. It was a disastrous move. The bankruptcies had involved many friends and supporters of the Society – the English province, for example, was affected to the tune of at least £1,000,000 by today's values. The French province's attempt to disclaim liability for the sins of an ex-Jesuit who had acted contrary to the rules looked very like a callous casuistical ploy. The Parlement, presented with a fine chance to deliver a *coup de grâce*, widened the issue, ordering settlement of the debts within a year and demanding a thorough check on the 'mysterious' Constitutions on which the Jesuits seemed to rely to get them out of trouble.

When Louis XV, advised to dispute the Parlement's right to handle the matter, insisted that the examination should be made by a specially appointed committee of the Royal Council, the enquiry into Lavalette's crash was transformed into a contest between Crown and judiciary to decide the fate of the Society in France. Ignoring the royal initiative, the Parlement decreed a public burning of books by well-known Jesuit authors, in particular Suarez and Mariana, as subversive of public morality, banned further recruiting to the Society, and ordered its colleges to be closed by August 1762. Trying to present the Jesuits as good patriots, the Royal Council drafted a declaration in which they were asked to repudiate tyrannicide, to accept the Gallican Articles of 1682 (which insisted that a general council of the Church was superior to the Pope), and to swear to obey the declaration even if their General ordered otherwise. When the Provincial, Étienne de la Croix, proposed to sign the Articles as 'theological opinions' rather than matters of faith, he was severely rebuked by Clement XIII and by Ricci for breaking the fourth vow. They also rejected Choiseul's solution of a French province ruled by a Vicar-General sworn to observe the statutes of the kingdom.

[183]

This fourth vow obstinacy amounted to a death warrant. Some eagerly, some reluctantly – the loss or disruption of nearly a hundred Jesuit schools was a considerable disincentive – the twelve regional Parlements followed the lead of Paris. Four Parlements, including Paris, banished the offenders from France and confiscated their property. Five suppressed but did not banish them. Three refused to take any action. In November 1764, remarking that 'I have no great love for the Jesuits, but every heresy has made them an object of contempt, which is to their honour,' and stipulating that they should receive a small annual allowance, Louis XV issued an edict proscribing the Society throughout France, but allowing ex-Jesuits to stay if they undertook to behave 'like good and faithful subjects' under episcopal authority.

A few ex-Jesuits temporarily solved their problems by accepting the hospitality of ideological foes who, with ironical magnanimity, were prepared to shelter these victims of sectarian strife (Voltaire set the fashion by taking in the lame and elderly Fr Antoine Adam, with whom he played chess in the evenings). Most, taking advantage of General Ricci's permission for release from their vows, worked as diocesan priests or schoolteachers. Ricci's efforts to find room for loyalists in other countries were not successful, but a handful of scholastics made their way to Poland to continue their studies.

In Portugal the dissolution was a painful business. Pombal's offer that all Jesuits who had not taken their final vows could remain if they 'apostasized' had little effect: it was estimated that eighty-five per cent stayed loyal. Some, including non-Portuguese missionaries, were imprisoned in conditions so appalling that few survived the ordeal. But more than a thousand, packed tight in the holds under guard, were shipped to Civita Vecchia and dumped in the Papal States. Jesuits or friends of the Society had to accommodate and feed them. Treasures were sold, food strictly rationed, and to raise funds the Pope was asked to give a dispensation from the rule that fees should not be charged for Masses.

Crammed on and between decks, about six hundred Spanish Jesuits arrived at Civita Vecchia in May 1767. They were barred entry, not only because the Portuguese exiles were already straining resources and tempers, but because the Pope, as a temporal prince, protested at the arbitrary unloading of exiles in his territory. An attempt to land them in Corsica was foiled by war on the island between the Genoese, the French, and Corsican separatists. Twenty-two ships remained at anchor and some Jesuits lived on board for five months. The trials of makeshift quarters in ramshackle churches, barns and stables killed off a number, and the arrival of nearly two thousand men from the colonies added to existing tensions.

This uneasy and bickering community was broken up when in May 1768 France acquired Corsica from the Genoese. The refugees were shipped to Italy and left to their own devices. Some were allowed to enter the Papal States. At least seven hundred obtained release from their vows in Rome and either drifted about the city embarrassing Jesuit headquarters by their raffish behaviour or returned to Spain. In due course a thousand wanderers were settled in and around Ferrara, thanks to the energy of José Pignatelli, an aristocratic Jesuit from Saragossa, who as well as arranging shelter and provisions raised morale by improvising a course of studies. More than half of the Jesuits in Naples (where they had been accused of causing Vesuvius to erupt) and Sicily chose to break with the Society and stay where they were. The rest, whittled down by sporadic desertions, joined the exiles from Parma in Ferrara, Bologna, and other reception centres.

The dissolutions and expulsions of 1759, 1764 and 1767 to 1768 had affected about half the total membership of the Society. Choiseul advocated steady pressure on the papacy to finish the job. Clement XIII, who died early in 1769, had resisted several Bourbon demands for total suppression. The new Pope, Clement XIV, was immediately besieged by Bourbon ambassadors and envoys; and on 8 June, 1773, after four years of relentless badgering from Spain, Portugal, France and Austria, he signed the brief *Dominus ac Redemptor.*

The Spanish ambassador, Floridablanca, had bribed two of the Pope's closest advisers, one of whom drafted the document, which was printed in the Spanish embassy. The formula of suppression appeared as a brief rather than a bull because it required only two as against twenty signatories and could be kept secret until the moment of execution – 16 August. It was also argued that the use of a brief, which carried less authoritative weight, signified that the Pope's hand had been forced and that the sentence could be more easily revoked. Certainly *Dominus ac Redemptor* was a gesture of appeasement which, while itemizing most of the charges that had been levelled at the Society ever since its foundation, managed to avoid actually endorsing them. Charles III's decree of expulsion had spoken of reasons which were 'hidden in the depths of his heart', and the same phrase was put into Clement XIV's mouth. The main emphasis was upon the dissension caused within the Church by Jesuit activities. 'Even at its inception the Society was plagued with germs of discord, riven with jealousies . . . The Fathers exalted themselves above other religious orders . . . There is scarcely any kind of serious accusation that has not been brought against it and in consequence the tranquillity of the Church has been disturbed.'

The furore surrounding the lengthy dismantling of the Society in France had been a godsend to a government eager to distract attention from the disastrous outcome of the Seven Years War. Father-General Ricci, who with ten other curial Jesuits was imprisoned in the Castle of St Angelo, could find some consolation in the thought that the sacrifice of the Society had not been in vain. It was the price paid to avoid a break with Rome by Spain, Portugal and France, the three 'Most Catholic' nations. There was, too, a feeling that though the Society had been suppressed it had not been condemned, and that the ordeal would somehow purify and strengthen it. In Italy Jesuit archives were ransacked and Jesuit libraries all over the world were dispersed or transferred. Novices, scholastics and brothers were dismissed, priests permitted to function as diocesan clergy or to join another order. But the enforcement of the brief varied greatly. In the Catholic cantons of Switzerland and in Austria ex-Jesuits continued to live in community and to teach in their schools. In the Austrian Netherlands crate-loads of paintings by Rubens, Breughel and Van Dyck were seized from Jesuit houses and sent to the imperial court in Vienna. In Poland, recently partitioned between Austria, Prussia and Russia, Jesuits were in a state of much confusion and distress, though some found work as school-teachers or private tutors.

All was not lost. In 1772 an unofficial approach had been made to Frederick II of Prussia, a nominal Lutheran and disciple of Voltaire, to act as the protector of the Society. This, though desperate, was not such a fantastic proposition. Clutching at straws, Ricci had been heartened when King George III's brother, the Duke of Gloucester, lunched with him and hinted at English support. Clement XIV had justified his prevarication by pleading that he could not suppress the Society without the consent of the schismatic or heretic powers – Russia, Prussia and England – who might take offence if they were not consulted. Here, perhaps, was the germ of survival. Jesuits had always led a precarious existence in Catholic lands. Could it be that the roads back to Rome might begin in Moscow and Potsdam?

CHAPTER FIFTEEN

Last Rites

'LET US EAT JESUITS!' cry the cannibals in Voltaire's satire *Candide*, published in 1759. By then the papacy itself had joined in the chorus and Pombal was making the first of the great clearances which by 1770 had wrecked the work of some three thousand Jesuit missionaries. Even in Tibet there was trouble with the Capuchins and Carmelites. 'Propaganda' missionaries, they resented the intrusion of Ippolito Desideri, who in 1716 arrived in Lhasa as the envoy of the Archbishop of Goa. After Desideri had spent five years in a Lama monastery, General Tamburini ordered him to leave and one more experiment in acculturation had been aborted.

The going was hard, too, in Protestant countries. In Holland, which by the 1660s had occupied Formosa, Cochin, Malacca and Colombo, Jansenists and Huguenot refugees were hostile. Jesuits were expelled from several provinces, in 1720 the Estates General denounced them as troublemakers, and like other Catholic missionaries they got short shrift in Dutch colonies. During the backlash that followed the exile of James II Jesuits were blamed as the main cause of the penal legislation aimed at Catholics in England. Their Continental seminaries were half-empty and intellectually stagnant. Missioners from the English College at Valladolid, who after years of residence abroad and lectures in Latin were unable to speak their own tongue fluently, seemed like foreigners. Jesuits were frequently banished from Scotland especially after the failure of the Jacobite rebellion of 1745. But they were persistent, moving about at night, hiding in caves or forests by day. 'What disguises have I not worn, what arts have I not professed!' wrote the Jesuit John Innes. 'Now master, now servant, now musician, painter, clockmaker, physician.' In Ireland, where Catholics were banned from the towns, Jesuits contrived to keep a few cellar-schools going in Dublin.

The resilience and romanticism of the Jesuit missionary drive were stronger than ever. In a moment of anger Antonio Vieira remarked that 'the Dominicans live off the Faith while Jesuits die for it'; and the last part of that statement was justified when of twelve Jesuits who sailed

[187]

for China in 1673 only one reached his destination. Sickness took the others. There was a passionate refusal to accept the closing of Japan as final. The Duchess of Aveiro, a generous benefactress of Jesuit missions, shared this obsession. Raimundo Arxo, a Spanish Jesuit, wrote to her in 1684 that he was going to China 'with the firm resolve to enter Japan . . . If it should chance that I am not able to learn to speak Japanese well, I shall not hesitate, if my Superiors allow me, to enter pretending that I am deaf and dumb and using sign-language to beg for alms, dressed in beggar's rags, until I can make my way far inland where we know that there are many Christians who have no priest to administer the sacraments.' The Belgian François Noel regarded his work in Shanghai as a preparation for 'my most glorious and so ardently desired Japan', which he hoped to reach via Korea. Remembering the glories and the martyrdoms, many Jesuits in the Philippines were also haunted by this vision of Japan as a promised land.

The first considerable signs of Protestant missionary effort acted as a spur. The Quakers in Pennsylvania emulated the Jesuits' protective attitude towards the Indians, and welcomed Jesuit priests to minister to German Catholic immigrants. In Massachusetts the Presbyterian John Eliot, who had studied Jesuit methods, gathered his Iroquois converts into fourteen 'Praying Towns'. From Germany the sudden outthrust of Count Zinzendorf's Moravian Brethren took them to Greenland, Labrador, the Antilles, South Africa, and even to Mongolia. Their missionary compounds resembled Jesuit reductions and their organization was so tightly-knit that they were compared with the Jesuits as eroders of civil authority. From Germany,' too, as the Hispano-Portuguese veto on non-Iberian missionaries was reluctantly abandoned, came a rush of Jesuits – eight hundred of them between 1670 and 1770. In the Caribbean and throughout the Americas they became, with increased numbers of Dutch, Italians, Belgians and Irish, the mainstay of the missions.

In Canada the missions remained entirely French and mostly Jesuit, though Robert de la Salle preferred the services of French traders and, for spiritual purposes, Recollects, on his voyages of exploration. This strange, impetuous character had not only been educated by Jesuits at Rouen but for seven years had been a Jesuit. When released from his vows, apparently because of his rebellious temperament, he emigrated to Montreal, was given rights to the fur trade among the Illinois by Governor Frontenac, and in 1677 was granted a monopoly of trade in the Mississippi Valley. His conflict with the Jesuits, whom he already detested, developed into a near-vendetta. In 1673, with six companions, Fr Jacques Marquette had set out from the St Ignace mission opposite Mackinac to 'seek toward the South Sea new nations that are unknown to us'. Entering the Mississippi from the Wisconsin River, they paddled 1,700 miles down as far as Arkansas before turning back. Nine years later La Salle, accompanied by Recollects, completed the exploration of the Mississippi to the Gulf of Mexico, claiming for France 'possession of that river, of all the rivers that enter it, and of all the country watered by them', and naming the territory Louisiana in honour of Louis XIV. There is a story, which Francis Parkman believed to be well-founded, that Jesuits conspired to assassinate La Salle in 1687 after he had been appointed Governor of Louisiana.

By the 1720s the Jesuits in Louisiana, working among the Yazoos, the Arkansas and the Illinois, were embroiled with the Capuchins who ministered to the French settlers. When in 1763 the Jesuits were expelled, their property, including Negro slaves and herds of cattle, was seized and auctioned. At New Orleans ornaments and sacred vessels were handed over to the Capuchins and the church destroyed. Fr Philbert Watrin reported that 'the shelves of the altar had been thrown down and the linings of vestments given to negresses decried for their evil lives', while a large crucifix and some chandeliers reappeared in a brothel. At Fort Charles in Illinois a royal procurator took charge and demolished the chapels. Exiled Jesuits were given six months' subsistence allowance and told to apply to the Duc de Choiseul for pensions to be provided from the sale of their property.

Along the borders of New England Jesuit missionaries among the Mohawks and Abenaki were inevitably involved in Anglo-French frontier skirmishes. In the 1680s Thomas Dongan, the Catholic Governor of New York, planned to use English Jesuits among the Indians to counteract the influence of their French brethren. In 1699 Lord Bellomont, Dongan's successor, offered the Indians a cash reward 'for every Papist priest or Jesuit delivered up', and in 1724 Fr Sebastien Rasle, who for thirty years had worked among the Abenaki, was shot by English soldiers on the Kennebec River in central Maine. Yet the English conquest of New France saved the Jesuits from expulsion. They and the Recollects were allowed to remain but forbidden to recruit. Even *Dominus ac Redemptor* left them unscathed, since the news of it was given confidentially by the Bishop of Quebec and not published. A dwindling band laboured on. One, Sebastien Meurin of the Illinois mission, was appointed Vicar-General in the West. The last died in 1800.

[189]

The obituary of Jacques Marquette records that 'he always entreated God that he might end his life in these laborious missions, and that like his dear St Francis Xavier, he might die in the midst of the woods bereft of everything. Every day he interposed for that end both the merits of Jesus Christ and the intercession of the Virgin Immaculate, for whom he entertained a singular tenderness . . . He obtained that which he solicited with so much earnestness; since he had, like the apostle of the Indies, the happiness to die in a wretched cabin on the shore of Lake Illinois, forsaken by all the world.' Jesuit missionaries took seriously Jean Brébeuf's advice that among the Indians practical skills and the ability to rough it were as important as book learning. None more so than Eusebio Kühn, usually known as Kino, a Tyrolean trained in the province of Upper Germany who for twenty-five years before his death in 1711 lived the life of a Jesuit frontiersman. Covering huge distances on horseback he set off from the mission chain in the Sierra Madre to range along the California-Arizona frontier, preaching, baptizing, catechizing, helping to erect makeshift chapels. Most of the time he slept in a blanket on the ground; but he managed to keep a detailed journal, was an accomplished map-maker, pioneered cattle ranching, introduced European fruits and cereals, and confirmed that Lower California was a peninsula and not an island. Sixty years after Kino's death the German Jacob Baegert began his excellent account of the Lower California mission with the words: 'Everything about California is so unimportant that it is hardly worth troubling to write about it.' But a century later Robert Louis Stevenson contrasted the constructive, self-sacrificial work of Kino and his successors with the behaviour of 'greedy land-thieves and sacrilegious gunmen . . . so ugly a thing may our Anglo-Saxon Protestantism appear beside the doings of the Society of Jesus.'

Even more gruelling than Kino's travels were those of the Czech Jesuit Samuel Fritz, who spent thirty-seven years, until his death in 1725, evangelizing along the Marañon and the Amazon. He took as his parish virtually the entire basin occupied by the Amazon and its tributaries – an area almost as large as Europe containing about thirty thousand miles of navigable water. His first journey, made alone, involved crossing the Andes, then travelling on foot or by canoe for more than a thousand miles through jungle of oppressive heat, awesome silence, and sudden, terrifying noises. Other journeys were much longer. The several dozen villages that he and his helpers turned into Christian communities – teaching, working as architect, mason, sculptor and carpenter – were raided by the Portuguese and he himself, with many of his converts, taken prisoner. This was a constant danger at a time when the boundary between the eastern and western part of the Amazon basin was undefined. Illness was another hazard. Fritz, who mapped the whole length of the Amazon and some of its tributaries for the first time, left a graphic account of three months spent lying in a hut in a flooded village prostrate with fever and dropsy and attended only by a young Jurinagua boy: 'In the daytime I felt somewhat easier, but spent the nights in unutterable burnings, for the river, passing but a handsbreadth from the bed, was out of reach of my mouth; and there was sleeplessness, caused not only by my infirmities but by the grunting of the crocodiles which all night were roving round the village.' His food was snatched by rats, which gnawed his spoon and even the haft of his knife.

In Brazil the opposition of frustrated colonists made life hardly less precarious for Jesuit missionaries. Twice, in 1661 and 1684, they were expelled from the north-east territory of Amazonia (Maranhao-Para). The supply of African slaves had proved expensive and in 1686 all missionaries had to accept an arrangement which virtually made them into procurers and trainers of Amerindian labour. They were to persuade tribes in the interior (what remained of those nearer the coast having fled inland) that they would be well advised to live as 'rational beings' in mission villages sited near Portuguese settlements. After being brought down-river they were to be catholicized and tamed for two years. Then they were to be made available for employment by the whites on the condition, seldom observed, that they would not be enslaved, would be paid adequate and regular wages, and would be properly clothed and fed. Indians who refused this offer were to be forcibly settled in mission villages. By 1730, despite more smallpox epidemics, more than twenty thousand Indians were being 'prepared' in the Jesuit villages.

The allegation that missionaries, and especially Jesuits, were making vast profits out of their 'slaves' was ridiculous, since all the transit centres were expected to be self-sufficient: that being one of the great attractions of the 'co-operative' system. But though Jesuit reduction estates made little profit, they were run with impressive efficiency. Their Indian cowboys were famous for their skill; Jesuit-owned ships carried hides to Europe; oxen, steers and horses were exported to other parts of Brazil. Sugar was the main crop, but cotton, rice, maize, tobacco and coffee were grown on a substantial scale. The corporate pride and energy behind all these enterprises attracted little but envy and hatred. Nunes' slanders began to be listened to in Lisbon, and royal edicts reproved the Fathers for enslaving and exploiting the souls entrusted to their care. Franciscan missionaries were said to be 'using the Indians for their convenience . . . living abandoned to sensuality to the great discredit of their Order.' This was the one fault of which the Jesuits were seldom accused. But for all their zeal and competence they were trapped in a squalid situation. Distrusted by the colonists, they had lost face with the Indians, who could no longer see them as genuine protectors. Portuguese 'ransoming' expeditions were pressing further west, even raiding the Christian villages established by Samuel Fritz; and missionaries, including Jesuits, were forced to go along to see 'fair play'.

To the south, in Spanish territory, the republic of Paraguay was thriving and expanding. The Abipones, the Guaycuru and other tribes in the Chaco had been gradually reduced. In the 1740s two Spaniards, José Cardiel and José Quiroga, and an Englishman, Thomas Falkner, began to contact tribes south of Buenos Aires in Patagonia. 'At first,' says one account, 'before oxen were sent, the Fathers lived on horse flesh, the daily food of those Indians. Fr Falkner, who wandered all over those plains, having no plate of pewter or wood, made use of his hat, which at length grew so greasy that while he slept it was devoured by wild dogs with which the plains were overrun.' In the Guarani reductions conditions were idyllic. The German Jesuit Anton Sepp, who founded one of them in the 1690s, described rivers teeming with fish and plains full of wild cattle. 'In two months my villagers rounded up 50,000 head for the year's food supply. . . . These animals did not cost me a farthing, and what is true of my village is true of the others. Our three ships took 300,000 hides to Spain.' The land was divided into three categories: communal land on which the Indians worked for three days a week; plots of family land; and church land, worked by boys under fifteen out of school hours.

Now spread over a region almost as large as western Europe, the Jesuit empire possessed the finest ranches and plantations in South America, with a system of road and river communications more efficient than has been achieved since its demise. The streets of the townships were paved a century before those of Buenos Aires or Lima. Some of the churches were as big and splendid as any in Europe. San Miguel, designed by a former professor of architecture in Milan and built of square-cut stone blocks, was 220 feet long. A thousand Indian families worshipped under the vaulted timber roof of the church at La Cruz. The church at Itapua, with transepts and three naves, was 194 feet long and more than 100 feet wide, and the sculptured arches over its windows were decorated in gold and vivid colours.

26. Rubens' painting of a miracle attributed to St Ignatius is a masterpiece of Counter-Reformation religious art.

24 (*Above*) The Gesù, the mother church of the Society in Rome, opened in 15

25. (*Below*) Interior of the Gesù: a prototype of the Counter-Reformation
church, with uncluttered nave, side-chapels and focus on the high

24 (*Above*) The Gesù, the mother church of the Society in Rome, opened in 1571.

25. (*Below*) Interior of the Gesù: a prototype of the Counter-Reformation church, with uncluttered nave, side-chapels and focus on the high altar.

26. Rubens' painting of a miracle attributed to St Ignatius is a
masterpiece of Counter-Reformation religious art.

27. St Peter Claver (1580-1654), known as 'the slave of the slaves', with
convert in South America.

28. (*Inset*) St Isidore, patron of farmers. His statue was carried to the fields
        by the reduction Indians.

29. A church in a former Jesuit reduction (missionary settlement) in
        Paraguay.

Fr Sepp, a keen musician as well as a capable architect, trained his choristers and took pride in an orchestra of 'four trumpets, eight shawmplayers, four harpists, four organists and a lutist' which sometimes went to Buenos Aires to perform at church festivals. He also taught small girls to dance and supervised the smithy, brickyard, mill and bakery, the kitchen garden, the butchers, carpenters, painters, sculptors, tilers and turners. Boy servants attended the missionaries, reading passages from the scriptures in Latin and the lives of the saints in Spanish. 'Six boys who live in the house wait on table,' wrote Sepp, 'all barefoot and bare headed, very modestly, like novices. They eat when I have finished. I always give them a piece of white bread, which they appreciate more than anything else, and often a little honey and plenty of meat.'

Punishment was such as 'a father would use with the children he loves'. But the Fathers did not administer the caning, leaving that to 'the first Indian who comes to hand – he beats the delinquent just as a father spanks his son or a master his apprentice in Europe. Old and young are punished in this way, women too.' There was, however, no capital punishment, expulsion from the community being the ultimate, and much feared, deterrent. The Guaranis' very natural fear and hatred of the Portuguese was encouraged by a Jesuit iconography which, apart from images of Ignatius, Xavier, Aloysius Gonzaga and Stanislaus Kostka, approved of Indian carvings that showed the Archangel Michael treading down a bearded, satanic *bandeirante.* Guarani males competed for the honour of enlisting in the Jesuit militia, ready not only to repel attacks from hostile Indians but, when requested by the Governors of Asuncion or Buenos Aires (which in the early eighteenth century had a population of only four thousand), to fight against Portuguese raiders or quell settler revolts.

The Reduction Cavalry, carrying firearms, was considered a crack formation. The infantry relied mainly on spears, clubs and slings, with a few sabres and muskets. The artillery consisted of stone mortars and perhaps a cannon. Each town mustered a regiment of about six companies of sixty men, a colonel, six captains, six lieutenants and a general officer. Fr Martin Dobrizhoffer recorded that 'on the point of death a Guarani captain puts on his boots and spurs, takes hold of his staff, and awaits the priest. "This," he says, "is the way for a captain to die."' Instruction was given by Spanish officers, manoeuvres (including naval exercises) being held on Sundays after vespers, with target practice and perhaps a mock battle. Uniforms were in French military style: an ostrich feather adorned the dragoons' caps, which bore the name of

Jesus in front and the emblem of a skull at the back. From the Mojos reductions, established by Jesuits from Peru, through the Chiquitos settlements fringing the Matto Grosso, on down to the Guarani towns, the Jesuit regiments held the frontier for Spain.

The work of Jesuit doctors and infirmarians who studied the herbal medicines of the Indians attracted the attention of the Royal Society, which in 1730 sent young Thomas Falkner, who had studied under Isaac Newton, to report on the medicinal properties of South American plants. Frequent consultations with the Jesuits resulted in his conversion and the Society gained another useful recruit. Herbal medicine was adequate in the treatment of local illnesses and for staunching wounds but powerless against smallpox. 'The pustules invade the whole body, burning the intestines. Thence comes the continuous flux of blood,' wrote Fr Sepp after one epidemic. 'It strikes even unborn children, expelling them with cruel anticipation from the womb . . . There were not enough of the living to dig graves . . .' Mass blood-letting was tried: 'My musicians and smiths opened the veins, or rather pricked the skin with knives or nails for lack of proper instruments. It was a horrible sight to see the streets reddened with spilled blood.'

In vain, too, did the Jesuits try to dispel rumours that their military strength was a sign of imperial ambition, that armed 'savages' might cut loose and massacre the colonists, that the main purpose of Jesuit armouries was not to protect Indians but to guard fabulous hoards of treasure. The fact was that by the 1740s Jesuit Provincials were protesting at the burden of military commitments as Portuguese raids became more frequent. So many Fathers were occupied with full-time organization that plans to open more reductions in the Chaco had to be postponed. The Indians themselves were beginning to grumble at long campaigns which kept them away from their families for months. Tax exemptions did not compensate for the disruption of industrial and religious routine, and when conscription for all able-bodied men was introduced the fears and rumours grew, sharpened by xenophobic resentment of non-Spanish Jesuits.

Incessant friction led to a resolve to end the frontier disputes. This in turn caused an Indian revolt which strained and split Jesuit loyalties. The Treaty of Madrid, concluded in 1750, was a belated recognition of the changes that had taken place in South America in the two and a half centuries since Pope Alexander VI had divided the New World between Spain and Portugal. It was based on actual control of disputed territory, except for one major item. The colony of Sacramento, a base for illegal

Anglo-Portuguese trade which had been used for attacks on Buenos Aires, was to be handed over to the Spaniards in return for the land occupied by seven Jesuit towns east of the River Uruguay in the fertile, cattle-rich region described by Fr Sepp. Along the Amazon, too, some lands were transferred from Spain to Portugal. In both areas the Jesuits were accused of obstructing commissioners, who travelled slowly north across the pampas erecting markers and haranguing the Indians. But in the seven towns, with a population of nearly thirty thousand Guarani, there was a spontaneous rebellion which the Fathers, despite frantic messages from Generals Frantisek Retz and Ignazio Visconti, could not control. The attitude of Luis Altamirano, a smooth courtier Jesuit who was sent out as Visitor Plenipotentiary in 1752 and treated the harassed missionaries as contumacious rebels, was no help at all in a tragic dilemma fraught with agonizing crises of conscience; and the whole sorry episode glaringly exposed the weakness of over-centralized Jesuit government in an age of poor communications.

While Portuguese settlers who left their homes in Sacramento were offered compensation, the Guarani were to be summarily evicted from their ancestral lands, taking only movable possessions and abandoning the plantations and towns which their labour had created to the Portuguese they had been taught to hate. Yet they were the most exemplary products of the civilizing missions, loyal, pious and industrious. Their military services had been rewarded with special charters and letters of gratitude. Small wonder that they knocked over markers, refused to move, and ignored appeals from the detested Altamirano and their own distracted Fathers. In 1754 they defeated a joint Spanish-Portuguese military force, and not until June 1756 did a second full-scale campaign end their resistance.

In *Candide*, which satirizes the split in Jesuit loyalties caused by the Indian revolt, the hero sails to Paraguay to fight against the Jesuits, but is persuaded by his servant Cacambo to fight with them instead: 'It is a wonderful system they have,' says Cacambo. 'The reverend fathers own everything, the Indians nothing – a masterpiece of reason and justice. I don't think I have ever seen such godlike creatures. They fight the kings of Spain and Portugal over here and give them absolution in Europe. In this country they kill Spaniards and in Madrid they send them to heaven.' After some delay a German Jesuit colonel receives Candide and provides lavish hospitality – 'an excellent dinner was served on gold plates, and while the Paraguayans ate their maize on wooden dishes in the open field in the full blaze of the sun, his reverence the Colonel retired to the shade of his arbour.' This passage encapsulates most of the current fantasies about the Jesuit empire and the missionaries' role in the Guarani War. And General Retz, equally ignorant of Paraguayan realities, suggested that if the Guarani could not be moved before the boundary commissioners arrived it might be possible to arrange for them to stay as Portuguese subjects. He insisted that only prompt obedience would prevent further rumours of secret riches and imperialist ambition which would rebound on the Society as a whole: and indeed reports from officers of the victorious military expedition described Jesuit overseers as 'living like lords' while Indian dwellings were 'worse than negro slaves' quarters . . . It is the height of poverty and slavery . . . the Indians are flogged with metal-pointed whips which cut to the bone.' In fact the humanity of the Jesuit régime was its real offence; and the living conditions of reduction Indians, vastly superior to those of many, if not most, European colonists, were an added provocation.

Missionaries along the Amazon – Carmelites and Mercedarians as well as Jesuits – were accused by Pombal's stepbrother, Governor Mendonça Furtado, of greed, brutality, virtual enslavement of Indians, forced marriages, and violent disruption of native customs. This indictment was the exact opposite of the criticisms made of Jesuit pliability in China. In 1755 the Jesuits were deprived of temporal authority over the Indians, two years later the deportation of missionaries from the Amazonas region in northern Brazil was begun and by 1759 the entire region had been secularized.

Some Paraguayan Jesuits, disgusted by the cowardice of Rome, deeply attached to their missions, and angered by rumours spread among the Guarani that they had sold out to Portugal, did oppose the boundary treaty. A few may have encouraged rebellion, some accompanied the rebels as chaplains or physicians. But Pombal, infuriated by the heavy expense of the Guarani campaigns, which coincided with the herculean task of rebuilding Lisbon after the earthquake, chose to make them collectively responsible. Pamphlets, and even an epic poem, showed the Portuguese as anti-racist liberators, the Jesuits as avaricious hypocrites, the Indians as innocent pawns, and rejoiced in 'the fall of the infamous republic'. The edicts of 1759 proscribing and expelling the Jesuits hysterically denounced them as 'corrupted and manifestly unsuitable because of their many, abominable and incorrigible vices . . . They have clandestinely attempted to usurp the entire state of Brazil . . . Notorious rebels and traitors . . . they are to be driven from my kingdom and Dominions, never to return.'

About six hundred Jesuits were removed from missions and schools throughout Brazil, victims of the first, strident anti-clerical offensive of the age of enlightened despotism. Putting into practice the Indian-protecting solution advocated by Fr Vieira a century earlier, Pombal speeded the importation of African slaves: in one year alone twenty-five thousand were unloaded in northern Brazil. Ironically, though blaming the Jesuits for the rebellion against the Treaty of Madrid, Pombal welcomed its annulment by the Treaty of Pardo in 1761. The Jesuits and Guarani returned to put the seven towns in order (vandalized and overgrown, they were full of jaguar dens). The Jesuit militia went into action against the Portuguese, driving them from positions which they had seized along the coast, and were congratulated by the Viceroy of Peru and the Governor of Buenos Aires.

More Jesuit missionaries were sent to Paraguay, some even as late as 1767, when the Spanish expulsion decree reached Buenos Aires. Though there was some scattered Indian resistance further north the Fathers, determined to do nothing that might provoke another and even more disastrous conflict, surrendered immediately to the officers who, with fifteen hundred troops, brought the news to the thirty Guarani reductions. The first shipload of Jesuits sailed from Buenos Aires in September 1767. Within a year some two thousand had been cleared out of the Spanish colonies in South America and Mexico. Some aged missionaries perished on the way to their ports of embarkation. Ignacio Chomé, the greatest living authority on the languages of the Chiquitos, had to be carried over the Andes in a hammock, and all his manuscripts were lost. Fr Martin Schmid, a seventy-three-year-old Swiss architect, survived a five-month trek to Panama, unlike eleven of his companions.

This operation, carried out with almost manic resolve, was dramatically abrupt, though there had been no lack of danger signals. In the Far East the Jesuit collapse had seemed inevitable for at least fifty years and was only postponed by a continuous rearguard action. On both sides of the accommodation debate feelings ran so high and pens so fast that in France alone more than two hundred books on the Chinese rites appeared in forty years. In India the quarrel between Lisbon and Rome was temporarily composed when it came to condemning the practices of de Nobili and his successors, French (Venance Bouchet) and Portuguese (João de Brito). Mgr Carlo Maillard de Tournon, appointed Apostolic Visitor for 'the East Indies, the Chinese Empire, and neighbouring Islands and Kingdoms', arrived at Pondicherry in 1703 already well-primed with objections by the Capuchins. Before leaving for China he

[197]

issued an edict, in terms suggested by the authorities at Goa, listing sixteen points which had to be observed under pain of censure. One alone, the insistence on using saliva and breathing on a convert at baptism, spelled ruin to the de Nobili experiment. Envoys shuttled to and from Rome. Luigi Lucino, a Dominican, argued that distaste for the use of saliva was clearly heretical since Calvin had considered it dirty and stupid. Antonio Brandolini, a Jesuit, pleaded that such reasoning took no account of complex realities in an ancient civilization. The fact was, he explained, that Hindus abhorred being daubed with spittle just as Europeans were repelled by the cult of cow-dung.

As tactfully as possible, the Jesuits were accusing their opponents of intellectual poverty and cultural illiteracy; while they, in a familiar gambit, preened themselves on their humble, orthodox ignorance in the matter of what had become known as 'the Malabar rites'. With some waverings and qualifications, the popes supported de Tournon and the europeanizers; and Benedict XIV's bull of 1744 *Omnium sollicitudinum,* though granting a ten-year period of grace on saliva and insufflation and overlooking the Brahman Christians' retention of the sacred cord and the tuft of hair, insisted that social distinctions so repugnant to Gospel charity must eventually be abandoned. Even before this decision, General Retz had been busy urging obedience and suggesting the formation of a special squad of 'pariah' Jesuits. This had barely got into its stride before the expulsions and the suppression ended the argument, and Pombal launched an attack on the ecclesiastical colour bar, recalling obstructive prelates and officials and instructing the new Viceroy to 'arrange matters so that the ownership of cultivated lands, the ministries of the parishes and missions, the exercise of public offices, and even military posts, should be given for the most part to natives of the soil irrespective of the colour of their skins.' Pombal's pressure did more to improve the status and prospects of the Indian clergy than any other single factor except perhaps the departure of the Jesuits, which, together with a sharp decrease in vocations from Europe, left a big gap to be filled.

In China, whatever progress had been made was entirely due to the much-reviled 'mandarin' or court Jesuits, who from 1688 were dominated by French scientist-missionaries. In 1689 Jesuit interpreters were active in negotiations which resulted in a Russo-Chinese peace pact, the first treaty made by China with a European power. Three years later the Emperor K'ang-hsi issued an edict granting freedom to preach and proselytize throughout his realms, a concession won by Jesuit diplomacy but exploited not only by Jesuits, of whom there were fifty-nine, but by twenty-nine Franciscans, eight Dominicans, six Augustinians, and fifteen secular priests, mostly from the Paris Foreign Missionary Society. By 1700 there were some three hundred thousand Chinese Christians, the great majority of them from the non-mandarin classes, a few Chinese priests, and ambitious plans for a network of bishoprics and vicariates. The obvious, simple strategy was to leave the Emperors in the capable hands of Jesuit astronomers and sinologists and use the opportunities which their influence alone created. But there was nothing simple or obvious in the situation. It was a Chinese box of contentions.

Navarrete's attack on Jesuit acculturation was continued by the priests of the Paris Foreign Mission. In 1693, shortly after the imperial edict opening the way to unobstructed evangelism, one of them, Charles Maigrot, Vicar Apostolic of Fukien, forbade the veneration of ancestors and of Confucius and criticized the Jesuits' choice of Chinese words for 'God'. For seven years Maigrot's evidence and that supplied by the Jesuits, including the Emperor's written assurance that the Confucian-ancestral ceremonies were civic, were considered in Rome. The verdict, announced in 1704, was in favour of Maigrot, who pointed out that though the rites might be purely civic among the intelligentsia they were permeated with superstition among the masses. De Tournon and the Vicars Apostolic were instructed to publish and enforce a decision which, as in India, rejected the possibility of an apostolate tailored to differing social strata. And the message was underlined by cartoons showing silk-clad Jesuit mandarins contemptuously surveying the activities of humble Christian missionaries.

This crude dichotomy ignored the Catholic chaos that was building up in China. The dioceses of Macao, Peking and Nanking were subject to the jurisdiction of Goa and the Padroado, a combination which resented the intrusion of Vicars Apostolic and Propaganda missionaries. Jesuit unity was fragile. The French contingent operated almost as a separate unit. The Portuguese, now heavily outnumbered, resented the successes of their French, German, Belgian, and Italian brethren. Jesuit missionaries in the provinces could be as scornful as the friars of the 'sybarites' in Peking. The mandarin Jesuits themselves were at loggerheads. Most favoured the scientific approach at court, but there were differences of opinion about doctrinal pliability. Some disapproved entirely; some were in favour up to a point; others, mainly French, alarmed their colleagues with theories that the Chinese classics showed many traces of Judaic origins, including some parallels with the Old and the New Testaments, an account of the Fall and the Redemption, and, if one looked closely enough, a hint of the Immaculate Conception. On the question of the rites and the Padroado allegiances were bewilderingly divided. Portuguese and Italian Jesuits usually supported both the claims of the Padroado and the Riccian interpretation of the rites. French Jesuits tolerated the rites but opposed the Padroado. Spanish Dominicans and Propaganda missionaries opposed both the rites and the Padroado. The Franciscans sometimes accepted the rites but, unless they were Portuguese, rejected the Padroado.

Faced with these permutations, de Tournon clung to the childish simplicity of his papal brief. K'ang-hsi warned him that he would not tolerate interference with venerable customs. Two Jesuit envoys were drowned in a shipwreck on their way to Rome to protest against the legate's actions: and de Tournon himself died in Macao, where he had been detained by the Emperor's order as a disturber of the peace. Clement XI supported de Tournon, and General Tamburini assured him that everything possible would be done to enforce obedience: 'If there should be any of Ours who should be of other sentiments – for where there are so many subjects human diligence cannot altogether prevent such a contingency – the general declares that the Society will hold him for degenerate and no child of hers; and to the extent of her power will ever restrain, repress and crush him.' Though the Portuguese Crown, fearful for the safety of Macao, urged the Pope to retract his condemnation of the rites, and though all missionaries who would not sign an imperial edict guaranteeing to abide by the rules laid down by Matteo Ricci had been banished, another papal legate, Mgr Carlo Mezzabarba, arrived at Peking in 1720 to promulgate a sharply-worded anti-accommodationist brief.

After reading a translation of it the Emperor remarked that 'these Europeans are small-minded people. Much of what they say makes one laugh... The papal legate is like an ignorant Buddhist or Taoist priest... Hereafter preaching by Europeans must be prohibited in order to avoid trouble.' Shaken by this threat and by Jesuit remonstrances Mezzabarba authorized some concessions. But these were repudiated in Rome, the agitation against the Society's disobedience reached a crescendo, and in 1742 Benedict XIV finally rejected the Riccian rites in the bull *Ex quo singulari,* to which all missionaries were required to swear obedience. Persecution was intermittent, and some missionaries in the provinces continued with a semi-clandestine apostolate. But the affront to racial pride caused Chinese Christians to leave the Church in droves.

[200]

The court Jesuits lingered on until after the suppression of the Society (the last one, Louis Poirot, died in 1814), reaching a zenith of cultural prestige. Fr du Halde's encyclopaedic *Description de l'empire de la Chine* (1735) and the *Lettres édifiantes et curieuses* (1702 to 1776) influenced Leibnitz, Voltaire, Montesquieu and Gibbon. Fr Ignaz Kögler was appointed President of the Tribunal of Astronomy. Two French Jesuits taught Latin at a school for diplomatic interpreters, six others were commissioned to make a map of China, Manchuria and Mongolia. Jesuit savants corresponded with the Royal Society and with the Academies of Science in Paris and St Petersburg. Fr Antoine Gaubil sent books, astronomical observations and botanical specimens to London, where his papers were published in *Philosophical Transactions*, receiving scientific works and two barrels of sherry in return. The Milanese Fr Castiglione (known as Lang Shih-ning), a master of the Chinese style, was the most celebrated of a number of court painters. At the command of Ch'ien-lung Jesuit architects and engineers constructed a group of white marble buildings in the grounds of the imperial palace of Yuan Ming Yuan. Surrounded with fountains and a symmetrical profusion of elaborately clipped trees, the result was a variation in miniature on the theme of Versailles.

In 1860 it was looted and destroyed by a British expeditionary force. Twenty-five years earlier a Vincentian missionary had discovered a defiant Latin epitaph on the wall of a house near Peking: 'In the Name of Jesus, Amen. Long unshaken but overcome at last by so many storms, it has fallen. Traveller, stop and read. Reflect for a few moments on the inconstancy of things human. Here lie the French missionaries of that very renowned Society which taught in all its purity the worship of the true God; which for two centuries and more gave to the Church martyrs and confessors. I, Joseph-Marie Amiot, and the other French missionaries of the same Society, under the patronage of the Tartar-Chinese monarch and with the support of the arts and sciences which we practice, still forward the divine cause. While in the imperial palace itself, amid altars of false gods, our French Church shines with a true magnificence, we, secretly grieving even to the last of our days, have erected here amid burial groves this monument of our fraternal affection . . . In the year of Christ 1774, on the fourteenth day of October, in the twentieth year of Ch'ien Lung, the tenth day of the ninth moon.'

CHAPTER SIXTEEN

Suspended Animation

VOLTAIRE SAW THE apparent extinction of the Society as perhaps the most momentous event of the eighteenth century. 'Once we have destroyed the Jesuits,' he wrote, 'we shall have easy work with the Pope.' The formidable Jesuit mind-moulding machine had been dismantled, and a palace revolution had replaced Jesuit confessors with apostles of enlightenment. *The Church and the Legitimate Power of the Roman Pontiff* by Justinus Febronius (the pseudonym of Nicholas von Hontheim, a prelate who had studied under the Jesuits at the German College) became the bible of a new breed of Catholic reformers. The bishops, as delegates of the community, were classified as the real source of spiritual authority; princes had the right to reform national Churches and to defend them against papal interference; the pope, though he might be accorded a primacy of honour, was to be essentially a master of ceremonies; and the eradication of papal abuses was seen as the best way of persuading Protestants back into the fold.

In Austria the 'Febronian' Emperor Joseph II suppressed hundreds of monasteries, opened state-controlled seminaries, revised the liturgy, launched a campaign against superstition, and snubbed Pope Pius VI, who travelled to Austria to plead for mercy. In Tuscany Joseph II's brother, the Grand Duke Leopold, proceeded along similar lines. His state Church, with the Bishop of Pistoia, Scipio Ricci (a nephew of the deposed Jesuit General) as spiritual head, was provided with a vernacular liturgy and a mass of pedantic rules and regulations. Mariolatry was condemned, the display of the Blessed Virgin's girdle and other relics forbidden, and the police ordered to enforce the new religious code.

There were, however, signs that disinfected Catholicism did not have a wide appeal. In Belgium the Archbishop of Malines' resistance was backed by a near-insurrection. In Florence the attack on traditional Marian superstitions caused popular riots. In Madrid demonstrators called for a return of the Jesuits. The masses did not take kindly to enlightened despotism, with its patronizing social engineer's logic. To them a rationalist millennium was anathema and deism repellent. Their sentiments were cynically summed up by the French revolutionary leaders Carnot and Barras, who after the failure of Robespierre's cult of the Supreme Being remarked that anyone who wanted to launch a new creed should first get himself crucified, for absurdity and unintelligibility were the two prime ingredients of a successful religion, and Christianity had them both. In 1797 Rivarol's *Discours sur l'homme intellectuel et moral* made the point that 'the radical defect of philosophy is that it cannot speak to the heart. Even if we consider religions as nothing more than organized superstitions they would still be beneficial to the human race.' All through the eighteenth century Marian devotions and the cult of the Sacred Heart gained ground.

Voltaire overestimated the effect of *Dominus ac Redemptor* and underestimated the extent to which he himself, educated at a showpiece college, had been influenced by the Jesuit double standard – a fair dose of sophistication for the élite, a less exotic curriculum for run-of-the-mill pupils in their many 'scratch' schools. This was precisely what Voltaire advocated, except that he would have reduced the number of schools and would not have taught the classics to the non-élite. He deplored Baron d'Holbach's atheist propaganda, since in his view a God of vengeance should not be *publicly* eliminated ('if the cook does not do his duty the whole structure of society trembles'), despised Rousseau's sentimentalism about human nature, and would certainly have loathed the anarchic free-for-all of the French Revolution.

But how far can 'the revolution' be regarded as a direct result of the dissolution of the Society in France? Some, mainly Jesuit, historians imply that forty thousand students were turned adrift and exposed to 'godless' influences after 'practically the last barrier to the forward march of revolutionary ideas affecting both the philosophy and content of education' had been wrecked. They also point out that the school-leavers of 1764 to 1770 who reached maturity in 1793 'had not had the hand of the Jesuits upon them', and that Desmoulins, Robespierre and Saint-Just had been educated in the progressive de-Jesuitized Lycée Louis-le-Grand. Hence, it is argued, 'important sections of the rising generation either had no education at all or received it from institutions whose academic atmosphere was saturated with the doctrines of naturalism, humanitarianism, anti-Christianism, and a philosophism obstructive of all authority.' Yet a fair number of Jesuit schools were kept open or reopened, staffed mainly by ex-Jesuits who had not turned into *philosophes* overnight. The secular priesthood was presumably strengthened by an influx of ex-Jesuits. Queen Marie Antoinette chose two Polish ex-Jesuits as her confessors. There was no concerted effort to impose a deist, let alone atheist, norm in schools. 'Progressive' teachers were in very short supply; and the Oratorians, Benedictines, Brothers of the Christian Schools, and other orders continued to provide non-infidel alternatives for displaced scholars. The linking of the Revolution with the Society's suppression would seem to be a myth concocted by Jesuits to justify the restoration of the Society in the eyes of those who sought to restore the monarchy.

In Austria and the Austrian Netherlands ex-Jesuits functioned as priests or teachers. In Spain, to which hundreds of Jesuits had returned even before the suppression after being released from their vows, many resumed teaching in a country where francophile ministers were still struggling to break the hold of the Inquisition (Pablo de Olavide, the author of a sweeping plan for educational reform, was charged with heresy and atheism and sentenced to be confined in a monastery for eight years). In Brazil the educational impact of the Jesuit withdrawal was disastrous, since there were comparatively few priests of other orders to take over. In Spanish America, where there was a Jesuit school in nearly every town of any size, teachers had sometimes been less inhibited than their brethren in Spain, to the extent of admitting Descartes and Leibnitz to the curriculum. But there had been no significant departure from the *Ratio Studiorum*. A gradual modernization of the universities did not begin until after the Jesuits had left; and the mendicants, particularly the Dominicans, who were far more numerous than in Brazil, filled most of the gaps.

More important perhaps than the problems caused by their removal from the classrooms of Latin America was the Jesuits' part in exile as historians and, in a sense, literary nationalists. Many wrote with passion of the countries they had been forced to leave. Francisco Javier Clavijero compiled a history of Mexico which some twentieth-century Mexican writers have seen as 'helping to establish the ideological basis for our emancipation'. Rafael Landivar, formerly Rector of the seminary of San Francisco Borgia in Guatemala City, became a parish priest in Bologna, where he wrote an epic poem in Latin, *Rusticatio Mexicana* (Mexican Country Scenes).* José Cardiel, who had served in Paraguay, founded the first Jesuit missions in Patagonia and been disciplined for his

*Landivar, whose remains were in 1950 moved from Bologna to a grandiose tomb in Antigua, the ancient capital, is rated as a national hero and poet laureate in Guatemala. It is said that taxi-drivers can quote from his epic – in its Spanish version.

outspoken criticism of the Treaty of Madrid, published a detailed account of the Guarani reductions, illustrated with some excellent maps.

Every Spanish colony had its Jesuit chronicler. Their enthusiasm was such that they were suspected of plotting with the enemies of Spain. Salvador de Madariaga thought it 'a curious coincidence that as a result of the well-meant but mistaken endeavours of a group of enlightened despots, the Jesuits were driven to co-operate with the other two international brotherhoods, the Freemasons and the Jews, in the destruction of the Spanish Empire.' In fact, though Jesuit historians helped to crystallize patriotic sentiment in the colonies of which they wrote so lovingly, only two are known to have been active conspirators in the movement for independence: the Chilean Juan José Godoy and the Peruvian Pablo Viscardo. The wars which from 1810 to 1825 had freed all but Cuba and Puerto Rico from Spanish rule owed far more to the open incitement of the Latin American clergy.

The withdrawal from the missions left a huge vacuum, especially in Latin America and in the Philippines. Brazilian mission villages were placed under the authority of lay directors. These were instructed to act with kindness in their work of civilization (which included encouraging mixed marriages). But the liberal tone of the edict was belied by the actual working of the system. The directors, entitled to a percentage of everything grown or gathered by their subjects, were expected to see that all males between the ages of thirteen and sixty worked for the settlers or on public works for the Crown.

In Spanish America Dominicans and Franciscans did their best to cope by reinforcing and redeploying personnel. But in China, where the Jesuit contribution was so distinctive, its extinction has been seen as a tragic event with enormous implications. The English Catholic writer and politician Christopher Hollis, for instance, reflected that Ricci's approach might not have been successful but that it did suggest 'the possibility that the expansion of Europe might have been a real expansion of Christendom. With the Jesuits hampered and eventually suppressed it was inevitable that the non-European world should look upon the European as his enemy and that instead of the brotherhood of man we should have the racial conflict by which our whole existence is threatened . . . a conflict which is as much the consequence of the suppression of the Jesuits as of any other single factor.' Yet while admiring the ingenuity, patience and scholarship of Ricci and de Nobili it is hard to see their essay as more than a brilliant tour de force with little chance of achieving any real meeting of minds. At Peking the

Jesuits introduced the technique of three-dimensional painting, but they could not put across a vulgar three-dimensional religion. Their internal bickerings shattered the image of quasi-oriental serenity so painfully contrived by Matteo Ricci, while the fact that Louis XIV and other royal backers saw their Jesuits as political and commercial agents did not escape attention and did not appeal to the Vatican.

At its peak the number of Chinese Christians was a minute fraction of the population, and, as Voltaire suspected, the persistence of the Confucian cult indicated not that the rites were purely civic but that they were perfectly adequate. Men like Ricci, Schall, du Halde and Gaubil must genuinely have loved the Chinese and their culture: and perhaps sometimes, like the South Sea Island missionary in Sylvia Townsend Warner's novel *Mr Fortune's Maggot*, they lamented that 'because of our wills we can never love anything without messing it about'. Surely some Jesuits longed to write the sort of letter which the central character, the Rev. Timothy Fortune, sent to his superior ('Dear Archdeacon: My ministry here has been a failure. I have converted no one, moreover I think that they are best as they are')? Perhaps some of them did, and their letters are buried somewhere in the massive archives of the Society. But probably they never went much beyond sighing over the exotic drudgery they suffered, in the name of Jesus, as representatives of European technology.

It was precisely as an admirable experiment in social engineering that the French enlighteners, magnanimous to a defeated opponent, praised the Jesuit republic in Paraguay. Making amends for the cynicism of *Candide,* Voltaire, in his *Essay on Customs* of 1771, described the republic as a system of truly benevolent despotism that went far to expiate the sins of the conquistadores. D'Alembert praised 'a monarchical authority founded solely on powers of persuasion'. Montesquieu, who thought that Jesuits had performed something of a miracle by making the Indians happy *and* making them work, concluded that 'the Society of Jesus may pride itself on the fact that it was the first to prove to the world that religion and humanity are compatible.' The Abbé Raynal commended his former brethren for raising the Guarani to 'a degree of civilization perhaps as high as a young people could reach and certainly far superior to anything achieved in the rest of the new hemisphere. The laws were respected, morals were pure, a happy brotherhood united every heart, all the useful arts were in a flourishing state, and even some of the more agreeable sciences; plenty was universal . . . a triumph of humanity.'

Among the Amerindians the Jesuits had been held in greater respect, even affection, than any other group of missionaries. When they were arrested and deported Indians tried to release them by breaking into the barracks where they were held, and substantial military detachments were needed to escort the Fathers to their ports of embarkation. The awe transferred from the shamans to their priestly successors was so strong that Charles III of Spain was warned not to weaken it ('the best way to quell unrest is to station a friar with a crucifix in the nearest plaza'). The Jesuits had spread this awe deep into the interior. Yet their going was often welcomed by rival orders which had not ceased to regard them as intruders; and fifty years after the expulsion the chapters on the Guarani missions in Robert Southey's *History of Brazil* set the pattern for many subsequent accounts: 'Equal care,' he wrote, 'was taken to employ and to amuse the people; and for the latter purpose a religion which consisted so much of externals afforded excellent means . . . Never was there a more absolute despotism; but never has there existed any other society in which the welfare of the subjects, temporal and eternal, has been the sole object of government; the governors, indeed, erred grossly in their standard of both; but erroneous as they were, the sanctity of the end proposed, and the heroism and persever-ance with which it was pursued, deserve the highest admiration.'

'But,' he continues, 'if the Jesuits were placed in circumstances where even their superstition tended to purify and exalt the character, it was far otherwise with the Indians; they were kept in a state of moral inferiority. Whatever could make them good servants and render them happy in servitude was carefully taught them, but nothing which could tend to political and intellectual emancipation. The enemies of the Company were thus provided with fair cause of accusation . . . If the system were to lead to nothing better, then had the Jesuits been labour-ing for no other end than to form an empire for themselves. In vain did the Jesuits reply that these Indians were only fully-grown children and that they knew not whether their obtuseness of intellect were a defect inherent in the race or the consequence of savage life . . . They dared not insist upon the first alternative, which would have been admitting all that the *encomenderos* and slave-dealers desired; but if there were no original and radical inferiority in the race, then was the fault in that system upon which the Reductions were established.' Southey concludes that despite its tendency to arrest development the Jesuit system was justified because of the far greater evils 'of the surrounding society into which it was proposed that these Indians should be incorporated'.

[207]

The Brazilian sociologist Gilberto Freyre considered Jesuit influence 'quite as harmful as that of the colonists who, moved by economic interests or pure sensuality, saw in the Indian only a voluptuous female to be taken or a rebellious slave to be subjugated and exploited.' Though inclined to see all missionaries as a menace, the Scottish writer R. B. Cunninghame Graham, who knew his subject well, felt that the Jesuits were at least courageous and more sincere than most. He was also one of the first writers to throw doubts on the widely-held assumption that when the Jesuits had left the reductions were immediately abandoned by the Indians, who fled into the forests. In the 1870s he had 'often met in the deserted missions men who spoke regretfully of the Jesuit times, who cherished all the customs left by the Company, and though they spoke at second hand, repeating the stories they had heard in youth, kept the illusion that the missions under the Jesuits had been a paradise.'

What caused the Indians to migrate was the incompetence of the new Spanish régime, in which authority was shared between priests and lay directors: an arrangement that, as in Brazil, led to bickering, break-down, and pillaging by colonists. Grandiose plans for an Indian university came to nothing, taxes were increased, the workshops languished. Many Guarani craftsmen found jobs in Buenos Aires, Montevideo and Santa Fe. Others, crossing into Portuguese territory – where such excellent soldiers and well-trained workers were very welcome – settled in a town specially constructed for them on the Jesuit pattern. Philip Caraman, the most recent Jesuit historian of Paraguay, states that as late as 1818 some Indians 'made a foundation of their own where they tried to keep their faith pure. Their sacristan and cacique acted as priests and their old folk remembered the Guarani prayers taught them by the Jesuits.'

The reductions were finally ruined by the colonial wars of independence and the interminable wars between the successor states. In the 1830s some were still functioning, though in melancholy decay, as W. P. Robertson, a Scottish traveller, reported after visiting Candelaria, whose former population of more than three thousand had dwindled to about seven hundred. 'The church was in a state of dilapidation; the rain pouring in through many apertures of the roof . . . the school was pretty much in the same state . . . Every fruit tree had been hewn down for firewood. Of the original huts and cottages scarcely a third were standing.' The balsa rafts which had once carried Indians across the Paraná to work had been destroyed, and 'it was with difficulty that the two *curas* [priests] could scrape together enough from the labour of the whole community scantily to feed and clothe the members of it.'

The last traces of the Guarani republic were obliterated during the six-year war from 1864 to 1870 between Paraguay and the combined forces of Brazil, Uruguay and Argentina, but the remote Chiquitos towns in tropical forests towards the Mato Grosso escaped destruction. Caraman points out that 'entire regions marked blank on the modern map, two hundred years ago formed part of the Jesuit Republic where travellers could go without fear and at each stage of their journey find peaceful villages policed by Indian officers. The Upper Amazon, the Chaco, the tropical forest of eastern Bolivia, today for the most part *terrae incognitae,* were then populous territories.' He also argues that the Jesuits created a Guarani culture and sense of nationhood by fashioning a sort of lingua franca from a multitude of dialects, and preserved it by publishing grammars, dictionaries and treatises on animal husbandry and pharmacy as well as books of devotion. But in South America as in all the mission lands the great weakness was that they had remained mission lands, with no, or few, native priests, let alone hierarchies. The hopes of Valignano, de Nobili and de Rhodes had been frustrated by Rome, by racial prejudice, by a certain lack of courage and conviction.

While the communities upon which they had lavished so much thought and care gradually declined, those missionaries who survived the forced marches and the long, crowded ordeal of rat-infested ships settled in the 'Paraguayan' colony in the small town of Faenza – the arrival in Italy within a decade of three waves of displaced Jesuits was said to be the largest influx of learned refugees since the fall of Constantinople. Clement XIV died in September 1774, according to some poisoned by the Jesuits, according to others the victim of a guilty conscience that drove him to pace his apartments at night crying 'Mercy! Mercy! They forced me to do it!' A year later General Ricci, having been interrogated to the point of exhaustion about allegedly hidden Jesuit riches, died in prison.

Through all the controversy the exiled Jesuits worked on at their memoirs, histories and maps. Literary feuds were not uncommon, as when Girolamo Tiraboschi was fiercely attacked for suggesting, in his vast survey of Italian literature, that Spanish influences had corrupted taste. Fr Boscovich, that versatile genius, was much in demand, binding the dome of St Peter's with iron bands when it started to crack, drafting a plan to drain the Pontine Marshes, acting as director of optics to the French Navy, publishing five more books, and retiring to a monastery at

[209]

the age of eighty-six. Some Fathers busied themselves with anti-Febronian polemics. Jesuit engineers went to Austria, Prussia and Portugal to build roads and bridges, prospect for mines, construct dykes and river embankments. Since they were now eligible for preferment, forty-six became bishops, including John Carroll, first Bishop of Baltimore and founder in 1789 of Georgetown University. There were nineteen Jesuits in Maryland and Pennsylvania. One commented that 'our dissolution is in every newspaper and I am ashamed to show my face . . . As a Jesuit, every fatigue I underwent caused a secret and inward satisfaction; it is now unpleasant and disagreeable . . . the Jesuit is metamorphosed into I know not what – a monster, a scarecrow.' In Ireland sixteen Jesuits formed a voluntary association, looking to the day when the Society would be revived. Wherever they found themselves, Ours were increasingly convinced that this would happen. 'I tell you,' wrote Giulio Cordara to a friend, 'the Society will rise again. God will move one of His good servants to restore our Institute.'

The Society was not wholly extinguished and constantly hovered on the verge of restoration. Frederick II of Prussia and Catherine, Empress of Russia, both of whom had acquired large Catholic populations by the partition of Poland and saw no reason to scrap Jesuit schools, were powerful enough to defy the displeasure of the Bourbons and anathemas from the Vatican. *Dominus ac Redemptor* was itself suppressed, the Jesuits ordered to disregard it, and as time went on and Bourbon rulers were beheaded, deposed, or scared into remorse, the papacy accepted and rather furtively blessed an anomaly which had at first caused much embarrassment. So, after appropriate heart-searching, had the Jesuits in Silesia and Byelorussia. They were not the first of their order to bend to the whims of a royal despot, though some of their brethren deplored a fate which had designated the schismatic, amoral Catherine as protectress.

Frederick II had already been teased by his rationalist friends for welcoming exiled Jesuits and employing them as teachers. 'Sire,' wrote d'Alembert, 'it will be a curious state of affairs if while the Most Christian, the Most Catholic, and the Most Apostolic Kings are destroying the grenadiers of the Holy See, your most Heretical Majesty should be the only one to protect them.' The wily monarch felt his way carefully, but in the bitterness of the moment there must have been many ex-Jesuits who rejoiced at the keen sting in the tail of a message that the Prussian representative in Rome was instructed to convey to Clement XIV: 'You will tell the Pope that with regard to the Jesuits, my resolution is to keep them in my states as they hitherto have been. I guaranteed in the Treaty of Breslau the status quo of the Catholic religion and I have found no better priests than they. You will add that since I am regarded as a heretic the Holy Father can absolve me neither from keeping my promise nor from behaving as an honourable man.' It was rumoured that 'the Reverend Father Frederick the Great' had arranged for some of the Jesuit treasure which the Cardinal Commissioners had failed to find to be smuggled into Prussia as a *quid pro quo.* 'I shall tolerate them,' he said of his protégés, 'so long as they behave themselves and don't strangle anyone.' Some papal face was saved by an ambiguous agreement that though the Jesuits could continue to function corporately as priests and teachers, they should do so as individuals under episcopal authority. In 1776 the Society was, after all, dissolved in Prussia, re-emerging as 'Priests of the Royal Schools Institute'. In 1800 King Frederick William III dissolved that organization too. But further east the Society was hanging on. During the invasion of 1812 Napoleon was astonished to find French Jesuits on duty in the classrooms of Russia.

Since the débâcle of the False Dmitri there had been a number of Jesuit forays in Russia. In 1612 Fr Szgoda had worked as a missionary among the Cossacks in the Crimea and in the 1680s three Jesuits had appeared at the court of Peter the Great. The last of these envoys, Fr Vota, was bold enough to raise the question of reunion with Rome. He was no more successful than Possevino had been with Tsar Ivan. Peter permitted the establishment of a Jesuit school in Moscow but in 1719 closed it and expelled the Fathers (who were convinced that he had done so at the prompting of 'Jansenists' encountered during a visit to Paris). Then in 1773 some two hundred Jesuits in the Polish and Lithuanian provinces of the Society found themselves under Russian rule. Their scruples about the suppression were swept aside, a novitiate was opened at Polotsk, and a Vicar-General elected. Bourbon protests were cut short by a threat to withdraw toleration of the Catholics in White Russia and to enter the American War of Independence on the English side, and in 1783 Pope Pius VI verbally approved Catherine's demand for recognition of the Society's continued existence in Russia. Tsar Paul founded a Jesuit college in St Petersburg and put pressure on Pius VII for a more explicit statement. This was given in the brief *Catholicae Fidei* (1801), which directed that the Vicar-General should henceforth be styled General of the Society of Jesus, 'duly charged with the requisite authority to follow and maintain the rule of St Ignatius Loyola'.

[211]

Two crypto-Jesuit groups had emerged in Europe: the Society of the Sacred Heart of Jesus, originating in Antwerp in 1794 and later moving to Hagenbrünn near Vienna, and the Fathers of the Faith of Jesus, originating in Rome in 1797 under the leadership of Nicolo Paccanari, a former officer in the Papal Guard. They merged at the suggestion of Pius VI, with Paccanari as Superior. But his refusal to consider union with the Society in Russia, and his decision to honour wealthy patronesses by allowing them to form a female branch under his direction, soon splintered the organization. Paccanarist missionaries, zealous and dashing, had quite a success in London, opening a retreat house, a boys' school, and a girls' school run by Paccanarist nuns at a convent in Kensington. But stolid English ex-Jesuits were suspicious of these foreigners flaunting a claim to the mantle of St Ignatius so soon after the Society had been dissolved. The language of Paccanari's letters seemed too flamboyant, and as one critic discreetly remarked: 'I cannot look upon the Society of the Faith as the same as our Society. I acknowledge that they are Jesuits, but they are also something more – and that *more* I don't like.' Some of Paccanari's subjects made their way to Polotsk, others formed an independent nucleus in France. Paccanari was arrested and imprisoned in 1807; and the French Fathers of the Faith also came under suspicion by encouraging the foundation of two female orders – the Ladies of the Sacred Heart and the Sisters of Notre Dame de Namur.

Catholicae Fidei was received with rejoicing. Yet, as in Silesia under Frederick II, the Jesuits in Russia were little more than a group of tame if slightly privileged teachers, forbidden to proselytize. Neither the papal brief, their activities, nor those of the Fathers of the Faith seemed of much significance at a time when French revolutionary anti-clericals were jailing and guillotining priests and nuns and experimenting with feasts of nature and cults of reason. Pius VI himself, having been arrested and taken to France, died in Valence, where the municipal officer certified the decease of 'the said Giovanni Angelo Braschi, exercising the profession of pontiff'. The concordat of 1801 signalled a resolve to use a puppet pope to humour Catholic-royalist elements, and in 1804 Pius VII was summoned to Paris to crown Bonaparte Emperor. A limited revival of religious orders was permitted, but Napoleon particularly instructed Fouché, his police chief, to keep a close watch on crypto-Jesuit groups ('under no circumstances do I wish to see the Jesuits referred to as such. Anything likely to call attention to this society must be avoided by the press . . . Order the prefects to guard against the possibility of an agitation for the return of the Jesuits even being initiated'). In 1809 Napoleon annexed the Papal States, declared Rome a 'free city', and proposed to allow the Pope an annual salary as the figurehead of a captive Church. Arrested for insubordination – refusal to abandon his temporal power – Pius VII was detained at Savona, near Genoa, for three years, then in 1812 deported to Fontainebleau.

The spectre of social revolution broke the unity of the anti-Jesuit Bourbon front. In England the government realized that Methodism, substituting religious sentiment for political rebellion, was a useful ally against notions of liberty, equality and fraternity. William Cobbett railed at 'dirty, canting Methodists . . . they always pray for the Ministry; I mean the ministry at Whitehall. They are most "loyal" souls. The THING protects them; and they lend their aid in upholding the THING.' And this, approximately, was the role for which the Jesuits were cast. Charles IV of Spain resisted appeals to re-establish the Society, telling Pius VI that in his opinion the atrocities of the French Revolution were due to, rather than threatened by, its 'impure teaching'. But the ever-energetic Fr Pignatelli prevailed upon the Duke of Parma and the King of Naples to reinstate the Jesuits, who would 'restore the fear of God to their schools'. Jesuit propaganda constantly represented the Society as the most effective bulwark against the infidel tide. Characteristic of many pamphlets was the title 'Concerning the danger which threatens complete ruin to the Thrones, the States, and Christendom, through the false system of enlightenment and the bold arrogance of so-called Philosophers'. In England, where refugee French priests, seen as victims of revolutionary tyranny, had done much to mollify a militant Protestantism, the Jesuits benefited from a situation in which all enemies of the Revolution were recruited into a holy alliance. The school founded by Parsons at St Omers eventually settled into a new home at Stonyhurst in Lancashire. In 1803 Gabriel Gruber, General of the Society in Russia, appointed Marmaduke Stone Superior of the revived English province, and a novitiate was opened at Hodder, close by Stonyhurst.

Restoration and counter-revolution were in the air, and the Jesuits, expelled and suppressed as foes of enlightened despotism, were now seen as the logical partners of an unenlightened, grimly orthodox despotism. Napoleon came to the end of his tether, and what a Catholic historian calls 'the heroic helplessness of the man in white' began to pay dividends. In May 1814 Pius VII re-entered Rome in a coach lent by the exiled, repentant Charles IV and escorted by Hungarian hussars.

[213]

During the last fling of the Hundred Days Murat invaded the Papal States, forcing the Pope to flee to Genoa. But not before the bull *Sollicitudo Omnium Ecclesiarum* had formally restored the Society of Jesus. Proclaimed in the Gesù on 7 August in the presence of kings, cardinals, and about a hundred and fifty aged members of the suppressed Society, it was a short but bombastic document. 'The Catholic world,' it claimed, 'unanimously demands the re-establishment of the Society of Jesus . . . We should consider ourselves culpable of a grievous sin in the sight of God if, in the great dangers to which Christendom is exposed, we should fail to use the help which the special Providence of God now puts at our disposal; if, seated as we are in the Barque of St Peter, we should refuse the aid of the tried and vigorous mariners who offer to face the storms which threaten us with shipwreck. . . . We have decreed, in virtue of the plenitude of Our Apostolic power, that all the concessions and faculties accorded by us to the Russian empire and the Two Sicilies shall henceforward be extended in perpetuity to all other countries of the world . . . Finally, we earnestly recommend in the Lord this Society to the illustrious kings and princes and temporal lords of the various nations, as well as to our venerable brothers, the archbishops and bishops and whosoever may occupy positions of honour and authority. We exhort them, nay we conjure them, not only not to suffer that these religious should be molested in any manner, but to see that they should be treated with the benevolence and charity which they deserve.'

In the United States news of the bull was received late in 1814. 'The Society of Jesus is then re-established!' wrote Fr Fenwick in New York. 'That Society which has been denounced as the corrupter of youth . . . degraded by the Church, rejected by her ministers, outlawed by her kings and insulted by her laity! Hitherto cooped up in a small corner of the world . . . she is now called forth as the only plank left for the salvation of a shipwrecked, *philosophered* world; the only restorer of ecclesiastical discipline and sound morality; the only dependence of Christianity for the renewal of correct principles and the diffusion of piety! What a triumph!'

CHAPTER SEVENTEEN

Second Coming

IN THE PREFACE TO *Loyola and Jesuitism in its Rudiments* Isaac Taylor was one of the very few authors to make a comparatively calm assessment of the restored Society, buffeted, like restored monarchs and the restored papacy, by 'the giddy tossings – the reelings to and fro – of the social system'. Writing when liberal-nationalist pressure was exploding in the rebellions of 1848 to 1850, when Marx and Engels were composing the Communist Manifesto, Bakunin (slightly adapting Voltaire's *mot*) was dreaming of an anarchist millennium when the last king should have been strangled in the guts of the last priest, Proudhon was defining property as theft, and the first loud mutterings of mass democracy were being orchestrated, Taylor saw the Jesuits as an overrated phenomenon: 'It is not my intention to signalize my Protestant zeal in an assault upon the ever to be dreaded Society . . . Nor do I think that Jesuitism could at this time substantiate its claim to be singled out as the most to be feared among the antagonists of truth. On the contrary, it is because Jesuitism is now, as I think, falling into its place among schemes that may be analysed without alarm that I have selected it from among those institutes which are likely to subsist a while and to exert some dying influence, although they be hastening to their end. The same might be said of all those products of the Middle Ages or of the season of convulsion which brought the medieval era to a close.'

The century that followed Pius VII's bull was one of almost unmitigated disaster for the Society and for all the reactionary elements to which it was, as the price of its own restoration, so closely tied. Where there was a demand for its services – and this was by no means universal – the terms were bleakly utilitarian. 'I am persuaded,' wrote Victor Emmanuel, King of Piedmont and Sardinia, in 1815, 'that the Jesuits alone are able to defy a revolution. As I am resolved to use my last man and my last coin to crush the revolution, it follows that I give the Jesuits liberty of action in my territories.' In the nineteenth-century counter-reformation 'the ideas of '89' replaced the challenge of a Protestantism to which those ideas were equally abhorrent. Metternich and Talleyrand were Voltairean cynics, Tsar Alexander a religious dreamer who was humoured by the realists. The Holy Alliance of 1815, reflecting the Tsar's sentiments, described the rulers of Russia, Prussia and Austria as 'merely delegated by Providence to govern three branches of One Family, thus confessing that the Christian world has in reality no other Sovereign but Him to whom power alone really belongs.' This document, which professed to speak 'in the name of the Most Holy and Undivided Trinity', was eventually endorsed by every monarch in Europe except the Prince Regent of England – and the Pope, who had not been consulted, was not mentioned, and was alarmed by a rival concept of Christendom dominated by a schismatic Tsar leagued with a Protestant and a Catholic.

The papalism, or in the fashionable phrase, ultramontanism of the Society had offended the Tsar's irenic fervour. Father-General Brzozowski would have nothing to do with the distribution of a Russian translation of the Bible sponsored by British and American Protestants and not approved by the Supreme Pontiff. In 1815, accused of seeking converts, the Jesuits were banished from St Petersburg. Brzozowski was refused permission to return to Rome, and immediately after his death at Polotsk in 1820 all three hundred and fifty teacher-Jesuits, who had extended their sphere of operations to Riga, Odessa, Saratov, Astrakhan and Siberia, were ordered to leave. Brzozowski's detention had hampered the government of the Society, and the twentieth General Congregation was almost as vexed an affair as that which had followed the death of Ignatius. The Society was far from homogeneous. Of the six hundred members of 1814 some were old men of pre-1773 vintage, others had come from Russia, some were ex-Fathers of the Faith, others secular priests recently admitted. Prelates who were less than ecstatic about the resurrection of the Jesuits proposed that a committee chaired by Cardinal della Genga should examine the Constitutions and supervise the election of a new General; and the indignity was avoided only after a sharp struggle.

At this stage the Society was dominated by a collection of rather bemused medocrities. Eager loyalists, they moved in a climate of almost universal mistrust, burdened with a legendary reputation for skulduggery and seldom, especially in Catholic countries, allowed to settle long enough to bring the antiquated *Ratio Studiorum* to bear effectively on the younger generation. Their main role in the next thirty years was to act as scapegoats for frightened legitimists or as ogres for ambitious demagogues. In a letter published in the *Courrier Français* in 1847,

General Jan Roothaan protested that 'the Society's purpose and vocation is greater than any party. Slander may delight in spreading false accusations of Jesuits participating in political intrigues. I have yet to be shown that a single member of the Order entrusted to my care has offended in this respect against its very definite rules'; and he piously quoted from the resolution of the General Congregation of 1581 warning that the Society 'would expose itself to great dangers by putting its hand to worldly concerns . . . that is why our fathers have very wisely ordained that we who serve God should not become involved in things from which our vocation must shrink.' But in Paris particularly, then at a height of anti-clerical frenzy, such a statement merely invited ridicule or indignant denunciation.

From 1824 onwards the French Jesuits were, at least in liberal propaganda, closely identified with the ultra-reactionary régime of Charles X, who was said to be an 'affiliate' of the Society. They had prudently refrained from seeking official recognition, being content to run a few schools and seminaries under the shelter of religious freedom granted in the 1815 charter. But in 1828 a law requiring all teachers to sign a declaration that they did not belong to an unauthorized body brought even this modest activity to a standstill. During the July revolution of 1830, mobs inflamed by anti-clerical fantasies, which represented all Jesuit establishments as arsenals of aristocratic repression, surged menacingly about them. Novices were sent to Italy or Spain, and only a few dozen undercover priests and brothers stayed in France.

Under Louis Philippe's tolerant rule the Jesuits returned and began to regroup, only to find themselves at the centre of a violent campaign launched by professors Jules Michelet and Edgar Quinet, who in their lectures painted a lurid picture of Jesuit infiltration culminating in a St Bartholomew's Massacre of the champions of progress. The circulation of the *Constitutionnel*, which specialized in exposés of Jesuit wealth and sinister Jesuit sodalities, soared, and in 1844 Eugène Sue's world best-seller *The Wandering Jew* set the fashion for a whole series of highly profitable anti-Jesuit thrillers.

In this novel the monstrous Fr Rodin, marshalling his forces to secure the de Rennepont fortune, is aided by a network of agents including a 'female Jesuit', the Princesse de Saint-Dizier, a salon despot with a shady past, and Dr Baleinier, a fashionable physician. There is a secret memoir by a de Rennepont ancestor describing how he was 'lured' into the Society and disillusioned by its part in the assassination of King Henry IV – 'the missions have thrown a scanty but pure light on the darkness of this Company of Jesus, founded with the detestable and impious aim of destroying, by a homicidal education, all will, liberty and intelligence in the people so as to deliver them, trembling, superstitious, brutalized and helpless, to the despotism of kings, governed in their turn by confessors belonging to the Society.' Young Gabriel de Rennepont, another disillusioned Jesuit, recalls the farcical pretence that his vocation was unforced: 'When, broken by three months of solitude, I was completely exhausted, you opened the door of my cell and said: "If you like, rise and walk. You are free" . . . The only desire of my soul was the repose of the grave; and pronouncing those irrevocable vows, I fell like a corpse into your hands.' In a tremendous dénouement Fr Rodin manages to liquidate almost the entire de Rennepont clan and nearly achieves his triple ambition: to seize the de Rennepont hoard, to become General of the Jesuits, and, 'having ascended the pontifical throne by corrupting the Sacred College, to incorporate the Society of Jesus with the Holy See'. Luckily he is foiled at the last moment ('Ha! – this morning – the holy water – poisoned – Cardinal Malipieri . . .').

The Wandering Jew, playing expertly on every liberal-bourgeois prejudice, caused such a storm of indignation that the novitiate was moved from Avignon to Nice on orders from General Roothaan. Jesuits in Paris were hastily redistributed, and in other danger spots there was a thinning and scattering of members. In the Chamber of Deputies the verbal battle between secularists and 'spirituals' produced some fine flowers of rhetoric. 'We Catholics refuse to be slaves,' announced the Comte de Montalembert, 'we are the sons of the Crusaders and we shall not recoil before the sons of Voltaire.' Other speakers thought it shocking that anyone could speak of 'that destestable Society, the poisoners of the pious Ganganelli [Pope Clement XIV], without cursing it'. Jacques Crétineau-Joly came to the rescue with a massive six-volume history of the Society. But this prodigy of industry and learning, rushed out in two years, could not compete with the popular impact of Sue's garish fantasy.

The Spanish experience was even more dramatic. Recalled by King Ferdinand VII in 1815, the Jesuits were expelled in 1820 by a Liberal government and came back three years later with the French armies that restored Ferdinand to power. During the civil war of 1833 to 1840 Jesuits provided much of the organizing ability for the Carlist rebellion which, with strongholds in the Basque provinces, Aragon and Catalonia, regarded liberalism as a latter-day version of the Lutheran heresy, demanded the return of the Inquisition in full austerity, and dreamed of a pogrom of Freemasons and atheists. An outbreak of cholera in Madrid was attributed to Jesuits and monks who were supposed to have poisoned the water supply. Seventy religious were killed in the riots that followed, among them fifteen Jesuits. In 1835 the Society was again dispersed, novices and junior scholastics being evacuated to Belgium, and operated in a semi-clandestine way for sixteen years. It was banned from Portugal until 1829, and after celebrating a minor triumph when four of Pombal's great-grandsons became pupils in a Jesuit school was expelled in 1834, not to be readmitted until 1858. Many exiles from Spain and Portugal sailed to the newly-independent countries in Latin America, where their existence was just as precarious.

In Switzerland too the path was far from smooth. The Catholic cantons, agitating for decentralized rule, formed themselves into a confederacy, and Jesuits became involved in a controversy which had something in common with the Liberal-Carlist clash. In 1847 civil war broke out. One of the declared aims of the Protestant leaders was expulsion of the Jesuits; after the Catholic defeat over two hundred and fifty went into exile, most of them to Germany. Unable to open schools or seminaries there, they had to be content with organizing retreats and missions, concentrating heavily on Catholics of wealth and political influence. The two most flourishing Jesuit provinces in Europe were those of Austria and Belgium – after the Kingdom of the Netherlands had been broken up in 1830 by an insurrection in Brussels which led to the independence of the Catholic Walloon population.

And Italy? Early in 1845 Charles Dickens crossed 'the dismal, dirty Papal Frontier' on his way to Rome. He took away a nightmare recollection of competing relics: '. . . fragments of the pillar of the Temple that was rent in twain; of a portion of the table that was spread for the Last Supper; of the well at which the woman of Samaria gave water to our Savour; of two columns from the house of Pontius Pilate; of the stone to which the sacred hands were bound when the scourging was performed; of the gridiron of St Laurence, and the stone below it marked with the frying of his fat and blood . . . The rest is a vast wilderness of kneeling people, curling incense, tinkling bells . . . of Madonne with their breasts stuck full of swords arranged in a half-circle like a fan; of actual skeletons of dead saints, hideously attired in gaudy satins, silks and velvets trimmed with gold: their withered crusts of skull adorned with precious jewels or with chaplets of crushed flowers . . .' He also, during High Mass at St Peter's, noticed 'stealthy Jesuits creeping in and out'.

Already the Jesuits were known as 'the pope's pen-holders' and execrated as 'the Austro-Jesuits', upholders of the Austrian military rule which had been clamped over most of Italy after the defeat of Napoleon. Most of them supported Pope Gregory XVI in his condemnation of the passionate plea by the Abbé Lamennais for the liberalization and democratization of the papacy. This alone, he thought, could give it any genuine spiritual stature. Coming to Rome to put his case, Lamennais found the Pope 'a cowardly old imbecile' and the papal court 'the most dreadful cesspit . . . the great sewer of Tarquin itself would have been incapable of dealing with such a mass of filth.' The Roman Jesuits had long and painful memories of that sewer and chose to swim with its tide. One, who suggested that the Society might be well-advised to sponsor a liberalism shorn of anti-clerical sentiment, was told by Roothaan that 'liberalism tends of its very nature towards a freedom from any restraint . . . up to the present its fruits in those countries which have a constitution have been bitter.' All the leaders of the Risorgimento – Cavour, Mazzini, Garibaldi – regarded the Jesuits as deadly enemies. 'Woe to the country, woe to the class that confides to them the education of youth!' wrote Cavour. 'They would in a century make a bastard and brutalized race.' The patriotic priest Vincenzo Gioberti, exiled in Brussels, wrote *The Modern Jesuit* in which the Company was described as the greatest single obstacle to spiritual and political renaissance.

In 1846 the election of Pius IX, who had the reputation of being liberally-inclined, roused hopes that the jesuitical party would be routed and the policies of Lamennais and Gioberti prevail. His refusal to bless the revolts of 1848 and his subsequent flight from Rome put paid to such ideas; and when Pius returned to the Vatican in 1850, after Louis-Napoleon's armies had broken a resistance led by Garibaldi, he was a changed man. The Jesuits had also fled, hooted in Naples as they took ship for Malta, mobbed in Rome, Venice and Turin. General Roothaan returned with the Pope in close, like-minded alliance. One of Pius's first moves was to encourage the publication of a new Jesuit journal, the staunchly ultramontane and anti-democratic *Civiltà Cattolica*. And it was announced that a new article of faith, for long advocated by the Jesuits, was to be proclaimed. Under the protection of a French garrison, the papacy and the Company prepared to counter-attack with the dogma of the Immaculate Conception of the Virgin Mary.

Time was to show that the Society's most promising fields of operation were in Protestant regions, particularly in the United States and England. This, however, was not immediately apparent. News of the restoration had not pleased English Catholics, who saw it as a threat to the possibility of a limited measure of tolerance. Lord Sidmouth, the Home Secretary, agreed that there were 'insuperable objections to the restoration of the Jesuits'; and to appease Protestant prejudice the Emancipation Act of 1829 forbade the Society to receive novices. To circumvent this clause, schoolboys registered as Jesuits while still at Stonyhurst; the novitiate was known as Mr Clarke's Finishing Academy; and well into the 1860s novices pronounced their simple vows in secrecy and patrolled the grounds on Guy Fawkes Night.

The opening of a college at Clongowes Wood, Kildare, in 1814 had provoked the *Hibernian Magazine* to comment that 'Ireland now stands in imminent danger. If Popery succeeds, our fairest plains will once more witness days worthy to rank with those of Bloody Mary, and the walls of Derry shall again become the bulwarks against Popish treachery and massacre.' By the 1840s Jesuits were figuring prominently in popular novels of religious conflict. A favourite theme was that of innocent young women robbed of faith, fortune or chastity (perhaps all three) by devious Roman priests, often Jesuits. In *Father Eustace,* written in 1847 by Anthony Trollope's mother Frances, the Jesuit General inhabits a Roman lair with a labyrinth of secret passages. The handsome, accomplished Fr Eustace fails in his mission to convert a wealthy heiress, persuade her into a convent, and inveigle her into bequeathing her worldly wealth to the Society. He realizes that he has been 'made the tool of demons' and Mrs Trollope concludes that 'the subjection of human hearts to a human rather than a divine will must be evil.'

Once more Jesuits were caught between two fires, the enmity of the re-established Catholic hierarchy (Cardinal Manning disliked all religious but especially the Jesuits) and the anger of Protestants who assumed that they were 'behind' the continental mumbo-jumbo of convents, lace surplices, fancy candles, and incomprehensible rituals. William Sewell's novel *Hawkstone,* published in 1845, gloated over the horrible fate of a sadistic Jesuit intriguer – devoured by rats in a cellar ('there were marks of bloody hands upon the walls . . . the extremities were wholly gone. The vitals must have been attacked last').

The infernal alliance of the papacy, Napoleon III and the Jesuits inspired the broadside of *Westward Ho!* and a whole series of solemn warnings, not always strictly fictional. At a time when such titles as *Popery: Its Character and Crimes, Six Months in a Convent, Scripture Light in Popish Darkness,* and *Puseyism Unmasked: or the Jesuit Abroad* (by 'Anti-Vatican') were tumbling from the presses, one of the choicer items was

[221]

Jemima Luke's *The Female Jesuit, or The Spy in the Family,* published in 1851. Billed as 'a true narrative of recent intrigues in a Protestant household', it purported to tell the story of a young Frenchwoman, trained in a continental convent of 'the Faithful Companions of Jesus', who posed as a Protestant convert to insinuate herself into respectable British families. G. B. Nicolini's *History of the Jesuits* of 1854 insisted that 'the Jesuit menace is at its height. Are Jesuits really English citizens? No! They claim the privileges which the name confers, but will not accept the obligations it imposes. Their country is Rome; their sovereign the Pope; their laws the commands of their General; and at the bidding of a superior they will commit any crime. England they consider an accursed land, Englishmen heretics whom they are under an obligation to combat. . . . Can no measure be taken against these aliens who reside in England purposely to trouble her peace?' According to Nicolini it was 'commonly reported in Italy and also believed in France that on the anniversary of Ganganelli's death the Jesuits, at least those who are in the deep secrets of the order, assemble in a room, and after one of them has addressed a volley of imprecations against Clement XIV's memory, every person present pierces his image with a poniard.'

Nearly thirty years later the success of two novels, one merely accomplished, the other a masterpiece, showed that the Jesuit of fiction was still flourishing. In *The Black Robe* Wilkie Collins sets Arthur Penrose ('a Christian Jesuit') as a foil to Fr Benwell, a Parsons-like intriguer who in one of his despatches to 'the Secretary, S.J., Rome' remarks, after describing a blatant betrayal of confidence: 'I make no attempt to excuse myself. You know our motto: THE END JUSTIFIES THE MEANS.' In *John Inglesant,* a brilliant defence of the virtues of Anglicanism much appreciated by Gladstone, J. H. Shorthouse managed what must be almost the only rounded, sympathetic fictional portrayal of a cultured, resourceful courtier Jesuit in his creation of Fr St Clare, while Inglesant himself is a study in depth of a half-sceptical, half-fascinated Jesuit 'agent'. But a further 'invasion' of England by Jesuit refugees (including Pierre Teilhard de Chardin) driven from France by the anti-clerical legislation of 1901 brought more jeremiads. A typical outburst was that of Hector Macpherson in *The Jesuits in History.* 'Up to 1860,' he wrote, 'the Society of Jesus was expelled no fewer than seventy times from countries which had suffered from its machinations . . . yet England, in the name of a spurious toleration, has become a Jesuit dumping-ground . . . Unless there is a change of policy this nation will one day pay a heavy penalty.' But the anti-popery passions that had been so inflammable in the 1850s had died down; and despite much publicity an attempt to brand and banish the Society by invoking the dead-letter clause forbidding recruitment in the 1829 Emancipation Act was defeated.

America, where separation of Church and State was written into the Constitution, was a Mecca for fugitive Jesuits throughout the nineteenth century. A Belgian Jesuit acknowledged in a letter to General Roothaan that 'on the whole and after the experience of recent centuries, liberty as realized in America is better for the Church than the protection of absolute monarchies.' Yet some at least of the Founding Fathers had been hardly more enthusiastic than Lord Sidmouth about the restoration. 'I do not like the resurrection of the Jesuits,' wrote John Adams to Thomas Jefferson in 1816. 'Shall we not have regular swarms of them here, in as many disguises as even the King of the Gipsies himself can assume? I have lately read Pascal's letters over again . . . If ever any congregation of men could merit eternal perdition on earth and in hell, it is the Company of Loyola. Our system however of religious liberty must afford them an asylum. But if they do not put the purity of our elections to a severe trial it will be a wonder.' Jefferson replied: 'Like you I disapprove of the restoration . . . for it makes a retrograde step from light towards darkness.'

By the 1840s, when about eighty thousand immigrants, many of them Catholic, were entering the United States every year, frigidly tolerant distaste was supplanted by a bigoted Protestant xenophobia culminating in the Know-Nothing Party which was hotly opposed to Catholic immigration. And prejudice was fanned by such publications as Hogan's *Auricular Confession and Popish Nunneries,* allegedly written by a former Catholic priest, with scheming Jesuits as the brains behind a papist conspiracy to infiltrate and overthrow American institutions.

One of Hogan's more fantastic anecdotes is that of a female agent who, arriving in New Orleans 'with the necessary shibboleth from the Stonyhurst Jesuits', had been placed by the Sisters of Charity as chambermaid 'in one of the most respectable Protestant families in the city'. From there she had moved to similar posts in Baltimore and Philadelphia, making copious notes at dead of night about 'anything which could serve a Jesuitical purpose, to be recorded in the secret archives at Stonyhurst, from which they were to be transcopied to those of the parent college in Rome.' Her next assignment was in Washington, D.C., where, dressed as a man, she procured employment under the name of Theodore at an hotel much frequented by unsuspecting politicians, who were so impressed with the young fellow's intelligence and discretion that 'they forgot their usual caution and left their most important papers and letters loose, saying, as they were going out, "Theodore, take care of my room and papers."'

Undeterred by occasional outbursts of mob violence exiled Jesuits from Spain, Portugal, Italy, France and Germany continued to cross the Atlantic. Catholics, forming eighteen per cent of the population, had become a force to be reckoned with; politicians were paying handsome compliments to the work of the Black Robes in pacifying and civilizing Indians exposed to a ruthless westward drive. Peter de Smet, a Belgian who in 1840 began his mission among tribes in the Oregon territory, was often praised for his efforts to reconcile the redskins to their manifest destiny ('you can do more for the welfare of the Indians in keeping them at peace and friendship with the United States than an array of banners,' declared Thomas H. Benton in 1852).

But his ambition to create an Oregon 'Paraguay', a huge reservation studded with Guarani-type reductions, was not realized. Though some Indians stayed in the settlements most continued to wander. But during a debate on the Indian Appropriation Bill of 1900 Senator Vest, raised a Presbyterian, paid tribute to the Jesuit achievement: 'My earliest impressions were that the Jesuits had horns and that there was a faint tinge of sulphur in the air when one of them crossed your path. Some years ago I was assigned to examine the Indian schools in Wyoming and Montana . . . I did not see a single school that was doing any educational work worthy of the name unless it was under the control of the Jesuits.'

Jesuits in America were often embarrassed by the 'triumphalist' campaign climaxed by the definition of papal infallibility at the First Vatican Council in 1869 to 1870. From their point of view, the main positive result was a sudden flow of distinguished refugees driven from Europe. The upheavals of 1848 produced a revulsion of feeling among many Catholics, including bourgeois liberals, who now saw the Vatican as a protective rock against waves of 'materialism'. Hungry for miracles to prop their faith and silence the sneers of unbelievers, they rushed to Lourdes and La Salette. The Virgin's alleged apparitions to young girls; the cult of a child-like submission to the Vicar of Christ ('I am Tradition,' was a favourite saying of Pius IX); the growth of a tabloid press purveying a populist Catholicism very different from that envisaged by Lamennais; all this offered an unexpected but welcome opportunity to armchair Jesuit militants.

Pius IX's frequent attacks on Freemasonry were backed by the *Civiltà*

"A WOLF IN SHEEP'S CLOTHING."

Mr. Bull (*to* Britannia). " WHENEVER YOU SEE ANY OF THESE SNEAKING SCOUNDRELS ABOUT, MA'AM, JUST SEND FOR ME. ` *I'LL* DEAL WITH 'EM, NEVER FEAR!!"

30. A sample of Victorian anti-Catholic sentiment, from *Punch*, June 1877.

31. (*Above left*) Gerard Manley Hopkins (1841-1889), whose poems now rank among the most remarkable of the period.
32. (*Above right*) George Tyrrell, dismissed from the Society and excommunicated in 1906 for his part in the 'modernist' movement.
33. (*Below left*) Pius XII. Roman Jesuits condoned his failure to condemn fascism during the Second World War.
34. (*Below right*) Pierre Teilhard de Chardin (1881-1955). Now a cult figure, but viewed as a near-heretic during his lifetime.

35. (*Left*)
Fr Daniel Berrigan, SJ, c. 1972:
the radical American jailed for his
protests against the Vietnam war.

36. (*Below*) May 1978: Fr Arrupe
(third from right), Jesuit general since
1965, presides at weekly general council
in Rome.

37. (*Above*) Rector and students at the Russian College, Rome, which celebrated its 50th anniversary in October 1979.

38. (*Below*) Many Jesuits, like these in the Philippines, now make the *Spiritual Exercises* 'in a spirit of charismatic renewal'.

and Father-General Pieter Beckx is said to have drafted the anti-masonic Allocution of 1865. French Jesuits who in the 1830s had had to be disciplined into renouncing the doctrines of Lamennais now approved such effusions as an episcopal sermon which identified three incarnations of Christ – in the Virgin's womb, in the eucharist, and in the person of Pius IX. Protected by French troops from the armies of the House of Savoy (which forty years earlier had called in the Jesuits as defenders of the throne), the Vatican experienced its own Risorgimento under the aegis of Napoleon III, who traded Catholic privileges for Catholic votes in a régime characterized at the time as 'a bawdy house blessed by bishops'.

This was the setting in which the Jesuit theologians Giovanni Perrone, Carlo Passaglia, Klemens Schrader and Johann Franzelin, sustaining a role similar to that of Lainez and Salmeron at the Council of Trent, laboured. Perrone and Passaglia were prominent in the drafting of the bull *Ineffabilis Deus* which, on 8 December 1854, in the presence of more than two hundred prelates, declared it an article of faith that the Virgin Mary had been 'from the first instant of her conception, by a singular grace and privilege of Almighty God, in view of the merits of Christ Jesus the Saviour of mankind, preserved free from stain or original sin'. This tawdry piece of theological adventurism, which lent authority to a pious superstition, affronted liberal Catholics but delighted the tabloids and flattered the 'child-like' Catholic masses. Schrader called it 'an act to which no former pontificate can show a parallel; for the Pope defined the dogma of his own sovereign authority, without the cooperation of a council; and this independent action involves practically, if not formally, another dogmatic definition, namely that the Pope is infallible in matters of faith in his own person and not merely when presiding at a council.'

Passaglia, convinced that the spiritual standing of the papacy was bound to suffer unless the Pope got clear of Napoleon III's unsavoury protection, left the Society in 1859 and collected thousands of priestly signatures to a petition requesting Pius IX to renounce the Papal States and thus remove the main obstacle to Italian unity. Carlo Curci, the original editor of the *Civiltà*, also left the Society – and the Church – in disgust. But Perrone, Schrader and Franzelin soldiered on. *Quanta Cura*, an encyclical of 1864 announcing that 1865 would be a jubilee year in which good Catholics might be rewarded by a plenary indulgence, was accompanied by a Syllabus of Errors tracing the tight boundaries of loyalism. Indifferentism, rationalism (absolute or moderate), liberalism, socialism, communism, secret societies, Bible societies were all condemned: so was any criticism of the 'civil princedom' of the Pope and his right to defend it. State education was forbidden to Catholics, who were expected to demand recognition of their faith as 'the sole religion of the state'. The absolute independence of the Church from civil authority even in spheres 'not affecting faith or morals' was asserted. Freedom of speech was declared suspect as tending to produce scepticism and disloyalty; and the catalogue ended with the words 'If anyone thinks that the Roman pontiff can and should reconcile and harmonize himself with progress, with liberalism, and with recent civilization, let him be anathema.'

Civiltà Cattolica, which referred to the Inquisition at the height of its power as 'a sublime spectacle of human perfection', fostered the cult of Pius IX and made acceptance of the dogma of papal infallibility (which, it said, should be defined by acclamation without debate or vote) the acid test of faith. The journal *Stimmen aus Maria Laach,* founded in 1865 specifically to defend the Syllabus, was even more extreme, lamenting that secular authorities no longer co-operated with the Church in punishing those condemned by an ecclesiastical tribunal with fines, flogging or exile. Schrader's *The Papacy and Modern Ideas* put a halo round the Syllabus, while Fr Francis Xavier Brors' *Modern ABC for Catholics of All Classes* wove its sentiments into an anti-liberal catechism that treated its theses as dogmatic truths. The editors of the French Jesuit journal *Études* came under suspicion for their silence on infallibility and were replaced. And at a time when a rebellion of Polish Catholics (rumoured to have been instigated by Jesuits) had been savagely suppressed by the Russians, Napoleon III's Mexican adventure, in which the Church was deeply involved, had pathetically failed, and Catholic Austria had been defeated by the Prussians in the war of 1866, Pius IX rose above the wreckage to announce that an ecumenical council would meet 'to seek with God's help the remedies necessary for the evils which afflict the Church'.

Few people were surprised to learn that the remedy lay in the definition of papal infallibility. Montalembert, a former ultramontane, wrote of 'justice and truth, reason and history' being presented as 'one great burnt offering to the idol set up in the Vatican'. Johann Dollinger, the most distinguished ecclesiastical historian of the time, pointed out that 'years ago the Jesuits began to agitate in favour of the proposed dogma in Italy, France, Germany and England . . . In 449 a synod was held which became known as a synod of robbers; the council of 1869 will be the synod of flatterers . . . the Jesuits and their pupils will sing hosanna . . . the world will look on indifferent. But a deep antipathy against the Italian priesthood will gradually grow.' Odo Russell, an

English diplomat in Rome, observed that 'the Jesuits have been sounding the opinion of the Catholic laity and clergy, and they know perfectly well how far they can count on the superstition of the former and the servility and stupidity of the latter.'

Primed by Schrader, Perrone and Franzelin, Pius IX denied that this was a new dogma – 'there is question only of affirming a truth known and acknowledged by universal Catholic tradition.' At Trent, Lainez and Salmeron had pressed for acceptance of the proposition that the pope, as 'trustee' of the Holy Spirit, enjoys personal infallibility and has no need of the concurrence of a council when he proclaims an article of faith, and Bellarmine had defended this thesis. It had to some extent become a traditional belief, but to dogmatize it as a corollary to the ultramontane Syllabus seemed inopportune to at least a fifth of the prelates who turned up for the opening sessions of the council. The clash of 'inopportunists' or 'unbelievers' and 'infallibilists' was conducted to the accompaniment of vigorous intrigue. The *Civiltà* insisted that all opponents of infallibility were 'ecclesiastical revolutionaries who desire an '89 for the Church'. Augustin Thenier, keeper of the Vatican Archives, was dismissed, allegedly at Jesuit instigation, for releasing 'classified' documents to 'rebel' bishops. Cardinal Hohenlohe wrote that 'stupidity and fanaticism are dancing a tarantella' – a statement which seems fully justified by the argument with which the Bishop of Poitiers, after consulting with Schrader and Franzelin, opened the general debate on 13 May 1870. St Peter, he said, had been crucified head downwards 'so that his head bore his body. Even so the Pope is the Head which supports the Body of the Church. But obviously he who bears is infallible, not that which is borne.' Pounded by such rhetoric and subjected to incessant lobbying, the Fathers still present at the final session on 18 July voted for the dogma, which was limited to matters of faith and morals defined *ex cathedra*.

The bull *Pastor Aeternus* ('the gates of hell are rising on all sides') was issued in the nick of time. The French garrison left Rome on 4 August. A month later the Prussian victory at Sédan ended Napoleon's régime. On 20 September a Piedmontese army occupied Rome and the unification of Italy was completed by annexing the Papal States. General Beckx urged Pius IX to flee from Rome in order to provoke 'European intervention' against the outrage. Instead, as King Victor Emmanuel II was installed in the Quirinal, the Pope, forcibly shorn of his civil princedom, assumed a martyr's role as 'the prisoner of the Vatican'.

The repercussions of the First Vatican Council soon added to the long list of Jesuit expulsions. During the joint Franco-Piedmontese campaign which cleared the Austrians from Lombardy the Jesuits too had been swept out, and at the same time Garibaldi was driving them from Sicily and Naples. Pius IX gave the fugitives a warm welcome. But his favours did not prevent yet another expulsion from Spain in 1868 and renewed chaos after the secularization of Rome in 1870. The Italian Parliament dissolved all religious orders. The Society's colleges, museums, libraries and observatories were seized. From 1873 to 1895 Jesuit headquarters were at Fiesole, and so hostile was the atmosphere in Rome that the General Congregation of 1892 assembled at Loyola, St Ignatius' birthplace.

The German 'Iron Chancellor' Bismarck gave credence (at any rate in public) to a theory that the Franco-Prussian war was the result of an 'ultramontane conspiracy' inspired by 'Jesuit principles'; and his campaign to reduce the powers of the Catholic Church (the *Kulturkampf*) selected the Jesuits as the most dangerous element in a Catholic obstruction of political, social and educational progress. In May 1872 Bismarck declared that 'after the dogmas of the Roman Catholic Church which have recently been promulgated, it will not be possible for a secular government to conclude a concordat with the papacy without humbling itself in a manner to which the German Empire at least will not consent.' In the ensuing debate on a bill for the banishment of the Jesuits, Redemptorists, Sisters of the Sacred Heart and other 'affiliated' religious orders, passed on 4 July and not revoked until 1917, the moderate Catholic Prince Hohenlohe remarked: 'What astonishes me is that the Jesuits and their friends wonder that the modern State abhors them. And yet the Society of Jesus has taken upon itself to make war on the modern State . . . Shall we allow this hostile multitude, which condemns as pernicious errors freedom of the press, freedom of education, religious toleration, and freedom of conscience, to spread their principles by the power which the cure of souls, the confessional and education give?'

The suffocating atmosphere of an aristocratic household under Jesuit spiritual direction in the Germany of the 1860s and 1870s is vividly described by Count Paul von Hoensbroech in *Fourteen Years A Jesuit*. Though both his parents were Prussians, Bismarck was anathema to them. Hoensbroech's mother put great faith in bottles of 'miraculous water' from Lourdes, phials of 'St Ignatius water', and various wonder-working unguents, and mixed soluble portraits of the Madonna – sold in sheets like postage stamps – with the family's food and drink. Paul, who made his first confession at the age of seven, was encouraged to enter the flowery world of Marian sodalities where a group of fifteen devotees was known as a 'rose', eleven 'roses' amounted to a 'Tree of God', and fifteen 'Trees of God' made 'a garden of the Most Holy Virgin'. As in some puritanical Protestant families, children's bodies were as far as possible always totally covered: a sack-like nightdress, an ankle-length costume for the bath. Brothers and sisters could play together only under supervision.

During the *Kulturkampf*, when some bishops and hundreds of priests were imprisoned, seminaries closed and Catholic journals suspended, Hoensbroech's parents sheltered fugitive Jesuits and the ancestral castle in Holland was placed at the Society's disposal. In 1872 Paul, then eighteen, was sent to Stonyhurst for a course in philosophy with the senior pupils. Having experienced the pious tyranny of the Jesuit school at Feldkirch, he was shocked by the laxity of the régime. His fellow 'philosophers', mostly from wealthy backgrounds, did a minimum of work. Some, he claimed, 'even kept their mistresses in little villages in the neighbourhood of the college . . . In March 1873 five of us hired a coach and drove to the Grand National Steeplechase, and it was the intention of my companions to finish the evening at some Liverpool brothel . . . My own philosophic studies consisted in reading English newspapers and novels, playing chess and billiards, and visiting at country houses, where I went fox-hunting and enjoyed myself immensely.' A visit to Lourdes strengthened Hoensbroech's romantic attachment to the faith and in 1878 he began his noviceship at Exaeten in Holland: 'I found the garb of the Order spread out on my bed. A long black upper garment reaching to the feet and fastened by a narrow girdle, with a little round black cap, the *calotte*, worn at the back of the head. Below the outer garment was a shirt of coarse linen, breeches of some rough material, and long black stockings kept in place by suspenders. Thick shoes completed the toilette, for drawers are unknown in a Jesuit household.' The novice master issued him with a scourge of knotted cords, to be used on the buttocks, and a 'penitentiary ring' to be fastened round the leg above the knee. There were daily readings of the *Imitation of Christ* and of Alfonso Rodriguez' *Practice of Christian Perfection,* a monthly reading of St Ignatius' celebrated Letter on Obedience; but the New Testament, he says, was read only as 'an exercise to strengthen the memory'.

The Society's dispersal in Italy and eviction from Germany was no bar to the esteem of Pope Leo XIII. As Bishop of Perugia he had been as ultramontane as Pius IX, as Pope he extended his approval to the Jesuits who specialized in denouncing Freemasonry in such works as *The Secret*

War Against Throne and Altar and *The Idol of Humanity.* In 1884
Humanum Genus, one of Leo XIII's eighty-six encyclicals, began in true
Ignatian style with a contrast between the two standards – the Catholic
faith and the masonic heresy 'working openly for the ruin of Holy
Church with the object of depriving Christian peoples of all those
blessings brought by the Redeemer'; and Fr Fiorelli, the Portuguese
Provincial Superior, instructed his subordinates 'to let slip no opportunity of fostering hatred against the Freemasons'. Jesuit professors were
keen champions of the neo-Thomism commended in the encyclical
Aeterni Patris, which was drafted by a Jesuit, Josef Kleutgen. But when
the Pope moved cautiously towards an expression of liberal sentiment, at
least one Jesuit, Matteo Liberatore, was on hand to help draft *Rerum
Novarum* (1891): an encyclical which plagiarized ideas that, when
advocated by Lamennais in the 1830s, had been condemned by the
Jesuits and by Pope Gregory XVI in the encyclical *Mirari vos.*

In France the anti-clerical campaign, interrupted by the Second
Empire, was resumed in the late 1870s. In 1880 the Society was again
dissolved, but even in exile some French Jesuits continued to intrigue for
a restoration of the monarchy or the setting up of a dictatorship that
would put an end to 'the dirty and impious republic'. They and other
die-hard ultramontanes were not inclined to accept Leo XIII's belated
ruling that the Third Republic should be accepted and obeyed by
Catholics. As on other occasions the Jesuits quietly returned from exile
to reopen their schools and seminaries when the uproar had died down.
They had hardly resettled themselves when in 1894 the Dreyfus case
burst upon the public. By comparison with the anti-semitic, anti-
republican ravings of Édouard Drumont in *La France Juive* and *La Libre
Parole* and the very similar editorials of Fr Vincent de Paul Bailly in *La
Croix,* which for years had been whipping up hatred against the Jews,
the Jesuits did not appear to be deeply involved in the 'crusade' against
Dreyfus. But the comment of *Civiltà Cattolica* that 'if a judicial error has
been committed, the Assembly of 1791 was responsible when it accorded
French nationality to Jews . . . the Jew was created by God to act the
traitor everywhere' helped to focus attention on the activities of Fr du
Lac, director of the Society's most fashionable school in Paris. A well-
known diehard, he had converted Drumont and was said to have
encouraged his anti-semitic journalism. He was also the confessor of
General de Boisdeffre, chief of the army general staff, and the Jesuit
historian T.J. Campbell glories in the fact that 'in the short respites that
were allowed them, the Jesuits filled the army and navy with officers who

were not only conspicuous in their profession but thoroughgoing Catholics. Marshal Foch is one of their triumphs.'

Joseph Reinach, a leading Dreyfusard, maintained that 'the Jesuits contrived this dark affair. For them, Dreyfus is only a pretext. What they want is to strangle the laity and the ideas of '89 . . . The orders of the day emanate from Père du Lac's simple cell. In it there is a crucifix on the wall and on the writing table an annotated copy of the Army List.' Émile Zola's famous *J'Accuse* article was a powerful Dreyfusard asset, and his recently-published novel *Rome,* with its picture of a Jesuit-educated (and manipulated) hierarchy conspiring to crush the noble visions of Pierre Froment, an idealistic young French priest, was reaching a large public. 'It is they, always they, who are at the bottom of everything,' says Don Vigilio, one of the Abbé Froment's few friends in Rome. 'The Jesuits! You fancy that you know them, but you haven't even an idea of their abominable actions and incalculable power – the Jesuit! Mistrust him when you see him gliding by in his shabby old cassock, with the flabby wrinkled face of a devout old maid . . . all Rome belongs to the Jesuits, from the most insignificant cleric to his Holiness Leo XIII in person.' Zola wrote almost admiringly of the Company's 'stupefying resilience . . . incessantly hounded, condemned, demolished, yet still and ever erect . . . even in the shadows the Jesuits are none the less triumphant, quietly confident of their victory.' This resilience was soon to be tested yet again. Taking office as premier in 1902 Émile Combes, a former priest who regarded the ousting of the religious orders as his main mission, got rid of all but five male orders and cut a swathe through female congregations. Abandoning their twenty-four schools and seminaries, the French Jesuits were on their way once more.

Their travels could be quite stimulating. Teilhard de Chardin, for instance, went first to Jersey, where he began a serious study of geology; then to Cairo to teach physics and chemistry in a Jesuit school; then, in 1908, to Hastings, where he completed his theology course and was ordained. Now a budding palaeontologist (he was deceived by the Piltdown Man hoax), he began to read the novels of R.H.Benson, Rudyard Kipling and H.G.Wells which played an important part in forming what he called 'the ambitious splendour' of his cosmology. Teilhard had chosen the Jesuits because he felt that they offered 'the most perfect example'. The battering which the Company in particular had taken from militant secularists seemed to him, as to von Hoensbroech and to Gerard Manley Hopkins, a token of grace. Neither he nor Hopkins fitted the conventional pattern of an organization clinging to past glories and hoary routine as it tried to refashion a cast-iron *esprit de corps*. Life in the Jesuit houses of Europe from the 1820s right through to the 1920s and even beyond was often oppressively stilted and stunting. A kind of fanatical mediocrity was the cardinal virtue, flair and flamboyance anathema. Not that this dim protective colouring was very effective. In *Twelve Years in a Monastery* (1897) S.J.McCabe, an ex-Franciscan who turned into a prolific anti-clerical propagandist, estimated that 'nine secular priests out of ten hate all monks, and nine priests (of any kind) out of ten hate the Jesuits – though in front of laymen there is a spurious professional solidarity.'

On 8 December 1975 a plaque was unveiled in the Poets' Corner of Westminster Abbey. Set in the pavement next to that of T.S.Eliot, it reads: 'A.M.D.G. Gerard Manley Hopkins, S.J., 1844-1889. Priest and Poet, Immortal Diamond.' Yet Hopkins' *Wreck of the Deutschland,* inspired by the drowning of six Franciscan nuns exiled from Germany during the *Kulturkampf,* was, in the opinion of the editors of *The Month,* a Jesuit magazine, too distinctive and disturbing to print. It has been argued that the obstacles which Hopkins himself as much as his superiors put in the way of writing poetry ensured that what he did write was supremely taut and good. He accepted the verdict of *The Month* and refused to have his work published anonymously in the secular press ('it may come to the knowledge of some of Ours and an unpleasant construction be put upon it . . . all that we Jesuits publish, even anonymously, must be seen by censors'). And this brilliant, hypersensitive aesthete, acclaimed at Oxford much as Campion had been acclaimed two centuries earlier, endured the drudgery of parish work and schoolmastering, for both of which he was ill-suited, with ascetic rapture ('this life, though it is hard, is God's will for me . . . which is more than violets knee-deep').

Hopkins' last recorded words were 'I am so happy.' But he had known sheer misery, depressed by his lack of the common touch, his failure to match the sterile Jesuit norm. Writing to Robert Bridges from Stonyhurst in 1871 at the time of the Paris Commune he said, 'I am afraid that some great revolution is not far off. Horrible to say, in a manner I am a Communist . . . It is a dreadful thing for the greatest and most necessary part of a very rich nation to live a hard life without dignity, knowledge, comforts, delight or hopes in the midst of plenty – which plenty they themselves make.' In another letter he admitted that 'our Society has contributed to culture, but only as a means to an end . . . We have had for three centuries often the flower of the youth of a country enter our body: among these how many poets, how many artists of all sorts, there must have been! But genius attracts fame and individual fame St Ignatius looked upon as the most dangerous and dazzling of all attractions. You will see then what is against me . . . but it may be that the time will come for my verses.'

There was, however, in Hopkins as in Teilhard, a lush *fin-de-siècle* streak typical of the age. On the one hand the priestly ideal, symbolized by the 'third sex' universality of the cassock, was that of a sombre sentinel who would keep free thought, Freemasonry, and infidel science at bay. On the other hand Hopkins' elaborately wrought sermons abounded with references to 'the Blessed Virgin's breasts' and with idealized pre-Raphaelite descriptions of Christ – 'his features straight and beautiful, his hair inclining to auburn, parted in the midst, clustering about the ears and neck as the leaves of a filbert . . . I look forward with eager desire to seeing the matchless beauty of Christ's body in the heavenly light.'

This, however, was perhaps preferable to the neo-medieval extravagances of many Jesuit manuals of devotion. According to one of them: 'When the cholera was raging at Bruges in 1839 it suddenly ceased through the use of St Ignatius water . . . which is also especially efficacious for birth pains.' A *Book of Relics* issued to Jesuit scholastics on a pilgrimage to the cathedral of Aix-la-Chapelle went into detail about 'the loin-cloth of Christ, the bridegroom of your soul . . . The sacred blood on it is dead, separated from the holy body and soul and not transfigured . . . still, we ought to honour it . . . Then there is the girdle of the Mother of God . . . Pray in your heart: "By thy girdle, oh most blessed Virgin, I beseech thee for the grace of purity."' The cult of the Sacred Heart, a Jesuit speciality, was spread through an Apostolate of Prayer, and the *Messenger of the Sacred Heart,* which by 1912 was being published in twenty-six languages, listed such prayer-miracles as a groom curing his horse's lameness; the recovery of some wine-casks lost in transit on the railway; the abandonment of a plan to build a 'Protestant' factory and the construction of a Catholic church on the site; and the resurrection of a dead baby cut from the drowned corpse of a pregnant woman.

Despite the many politically-motivated interruptions a full Jesuit training was expected to occupy at least fifteen years. There were two years in the novitiate; two in the 'juniorate' for Greek and Latin studies (as a novice the Jesuit was called 'Brother', as a junior he was called 'Mr' and became a scholastic); three years in the philosophate, taught in Latin; a three-year 'regency' period of work in a foreign mission or teaching in a Jesuit school; a four-year theologate where teaching was again in Latin (with ordination at the end of the third year); last, the Tertianship, or Schola Perfectionis, a final year of study and rededication. Teilhard entered the novitiate at Aix-en-Provence in 1898 at the age of seventeen after attending the Jesuit school at Villefranche-sur-Saône. In the same year Cyril Martindale, a nineteen-year-old Anglican convert, started his noviceship at Manresa House, Roehampton. They met at Aix-en-Provence, where they took baths in thick blue serge robes, afterwards removed in a linen tent. Martindale, a brilliant scholar with a lively mind, found the training a tedious compound of funk and prudery. He felt it was wrong that a novitiate should try to standardize minds and operate in a pious vacuum. At Aix one of his 'experiments' was to work in a home run by the Little Sisters of the Poor; yet St Ignatius, he remembered, had sent his novices out on long pilgrimages, begging their way, or into Roman hospitals where they would be exposed to a full blast of blasphemy, obscenity and life in the raw.

At Manresa House, where novices irrespective of age performed such penitential tasks as sweeping leaves against the wind or weeding with a nail and a flowerpot, he shuddered at the vulgarity of the pious shrines in the Long Gallery and was saddened that the Church should be so dependent on the support of rich bourgeois and so blatantly reflect their values. Martindale had been drawn to the Society by an admiration for Aloysius Gonzaga, and later wrote a biography which removed some of the more nauseous layers of legend around that sainted youth. But a visit to Jesuit houses in Italy, where the tone was one of spiteful, spinsterly conservatism and Aristotle still reigned supreme, appalled him.

Thomas d'Esterre (later Archbishop) Roberts, who joined the novitiate at Roehampton in 1909 at the age of sixteen, straight from St Francis Xavier's College, Liverpool, found the devotional literature a penance in itself ('things like visions of souls falling into hell like leaves in an autumn wind'). The routine was so rebarbative that eleven out of twenty-two novices failed to stay the course. A senior novice issued a knotted 'discipline' for twice-weekly, supervised self-flagellation, and a spiked chain to be fixed round the leg, also twice a week. A lay brother's shouted 'Deo Gratias' began the day at 5.30 am and from then on every minute was regulated – meditation in chapel, then in cubicles, kneeling, standing, sitting; then Mass. At night there would be another meditation and a detailed examination of conscience (entries to be made in the ruled notebook prescribed by Ignatius). The dominant impression was of controlled hurry. When faced by a situation which had not been legislated for, the general rule was to go against one's natural inclination. The experience made Brother Roberts suspect that this was not the sort of intelligent obedience which the founder had had in mind.

Edward Boyd Barrett, who decided to become a Jesuit when he was a thirteen-year-old schoolboy at Clongowes in the 1890s, entered the novitiate some years later at Tullabeg in the midst of a dreary Irish moor. There he 'thanked God every day for the happiness and honour which He had bestowed upon me in making me a Jesuit'. Sent to Louvain for philosophy, he tried to emulate the heroic virtue of St John Berchmans. But back at Clongowes as a teacher in 1911, he was reprimanded when he showed interest in Sinn Fein and sympathy with underpaid college servants who joined a union and went on strike. Theology at Milltown Park near Dublin was a purgatorial chore under an acidulous martinet known as 'Little Albie', who had written a booklet entitled *Little Nellie of Holy God* about a four-year-old saint. But the tedium was broken when students set each other imaginary problems in moral theology *De Sexto* (about the Sixth Commandment) – 'one hears all round one, all day long, Jesuits spinning out yarns of abominable imaginary crimes . . . "Habui rem cum puella, etc. . . ." (I made illicit love to a girl and . . .). Then the tale winds up with a "Quid faciendum, Pater?" (What am I to do, Father?)'

In general much scholarly endeavour went into the task of compiling histories of the Company in various countries and of collecting and editing documents relating to Jesuit origins – the *Monumenta Historica Societatis Jesu* now run to over a hundred large volumes. The lifting of the ban on the Copernican 'theory' freed Jesuit astronomers, among whom Angelo Secchi was eminent, from the limitations which had hampered them. Giuseppe Marchi, investigating the catacombs in Rome, pioneered new archaeological techniques. By the end of the century Jesuits had re-entered most of their former mission fields. In India the conversion of a number of Brahmins caused the feminist and theosophist Annie Besant to denounce such meddlesome presumption. There was no lack of courage or initiative, as when in 1879 four wagons set out on a massive trek from Grahamstown, S. Rhodesia, into the territory of King Lobengula. Fr Augustus Law died an exemplary Victorian missionary's death in a Kaffir kraal, comforted by readings from the *Imitation of Christ*. But there was little scope or inclination for the unconventional daring of Ricci, de Nobili or de Rhodes.

The Society was sunk in the long trough of defensive conservatism against which reformers strove in vain. Teilhard was later to be told that it was not a society of pioneers: and George Tyrrell, an Anglican convert prominent in the 'modernist' movement which sought to reinterpret Catholic doctrine in the light of recent biblical scholarship and theological speculation, was dismissed from the Society in 1906, and a year later excommunicated (for defending his beliefs in a letter to *The Times*). Pope Pius X's encyclical *Pascendi,* condemning the heresies of Tyrrell, Loisy and other modernists, was in part drafted by the Jesuit Cardinal Billot, an admirer of Drumont and the anti-semitic movement called Action Française. Tyrrell, a well-known Thomist scholar who was widely regarded as Newman's logical successor in the liberal Catholic leadership, had dared to imply that Catholicism could be analyzed and criticized in the same way as any other religion and could not rely on anathemas. But *Pascendi* was the signal for an ecclesiastical reign of terror, all Catholic clergy being required to subscribe to an anti-modernist formula. Tyrrell's ideas, like Teilhard's, had to wait until the Second Vatican Council before becoming respectable.

While still in the Society Tyrrell had in private letters poked fun at Jesuit clichés. 'For the greater glory of God' really meant 'for the greater convenience of superiors'; 'Divine Providence' was a euphemism for 'the misgovernment of the General'. Like Hoensbroech, who left the Society in 1892, and like a good many Jesuits who stayed on, he felt that obedience had degenerated into a slavish servility. Ignatius had spoken to a small company of mature, spontaneously united friends, not to 'an ecclesiastical militia of mentally and morally average men'. He was, again like Hoensbroech, repelled by fashionable sacerdotalism ('the Farm Street confessor, lady's-lap-dog sort of life') and hoped that women's emancipation would gradually end 'Jesuit mumbo-jumbo influence'. He contrasted the bold attitude of Ignatius, Lainez and Aquaviva towards the popes with abject 'papolatry' of post-restoration generals, and ridiculed the leadership of 'infallible' popes ('a pair of critical platitudes once in four years'). Finally, he criticized the exclusivity, quite as prevalent as when Cordara lamented it in the 1770s and largely responsible for the pseudo-monastic routine of many Jesuit schools.

Fearing that the Jesuit system of 'espionage', combined with an antediluvian curriculum, would prove an obstacle to the conversion of wellbred Englishmen, Cardinal Newman had founded his Oratory School as a more progressive alternative. From 1820 onwards there had been talk of revising the *Ratio Studiorum.* But the demands of state education made futile any attempt to draft a 'universal' Jesuit scheme, and Protestant suspicions intensified traditionalist sentiment. In 1874, when

Stonyhurst played its first-ever cricket match against a Protestant school (Rossall), the *Rock,* a rabid Protestant journal, warned that 'all these comminglings with Papists act as so many enticements to idolatry . . . We would advise parents who have sons at Rossall to keep a sharp look-out.'

In 1854 General Beckx, writing to the Austrian Minister of Public Instruction, had asked: 'How can we place reliance in modern philosophy when its four great schools which under Kant, Fichte, Schelling and Hegel by turns captivated the whole of Germany, finally melted away into pure atheism and confusion . . . The truly Catholic Universities were always agreed on the Aristotelian system as the basis of sound philosophical thinking.' Twenty years later a Jesuit professor in Prague described contemporary philosophies as 'futile vagaries, a charlatanism of boastful, empty phrases expressed in repulsive, unintelligible jargon . . . reaching a climax in the blasphemies of that monstrous abortion, the Philosophy of the Unconscious.' A cry of anguish which must have been echoed by many a teacher struggling to find a patch of firm ground in the quicksands of intellectual fashion.

Hoensbroech, writing of his time at Feldkirch school in Austria in the 1860s, recalled that all letters to and from parents were read by a censor. Marks for 'industry' and 'purity' were read out at the end of each week, though allowances seemed to be made for the sons of particularly rich or resoundingly titled parents. Pupils were exposed to alarming tales about the devilries of Freemasons and liberals ('Fr Dumont assured us he had known a man who carried about with him a consecrated host in a little box, which, in accordance with the principles of freemasonry, he bespat and pricked every day with a needle'). Jesuit authors, however undistinguished, were preferred, and this held good through the whole range of his training. He heard or read Jesuit teachers who furiously denounced German cultural heroes – 'We Germans should be ashamed to possess such a literature . . . Whilst Lessing endeavours to undermine Christianity, a St Francis Xavier wins whole kingdoms for Christian morality. Whilst Goethe welds his whole life into a chain of excesses, a St Benedict throws himself into nettles to overcome the temptations of the flesh.'

In *A Portrait of the Artist as a Young Man,* James Joyce reflected on his schooldays at Clongowes and Belvedere – the statues of the boy saints, so often held up as patterns of virtue, in the corridor; the hell-fire sermon after the *Exercises;* the feeling that the Jesuit teachers could all have been great men in the world if they had so chosen, and in any case were 'the fellows that can get you a position'; the fishing for vocations. But he took to 'monkish learning' and thought the Fathers 'intelligent and serious priests . . . men who washed their bodies briskly with cold water and wore cold clean linen'. Arthur Conan Doyle, who was at Stonyhurst in the 1870s, found the curriculum stupefying and the incessant supervision tiresome, and he never forgot his teacher's prediction, at the end of his last term, that 'he would never come to any good', being too much of a rebel. His masters were, he thought, 'keen, clean-minded, earnest men, no more casuistical than their neighbours', but their theology was narrow and he remembered his horror when 'Fr Murphy, a great fierce Irish priest, declared that there was sure damnation for everyone outside the Church.' The 'pandyings' – hand-beatings with a piece of thick, tough rubber – he found excruciating, but they were probably no worse than the floggings in non-Jesuit public schools.

Martindale was appalled by the academic standards at Stonyhurst compared with those at Harrow, where he had been educated. But on the Continent the most distinctive feature of Jesuit schools seems to have been their relentless, prettified pietism. This aspect is brilliantly conveyed by Roger Peyrefitte, who himself went to a Jesuit school, in his fictional account of St Claude's College in *Special Friendships*. Readings from the Martyrology at luncheon, from the *Imitation* at supper; a bed-time prayer in the dormitory ('Sleep is the image of death'); M.le Superieur gloating over the sacramental statistics – 'This year, up to and including this morning, there have been 43,793 communions'; a guest preacher's awful warnings – 'instances of the Host bursting into flames or sweating blood as it came into contact with sacrilegious lips. Cases of sudden death following wicked communions . . .'

But if Jesuit pupils and teachers sometimes suffered from a claustrophobic, out-dated régime, the Society could point to at least one worldly success. Fr Bernard Vaughan, equally at home in Rome, in Mayfair, on the French Riviera, and with the Prince of Wales, filled the pews with his melodramatic sermons. When he preached at Farm Street on the sins of society, hostesses organized Vaughan luncheons and actresses studied his oratorical technique. Even in the educational field there had been one great change. In 1833 Roothaan, yielding to pressure from America, petitioned Pope Gregory XVI for a dispensation to allow tuition fees to be paid. At first confined to England, Ireland and the United States, this was in 1853 extended to any college that found it necessary due to 'extraordinary circumstances' – shrinking endowments, falling donations, a reluctance to accept state subsidies where these were available.

In England and America the Jesuits, in common with other teaching orders, addressed themselves to the problem of schooling the hordes of Catholic immigrants. By 1851 nearly two-thirds of the Catholics in England had been born in Ireland, and eight years earlier the first Jesuit school designed for a new clientèle had opened in Liverpool. 'Religious and moral instruction will form the first care of the teachers,' said the prospectus. 'Pupils will be taught the different branches of education usually taught in such schools and, when parents wish it, French, Latin and Greek also. The terms will be £2·10s per quarter, payable in advance. Pens, ink and paper will be provided. School books will be the only extra charge.' In America the fathers were able to exploit national rivalry, as when in Seattle Irish and German Catholics vied with each other to finance and build a church and school. By 1910 the educational pattern had been adapted to the eight-year high school/college sequence, split into two four-year periods and catering for students between the ages of fourteen and twenty-two. Along the east coast, where Harvard and Yale preserved the European tradition, Jesuit schools and colleges were able to stay closer to the old ways. But Roothaan was saddened by the neglect of Greek and Latin in the Midwest, where St Louis began the practice of offering a course in 'mercantile education' and a Jesuit Visitor heard that the *Ratio Studiorum* was 'a document rarely met with in our houses'. At the end of the century General Franz Wernz acknowledged that flexibility was imperative and soon afterwards Jesuit high schools began to apply for official recognition by accrediting agencies. As schools and colleges multiplied more and more lay teachers had to be employed and paid. Fund-raising became the main function of many a Jesuit administrator.

If the Americanization of the *Ratio Studiorum* grieved the purists, the liberalism of the American Church was equally alarming, with its low priority for learning and ritual, its preference for a 'social gospel', and its fondness for ecumenical extravaganzas such as the International Congress of Religions held at Chicago in 1892, when Catholics debated with Protestants, Greek Orthodox schismatics, Buddhists and Brahmins. But the American Church was too robust, fast-expanding and rich to be too openly rebuked, by popes or Jesuit Generals. In 1914, of nearly seventeen thousand Jesuits, more than two thousand were in the United States, whose four provinces had been assigned foreign missions in Alaska, British Honduras and Jamaica and were publishing their own weekly, *America*. Once again it seemed that the New World might compensate for defeats and disappointments in the Old.

CHAPTER EIGHTEEN

A Cool Scene

INTERVIEWED IN April 1970 shortly before he was due to begin a three-year prison sentence for his part in destroying Vietnam draft files, Fr Daniel Berrigan SJ remarked that the special relationship between the pope and the Society had always had its dangers: 'Even recently Paul VI invoked that image of running to horse when the pope speaks. *Humanae Vitae,* the encyclical on birth control, was a loyalty test that the Jesuits above all others were required to pass. It's the most horrendous kind of Machiavellianism.'

Appeasement of the papacy had not averted suppression. Identification with it had given the restored Society an unsavoury reputation. In 1640 when, as a sop to public clamour, Urban VIII had appointed a committee to investigate his blatant nepotism, Vitelleschi had endorsed the verdict that the pope had been well within his rights. In the 1830s and 1840s most Italian Jesuits had approved of the crushing by Austrian troops of revolts in overtaxed, corruptly governed Papal States. They had not protested against the censorship of books, the muzzling of the press, the closing of universities, Leo XII's veto on vaccination against smallpox as a violation of the law of nature, or the forcible return of the Jews to the ghettos. From 1850 to 1870 they had been the chief architects and trumpeters of a meretricious papal triumphalism. Their part in Leo XIII's encyclical *Rerum Novarum* had annoyed socialists, their share in attacks on Freemasons and in the onslaught on modernism had angered liberal Catholics.

Papal bouquets, and there were many, intensified Protestant suspicions. In America it was rumoured that Wilkes Booth, the assassin of Abraham Lincoln, was 'a tool of the Jesuits' and in *Fifty Years in the Roman Catholic Church* a former priest alleged that not long before his death the President had said that 'it is to Popery that we owe this terrible civil war . . . from the Vatican, from the colleges and schools of the Jesuits, from the convents of nuns and from the confessional the papists have spread hatred against our institutions.' The popes were represented as being as much prisoners of the Jesuits as of the Vatican. A tract of 1909, *The Papal Conquest: Italy's Warning – Wake up, John Bull!* by the Rev. Alexander Robertson, claimed that Pius X was 'locked in his palace with the key in his pocket, or rather in that of Father-General Francis Xavier Wernz, the Black Pope.' Kaiser Wilhelm had 'by secret negotiations with the Pope, and as proof that their interests in certain matters were identical', secured the election of Wernz, who would make certain that the Kaiser was 'the willing tool of the Vatican for the humiliation of England'.* It was whispered in France that the Jesuits had 'engineered' the Dreyfus affair in order to divide the nation, foster antimilitarist sentiment, and thus ensure the victory of the Central Powers – the Vatican's new champions after Bismarck had called off the *Kulturkampf* and come to terms with Rome in the crusade against socialism.

The campaign against liberal Catholicism unleashed by Pius X and his Secretary of State, Cardinal Merry del Val, an aristocratic Spanish reactionary who was a pupil and ally of the Roman Jesuits, did not improve their image. To counter an alleged modernist conspiracy centred in France, Merry del Val ordered the compilation of dossiers on 'unsound' clerics (Angelo Roncalli, later Pope John XXIII, was on a list of suspects in the files of the Holy Office) and established a denunciation network, the Sapinière, which was exposed when in 1915 German Army Intelligence published some incriminating documents found in Belgium. The story went that 'the Jesuit counsellor of King Albert of the Belgians' was finally responsible for persuading him to resist the German occupation; and in Ireland Fr Peter Finlay SJ was credited with stiffening the Catholic hierarchy's hostility to Sinn Fein, thus ensuring that the nationalist movement would be forced into armed rebellion.

In Britain and the United States hard-working Jesuits were too busy teaching and raising funds for new schools and churches to be much affected by the odium attached to the Society elsewhere. In 1910 Wernz reported 'five new provinces; a revival of the professed houses; new novitiates . . . The province of Germany, though dispersed, has built in Holland an immense novitiate and houses of retreat . . . France is dispersed but it has furnished excellent professors for the Biblical Institute and the Gregorian University. In the mission of Calcutta 130,000 pagans have been brought to the faith . . .' Soon after this report was circulated, another political upset in Portugal led to another Jesuit

---

* But Jesuit historians claim that Pius X wanted to depose General Wernz as insufficiently subservient.

expulsion. But as late as June 1914 'Black Pope' Wernz was solemnly writing to Fr Anthony Maas, Provincial Superior in Maryland, on the subject of American football. After considering various reports he had come to the conclusion that '(1) the game itself, as regards the ferocity with which it is often played, must be moderated . . . nor should it be played with those extern colleges who play with such violence; (2) the frequency of playing this game with extern colleges must be limited; (3) sparingly and with definite safeguards must the game be played with other colleges when it is necessary to be away overnight . . . I ask that these norms be published as guidelines in all our colleges, that they be read at table and forthwith put in execution.'

Impetus was being smothered in a passion for real estate and pedagogic minutiae. Nor was the long generalship of Wlodimir Ledochowski, which spanned the pontificates of Benedict XV, Pius XI and Pius XII, two world wars, the Spanish Civil War and the rise of Fascism, remarkable for much but a clinging to Jesuit tradition. Ledochowski, an aristocratic Pole with a powerful hatred of Russia, was described by Boyd Barrett as 'a dry, dark, foxy little man with piercing eyes and a nervous, restless manner'. By 1938, under the strain of social and political upheavals such as not even Aquaviva or Lorenzo Ricci had experienced, Ledochowski was in poor physical shape, suffering from insomnia and dependent on sleeping draughts. Cyril Martindale, who attended the twenty-eighth General Congregation called in that year to choose a Vicar-General to assist Ledochowski, was troubled by 'the apparent loss of dynamism'. He found the Congregation tedious in its overriding concern with administrative machinery and thought the General 'a curious man, somewhat hampered by being a Pole, having an enormous ancestry, and having been trained only in court circles . . . He is as weak as a feather, with unbelievable energy; minute and mouse-like until he turns into a sort of eagly, steely-wristed (not taloned: he seldom scratches) creature.' Ledochowski himself seemed to share Martindale's view that the Congregation was ineffectual and the Society too large to be governed in the old manner even with the help of a proliferating bureaucracy in Rome. 'You *must* realize, Fathers,' he protested, 'that you will be going back to a totally different world. We need *totally* new men.' But no one seemed to know how these new Jesuits were to be produced or even, after the Teilhard de Chardin scandal, to believe they were needed.

If pacifism is a sign of logical, courageous Christianity the Jesuits had not seemed to be aware of it in 1914. Benedict XV's impartial stance provided a noble façade behind which the Catholic clergy rushed to the colours. Over two thousand Jesuits served as soldiers, stretcher-bearers or chaplains. It seemed a good chance to prove their patriotism and raise the barriers which had been erected against them as papal fifth columnists. Fr Bernard Vaughan urged his fellow countrymen to 'exterminate the Hun rats'. And when the war ended the Company's chroniclers proudly catalogued the decorations awarded to Jesuits enlisted on various sides in a conflict where religious affiliations had been almost irrelevant, with Protestant Germany, Catholic Austria, Orthodox Bulgaria and Muslim Turkey facing Protestant Britain, Catholic France and Italy, Orthodox, and after 1917 officially atheist, Russia.

Idealists and ideologues, Christian or otherwise, had competed to charge the interminable, mechanized slaughter with 'meaning'. Often the attempts were banal – God as German, French, or whatever, Christ blessing a just war. But Teilhard de Chardin, who served as a corporal stretcher-bearer, was an apocalyptic of a peculiar kind. His vision combined the insights of an artist, a technocrat and a speculative theologian in the baroque tradition. In one sense Teilhard was a simple patriot, seeing the war as 'a struggle between two moralities . . . We are fighting for Christian justice.' His coolness under fire won him the Croix de Guerre and the Military Medal, but he regretted being a mere medical orderly, writing to a friend that 'I'd rather be handling a machine gun . . . I feel that doing so I would be more a priest. Isn't a priest a man who must bear the burden of life in all its forms?'

Teilhard's rare moments of depression came when he was withdrawn from the 'unifying' furnace of the front and watched men relaxing in drunken bawdiness. Much influenced by the evolutionary philosophy of Henri Bergson, he saw death as a barrier against which human beings should eagerly press to enter the next, assumedly higher, stage. In a story called *The Pyx* he wrote of a coming battle as 'a grandiose, almost fantastic advance in the liberation of souls . . . I shall go into this engagement in a religious spirit . . . unable to distinguish where human emotions end and adoration begins. If I should not return from those heights I would like my body to remain there, moulded into the clay of the fortifications like a living cement thrown by God into the stonework of the New City.' In July 1918, soon after making his profession in the chapel of a Jesuit novitiate, Teilhard composed *The Priest,* an ecstatic statement of that cosmic optimism towards which he had been moving: 'I see your flesh, Lord, extend throughout the entire universe, there to be mingled with it and so extract all the elements which can be made to serve your purpose . . . Was there ever, my God, a humanity more like, in the shedding of its blood, to a sacrificed victim – more ready, in its ferment, to receive creative transformation – more rich in energy that can be sanctified – closer, in its agony, to the supreme communion?' The priest, he felt, had 'a universal function to fulfil: the offering to God of the entire world. Going far beyond the bread and wine the Church has put in your hand, your influence is destined to extend to the immense host of mankind.'

George Tyrrell had defended 'the right of each age to adjust the historico-philosophical expression of Christianity to contemporary certainties, thus putting an end to this utterly needless conflict between faith and science, which is a mere theological bogey.' Teilhard expanded on this theme. He argued that 'it is time for our religion to draw new youth from a substantial infusion of the earth's passions and spiritual energies . . . We must proclaim from the housetops that it is from the visible world that the soul draws the elements which grace divinizes . . . Science, the arts, industry, social activity – all these are necessary if we are to offer worthy material for Christ's influence.' Religion had been enfeebled for lack · of 'a sufficiently passionate admiration of the universe'. Even the capacity for genuine detachment had been damaged, for 'one must have a great love for the world if we passionately wish to renounce it'.

Few of his wartime essays were submitted for publication. *Études* printed one, but only after cutting a final paragraph comparing the terrific splendours of a front-line barrage with prehistoric catastrophes of which the only witnesses had been creatures without the power of reflection. Other manuscripts, privately circulated, caused misgivings about Teilhard's orthodoxy. His vision of the universe as a vast, palpitating Sacred Heart or 'single giant Host' seemed to tremble on the brink of a gnostic pantheism, while his scientific-poetic use of symbols savoured of 'modernism'. His postwar career was one of unbroken academic distinction. With Édouard le Roy of the Collège de France he coined the term 'noosphere' to describe the gradual development, with the evolution of man, of a 'thinking layer' round the world. Devotees transcribed and distributed the texts of lectures in which he attempted a new, and he hoped rigorously scientific, synthesis of faith and reason.

His mission as an apostle to scientists was off to a brilliant start. But bold speculations, for instance that original sin was a passing flaw which would vanish as the creation evolved towards its omega point, though clearly sympathetic to the Ignatian emphasis on consoling truths and human perfectibility, alarmed his superiors. So did the concept of Christ 'fulfilling himself gradually through the ages in the sum of our individual endeavours . . . Without the process of biological evolution which produced the human brain, there would be no sanctified souls; and similarly without the evolution of collective thought, how can there be a consummated Christ? The whole of the world's industrial, aesthetic, scientific and moral endeavour serves physically to complete the Body of Christ.' Teilhard's enthusiasm for such agnostic humanists as André Gide and H. G. Wells was deeply suspect; and yet his immense popularity as professor, preacher and retreat-giver made him a cult-figure. Permission to publish his masterpiece, *Le Milieu Divin*, was refused, and under pressure from Cardinal Merry del Val, now secretary of the Holy Office, Teilhard's superiors compelled him to sign a document repudiating his 'heretical' views on original sin. His limitless scientific curiosity enabled him to treat his exile to China as an opportunity for further geological and palaeontological investigation, though he confessed to having lost faith in 'the immediate and tangible value of official directions and decisions'. In China, as in Paris, he was subject to a surveillance that did not scruple to filch manuscripts from his desk to be sent to Rome for scrutiny. It was the start of a lifelong stifling of his 'non-scientific' works: a triumph of mediocrity enforced in a period when Jesuit theologians laboured to draft and defend the flaccid clichés of Pius XI and Piux XII.

Edward Boyd Barrett's experience as a Jesuit in the 1920s was, it seems, equally frustrating. In 1917, when he was ordained and said his first Mass in Dublin, he was a model priest who still believed that, in the words of General Roothaan, the Society was 'a splendid depository of learning, piety and virtue; an august temple extending over the earth, consecrated to the glory of God and the salvation of souls.' The tertianship of 1919 to 1920, coming after fifteen years in the order, severely tested his illusions. It began with a full thirty-day course of the *Exercises*, followed by a strict routine of prayer, devotional reading, and study of the Constitutions. Twenty mature Jesuits, including ex-army chaplains, had to pretend to be novices all over again, 'subject to the minute and trying rules under which we had lived in our first days. We were to keep silence, observe bounds strictly, read no papers, discuss no politics, write no letters, sweep, dust and clean corridors.' The thirty-day retreat did for a time generate a kind of spiritual frenzy. 'Cursed be he who doth the work of the Lord carelessly,' wrote Boyd Barrett in his notebook. 'Dear Christ, give me understanding! Make the seed of truth to grow in my soul!'

After two months the fervour evaporated. Newspapers were smuggled in, and there were discussions about 'the physical charms of some of the young novices'. Boyd Barrett secretly visited Fr James Tomkin, a rogue Jesuit who was a personal adviser of Eamonn de Valera and took the confessions of volunteers about to do battle for independence. Why, asked Fr Tomkin, should it be wrong for Irish patriots to risk their lives in such a cause, when it was considered right and proper for Englishmen, Frenchmen, Germans and Italians? At the end of the tertianship – which, he felt, should be an optional extra for those who felt a need for it – Boyd Barrett was handed his character assessment forwarded from Rome. It hinted at insufficient obedience to superiors and lack of humility.

But the privilege of a 'biennium', a two-year course of advanced studies in biology and psychology at London University, seemed to prove that he was trusted. The professionalism and dedication of his teachers greatly impressed him by contrast with Jesuit teachers who were interested in policing rather than extending knowledge. His studies prospered and when a number of priests, among them Jesuits, consulted him about their 'nerves', he conceived the idea of becoming a priest-psychiatrist. He had seen the wretchedness caused by 'breakdowns' which few spiritual directors would dare to diagnose honestly. Many of those afflicted were ashamed to seek medical help, and most Jesuits, like almost all professing Christians, were hostile to psychiatrists and psychoanalysts as professional rivals to the confessor, whose power to absolve was held to be the only acceptable and efficacious form of mind-healing. Not for many years would there be any attempt to assimilate the insights of Jung and Adler, while Freud was particularly execrated.

Yet Boyd Barrett cherished the hope that his superiors would recognize a parallel between the joy of Ignatius when he gathered a group of intellectually able men to serve the Church and his own plan to 'put to the service of God the science I had so painstakingly acquired'. His idea was to select and train a group of priests, well-versed in the problems of their patients, who would open psycho-spiritual clinics for the treatment of 'scruples, delusions, sex-troubles and all forms of semi-religious morbidities', enabling 'those who entered religion under the influence of deceptive emotion to secure honourable exits from a life that was driving them insane'. This ambition, together with Boyd Barrett's known Irish Republican sympathies, brought retribution in the

form of a letter from his Provincial telling him that his final vows had
been postponed. Banished to a school in Mungret, a remote country
town in southern Ireland, he was, despite a further reprimand for
publicly reading prayers in Gaelic at the request of relatives of IRA
prisoners, awarded his 'colours' in 1924.

This honour – the equivalent of tenure or establishment – now
seemed almost an insult. Boyd Barrett was depressed by the persistence,
at least in Ireland, of medieval play-acting in the way of penances: 'Were
one to glance through the window of a refectory at the beginning of
dinner or supper on an ordinary Friday or on the vigil of a feast,' he
wrote, 'one would see quite a number of Jesuits saying grace on their
knees with outstretched arms; crawling around under the tables and
kissing the toes of those already seated . . . others calling out in a loud
voice that they were guilty of some breach of order or of charity. In some
countries the lights are lowered and the Fathers, taking from their
pockets small scourges made of knotted cords, bare their shoulders and
whip themselves.' There was a movement to canonize Fr William Doyle,
a highly eccentric Irish Jesuit who pushed asceticism to the limit by
rolling naked in nettles and lying in a bath of cold water in midwinter.

Irish Jesuit censors had vetoed Boyd Barrett's articles, and though his
book *The New Psychology* was passed for publication in America its
appearance was delayed until he had cut some passages and inserted
others in praise of scholastic (Thomist) wisdom. Soon after his profession he was offered the chance of two years in New York with special
facilities for the work of his choice. In fact he was assigned to
Georgetown University where the Dean, Fr Edmund J. Walsh, noted for
his anti-Bolshevik tirades, set him to menial tasks. The editor of *America*
was forced to reject his articles. Lectures given under the auspices of
Fordham University had to be bowdlerized, a Jesuit professor urging
him to 'keep off sex, ram down the freedom of the will, the spirituality of
the soul, the distinction between essence and existence'. At Georgetown
Boyd Barrett was allowed to conduct a short course in heavily vetted
psychology, but in June 1925, after twenty years in the Society, he was
refused admission to the Jesuit house in New York – a bar which he
interpreted as virtual expulsion.

Irish-American Jesuit Superiors had proved no more accommodating
than those in Ireland; and there were, he thought, other similarities.
Without the backing of the nuns and pious female Catholics of Dublin
and Limerick, 'Jesuit collection plates would have been bare, their
schools empty, their booklets unsold, their retreat-givers out of commis-

sion.' In America some Fathers conjured tidy sums from expectant mothers by peddling a nostrum which ensured a safe delivery, a picture of the Virgin to be dissolved in water and swallowed. Offerings for Masses averaged about five dollars. The American and Irish editions of *The Messenger of the Sacred Heart* not only had enormous circulations but advertised badges, medals and oleographs of the Sacred Heart which sold briskly. The poverty of the individual Jesuit in his spartan room was offset by a corporate wealth which, so long as he conformed, provided him with total security in the way of food, lodging, medical care, holidays, and magnificent facilities – 'splendid halls, sumptuous libraries, perhaps a delightful garden, situated probably in the most exclusive part of a city where each square foot represents a fortune.' For real poverty one had to go to the slums.

Boyd Barrett, who became an American citizen and built up a psychiatric practice in New York, had to fight off determined efforts to reclaim or discredit him. His desire to minister as a secular priest had been frustrated. His Irish Provincial pleaded that he should return to the Society 'for your own sake, for the sake of your mother, whose heart would break if she should hear of your defection.' A Jesuit at Georgetown exhorted him to 'come back as a simple, trusting child . . . come back, dear Boyd, to Jesus and his Little Society.' A rumour circulated that before the publication in 1927 of his book *The Jesuit Enigma* he had tried to blackmail the Society into paying him to keep silent. His 1929 critique of the Church, *While Peter Sleeps*, was violently attacked in the ultramontane press. 'Barrett's unhappy spirit was no doubt fertile soil for the pernicious thoughts and wild desires that have brought him into a morass where he wallows in slime surrounded by serpents,' wrote one agitated reviewer, adding that 'when a man leaves his Order and devotes his abundant time and meagre ability to the task of biting the hand that fed him and befouling the nest that sheltered him, then decency as well as religion disowns him . . . even the devil despises him!' Boyd Barrett himself came to see his twenty years in the Company as a painful but ultimately rewarding ordeal, quoting Fr Tyrrell's conclusion that 'it is a good life's work to have arrived by personal experience and reflection at the solution of so plausible and complicated a fallacy as that of Jesuitism.'

The English Jesuits, though generally conservative, showed flickers of vitality. Fr Herbert Thurston, a formidable controversialist who crossed words with Rider Haggard, Conan Doyle (as an apostle of spiritualism) and Dr G.G. Coulton, a celebrated medievalist, occupied the same room

in the Jesuit house at Farm Street for forty-five years and spent most of
his working hours in the British Museum Reading Room. Alban Goodier
resigned as Archbishop of Bombay after a jurisdictional dispute with the
Portuguese Primate of Goa during which, at an official reception, an
'enemy' priest spat on his episcopal ring. Boyd Barrett found his London
superior, Fr Frank Devas, refreshingly sophisticated – 'he held that the
true Catholic spirit was a mixture of ritual and freethinking . . . was
delighted when it was pointed out that some of his own habits, such as
sucking his pipe-stem, had a sexual significance according to Freud's
symptomology . . . and not shy about illustrating, from the rich harvest
of his own experience, such abnormalities as we discussed.' One Jesuit
studied experimental psychology in Prague after his ordination in 1930
and lectured in the school of psychology at Oxford. Eric Burrows,
official cuneiformist with Sir Leonard Woolley during the excavations at
Ur, invariably dressed in black and erected an altar of packing cases
surmounted by a slab of Sumerian masonry.

Fr Martindale, who combined a prodigious literary output and
popular radio talks with a mission to seamen and a series of clubs for
working men and down-and-outs, did not hide his impatience with
pomposity and stupidity, though accepting that they were an inescapable
part of the divine scheme. One evening in Bradford he forced himself to
endure 'some schoolgirls acting the *whole* of *The Gondoliers*, followed by
speeches from several aldermen *and* the local Director of Education,
who talked for an hour solid, in a cold room, on the Rudder of Mind, the
Keel of Character, the Wind of the Sense of Beauty and much more
ungodly tosh, all of which I thought I ought to go to in order to
encourage the local nuns of the Cross and Passion. Would you believe
it?' In 1933 he led a pilgrimage of unemployed Catholics to Rome,
insisting that at a public audience with Pius XI they should not, as
planned, sing Cardinal Wiseman's hymn *Full in the Panting Heart of
Rome*, but the Credo in plainchant and in Latin. He was denounced to
the Holy Office for belittling St Margaret Mary Alacoque in an article in
the *Tablet*, and suspected of 'modernism' as a result of such statements
as that in which he declared that the Church was 'suffering from
hopeless confusion as to what is or is not Socialism, so that tens of
thousands of honest lads are damned as Bolsheviks when they are only
asking for social reforms considered just by Leo XIII.'

Turning his back on an academic career to become a people's priest,
Martindale concealed his intellectualism under a rather hearty *persona*
('the Exquisite is always going in for a sort of spiritual self-abuse . . .

[249]

When the athlete plays rugger, he is somehow in love with God. When I say athlete I mean also clerk, policeman, navvy, taxi-driver, porter, sailor . . . For God's sake remain kiddish'). Fr Martin D'Arcy, allegedly Evelyn Waugh's model for the urbane Fr Rothschild in *Vile Bodies*, made quite an impact as a scholarly-worldly Jesuit, mingling the fashionable appeal of Bernard Vaughan with something of the fastidious intellectualism of the young Newman. But as master of Campion Hall, Oxford, from 1933 to 1945, he was criticized for his too evident relish of high society. In 1930 he had received Evelyn Waugh into the Church at Farm Street, and the novelist's diary is full of references to their meetings. 'Went to Fr D'Arcy at 11. Blue chin and fine, slippery mind. The clergyhouse at Mount Street superbly ill-furnished. Anglicans can never achieve this ruthless absence of "good taste". 'We talked about verbal inspiration and Noah's Ark . . . Went to Fr D'Arcy and talked about infallibility and indulgences.' The newly-built Campion Hall, designed by Sir Edwin Lutyens, was adorned with items known as *objets D'Arcy*, which Waugh described as 'bric-à-brac. A fine Murillo, probably genuine, fine vestments, a lot of trash including watercolours by undergraduates and bits of china.'

D'Arcy stayed with Waugh over Christmas 1936. Waugh found him 'very dotty', and when he officiated at the writer's second marriage in 1937, noted his 'sensational ignorance of the simplest professional duties'. But it seems at least possible that the eminent Jesuit's gamey conservatism may have influenced some of the quirkier anti-progressive attitudes developed by Waugh, who also made good use of Catholic missionaries, including Jesuits, on his extensive post-conversion travels. In 1933 he was in Brazil, reading Cunninghame Graham's *Lost Arcadia* on the Jesuit reductions in Paraguay and staying in the St Ignatius Mission at Bon Success: 'Thatched two-storey dwelling-house; two bedrooms, gallery, downstairs store and dining-room. Tame toucans, ponies, mocking bird, toad (eats cigarette cards etc). Fr Mather infinitely hospitable and kind; talked of Stonyhurst. Church tin sides, thatched roof, mud floor. School, rest-house and Indian dwellings scattered in neighbourhood.' Fr Mather made a pack-saddle and a walking-stick for his guest, mended his watch-glass, and gave him a stone axe-head and 'two cigarette holders to take to J. B. Priestley'; but Waugh found the learned and energetic Fr Keary, who snored and was much given to early Masses, less agreeable as a travelling companion.

Typical, however, of what a Jesuit journal calls 'the traditional plan for Ours in those days', was the *curriculum vitae* of Fr James Brennan.

'Straight from a Jesuit college to noviceship, juniorate, philosophy . . . then teaching at St Francis Xavier's, three years' theology leading to ordination in 1937, followed by fourth year theology, tertianship, and a life-time of teaching . . .' Fr Clement Tigar, Superior and Prefect of Studies at Campion House, Osterley, for thirty years, was one of the hard-driving 'characters' who moulded generations of Jesuits. Much involved in a cult of the Blessed Sacrament, with its concomitant Knights, Handmaids and Pages, he was given to terse dicta ('meekness is not weakness, it is restraint of strength'). Meals were accompanied by readings from the *Imitation* or excerpts from the lives of the English Martyrs. Over-idealistic applicants were firmly rejected ('what a lot of trouble I have saved the bishops'); as an exercise in voice production students were taken to the rooftop to proclaim Campion's *Brag* or passages from *Paradise Lost*; and there was an array of proverbial end-of-term quips ('If there is a dance in your parish when you go home for Christmas, go by all means; and if there is a pretty girl you want to dance with, do so.' Pause. 'But don't come back here in January!').

In the United States, Jesuit training made few concessions to the twentieth century. Daniel Berrigan, reared in a turbulent Irish-American household at Syracuse, New York, remembers that when, at sixteen, he and a friend applied to various religious orders for prospectuses, what impressed them about the Jesuits was that 'they didn't seem to want us. All the other orders were trying to rope us in with photographs of jazzy swimming pools. But the Jebbies just had a couple of tight little quotes from St Ignatius in a very stark pamphlet. We thought that cool scene was revolutionary.' Two years later, in 1939, he entered the Jesuit seminary near Poughkeepsie. No home visits were allowed during the two-year novitiate and only four visits a year from his family. Berrigan, a very conscientious seminarian, did not go home for seven years.

George Riemer, who joined the Society at St Stanislaus, Florissant, Missouri in September 1940, found himself caught in 'a maze of brief activities controlled by bells'. There were strict rules against room visiting, physical contact, and 'particular friendships' (never the same two companions on a walk). Long sleeves were obligatory even when playing tennis or handball. So much time was spent in prayerful meditation that novices developed 'monk's knees' and compared callouses. Strictly limited conversation was held in Latin except at specified times. There was a little light relief in the way of puns – *sub ubis* ('under' plus 'where') for underwear, *quercus* (oak) for okay. First and second year novices were known as *primianni* and *secundianni*. The meeting room was called the ascetary and it was there that the regular *exercitium modestiae* took place. Novices, arranged in a horse-shoe with the novice master at the opening, admonished each other 'objectively and without rancour'. It was not only an exercise in humility but a way of releasing tensions. An exercitant might be peppered with twenty or more criticisms ('Brother has a shattering, loud kind of laugh . . . He comes too close to your face when he talks . . . He is always clicking his ball-point pen'), and was expected to write these down and take them to the novice master for discussion. Looking back on those days, Riemer admitted that some of the Jesuits who later became firm friends were men he would have avoided if he had been given a free choice. But he also wrote that 'September being the month school starts, I've had a lot of bad Septembers, but I can't remember any September that was as bad as the first one at Florissant.' Sometimes he would stand in a field looking down wistfully at the distant lights of St Louis, the wicked, beckoning city. In 1947 he left the Society because he wanted to be a writer and a Jesuit, and 'back then you couldn't be both without getting into trouble . . . no good Jesuit would have dreamed of picketing a bishop or of demonstrating against a Jesuit university. He would never have talked to the press about contraception or abortion or trial marriage without first getting his ideas cleared through his provincial . . . As a member of a historic international organization I had to respect that organization's image and help protect it.'

CHAPTER NINETEEN

New Orders

WRITING IN 1938, Fr Martindale suggested that Catholics should 'vigorously demand social justice . . . As to Communism, we spoil our denunciation of its iniquities by not owning up in considerable detail. The Communists and we see the same things but recommend different methods. We cannot dare to leave the acknowledgement of facts wholly to them . . . *The Clergy Review* has asked to print an article of mine on condition that everything I say about the life of stewards on ships be omitted; for they say that the Shipping Lines might take out a libel action. But it is terrible if Catholics are to remain always within harmless generalities.'

There had been little sign of such thinking at Rome, either in the papal or the Jesuit curia. Under Pius X and Merry del Val papal policy had aimed to crush not only 'modernism' but independent movements towards Christian democracy, ordering their dissolution and replacement by the right-wing, Vatican-controlled Catholic Action. Far more tolerance had been shown to Action Française, led by Charles Maurras, an atheist who regarded Catholicism as an instrument of social discipline much in the manner of Voltaire. Pius X refused to condemn Maurras publicly, describing him as 'a doughty defender of the Church and the Holy See'. Pius XI reluctantly condemned Action Française in 1927 but was hostile to the Partito Popolare, a mass party of Catholic workers with a socialist flavour, and regarded Bolshevik Russia as a satanic foe. Yet in the early years of the Bolshevik régime, when civil war, famine and industrial chaos had brought it close to collapse, the Vatican tried to exploit the situation. Once again, as in the time of Possevino and the episode of the false Dmitri, Jesuits figured prominently in a bizarre interchange conducted in an atmosphere of complete mutual distrust.

Legend insisted that Pius X had died of grief in August 1914 at the news that war had broken out; but another version was that he had succumbed to a paroxysm of joy, having done everything possible to encourage the war so that Catholic Austro-Hungary might open Orthodox Serbia and Russia to the true faith. During the Balkan Wars of

1912 to 1913 Pius X, Merry de Val and Ledochowski, a fervent Polish patriot, had been involved in an elaborate plot for the liberation of Poland and a Bulgarian occupation of Constantinople. The wild hope was that all the Eastern Orthodox who feared Russian occupation might somehow be coaxed back to the Roman obedience. In 1918 the Jesuit General, according to some historians, conceived the 'Ledochowski Plan' for a federation of Catholic states in central and eastern Europe – Bavaria, Austria, Slovakia, Bohemia, Poland, Hungary and Croatia – aimed primarily against Soviet Russia. Mgr Pacelli (later Pope Pius XII), then papal nuncio in Munich, is said to have been a strong supporter of the plan, together with Mgr Ratti, the nuncio in Poland (who became Pope Pius XI in 1922).

As a fanatically anti-Russian, anti-Bolshevik bastion, Poland had by the Treaty of Versailles been awarded two large provinces, formerly part of the Russian empire, containing several million Russian Orthodox Christians and Greek Orthodox Uniates (who practised the Greek rites but recognized the authority of Rome). A campaign to catholicize these schismatics was immediately launched, Orthodox priests arrested, dragonnade techniques applied; and in Soviet Russia Catholic priests were, understandably, classified as political agents of the Polish government. Yet while condoning the Catholic terror in Poland and protesting at the persecution of Catholic priests in Russia, Benedict XV and Pius XI began discreetly to negotiate with the Bolsheviks. Cardinal Gasparri, the Secretary of State, had warned that 'the victory of Tsarist Russia, to whom France and England have made so many promises, would be for the Vatican a disaster greater than the Reformation', involving the occupation of Constantinople and a militant Orthodox challenge to Rome. The fall of the Tsar, the disestablishment of the Orthodox Church, the ravages of civil war, and the eagerness of Bolshevik leaders for some kind of recognition offered a chance which could not be ignored. If the Vatican could supply food and *de facto* recognition, there was a possibility not only of securing tolerance for the Catholic Church in Russia but of replacing the Orthodox Church – at that time notoriously anti-Communist – as the main state-sponsored religious organization.

Osservatore Romano, the official Vatican journal, commented that 'the moment for rapprochement has arrived, inasmuch as the inner circle of caesaro-papism which closed Russia to all Roman influences has been broken.' Italian newspapers ran sarcastic cartoons showing Pius XI blessing the red atheist persecution of Orthodox Christians. Polish

Catholics, whose bid to romanize the Ukraine and overthrow Lenin had failed in 1920, were infuriated by the Vatican's treacherous alternative, knowing that one of the main conditions laid down by Bolshevik negotiators was the exclusion of Polish priests from Soviet territory. But in September 1922 a relief mission led by Fr Edmund J. Walsh, SJ, began work on the understanding that it should refrain from religious propaganda. In the next two years a chain of relief centres catering for about a hundred and fifty thousand people was established. But, perhaps on the widely-held assumption that Bolshevik rule was so precarious that a show of belligerence might help to undermine it, Walsh ignored the agreement.

The mission, in his view, was missionary. It arrived with a million parcels inscribed 'to the children of Russia from the Pope in Rome'. Walsh's attempts to smuggle in foreign priests as relief-distributors were prevented, and his close liaison with President Hoover's American Relief Administration was interpreted as confirming his 'solidarity with western imperialism'. His suggestions for transferring money from abroad to Russia and vice versa were construed as a plot to establish financial links between Russian Catholics and White émigrés, or as evidence that the Jesuit was an agent of the United States Steel Corporation headed by the arch-capitalist J. Pierpont Morgan. Walsh's exasperation was not surprising, but his undisguised enmity caused Bolshevik complaints that he was 'objectionable, haughty, and inclined to make a terrible scandal of every little issue' – though some of the issues, notably the question of whether Catholic property should or should not be nationalized, were regarded as of prime importance by the Vatican. The threat of a second Polish invasion led to the arrest of some Catholic prelates as counter-revolutionary agents. One was executed. But though the Polish, French and British governments made official protests, Pius XI did not. A Bolshevik envoy, Jordansky, reopened negotiations in Rome with Fr Pietro Tacchi-Venturi, a Jesuit scholar-diplomat who was the Pope's main contact with the Fascist leader Benito Mussolini.

In 1924, when the Communist régime had obtained *de jure* recognition from Britain, France and Italy, attitudes changed. The Bolsheviks began to negotiate with the Orthodox Patriarch, and the Vatican concentrated on the conversion of White émigré leaders. The Walsh mission was withdrawn at Soviet demand, the Pope proclaiming that the Reds 'preferred to doom thousands of innocent people to death rather than see them fed by Christian charity'. But the breach was less complete than appeared. In 1925 Chicherin approached Mgr Pacelli, the papal nuncio

[255]

in Berlin, with a detailed plan to regularize the status of the Catholic Church, including the appointment of bishops. Again, the main point demanded in return for the legalization of the Church under government surveillance was the banning of Polish priests from Russia.

Perhaps the sowing of discord was Chicherin's main object. With Polish Catholics already bristling, Pius XI could not accept such a condition, as Ledochowski made very clear. But with the Russian Orthodox Church edging back into favour and the persecution of Catholics likely to increase, some sort of gesture seemed needed if the situation were not to slip completely beyond control. One possibility put forward was the clandestine consecration of Russian bishops who would provide an emergency leadership with special powers. The idea came from a French Jesuit, Michel d'Herbigny, who suggested that the job might be done by an envoy travelling on the trans-Siberian railway to China. He himself was selected to go. Thus began a tragi-comic episode which must surely rank as one of the murkiest in the annals of Jesuit-Vatican politics. Except for his undoubted courage d'Herbigny seems to have been singularly ill-equipped for the role of secret agent. Born in Lille in 1880 and educated by the Jesuits, he became fluent in German and later specialized in Russian studies. By 1912, as a teacher of theology in Belgium, he seemed to have settled into a pedagogic routine. But his reputation as a student of Russian affairs sucked him into the world of political intrigue when Count Orlowski contacted him to expound the programme for Polish liberation and a Rome-oriented Balkan federation in which Pius X, Merry del Val and Ledochowski became interested. Much in demand as an interpreter in Belgium during the war, d'Herbigny was given the Legion of Honour; the citation stated that he had supplied French Army headquarters with 'useful information' about the final German offensive.

In 1921 he was teaching at the Gregorian University when the Society was asked by the Vatican to supply Apostolic Visitors to Lithuania, Estonia and Latvia. D'Herbigny, who supervised their training, was in 1923 appointed head of the Pontifical Oriental Institute and in October 1925 visited Moscow as official French observer at the Orthodox Church Council. Back in Rome he made a full report to the Pope, which among other details dealt with the peculiarities of the water-closets in Moscow. In his hotel, he said, it had been forbidden to flush down used paper, which had to be placed in an 'evil-smelling' basket. After burning a piece of paper on which he had noted an address, he had dropped the ashes, and the match, into the pan, but his Russian 'shadow' had verified that the spent match resembled those in a box in d'Herbigny's possession.

Clandestinity now enveloped him. His consecration as bishop (of Ilium – Troy) was performed in Berlin in 1926 by Mgr Pacelli, with one witness, sworn to secrecy. Pius XI and his advisers worked out a paper redistribution of the one and a half million Catholics in Russia into five Latin-rite dioceses and one exarchate for those using the Slav-Byzantine rite. Cardinal Gasparri joked that if d'Herbigny managed to consecrate a few bishops and was then martyred by the Reds 'we will get you canonized before long'. Ledochowski was not enthusiastic. Muttering about Polish hostility, he promised to pray for d'Herbigny, but insisted that no information about the assignment should be revealed even after its completion. D'Herbigny was, for all public purposes, to remain simply a member of the Society of Jesus. His mission did not stay confidential for long – it seems likely that a woman in the same compartment on the train was a Soviet agent and that the bishop was pumped – but in Moscow, after various alarms and excursions, three bishops were consecrated. Two years later d'Herbigny made one more sortie to consecrate a Vicar-General for Leningrad, and in 1929 took over direction of the Pontifical Russian College (the Russicum), whose chief function was to train priests to work among the many refugees in Europe, the United States and Australia.

Almost from the start of this appointment, the reward of an apparently successful mission, he was in trouble. News filtered through that two of the newly-consecrated bishops had been sent to prison camps, many priests arrested, and an obviously well-informed persecution launched. D'Herbigny was blamed for a leakage which was later traced to one of his enemies in the papal entourage, and there were other repercussions. Herbette, the French ambassador in Moscow, who had taken a close interest in d'Herbigny's missions, was rebuked; Franco-Soviet relations were affected; and Count Brockdorff-Rantzau, the German ambassador, who had sometimes acted for the Vatican in dealings with Foreign Commissar Chicherin, protested at Herbette's reckless attempt to extend French influence among Russian Catholics.

Herbette complained that d'Herbigny's naïvety made him a bad security risk, an assessment which seemed correct when the harassed Jesuit failed to realize that some 'fanatical' Russian Catholics who came to the Russicum with pleas for help with underground journalism and propositions for gun-running were Soviet *agents provocateurs*. Maurras was convinced that d'Herbigny (who was on the Sapinière's black list) had influenced the Pope to condemn Action Française. The Soviet embassy in Rome suspected that he was involved in arranging the Mass of Expiation in St Peter's on 19 March 1930 when, with Pius XI himself presiding, a huge congregation that included many Russian exiles commemorated the victims of Soviet persecution. When Cardinal Pacelli succeeded Gasparri as Secretary of State d'Herbigny had few allies in the Vatican. Pacelli had been irritated by the secret consecration which he had been forced to perform at short notice, and in any case considered that he was far more competent to deal with Soviet affairs. The next blow came when Pius XI directed that an account of a pontifical Mass conducted in Moscow by his protégé should appear in the *Osservatore Romano,* thus making public his episcopal status. Ledochowski, who had always had misgivings about the affair, was furious. Not without reason, for the dictator Josef Pilsudski threatened to deport all the Jesuits in Poland to Russia in army trucks unless d'Herbigny was sacked from the Russicum, and the Polish hierarchy promised to resign en bloc.

Pius XI now abandoned d'Herbigny to the wolves. An inquisition conducted by two Jesuits convicted him of carnal relations with two women, fathering an illegitimate child, baptizing a man who turned out to be a Russian agent. They concluded that he was either an imbecile or a traitor, perhaps a bit of both. The Russicum continued under Jesuit direction. When Walter Ciszek, who had entered the Society's novitiate six years earlier at Poughkeepsie, New York, arrived in Rome in 1934 to study Russian language, liturgy and history, he found twelve other candidates in training – Belgian, English, Spanish, Italian, Russian, Polish and Rumanian. All were hoping to be sent to Russia, which for Jesuit missionaries now had the sort of baleful attraction which China and Japan had once possessed. There was at least one more secret mission to Moscow, involving two Jesuits who tried to set up a parish or seminary. But by that time d'Herbigny, who had been forced to sign a statement admitting his guilt and to resign his offices in Rome, was well out of the picture. First banished, like Teilhard, to China, where he was kept under close watch, he spent the last twenty years of his life under house arrest at Jesuit residences in Belgium and France. During this time he wrote a number of books, none of them published but all dutifully read and shelved by the censors. He was, in his own phrase, 'buried alive'. When he died in 1957 the inscription on his grave described him simply as 'Père Michel', neither bishop nor SJ.

The full story will perhaps never be known: certainly not unless the relevant files in the Vatican and in the Jesuit archives are opened to inspection – and are still intact. But a book published in 1973 which draws heavily on the d'Herbigny episode tells the thrilling and convincingly contexted story of a 1935 mission, complete with a specially-created Russian-American bishop called Alexander Ulanov, a protégé of Pacelli chosen because of his socialist sympathies. In *The Jesuit* by John Gallahue (a former member of the Society in the United States) Ulanov's brother, who against instructions is included in the team, turns out to be a Communist agent. In a dramatic finale Pius XI strips Ulanov of 'each and every function, honour and privilege of the office of bishop and of priest', sentencing him to '"be transported to the property of the Jesuit order at Toulouse . . . There you will spend the remainder of your days on this earth. You shall speak to no man nor be spoken to by any, excepting the one person designated by your Father General as your confessor . . . Everyone who has ever manifested a religious sympathy in Russia in relationship, however indirect, to this mission . . . every one of them" – the Pope rose suddenly from his chair and shouted in the chapel – "is dead or in Siberia or in Lubyanka prison or being tortured or hunted, at this very moment . . . You, our representatives, have destroyed the Church in Russia . . . I die with your dead on my soul. I too must answer to God."' After a long period of oblivion the strange case of Michel d'Herbigny seems likely to be re-examined. But French Jesuits are opposed to any attempt at rehabilitation.

Ledochowski, who had so reluctantly endorsed Pius XI's romantic enthusiasm for the Russian venture, acted promptly and ruthlessly to silence d'Herbigny for the honour of the papacy and the good of the Society. But he did not restrain the *Civiltà Cattolica,* which, when Action Française was belatedly denounced by Pius XI, appeared with a subdued version of the anti-semitic opinions it had expressed during the Dreyfus Case. In the 1890s it had charged the Jews with controlling 'half of Bohemia' through the Rothschilds, championing state-directed education in the United States out of hatred for Catholics, contriving the secularization of Rome, and 'de-Christianizing' France. In 1927 it declared that 'the Judaic mentality is a danger to the world . . . the Jews are double-dealers . . . the Jewish religion is double-dealing also because, in spite of its merits, it is profoundly corrupt.'

There were, however, signs that Jesuits and Freemasons were drawing closer together in face of a common enemy. In Soviet Russia the Masonic movement had been banned as an instrument of bourgeois counter-revolution and in Europe Social Democratic parties saw it in much the same light. Prolonged and delicate negotiations resulted in a conference held in June 1928 at Aix-la-Chapelle, where Fr Hermann

Gruber, a leading Jesuit writer on Freemasonry, met representatives from the Grand Lodges in New York and Vienna. Fundamental differences were not denied, but both sides agreed to minimize public controversy. Fr Gruber substituted 'deism' for 'godlessness' in his next anti-masonic publication, expressed a desire that differences 'should be discussed with suitable earnestness, in the spirit of true Christian, or if you prefer, humanitarian charity . . . with no other object than that truth may prevail in the interests of all,' and conceded that 'the childish, false ideas regarding Freemasonry which are still so deplorably widespread should be discreetly combated.' Falling into line, *Civiltà Cattolica* and *Études* did their best to conciliate the organization which for so long had been a main target for editorial thunderbolts.

Jesuit theologians had helped to formulate Leo XIII's social encyclical *Rerum Novarum,* and Jesuits now laboured to expound and expand this antidote to Marxism. The moral theologian Victor Cathrein explained that 'like everything else property may be, and often is, misused . . . nevertheless inequality in the distribution of worldly goods is of exceptional importance as the means by which God is able to try us and by which we can exercise virtue and so attain to everlasting life. By this unequal distribution rich and poor are drawn together for mutual assistance in carrying out the divine purpose.' Though admitting that socialist critics had performed a service in calling attention to the evils of uncontrolled capitalism, Cathrein suggested that the answer was not state capitalism but a recognition by employers and employees that 'man's relationship to God is that of a steward who together with privileges has incurred obligations.'

In a five-volume exposition of what he called Christian Solidarism the economist Heinrich Pesch attempted to strike a 'healthy balance' between over-individualistic capitalism and over-collectivist Marxism. Gustav Gundlach implied that Jesuits, trained 'to apply effort to the best advantage' and to 'make a positive valuation of the world', were peculiarly fitted to indicate a solution to the difficulties raised by 'the quickened rhythm of life in our modern industrial society'. Yet another German Jesuit, Oswald von Nell-Breuning, whose development of the ideas of Pesch and Gundlach was known as 'subsidiarism', played a considerable part in drafting Pius XI's encyclical of 1931, *Quadragesimo Anno.* The Jesuit legend was still sufficiently powerful to ensure that Marxist commentators took it very seriously. 'Catholic Christian Social-ism, the most insidious form of Fascism, has been officially founded,' wrote one, pointing out that 'this encyclical is more practical than *Rerum*

Novarum. It recommends the necessity of "humanizing" labour legislation and founding workers' cooperatives and savings banks, and makes a fundamental distinction between the "right" to property and its "use". Private property, as St Thomas Aquinas stated, was created by God, but it has certain "social duties". The "family wage" and social insurance are the methods by which employers are to fulfil these duties.'

In *The Civil War in Spain* (1938) Frank Jellinek argued that the Jesuit-papal master-stroke made it 'easy for Catholic Christian Socialism to base itself on the eternal emotional platitudes which have not yet lost their attraction for the uneducated masses: Religion, Family, Patriotism, Property, Discipline . . . the real Fascism in Spain was never young Primo de Rivera's pistol-dramatism but the insidious Catholic propaganda for the brotherhood of master and man. When the clergy were forced out into the open to defend this Fascism with guns, the Spanish masses realized the danger and burned the churches.' Making due allowance for such crude over-simplification, it is hard to deny that the neo-Thomist convolutions of Cathrein, Pesch, Gundlach and Nell-Breuning could look provocatively trite when stripped of verbiage as in this editorial sermon, based on *Quadragesimo Anno,* which appeared in *Trabajo,* a labour-oriented Spanish Catholic paper: 'It is untrue that you hate Capital, friend worker. No, you want it yourself, as we all do . . . You do not hate Capital, but the Capitalist who does not fulfil his obligations towards you. To a certain extent you are right. But you cannot defend yourself with hatred. You will only answer injustice with injustice . . . To sum up, friend worker, Capital is not an abuse, only those that abuse it. Against these abuses there should be a legal rate of interest for loans, legal regulation of labour contracts, State protection of the worker, non-political means to deal with other abuses . . . You agree? Then in future, friend worker, don't say you hate Capital!'

In *The Jesuit* John Gallahue imagines Pius XI, flanked by Cardinal Pacelli and General Ledochowski, justifying Vatican foreign policy to Bishop Ulanov on the eve of his departure to Russia. 'Is it not a fact that we are the only institution left confronting the nation states with the limitation of their powers? Is it not we alone who deny the primacy of Mammon and Caesar, and shall they not hate us – liberal, Fascist and Communist alike? I had, it is true, to negotiate with Mussolini, but I negotiated precisely to force the surrender of those religious prerogatives he was asserting. Insofar as he conceded these claims, he gave up his Fascism. . . Of course we are in no position to depose any leader. But with the few fragile weapons in our possession we do fight to prevent the

[261]

people being destroyed by their own leaders and to protect the true primacies of salvation and freedom. However inadequate we are to this task, who else is there? Who else can speak for mankind as a whole, for each individual's meaning, beyond a national destiny and economic success?'

That, in broad outline, was and remains the official version. But one did not have to be an atheist or a cynic to see that it needed plenty of qualification. Excluded from the peace conference and the League of Nations, the papacy was a political outsider which sought allies where it could find them, often among other political outsiders. In the seventeen years of Pius XI's pontificate, fifteen concordats (Church-State deals) were made, among them those with Italy, Germany, Austria, Poland, Portugal, Rumania and Czechoslovakia. Democratic freedom was the last consideration in any of these bargains. Ever since Constantine the papacy had been used to negotiating with autocrats. Mussolini and Hitler, with large Catholic populations to manage, had a need, however temporary and resented, for respectability and recognition which ignored ideological barriers. The concordats could hardly be said to have acted as a brake on nationalist aggression. As nuncio in Berlin and as Pope Pius XII, Pacelli worked to destroy Christian democracy as an obstacle to agreement with the Nazis. In Italy the 'leftist' Partito Popolare was dismantled and its leader, the Sicilian priest Don Luigi Sturzo, forced into exile. One of Pius XII's first moves on becoming pope in 1939 was to revoke the ban on Action Française. The papacy and the various hierarchies, rather than the Catholic populations of Europe, benefited from a 'protection' that was morally dubious and minimally effective.

There was probably little that the Jesuit curia could have done to halt or modify papal policy. But the Society's reputation for fishing in troubled political waters and for manipulating autocrats was such that Pius XI, with his Jesuit confessors, was rumoured to be a secret Jesuit himself. Ledochowski was even more optimistic than the Pope about persuading Mussolini to settle the 'Roman Question' in return for Vatican backing. In 1921 a speech by Mussolini praising the papal contribution to the greatness of Rome, which publicly indicated the Duce's desire for a deal, was said to have been drafted by Tacchi-Venturi, who took part in a series of confidential talks soon after the Fascist march on Rome in 1922. After more than half a century of 'persecution' by democratic politicians the prisoner of the Vatican and his Jesuit advisers scented a kind of revenge.

The Lateran Agreements of 1929, negotiated by the lawyer brother of Cardinal Pacelli, solved the Roman question by recognizing the 'sovereign rights' of the Pope in a tiny 'papal state' known as Vatican City. The Holy See graciously accepted a largesse of 750 million lire plus the interest on 1000 million lire of State Bonds as 'a definite settlement of its financial relations with Italy in connection with the events of 1870'. There were also tax exemptions, immunity for Vatican diplomats and for foreign diplomats accredited to the Vatican, safeguards for the Pope's life and 'honour' as stringent as those for the King, the introduction of religious teaching in State schools, and a veto on divorce.

Though Pius XI's major denunciations of totalitarian dictatorships were infrequent, Fr Tacchi-Venturi, until the collapse of the Fascist régime in 1943 the Vatican's link with the Duce, was quite often called in for consultation. 'Had a talk with Fr Tacchi-Venturi,' Ciano recorded on 9 August 1938. 'We agreed about the advisability of taking steps to avoid a conflict between the Holy See and Fascism. . . The friction with Catholic Action is unimportant and may easily be kept within bounds if there is goodwill on both sides.' In the course of his unenviable duties, the Jesuit had to endure a good deal of rhetorical thunder from Mussolini. 'It seems,' noted Ciano, 'that the Pope made another disagreeable speech yesterday about exaggerated nationalism and racial ideology. The Duce has summoned Fr Tacchi-Venturi for this evening and proposes to deliver an ultimatum.' The Duce rehearsed his speech: 'Contrary to what is believed, I am a patient man. But if the Pope continues to talk like this I will tickle up the Italians and turn them into anti-clericals again. The men in the Vatican are mummified. No one believes in a God who bothers about our petty troubles. I should despise a God who bothered about the personal affairs of the policeman standing at the corner of the Corso.' But Tacchi-Venturi (the author of a classic history of the Jesuits in Italy) was able to discount the bluster, knowing that, as Ciano put it, 'in the present difficult international situation a conflict with the Church would help nobody.'

Pius XI's full-dress condemnations of Hitler and racism were the signal for an attack on the Church in Germany. They had been long delayed because the concordats of 1929 with Mussolini and of 1933 with Hitler were in effect continuations of Leo XIII's anti-socialist pact with Bismarck. The Church had agreed to support the State if the State kept Bolshevism at bay. But there is evidence that after years of diplomatic restraint Pius XI's conscience was troubling him. In June 1938, old and ill, he commissioned three Jesuits to draft an encyclical firmly denouncing racist nationalism in general and anti-semitism in particular. Cardinal Pacelli, now Secretary of State, who had spent twelve years in Germany and whose entourage included two German Jesuits, was watching closely, and the draft was held back by Ledochowski. When Pius XI died a few months later – there was a rumour that he had been poisoned – Fr La Farge, one of the drafters, was told that he could publish the 'paper', but only as a private opinion.

The years of the Second World War and the prelude to it were full of incidents or coincidences for those intent on reviving the 'black legend' of the Society. In 1939 a certain Albert Hartl, who had become a priest at the persuasion of his Jesuit teacher but in 1933 left the Church to join the SS and become 'Chief of Church Information', sought an opinion on the Nazi euthanasia programme from Dr Josef Mayer, professor of moral theology at the Catholic University of Paderborn. Employing what he called the Jesuit technique of probabilism, Dr Mayer argued that 'most moral decisions are dubious . . . if there are reasonable grounds and authorities in support of personal opinion, then such personal opinion can become decisive even if there are other reasonable grounds and authorities opposing it.' He concluded that as there were 'reasonable' grounds for and against euthanasia of the mentally ill it could be considered 'defensible'. Mayer's verdict, complete with a lengthy historical summary and quotes from St Thomas Aquinas, was shown to Protestant and Catholic leaders, including the papal nuncio, Cesare Orsenigo. There was no outright condemnation and the programme was launched.

Heinrich Himmler was notorious for his belief that the SS, which he saw as a religious élite, was the Nazi equivalent of the Society of Jesus, and in his book *The Secret Front* (1953) the former SS officer Walter Hagen alleged that Ledochowski was 'ready to organize, on the basis of anti-communism, some collaboration between the SS and the Jesuit Order'. Hitler, a lapsed Catholic who was inclined to make fun of Himmler's religious mania, remarked that 'I can see him as our Ignatius Loyola' and told the author-politician Hermann Rauschning that he himself had 'learned much from the Jesuits'. Walter Schellenberg, a former SS general and close confidant, wrote that Himmler 'possessed the largest library on the Jesuit Order and had studied it for years . . . he modelled the SS organization on Jesuit principles. The Constitutions and Exercises of Ignatius Loyola served as foundations. The highest command was absolute obedience, the execution of every order without contradiction. Himmler himself, as Reichsführer of the SS, was the general of the order. . . A restored medieval fortress at Paderborn in Westphalia was, so to speak, the SS monastery to which Himmler summoned his secret consistory once a year. Here everyone had to undergo meditation and exercises in concentration.'

Himmler would seem to have studied the legend rather than the history of the Jesuits. But years later Pierre Dominique, a French historian, was in no doubt that Jesuit influence was ubiquitous and nefarious. 'Some will say that I see them everywhere,' he says in *La Politique des Jésuites* (1955), 'but . . . they were behind the monarchy of Alfonso XIII of Spain, whose confessor was Fr Lopez. . . When the Spanish monarchy was ended and their colleges burned, they were found again behind Gil Robles, then, when civil war broke out, behind Franco. In Portugal they uphold Salazar. . . In Austria and Hungary the Emperor Charles was dethroned three times (what part did they play in those attempts to regain the throne of Hungary?). . . Monsignor Seipel, Dollfuss and Schuschnigg are from their ranks. In Italy they support first Don Luigi Sturzo and then Mussolini . . . Fr Tacchi-Venturi served as the middleman between Pius XI, whose confessors were the Jesuit Fathers Alissiardi and Celebrano, and Mussolini. . . The Jesuits have their secret abode in the Vatican. . . From there they survey the Universal Church with the cold, calculating eye of the politician.' Another Frenchman, Frédéric Hoffet, argued that with Hitler, Himmler and Goebbels all brought up in the faith 'the National Socialist government was the most Catholic that Germany ever had. . . On this subject nothing is more instructive than Joseph Goebbels' works. He had been educated in a Jesuit college . . . every line of his writings recalls the teaching of his masters . . . he stresses obedience, the contempt for truth – "Some lies are as useful as bread," he proclaimed, by virtue of a moral relativism extracted from the works of Ignatius Loyola.' In *The Secret History of the Jesuits* Edmond Paris startlingly maintains that *Mein Kampf* was 'written by the Jesuit Father Staempfle and signed by Hitler. It was the Society of Jesus which perfected the Pan-German programme and the Führer endorsed it.'

There was a persistent rumour that the assassination of King Alexander of Yugoslavia and the French Foreign Minister Louis Barthou in Marseilles on 9 October 1934 by a Macedonian terrorist had been master-minded by another Jesuit, Fr Korochetz, who had been banished by King Alexander. After the assassination Korochetz, according to one account, 'was recalled from exile and began to conspire with the Regent, Prince Paul, and with Mussolini and Goering to bring Yugoslavia into the Nazi-Fascist orbit.'

In Spain the Jesuit legend, and the Jesuits, were both flourishing. Dispersed in 1767, 1820, 1836 and 1868, the Society had grown richer and more powerful than ever in the years between its return in 1876 and the proclamation of the Republic in 1931. This seemingly almost miraculous achievement was due in part to a system whereby Jesuit property was held through limited companies or individual agents. Frank Jellinek stated that 'in 1879 three English Brothers were entrusted with the nominal ownership of the Spanish Province's property' and that the third party arrangement worked perfectly until the outbreak of civil war in 1936. In 1912 it was estimated that, with the help of heavy investments from the general funds, the Company controlled one-third of the country's capital wealth.

By the 1920s Jesuit commercial activity had, in popular gossip, reached mythical proportions. It was confidently asserted that they 'ran' the antiques business, supplied Madrid with fresh fish and owned the liveliest of its cabarets. Their financial expertise was rated as second only to that of Juan March, the Majorcan buccaneer capitalist, and in the 1930s a sharp-eyed researcher noticed that the Society's legal adviser appeared as president of nine companies, vice-president of six, and director of twenty-nine. A lot of money was pumped into subsidies for Jesuit schools, which were able to undercut clerical rivals (a manoeuvre that roused much ill-feeling). Their teaching was impregnated with the spirit of the Church Catechism as represented in the following excerpt: 'What does Liberalism teach? That the State is independent of the Church. What kind of sin is Liberalism? A most grievous sin against the Faith. Why? Because it consists of a collection of heresies condemned by the Church. Is it a sin for a Catholic to read a Liberal newspaper? He may read the *Stock Exchange News*. What sin is committed by him who votes for a Liberal candidate? Generally a mortal sin.' All this was a far cry from the sixteenth century, when Juan Mariana, a Jesuit black sheep for all his brilliance, had proclaimed the immorality of private ownership in land and demanded State intervention to ensure that natural wealth was justly distributed; and when José de Acosta, in his *Natural and Moral History of the Indies,* had recommended the application of Inca state socialism to Spain.

Primo de Rivera's proposal to allow Jesuit colleges to grant degrees caused violent protests in the universities and was an important factor in the collapse of his dictatorship. The Republican Constitution of 1931 secularized education, legalized divorce, forbade religious orders to indulge in commerce, and dissolved the Society of Jesus. Dozens of churches were destroyed, among them a new Jesuit church in the centre of Madrid on whose blackened walls was scrawled 'The Justice of the People on Thieves'. Visiting Loyola at this time, Walter Starkie was told by a young Jesuit that the place was 'crowded with members of our order who have had to flee from the incendiarists in the cities. . . We are ready to leave at any moment. But we shall return to the Casa Santa of our founder, even if they scatter us to the ends of the earth. . . In this hour of peril for Spain there is only one hero to lead – Saint Ignatius.' And sure enough, Jesuit enterprise, together with left-wing dissensions, played a considerable part in the revival of the Right which brought victory in the elections of November 1933. Already possessing a large interest in a film company dedicated to furthering 'patriotic and religious ideals' and controlling *El Debate,* one of the most influential daily papers, the Society helped to channel monarchist, conservative and Catholic sentiment into Acción Popular, the political branch of Catholic Action, with Gil Robles as a potential Duce.

The victory of the reorganized Popular Front in 1936 was, according to *El Debate,* a victory for 'communism . . . infinitely more dangerous when disguised with the mask of governmental collaboration'. During the anti-clerical fury of the first months of the civil war Jesuits were inevitably among the victims. But in May 1939 an edict of General Franco's not only welcomed the return of the Jesuits but loaded them with privileges and responsibilities.

Pius XII broadcast an apostolic benediction: 'With great joy we address you, dearest sons of Catholic Spain, to express our paternal congratulation for the gift of peace and victory with which God has chosen to crown your Christian heroism.' But his celebrated silence about the Final Solution and about Nazi atrocities in general seemed to many people, Catholics included, one of the shabbiest aspects of the Second World War. According to Edmond Paris, Hitler, Mussolini and Franco were 'in spite of appearances, but war pawns manipulated by the Vatican and its Jesuits'; and after the fall of France Ledochowski 'already spoke arrogantly about the General Congregation the Company would hold in Rome when England had capitulated'. But though some Jesuits, and other priests, came to terms with the New Order, others were deeply involved in resistance. Just before he was strangled in Plotzensee camp, one of them, Fr Alfred Delp, wrote with commendable moderation that 'an honest history of religion will have to include bitter chapters on

[267]

the support given by the Church to the rise of totalitarianism and the dictator principle.' These chapters were already being written. In 1943, when Pius XII protested so vigorously about the Allied bombing of Monte Cassino and the accidental fall of a few small bombs in the grounds of the Vatican, the Polish underground press jeered that he 'showed himself to be no more than a bishop of a Mediterranean peninsula . . . the Vatican had tied itself up with the Nazis so as to conquer Russia for Catholicism and to this end sacrificed Poland.'

Hitler had defined 'pure Christianity' as 'whole-hearted Bolshevism under a tinsel of metaphysics'. Pius XII's Christianity came perilously close to being whole-hearted anti-Bolshevism under a tinsel of metaphysics. The Soviet invasion of Finland in 1939 was condemned by the *Osservatore Romano* as 'a calculated crime . . . the most cynical aggression of modern times', but there was no papal comment on the German invasion of Poland, nor on the Hitler-Stalin pact which left eastern Poland under Soviet occupation – perhaps because it was understood that this would be temporary (Polish Jesuits are said to have alerted the Vatican well in advance of the good news of the German invasion of Russia in 1941). When the tide turned at Stalingrad, the Pope's concern to save Europe from the red menace caused him to plead Hitler's case for a negotiated peace, to reject President Roosevelt's plea that he should call on the Catholic world to fight Nazi Germany ('because the Vatican is unable to identify itself with the war aims of any group of belligerents'), and finally to proclaim that 'the declaration of Casablanca, demanding the unconditional surrender of the Tripartite Powers, is completely incompatible with Christian doctrines.'

Non-Catholic religious leaders with similar misgivings had approached the Vatican in the hope of creating a common front to condemn total war in *all* its forms: but this would not only have involved speaking out against Hitler but co-operating on a basis of equality with heretics and schismatics. Were the Roman Jesuits particularly guilty of justifying the conspiracy of silence and encouraging the Pope's fantasies? Insofar as they were peculiarly well-placed to influence him, the answer would seem to be 'Yes'. Robert Leiber, who from 1924 until Pius XII's death in 1958 was his private secretary and confidant, is known to have written a number of the Pope's almost invariably nauseating radio speeches, for instance the Christmas 1941 broadcast ('We love all peoples without exception and with equal affection . . . We have imposed the maximum reserve on Ourselves so as to avoid even the appearance of being contaminated with the Party spirit'), or that of 1942 with its ambiguous talk of a 'holy crusade' to ensure that 'the star of Peace, the star of Bethlehem, should burst forth once again in its shining light, in its pacifying comfort, as promise and augury of a better, happier future' (of this effusion Mussolini remarked that it was 'full of platitudes and might just as well be by a village priest'). Not long before his death in December 1942 Ledochowski is said to have seconded a German approach for a cease-fire; and he apparently saw nothing reprehensible in the fact that the Society was (to quote a report of August 1958 in *Der Spiegel*) 'earning money from both sides with this raw material [mercury]. While the Spanish firm supplied the Allies and the Russians, the Italian mines serviced German armament factories.'

Ledochowski's loyalty to his grotesque chief was such that he accepted the agony of Poland as a necessary prelude to the Russian crusade, geared up the Russicum for the great opportunity, and urged Polish Jesuit Superiors to defend the strategy. A Polish Home Army report described the Jesuits as 'representing the Vatican element . . . Their activity is preeminently political . . . they try to be discreet and to influence many circles . . . Typical of Rev.17 [code] is his last statement, according to which the German clergy should not be indicted . . . Jesuits are in close touch with the secret nuncio of the Vatican – an Italian priest hostile to the Poles. His attitude is illustrated by his phrase "the Poles are responsible for their fate".'

'How many divisions has the Pope?' asked Stalin sarcastically. None of his own to be sure, but that did not prevent him or Ledochowski from using any force that seemed likely to open the way to catholicization, above all at the expense of the Orthodox Church. A Jesuit had been linked with the assassination of King Alexander of Yugoslavia in 1934, and the Jesuits were involved in the frightful pogroms of Orthodox Serbs in Croatia. After the invasion of 1941 Yugoslavia had been partitioned: Serbia under German occupation, Croatia an Italian puppet state ruled by Ante Pavelic, whose nationalist organization, the Ustase, had since 1919 been agitating for independence from Orthodox Serbia. A fanatical Catholic-Fascist, Pavelic offered the two and a quarter million Serbs in Croatia the choice of expulsion, conversion, or death. In the next four years the papacy stayed silent while three hundred thousand Serbs, including Jews, were deported, more than half a million massacred and a quarter of a million forcibly converted. Pius XII received Pavelic and members of the Croatian SS, and in *Civiltà Cattolica* a Croatian Jesuit glorified 'Catholic crusaders' whose victims were lucky if they had their throats slit rather than being axe-hacked into mass graves or bound with barbed wire and buried alive.

Archbishop Stepinac of Zagreb failed to indict the crusaders. A papal observer, Abbot Marcone, failed to restrain their zeal. Though the Franciscans were particularly prominent as terrorist leaders, marching crucifix in hand at the head of the columns, Jesuit chaplains too slaughtered and sacked their way through Bosnia and Ustase bands. During one of the most appalling civilian massacres on record Ustase representatives from 'Holy Croatia' were careful to keep in touch with the Jesuit curia, which, as one of them reported in June 1942, 'faithfully reflects the Vatican. The General loves the Croats personally and is pleased at their independence; but there are two Slovenes in the Curia . . . and the Assistant for Slav jurisdiction, Fr Preseren, is all for the resurrection of Yugoslavia.' After a talk with Ledochowski, another envoy – a Vatican chamberlain called Lobkovicz – sent word to Zagreb that 'he received me with great cordiality, assuring me repeatedly that he will help me in every way.' Ledochowski ('certainly one of the finest Generals of this powerful and famous Order') died a few weeks later and, pending the time when a General Congregation could be called, was replaced by Alessio Magni, General Assistant for Italy. 'According to definite information,' reported Lobkovicz, 'Magni is not kindly disposed towards the Croats . . . a man of limited outlook.' But there were compensations. Fr Preseren seemed more friendly and Fr Leiber, professor of ecclesiastical history at the Gregorian University, was, though cagey, not discouraging: 'Among other things he said that the ideal state in Europe was Portugal, because on the one hand it puts its Catholic principles into practice, and on the other – unlike Dollfuss's Austria – does not compromise the Church and its teaching.' This oblique criticism of Ustase methods was followed by a denial that the Vatican's lack of positive support was due to a predominance of Italians ('Leiber insisted that the Pope, like the Secretary of State and their closest collaborators, was above any kind of national prejudice'). Lobkovicz was persistent: "We must keep in touch with Leiber, since he is one of the Holy Father's closest advisers. I gave him a copy of *Ustase Principles* and managed to arouse in him a great interest in our case. I think he will help us.'

But the deviousness of curial politics, the actions of a few Jesuit thugs in Croatia, and the papalist-collaborationist attitudes of some Jesuits elsewhere should not obscure the fact that Fr Delp was by no means the only member of his order to show the courage of his own convictions.

More than thirty German Jesuits were interned and two executed. About fifty Jesuits – Polish, German, Austrian, French, Dutch, Belgian – died in concentration camps, mainly in Dachau. Riccardo Fontana, the idealistic young hero of Rolf Hochhuth's play *The Representative,* is one of the very few examples of a 'good' Jesuit in recent fiction; and the exploits of Jesuit *résistants* drew tribute from Daniel Berrigan not only in the form of poems and essays but in similarly motivated action. About a hundred French Jesuits were active in the Resistance, notably in the Temoignage Chrétien group, founded at Lyon in 1941 by Fr Pierre Chaillet, which included Frs Henri de Lubac, Desqueyrat and Henri Chambre. It printed and distributed a clandestine journal and helped Jews to hide or escape. Other Jesuits took part in Maquis guerrilla operations. About twelve were shot or deported.

Stranded during the war in a Jesuit residence in Copenhagen, Fr Martindale was repelled by the dusty aspidistras, puzzled over what to say to Catholic partisans who asked him 'Can I lawfully kill so-and-so?', and tormented by the problem of how he should behave to the German priests in the house. After watching a triumphal parade of German troops through the city he had noted that the men were Sudetens, 'small, ruddy and very non-Prussian . . . another multitude to embrace with all one's heart.' But it was impossible to sustain this mood of Olympian charity. 'What,' he asked himself, 'would be the Christian way? Is it compatible with quiet unyielding dignity? With plain-spokenness? Must one try to be positively friendly also in manner, with the certainty of being misunderstood?' Immobilized by two heart attacks and fretting at his inactivity, Martindale nevertheless completed a biography of St Camillus de Lellis who in 1584, horrified by hospital conditions, had founded the Servants of the Sick, insisting on such innovations as open windows, sensible diet, the isolation of contagious cases, and making sure that patients were really dead before they were buried. In the last months of the German occupation, with the noise of looting and sniping in the streets, he reflected upon the energy and daring of SS Ignatius and Camillus and wondered how the Church – and the Society – would tackle the need to present the faith freshly and arrestingly in a churned-up world. 'The clergy,' he wrote in his journal, 'will never do this unless awful disasters and all but extermination come upon us or unless we have a quite miraculous and heroically audacious Pope.'

CHAPTER TWENTY

New Directions

IN 1946 THE TWENTY-NINTH General Congregation elected a fifty-seven-year-old Belgian, John Baptist Janssens, as General. The thirtieth General Congregation, in 1957, elected a Canadian, John L. Swain, as Vicar. Janssens' health, like that of Ledochowski, had begun to fail under the burden of office. In eastern Europe the Soviet empire had engulfed sixty million Catholics, in China the Communist revolution had virtually destroyed Christian missions, in Africa and Asia nationalist, often quasi-Marxist, sentiment challenged missionary paternalism. Among Jesuits there were the first mutterings of rebellion against the Society's ultramontane image which were part of a general restlessness that by 1959 had forced the papacy, in the person of John XXIII, to call for a Second Vatican Council. When after three years of deliberation the Council ended in 1965, the year of Janssens' death, the Society of Jesus found itself in a curious and somewhat exasperating crisis.

An *Atlas Geographicus* issued in 1964 to commemorate the hundred and fiftieth anniversary of its restoration showed that the Sociey was more populous than ever. There were nearly thirty six thousand Jesuits – more than eight thousand 'of them Americans – as compared with seventeen thousand in 1914. The organization embraced eight Assistancies with more than eighty provinces and vice-provinces, and put out over a thousand publications in a hundred and fifty languages with a yearly printing of a hundred and fifty million copies and fourteen million subscribers. Nearly seven thousand Jesuits were manning some thirty mission fields. About twelve thousand Jesuits were teachers or administrators in over four and a half thousand schools with fifty thousand non-Jesuit teachers and administrators and at least one and a quarter million students. In 1956 even Norway had relented to lift a four-century-old ban on the Society. And at this point it was, like other orders, asked to search its soul and decide whether these triumphant statistics did not conceal an urgent need for renewal by 'a return to the sources of Christian life and the original inspiration of the founder'.

During Pius XII's reign, which did not end until 1958, the Society, like the Church as a whole, was bathed in an Indian summer of papal triumphalism. Frs Leiber and Hendrich, Jesuit archivists and confidants, continued to live in the Vatican just above the Pope's apartments, the German Jesuit Augustin Bea was the Pope's confessor. All three, perhaps, helped to make him a master of public relations and to inspire that parody of Ignatius' catholicizing fervour which led him to pronounce, in suitably technical detail, on the moral obligations of doctors, dentists, lawyers, architects, journalists, engineers, actors, film producers and cinema managers (to name but a few recipients of his promiscuous wisdom). Like Pius VII in 1815 and Benedict XV in 1914 he firmly blamed the horrors of war and its aftermath of international tensions on the failure to heed the Vatican. The enemies of the Church – Communists, heretics, schismatics – had not changed, nor could there be any question of dialogue with them; the United Nations, like the League of Nations before it, was a promiscuous travesty of the only true International whose centre was in Rome.

Two Italian Jesuits, Fr Lombardi, a sort of Catholic Billy Graham famed for radio sermons beginning with the words 'Jesus Christ is speaking to you,' and Fr Rotondi, founder of the 'For A Better World' movement, were much favoured by the Pope. His authorization of the use of the 'safe period' as a 'natural' method of contraception was applauded by a Jesuit theologian ('the woman who uses a diaphragm seals off the most intimate part of her body and thus, in symbol, closes the depths of her spirit to her husband'). Visiting the Jesuit curia in the Borgo Santo Spirito near St Peter's in the early 1950s Bernard Wall, an English Catholic journalist, was struck by the surliness of the lay brother at the entrance and the hideousness of the furnishings in the reception parlour. 'It isn't just absence of art, it is anti-art. Some Catholic orders are inclined to indulge in sentiment . . . a Victorian-Gothic window, a reproduction that sends our thoughts to Higher Things. Not this one. What do these Jesuit parlours remind me of most? Rooms in a barracks . . . the air of a requisitioned house.' Yet from this bleak building the activities of some thirty thousand Jesuits were controlled. Jesuits were in charge of the Vatican observatory at Castel Gandolfo and of Vatican Radio. It was 'impossible to probe far into the organization of the Vatican without coming across Jesuits . . . their power is far greater than that of many of the grandiose figures whom one may think of as important'; impossible, too, not to be impressed with recent statistics of the Society's missionary achievement – eleven per cent of all Catholic missions, twenty-four per cent of Catholic missionary schools,

[273]

twenty-three per cent of the Catholic press, sixty-two per cent of the universities in mission territory, thirty-one per cent of non-European prelates Jesuits.

The Russicum was still a focus of speculation and rumour. The Soviet press insisted that clandestine missionaries were still being sent and referred to them as 'the Vatican's parachutists'. Edmond Paris quotes an interview in the newspaper *Il Paese* of 2 October 1954 with Fr Alighiero Tondi, formerly a professor at the Gregorian University, who stated after leaving the Society that 'the activities of the Russicum and other organizations linked to it [e.g. the Pontifical Oriental Institute] are many and varied. For example together with Italian fascists and Nazi remnants, the Jesuits co-ordinate anti-Russian groups . . . The ultimate aim is to be ready to overthrow the governments of the East . . . These same men would readily tear their cassocks apart in simulated horror when accused of meddling in politics and urging the bishops and priests of the East to conspire against their governments . . . When talking to the Jesuit Andrey Urusov I said that it was disgraceful to affirm in the *Osservatore Romano* that the Russicum's unmasked spies were "martyrs of the faith". Urusov laughed . . . "Today the Vatican *Ostpolitik* needs martyrs," he said, "so they are fabricated."' (In 1979 Urusov was reported to be living alone like a hermit in Oregon.)

In a long success-story feature on the Jesuits in America, *Life* magazine of 11 October 1954 saw Ignatius Loyola as a man whose *Spiritual Exercises* 'endeavoured to make perfection a goal of ordinary people' instead of 'something attainable only by monks and mystics, God's elect'. Among the thirty-one million Catholics of the United States, the Jesuits exercised a peculiarly effective ministry: ninety-nine schools, including important universities like Georgetown, Fordham and Marquette; twenty-five periodicals; a wide span of operation as parish priests, prison chaplains, leaders in scientific research, mediators in labour disputes. Photographs showed cassocked novices rather self-consciously harvesting grapes in California, a 'flying Jesuit' who taught aeronautics at St Louis University, a language laboratory at Georgetown, a censer-waving priest in St Andrew's Church, Los Angeles ('Jesuits trained in Byzantine rite, which is similar to Russian Orthodox, usually wear beards and speak to each other in Russian'), and an array of Jesuit notables – Fr Walshe Murray, 'Hollywood Counsellor often called in to give his unofficial opinion of the propriety of scripts'; Fr Dennis Comey ('dispute adjuster') with longshoremen in Philadelphia; John LaFarge, liturgiologist and writer on international problems; explorer-geologist

Fr Francis J. Heyden ('has travelled all over the world studying eclipses of the sun'); seismologist Fr Daniel Linchan ('making tests for a power company to determine the site for a dam. The pay he receives goes to the order'); theologian John Courtney Murray, Thomist scholar and author of a learned justification of the compartmentalized Church-State relationship which helped to reassure Protestants and made him popular with the Kennedy family.

The impression left by the *Life* coverage, as by the leadership of Pius XII, is of an elaborate, superficial pantomime. Specialists are specializing away at their 'concerns' with the backing of an efficient, respectable and wealthy organization. But no Jesuit writer had the vogue or the talent of the Trappist Thomas Merton. Most of what they said, did or published was forgettable and emollient. They provided services, not challenges. Joseph McCarthy had nothing to fear from these Jesuits. Beside them Archbishop Roberts, then in his sixties, was an *enfant terrible*. As Archbishop of Bombay from 1937 he had shown a Xavier-like flair for dissolving class and ethnic rivalries. In 1946, with India on the verge of independence, he decided, without waiting for permission from Rome ('it might take years'), that the Church should make a gesture by appointing an Indian archbishop, and persuaded the authorities to let him take leave of absence while an Indian 'caretaker' settled in. Five years later he formally resigned, returning to England as an ordinary priest. His forthright views on the abuse of authority (he wrote of the cruel absurdity of official Catholic teaching on contraception as applied to poverty-stricken Indian peasants), his vigour in the campaign for nuclear disarmament and as a trustee of Amnesty International, his contempt for curial disingenuity (the official version was that he had resigned 'because of ill-health'), and irreverent comments such as that on Pius XII's fulsome praise for Portugal's missionary work ('the language of diplomacy, while telling the truth, does not necessarily exhaust it'), indicated that for him Jesuit loyalty included the right to criticize. In 1960 he was denounced to Rome by the Apostolic Delegate in England.

A more serious challenge to the Catholic establishment was the worker-priest movement in France. Most of the priests involved, Jesuits among them, had been active in the resistance, and some had been deported. Their concern was for the millions of workers, urban and rural, who had no religion and were impervious to conventional approaches. Their method was to become as nearly as possible workers themselves. Wartime experiences had for many of the new-style missionaries made nonsense of hieratic divisions between clergy and laity.

[275]

Liturgical improvisation had come naturally in a time of shared risks when Mass was said in fields, factories or private homes. Worker-priests in factories shared the hardships – and the taverns – of those they sought to evangelize. They also tended to share their political views, often socialist, anti-colonial, and very cynical about American dollar imperialism. Two worker-priests were arrested when leading a demonstration against NATO and General Ridgway. Eyebrows were raised when another accepted nomination as Secretary of the Paris Steelworkers' Federation, said to be Communist-controlled. Henri Perrin, a Jesuit who had come back from German concentration camps, was a prominent activist. In 1952, while working as a navvy on the construction of the Isère-Arc dam, he was involved in a strike over poor pay and working conditions which he reported in a circular letter: 'Dear Everyone . . . Above all what we have gained is that the management has really woken up, the worksite is running better than ever before . . . Better still, the bosses, far from trying to take reprisals, treat the strike leaders with obvious respect. They consult us and listen to us. In a word, the situation is good.'

For some young Jesuits outside France the experiment came as a revelation. Daniel Berrigan, studying theology in the late 1940s, discussed it with his brother Philip, a member of the Order of St Joseph. After his ordination he was sent to France for a year in 1953 and met some of the worker-priests, an encounter which transformed his view of the priesthood. 'The American Church, at the time, was an Irish ghetto,' he said years later in an interview. 'I had never been politically aware . . . I remember defending the altruism of foreign aid programmes, the execution of the Rosenbergs . . . The worker-priests radicalized me, gave me a vision of the Church as she should be. The French had just lost Dien Bien Phu and were forced out of Indo-China, and my friends woke me up to the evils of colonialism. To make it all the more traumatic, I saw this movement which I so admired squashed before my eyes. In the winter of 1954 our icebox Pope, Pius XII, had it dissolved in one swift stroke, ordering every worker-priest to report to his bishop.' In 1959 John XXIII banned the movement altogether and Henri Perrin, among others, left his order. Yet in a sense the worker-priests attempted spontaneously to achieve what Vatican II ponderously and belatedly recommended – an updating, an adaptation of the Church to a world in which it had become so irrelevant that the vast majority of Catholics were hardly even nominal. With a minimum of fanfare the Council approved a resumption of the experiment. In 1967 more than fifty priests – half of them, including five Jesuits, from religious orders – were working full-time in factories.

Pius XII preferred to encourage the rapid growth of secular institutes, comprising single men and women, to penetrate 'the world'. If, like some worker-priests who dropped out to marry, they fell by the wayside, the scandal would be less; while unordained female missionaries could take over the apostolate to working women. Taking the three traditional vows of a religious, these lay apostles were a logical development of that loosening of the monastic structure which the Jesuits had fought so hard for in the sixteenth century. But the steady growth in their numbers, helped by a sharp decline in vocations to 'real' religious communities, brought sharp criticism from the traditional orders, not least from some Jesuits. Spanish Jesuits were much disturbed by the success, in terms of high-level influence, of Opus Dei, the most powerful of the lay orders. Founded in 1928 by José Maria Escriva de Balaguer, a lawyer who became a priest, it also attracted the sort of sneers which the Company of Jesus had once monopolized. Under the patronage of the very conservative Cardinal Tardini and with headquarters in Rome, its members, vowed to secrecy, included in 1960 about half the Franco Cabinet, generals, bankers, financiers, professors, publishers, and film producers, who used Escriva's testament, *Camino*, as a practical and spiritual guide in rather the same way as they might once have used the *Spiritual Exercises*. Though strongest in Spain, Opus Dei was said to be operating in thirty countries, including some in the Soviet bloc, particularly Poland.

Daniel Berrigan had been drawn to the Society by its unstrident prospectus. But his visit to France had made him realize that conservatism could imply aridity and timidity. The worker-priest movement was not the only example of much-needed spiritual vitality. The oddly-named Little Brothers (and Sisters) of Jesus had a panache inspired by an aristocrat with a rakish military past and a personal odyssey as remarkable as that of Ignatius Loyola. Charles de Foucauld, a dashing cavalry officer in Algeria until he was cashiered for keeping a mistress, had spent seven years as a Trappist monk and three years as handyman to a convent of Poor Clares in Palestine before, as Fr Charles of Jesus, he travelled deep into the Sahara to live among the Tuareg as a Christian hermit. He was shot by raiders in 1916 but the rule he composed was preserved and from the 1930s men and women began to put his idea of 'submersion' into practice. By the 1960s there were two hundred and fifty Little Brothers and about a thousand Little Sisters scattered in twenty-eight countries, always living at the lowest level, whether in an industrial urban slum or an African or Brazilian shanty town. They worked in local factories, as lorry drivers, blacksmiths, living in community in groups of five or less, never talking about religion to their workmates unless the subject was broached, existing on one and a half wage packets and donating the rest to their order's funds or to charity. Their drastic interpretation of the vow of poverty challenged Trappist shut-aways at one extreme, property-heavy Jesuits at the other.

The apparently prospering Society was faced not only with these challenges but with a certain coolness at Rome. John XXIII underlined his view that the secular clergy were the backbone of the Church by replacing his predecessor's German Jesuit trio with ordinary Italian priests. This, and his distant attitude towards Pius XII's favourites, Frs Lombardi and Rotondi, proved, according to Vatican gossip, that the reign of the Jesuits was over. But Fr Bea, a noted theologian, was made a cardinal, and a team of four Jesuits – Pierre Blet, Robert A. Graham, Angelo Martini and Burkhart Schneider – was soon tackling the formidable task of sifting and editing the fat files of reports, memoranda and letters sent to and from the Vatican between 1939 and 1945. The honour of the papacy had to be defended, the silences of Pius XII justified. Paul VI, who became Pope in 1963, had already as Archbishop of Milan protested at the rough handling of Pius XII in *The Representative* (which was not allowed to be staged in Rome). The Catholic press followed suit and Jesuit experts were brought into play. For the honour of the Society, too, was at stake. 'The Jesuits,' says Riccardo Fontana, 'have for years been training specialists for Russia, who were to follow the German army to prosyletize the Russians.' There is a scene in which Pius XII and his advisers discuss the Jesuit supplies of mercury (from mines in Texas, Spain and Italy) to the USA, USSR, Germany and Italy, talk about the Society's holdings in 'the four largest aircraft factories in America', and gloat over the large donations to Vatican funds that result from this commercial acumen.

Asked by the *Frankfürter Allegemeine Zeitung* to comment on Hochhuth's polemic, which had been performed in Berlin on 17 February 1963, Fr Robert Leiber maintained that 'Pius XII did not know what was really happening. Nor did the Allies. It was not until after the war that they were able to realize the extent of the Nazi crimes.' This was a neat way of pointing out that the papacy had not been alone in its political reticence. But it was unfortunate that in *Civiltà Cattolica* on 30 June 1961 Fr Fiorello Cavelli SJ had written of the situation in spring 1942 that 'anguished appeals for help had reached the Vatican from the Jews and their governments in many countries, through the British Minister to the Holy See, President Roosevelt's personal representative to the pope [Myron Taylor], the Apostolic Delegates in Great Britain, the United States and Turkey, and the Nunciatures in Rumania, Hungary and Switzerland.' Even in June 1964, when Roman ranks were being closed against Hochhuth, Fr Martini, immersed as he was in wartime documents, did not feel able to give unqualified support to Fr Leiber's position. Pius XII, he wrote in the *Civiltà,* had spoken 'according to his duty and his knowledge of the facts . . . the decision to adopt the final solution was *suspected* from the middle of 1942, but the details were clear only when the extermination was completed, i.e. after the defeat . . . The Pope received news, but unfortunately these data lacked the verification needed to provide grounds for denouncing them as facts.'

In 1966, breaking the rule that papal documents should not be published for a century after their date of origin, the Vatican press brought out the first of ten volumes of *Acts and Documents of the Holy See Relative to the Second World War,* the fruit of several years of multinational Jesuit labour. The Vatican press spokesman, Mgr Vallainc, was at pains to emphasize that it was 'not an apologia but an objective historical work'; and despite the omission of a number of damning items, including a series of memoranda from the Polish ambassador Kasimierz Papée (for instance one dated 19 December 1942: 'The Germans are liquidating the entire Jewish population of Poland . . . it is estimated that the number of Polish Jews exterminated has passed a million'), the general effect of the huge tome on *The Holy See and the Religious Situation in Poland* was to justify Hochhuth's version. Frs Blet, Graham, Martini and Schneider produced abundant evidence that Fr Leiber's contention was completely untenable. Pius XII is shown vetoing a Radio Vatican series on the plight of the Church in Poland after a protest from the German embassy, fussing for months over the text of a 'stern' note to Foreign Minister Ribbentrop (mainly intended, according to Cardinal Tardini, to 'bear witness to the prudence and constancy of the Holy See'), and managing, in his least muffled radio message, to say no more than that 'in certain parts of the Catholic world the faithful are being persecuted in such a fashion as to awake grave fears for the future of their faith.'

The Jesuit team, chained to the archives in what was surely one of the most distasteful of all the Society's papal chores, was also on call to deal with inquisitive journalists. Fr Graham assured a press conference that the Vatican had been under such awful pressure that in 1943 'personnel had been advised to keep a bag packed for sudden flight'. In 1973, interviewed by Gitta Sereny, the team leader Fr Schneider was still arguing that 'people just don't realize . . . that the Vatican was merely a tiny, powerless enclave encircled by Fascists and Nazis . . . the Vatican Radio was virtually unheard . . . If the Allies had used a protest by the Holy See for their own propaganda it would have undone any good such a protest might have achieved . . . The Vatican has to be very careful. It has no bombs, no arms, no power in that sense. If it is to remain effective as the centre and focus of the Church it must above all remain in touch. Towards that end it must – as far as possible – go along with ruling governments.'

To maintain the pope as the centre and censor of the Church Pius XII and his advisers had been willing to make enormous concessions to anti-Communist governments; but woe to unorthodox theologians who had a different interpretation of keeping in touch, among them several Jesuits. In 1950 the encyclical *Humani Generis* (Concerning Certain False Opinions) was clearly aimed at, among others, Teilhard de Chardin and Henri de Lubac as the heresies of Fr Tyrrell had been one of the targets of Pius X's anti-modernist blast of 1907. Over-bold speculators were warned not to treat the 'wisdom of the ages' as 'an interesting ruin . . . It is not for the Christian, be he theologian or philosopher, to give every latest fantasy of the day a thoughtless and hasty welcome . . . It does not appear how such views can be reconciled with the doctrine of Original Sin as guaranteed by Scripture and tradition.' Daniel Berrigan, who was as sickened by *Humani Generis* as Martindale had been by *Pascendi,* later referred to it as 'that shameful document directed against the great French theologians who had nourished me for years. I saw at close hand intellectual excellence crushed in a wave of orthodoxy like a Stalinist purge.'

Teilhard's unpublished but subterraneously influential writings, which some have seen as a twentieth-century equivalent of the *Summa* of St Thomas Aquinas, were censored not only by his Jesuit superiors but by the theologians of the Holy Office, notably the Dominican Garrigou-Lagrange. Immobilized in China by the Japanese invasion, he had written his most celebrated book, *The Phenomenon of Man.* Returning to Paris in 1945, he was allowed to contribute to scientific and philosophical periodicals and conferences; he was used as a prestige Jesuit champion in public debates with existentialist spokesmen, and acted as a consultant to UNESCO, with whose then director, Sir Julian Huxley, he shared much common scientific ground. But though permitted to lead the life of a distinguished savant, he was prevented from casting his dangerous spell over large student audiences. The publication of *The Phenomenon of Man* was vetoed and he was forbidden to seek appointment to a chair at the Collège de France. In 1951, at the age of seventy, he was again exiled from France and spent the next four years in South Africa and the United States on palaeontological research as a Fellow of the Wiener-Gren Foundation, dying in New York in 1955. In a moment of depression he had asked friends, 'Pray for me, that I may not die embittered.' But his cosmic optimism was proof against more than temporary resentment. Absorbed in his work, he felt little inclination to kick against Company or papal pricks, and thus gave an impression of humble obedience. And there was always the consolation that if his works were not to be published in his lifetime, he could write with less constraint.

In the atmosphere of 'dialogue' promoted by Vatican II, once suspect Jesuit theologians suddenly found themselves in favour. Paul VI quoted with approval Henri de Lubac's dictum that 'man can organize the world without God, but in the last analysis he can only organize it against man. Exclusive humanism is an inhuman humanism.' Karl Rahner's gift for the ecumenical phrase ('anonymous Christians' for agnostics or people of goodwill was reminiscent of Canisius' tactful 'our separated brethren' for Protestants) and the liberal aphorism ('anthropology is theology') exactly suited the mood of the moment. Jesuit influence was hardly less noticeable in the 'open' style of Vatican II than it had been in the dogmatic exclusivism of Trent and Vatican I. De Lubac and Rahner were on the Theological Commission. Jean Daniélou and Josef Jungmann, liturgiologists, were much consulted. Cardinal Bea, President of the Secretariat for Promoting Christian Unity, prepared a 'Declaration on the Jewish People' which learnedly exonerated them from guilt for the murder of the Son of God. John Courtney Murray was a chief architect of the Declaration on Religious Freedom.

By the early 1960s the simple grave of P.Petrus Teilhard de Chardin in the cemetery of the novitiate at St Andrew's on the Hudson had become a place of pilgrimage and the Jesuit leadership was beginning to extend a justifiably guarded welcome to his *Summa*. His vision of the creation moving, through whatever agonies and seeming reverses, to an apotheosis or universal culmination owed much to Aristotle's teleology; but his scientific zest inclined him to give an excited, even indiscriminate, blessing to the wonders of high technology. He addressed himself to 'the spiritually stateless – torn between a Marxism whose depersonalizing effect revolts them, and a Christianity so lukewarm in human terms that it sickens them,' but his version of vital Christianity began to resemble the wishful One World clichés of the 1950s, though with a rhetorical sweep which gave it an oracular intensity. World war, totalitarian collectivism, over-population, could be seen as 'successive turns of the screw' forcing a recalcitrant humanity towards a final stage of 'planetization' or 'totalization' which would herald the millennium. The explosion of the first A-bomb in New Mexico was for him pure victory, 'our first bite at the fruit of the great discovery . . . a taste for super-creativeness that can never be washed away.' What possibilities for liberation did the future not hold? 'The vitalization of matter by the creation of super-molecules. The remodelling of the human organization by means of hormones. Control of heredity and sex by the manipulation of genes and chromosomes. The readjustment of our souls by direct action upon springs gradually brought to light by psycho-analysis . . . Is not every kind of effect produced by a suitable arrangement of matter? Have we not reason to hope that in the end we shall be able to arrange every kind of matter, following the results we have obtained in the nuclear field?'

Teilhard's mysticism, or mystique, of matter and its 'arrangement' by a dedicated élite was big-scale thinking with a conceptual jargon of its own ('ultra-personalization', 'collective super-consciousness', 'noosphere', 'Christogenesis'). In his novel *The Shoes of the Fisherman* Morris West introduced Teilhard in the lightly-veiled character of Père Jean Télémond, a misunderstood palaeontologist whose book, *The Progress of Man*, serves as the theological and philosophical justification for a triumvirate – pope, Russian premier, American president – which enforces world peace. 'All men who arrive at authority have certain attitudes in common,' says the liberated pope: even a Marxist politician, having achieved supreme power, has 'begun to breathe a freer air'.

It is something of a relief to turn from Teilhard's power fantasies to the homelier scope of Archbishop Roberts, who in several respects represented average reactions to injustice and to the problem of suffering and redemption in general. When, after he had been promised an enquiry into the anonymous charges against him, he was told that though this had not been forthcoming he could interpret silence as vindication, he protested that 'this is not an argument which would be understood outside totalitarian countries'. There could, he said in a

1964 television interview, be just wars but never a just nuclear war. Politicians might be excused for moral compromise, but not Christian leaders: 'God did not intervene on Calvary. Christianity tells us that as long as we are in this life we shall be the victims of injustice, cruelty, stupidity and perversity. It also says that all those things *can* be steps to heaven. But they are *not* steps that we must put if we can avoid it.' He was also blunt about the shortcomings of Vatican II and the real purpose of dialogue. The Catholic Church remained *the* Church – 'if anybody is going to change it is the Protestants'. He was angry that the question of nuclear disarmament was not high on the Council's agenda; suggested the need for ombudsmen to investigate cases of injustice within the Church ('there are whole classes of Catholics unrepresented at this Council – nuns and all other women'); and criticized the long-windedness of the gathering, with its plethora of committees.

Recruits to the Society, even when they came from pious Catholic families and Jesuit schools, tended to be far more critical than in the 1940s and 1950s. In *Against All Reason*, published in 1969, Geoffrey Moorhouse quotes an interview with an English scholastic of twenty-five who, though appreciating the comradeship of the order, had serious doubts about the value of some assignments imposed to 'give experience' or 'test obedience'. He was also 'out of sympathy with hours of rising and retiring unnecessarily out of conformity with the society in which we live', thought it 'a scandalous waste of time and benefactors' money' to put non-academic Jesuits through an elaborate academic training; and felt that this training took little account, in theory or in practice, of the actual problems of people in a relentlessly collectivist society. He was inclined to attach less importance to 'the hierarchical Church' than the founder, but felt that Ignatius' principle of making the best possible use of a man's talents was fundamental ('if at any stage I decided that I could make better use of my talents outside the order I think I should leave'). He had thought carefully about the triple vow. That of poverty was 'a challenge to the rat race' – but 'how effective this can be when one is a member of a large organization with substantial funds remains question-able'. The vow of chastity was not only 'a challenge to the place of sex in the modern world' (what Daniel Berrigan calls 'a hot-crotch culture'), but a near-requisite in Berrigan's view for voluntary danger-duty which might involve prison or death; no family to warp one's judgement. The vow of obedience challenged the facile over-valuation of independence. 'I would like it also to suggest that we can go a long way by trusting men who make mistakes like everyone, while remaining realistic about the mistakes – a public acceptance of the fact that nothing can be perfect and that we must do our best with what we have.'

In the hubbub of unofficial debate, signalling a crisis of authority, which accompanied and followed Vatican II, Jesuit radicals figured prominently. In so far as they sought inspiration from Jesuit thinkers they were more likely to find it in Frs Desqueyrat or in Karl Rahner than in Teilhard. Desqueyrat, attacking the cult of science and positivism, argued the need for a 'revolutionary mysticism' which recognized that there were regions of mystery, a place for the 'irrational', and a need for 'holy activists' to question the iron determinism of modern industrial society. Rahner, who, in the opinion of many qualified judges, may well come to be seen as the greatest Catholic theologian of this century, insisted that the Church, being a human institution, is imperfect at all levels, lay or clerical; that belief meant risk, adventure, taking a chance with a sinful but aspiring Church. Berrigan referred to the Bride of Christ as 'a sinner, but my Mother', and in an essay which became a radical Jesuit classic declared that the best way to discover the true meaning of faith was to confront 'the world . . . the only stage of redemption, the men and women who toil in it, sin in it, suffer and die in it. Apart from them . . . the priesthood is a pallid, vacuumatic enclosure, a sheepfold for sheep.'

In the liturgical and theological turmoil of the times Holland, once noted for rigid orthodoxy, became notorious as a laboratory of experimental religion: Dutch Jesuits showed a determination not to drag their feet in the merry dance. Fr Huijbers composed liturgical music in a modern idiom. In 1962 Cardinal Alfrink rejected a demand from the Holy Office for the resignation of Fr van Kilsdonk SJ, chaplain to students at the University of Amsterdam, who had openly criticized the reactionary attitudes of the papal curia. Despite vehement protests from the Dutch provincial, Fr Terpstra, General Janssens felt obliged in 1964 to close down two Jesuit periodicals which had carried 'unsound' views on clerical celibacy, the presence of Christ in the eucharist, and the Roman censorship, with particular reference to restrictions imposed upon Fr Rahner. A Swiss Jesuit complained of the callowness of young hotheads, who 'would abolish all tensions between Church and world, hierarchy and laity. . . The effect is to turn the service of God into a service of man, to regard evolution as the source of revelation, and to degrade Christianity to a mere method for the improvement of human relations.' There was more trouble in 1966 when a new catechism, which cast doubts on the virginity of Our Lady and on the accepted version of the Resurrection, was denounced to .Rome and defended by a Dutch Jesuit theologian.

The thirty-first General Congregation (consisting of the provincials and two elected representatives from each province) which met on 7 May 1965 to elect a successor to Janssens had a difficult task. The Dutch commotion was not the only sign of restlessness in younger Jesuits affected by the 'revolution of expectation' aroused by Vatican II. Pope Paul VI, an experienced curialist, was known to favour 'the church of the silent majority' and to be particularly irritated by the behaviour of the radical Jesuit fringe. The new leader would be faced with the problem of appealing to what amounted to two Societies within a much divided Church. 'We need a general who will ever keep the Society united with the world to which the word of salvation is to be carried,' said Fr Maurice Giuliani in the customary exhortation to the assembled delegates. 'It will not be enough for him to be taken up with continuing and enlarging particular projects arising out of local needs. . .' He would have to reinterpret the spirit of the founder in the democratic (but not anarchic) sense of Vatican II's nebulous *aggiornamento.* The choice fell upon Pedro Arrupe, aged fifty-eight. Born in Bilbao, he was the first Basque General since Ignatius, and even looked remarkably like him. Intellectually distinguished and very much a citizen of the world, he had been a medical student before entering the Society in 1927. After the expulsion from Spain in 1932 he had done most of his Jesuit training in Belgium, Holland (where he was ordained), Germany and the United States. Since 1939 he had been in Japan. On 6 August 1945, when the A-bomb fell on Hiroshima, he was a novice master in a house on the outskirts of the city and was praised for his skill and devotion in tending the wounded. Later, as provincial, he had gained a reputation as a formidable scholar, with eight books in Japanese to his credit.

'The voice of young Jesuits is the voice of the modern world within the order,' Arrupe declared. He supported a move to replace the system whereby Provincial Congregations consisted of the forty senior professed fathers – not likely to be over-responsive to the voice of youth – with an elective body. He also welcomed a suggestion that, to mitigate the burdens and delays caused by centralization, he should be helped by a 'cabinet' of four General Assistants elected by the General Congregation. The possibility of abolishing the distinction between the professed of the four vows and spiritual coadjutors was raised but not fully resolved. A decree on the reform of studies reduced the number of lectures (which were no longer to be in Latin), recommended teaching by tutorial as far as possible, and made other minor curricular changes. These adjustments did not substantially alter the labyrinthine ordeal of a 'formation' imposed four centuries earlier, in a very different context, by a founder superstitiously obsessed with the importance of making every Jesuit re-enact in cold blood the sequence of his own long intellectual pilgrimage. But the tone of the Congregation seemed to promise a loosening of autocratic bonds; an impression which was reinforced by General Arrupe's inauguration of a public relations policy that did not flinch from press conferences and television interviews, and opened a 'dialogue' with his subjects in the form of regular bulletins explaining what he proposed to do, and why.

After two months the Congregation adjourned, postponing its final sessions until the decrees of the Vatican Council had been published. Delegates had more than a year in which to mull over the Pope's special assignment for the Society. Much influenced by Henri de Lubac's book *The Drama of Atheist Humanism* and by the creakings of another piece of dialogic machinery, the Secretariat for Non-Believers, Paul VI ordered the Jesuits to 'stand in the path of atheism'. Since this was a function which they, in common with every Catholic order, had been performing for some time, it was difficult to grasp exactly what was expected of them. Were they to engage the whole spectrum of Christless humanism in all its ramifications? At a press conference General Arrupe himself seemed to be groping. 'The Pope's call,' he explained, 'must make us direct our efforts to unbelievers as well as believers. . . We must try to penetrate the mind of the modern atheist and look for the motives of his confusions and prejudices.' This, apparently, entailed combating racial antagonism, preaching peace, promoting equality, helping the underdeveloped and exploited. *El Correo Español,* a Bilbao newspaper, quoted Arrupe as saying that 'the battle against atheism is in part identical with the battle against poverty which was one cause of the mass exodus of the working classes from the Church.' The Congregation's decree was, however, more vaguely and upliftingly phrased: 'Since also the legitimate desire that the human sciences should be autonomous often leads men to raise objections against God or even to present irreligion as the liberation of man, Jesuits should strive to bring it about that faith should inform and illumine the whole of life . . . that human values, developed without pride, and the whole universe, cleansed from corruption, should be illuminated and transfigured. . .'

In a carefully balanced opening address in September 1966 Arrupe conceded that the Company was facing 'a crisis of confidence'. Could an order originally designed to serve a Church Militant and long notorious for its support of papal triumphalism adapt itself to the needs of a Church of Dialogue? The new General admitted that the *Spiritual Exercises* had too often been so unimaginatively construed as to rob them of impact and put undue stress on a servile obedience far removed from the intention of the founder. But the *Spiritual Exercises* were not at fault. The need was not to jettison but to reinterpret them, and to modify the over-authoritarian attitudes into which some superiors, being fallible instruments, had fallen. This, however, did not mean a reckless rejection of the past or a refusal to build on solid foundations. Arrupe was soon telling journalists that 'we must start to prepare our novices for the twenty-first century' and suggesting that the 'superior-within-the-community' should replace the 'superior-over-the-community'.

There was something for most Jesuits, it seemed, in this conservative-liberal blend: but Paul VI's valediction of September 1965 – 'Christ chooses you. The Church sends you. The Pope blesses you' – was offset by a stern allocution delivered at the closing session of the Congregation in November 1966. A news agency report stated that 'Pope Paul reproached the Jesuits this morning and said that he had heard strange and sinister rumours involving spiritual slackness and worldliness. He told Father Arrupe and 220 priests that he was astonished and grieved . . . He did not specify what the charges were.' A résumé issued by the Jesuit Information Service said that the Pope 'had spoken frankly of the fears some had been communicating to him about the future of the Society. These rumours suggested that the Jesuits intended to embark upon revolutionary changes or were abandoning the traditions that had for centuries made them such a powerful force in the Church.' The Jesuit Information Service also pointed out that the agency report had omitted to quote the rest of its bulletin: 'Pope Paul reassured his hearers that he was completely satisfied that the Society of Jesus had in fact simply worked out a programme of inner renewal and reform that answered the demands of the Second Vatican Council . . . He wished to take advantage of this occasion and of the setting of the historic Sistine Chapel to make a solemn declaration of confidence in the Society.'

Even with the qualifications this was a sharp rebuke, intended perhaps to arm General Arrupe and other leaders for their forthcoming engagements with rebels in the ranks and to reassure old-guard Jesuits that the Vatican sympathized with their feelings. Many of them, bewildered by the experimental exuberance around them, might have agreed with Evelyn Waugh's comment that 'it was fun thirty-five years ago to travel far and in great discomfort to meet people whose entire conception of life and manner of expression were alien. Now one only has to leave one's gates': except that they did not necessarily have to leave their gates.

Revisiting the novitiate at Florissant in 1969, twenty-five years after he had left there, George Riemer asked himself 'Will Jesuits be the new Protestants?' Much had altered. Meals were served in a cafeteria; beer was bottled; microphones made 'voice exercises' in the basement unnecessary; folk songs and guitars were in vogue ('no scholastic has ever heard "We hail thee, Francis Xavier", let alone knows the words'). He met cassockless novices returning at 11.30 pm from St Louis, where they had been to see *Midnight Cowboy*, and remembered that during his four years at St Stanislaus he never visited St Louis nor saw a film. The training period, still around fifteen years in 1960, had by 1970 been cut to ten years (theology being reduced from four years to two). Choice of occupation during the post-degree regency period had widened considerably. Yet liberalization had coincided with a steep drop in membership and vocations. Between 1965 and 1970 nearly three thousand priests and scholastics had left the Society, five hundred of them Americans. In 1960 there had been four hundred new entries; in 1967 there were only one hundred and forty-nine. Superiors and novice masters were bending over backwards to meet the democratic requirements of the last General Congregation. Theologates were moving from rural mansions to inner city slums in the effort to 'connect'. The hope was that a less formal, more flexible style would force the Society nearer to the spirit of its origins.

But old hands felt that when the Woodstock Theologate moved from Maryland to New York's West Side it was like pouring incense down a drain. Young Jesuits, eager for unconventional action, were often equally disgruntled. There was so much 'revolutionary' jargon, so little revolution. Why, complained a typical malcontent, 'give up having a son just to prefect a study hall? Any married teacher can do that. If the superior just sits on his ass and convinces me that this is his society, I'm getting out. It's not the game I signed up for.' Daniel Berrigan readily admitted that being in 'authority' was hell, as Fathers formed in the cloistral discipline of the 1930s struggled to adjust to a Society in which one Jesuit (Berrigan) was a fugitive from the FBI, another (Robert Drinan) was Congressman for the State of Massachusetts, Latin was an optional extra, and novices learned to dance and drink cocktails.

Reflecting on this transitional chaos Riemer surmised that Ignatius, when commending 'corpse-like obedience' to superiors, had assumed that superiors would themselves be vital, radically-minded militants. 'If Ignatius Loyola's image of swift military obedience isn't relevant today, it's because Jesuit superiors in the United States are too prudent, safe and sedentary. The provincial's visit is less the tense, electric Paul Revere kind of contact and more the small town watchman's making sure the lights are all out . . . The only orders that I've seen requiring military speed and detachment have come from superiors who suddenly wanted to get rid of a problem Jesuit – like Heithaus sent to Milwaukee or Dunne sent to Los Angeles or Berrigan to South America.'

There were limits to experimentalism. Fr Arrupe condemned a 'third way' (of 'inspiring spiritual intimacy' with a woman) explored, with predictably disintegrating results, by some Californian Jesuits. But the membership crisis was almost universal: even in Spain there were in 1970 a mere forty novices compared with the four hundred of comparatively recent times. The attempt to modernize, to readjust, was also universal. Some Spanish Jesuits were arrested for leading anti-Franco student demos; others, horrified by such developments, tried to set up their own 'strict observance' Society. The English province did its best to wake up. In the 1950s Fr Martindale, never conformist, had felt oppressed by the mock-Gothic rest home in Sussex, where ill health kept him confined with six ailing brothers and a few sick or aged priests: 'one's life is like a bracket that must soon close . . . better plain walls that shoddy oleographs and meaningless pictures of "A Monk with Two Cows" or prints of Old Masters crookedly mounted.' But as in the United States, closure and mobility were in the air. Heythrop College, Chipping Norton, was sold and the theologate moved to London, where it became part of the university. Beaumont College was closed. Between 1951 and 1971 the novitiate, originally at Roehampton, moved house six times, with recruitment dipping from an average of twenty a year to about five. Dismayed by Vatican II and its sequels, many of those who joined in the 1950s dropped out at the scholastic stage.

Macdonald Hastings, educated at Stonyhurst like his father and grandfather before him, was shocked in 1969 to find female teachers in the common room. In the novitiate, then on the outskirts of Edinburgh, he found an ageing superior lamenting the laxity of the new order. No censorship of letters, no more little ruled notebooks for the Daily Particular Examination of Conscience; newspapers, table tennis and a TV set; frequent visits to or from families; 'experiments' in factories or nursing the mentally sick. But the general impression was still quite spartan. Corridors were adorned with prints of illustrations to the *Spiritual Exercises,* chapels bare, dormitory cubicles doorless. The rules against *tactus,* room visits, and particular friendships were still in force; novices still put in a highly-fragmented seventeen-hour day; the fault-finding 'repetition' (*exercitium modestiae*) was still regularly practised, novices and tertians swept, scrubbed, cleaned toilets, washed their clothes, prepared vegetables. The most depressing thing was the number of empty beds. Examining boards, including a psychiatrist, began to screen applicants more thoroughly, showing a preference for graduates with knowledge of the world rather than for youths fresh from school. For more mature entrants with university degrees training could be further abbreviated, and the risk of fall-out was perhaps lessened.

No Catholic grouping took Vatican II's cloudy summons to renewal more seriously or tried so hard to work out in detail its implications. But with the Machiavellian Jesuit image still easily revived, almost every initiative was open to misconstruction. In 1966 Arrupe wrote to the Latin American provinces criticizing a tendency to put too much effort into educating a Christian élite which had failed to produce Christian leaders who challenged social injustice. The Instituto Patria, probably the best private school in Mexico, was closed and the provincial explained that 'the education we provide is meaningless if it does not include a determined effort to resolve social problems and overcome the egoistical attitudes of liberal capitalism.' Right-wing journals called the Jesuits 'Communists, confederates of a Mao, Castro, Moscow-inspired subversion'. Marxist politicians and union leaders resented competition from a 'revamped paternalism'. General Arrupe's extensive travels caused more contention. If he visited young Spanish activists, Franco and old-guard Jesuits took umbrage. If he paid a courtesy call on Franco or Salazar younger Jesuits were up in arms. Even his cautious rehabilitation of Teilhard fell rather flat: too tepid for some, too complimentary for others. Led by Daniel Berrigan, radical American Jesuits were challenging that high technology euphoria which Teilhard had seemed to bless and which in their eyes was on trial in Vietnam. Nor were they enthusiastic about the State-toadying Catholic Church which the American Jesuit John Courtney Murray had sanctified with such a wealth of erudition.

It was just the sort of concordat which Berrigan and his disciples regarded as blasphemous and, in the context of the war in Vietnam and the backing it received from the Catholic hierarchy, reminiscent of the

Nazi-Catholic understanding. In April 1970, as one of the Catonsville Nine convicted of burning draft files with home-made napalm, Berrigan evaded arrest and went 'underground' for three months. He was then forty-eight, contemptuous of woolly-minded radicals who ducked out of institutional religion rather than trying to revitalize it, and deeply attached to the Society. He sent 'a word of love to the brethren, who have been for these thirty years my bloodline, my family, my embodied tradition and conscience.' But he quoted Dietrich Bonhoeffer – 'the task is not only to bind up the victim beneath the wheel, but also to put a spoke in that wheel' – and managed his resistance campaign with a gaiety, an ingenuity, and a flow of rhetoric worthy of his heroes Campion and Southwell. 'Caesar's embarrassment,' he wrote, 'will pay tribute to my freedom . . . I have changed domicile some six times; this in strict accord with a rule of the Jesuit order making us, at least in principle, vagabonds on mission: "It is our vocation to travel to any place in the world where the greater glory of God and the need of our neighbour shall impel us." Amen, brothers.' His friends, he reported in a bulletin smuggled out from prison in Connecticut, were 'resisters, priests and nuns, some Black Panthers, many men and women at present serving time . . . my mother, Kurt Vonnegut, John of the Cross and his road map for a dark night, the Vietnamese.'

Berrigan was aware that his self-imposed ordeal was a form of guerrilla theatre. In 1965 hundreds of young Jesuits had threatened to leave the order when he was 'exiled' to South America, and he had returned in triumph. He knew that he was unlikely to be dismissed, for if he were it would be 'bye-bye to a thousand seminarians'. But the show had to go on, if only for the good of the Society. 'The courts have become the instruments of the warmakers,' he said in *Letter to the Jesuits*. 'Can Christians unthinkingly submit before such powers? We [he and his brother] judge not. To act otherwise would be a betrayal of my love for the Society.' In *Letter to the Young Jesuits,* written on St Ignatius Day 1971, he passionately bombarded his 'brothers beyond the wall'. Could they not see that 'resistance to the war-ridden, blood-shot state is the form that human life is called to assume today'? Was it not high time 'to disrupt the business of death as usual . . . stop making liturgy an excuse for inaction . . . and communities a compound for cultural Brahmins'? He wished that he had taken costly action earlier and drawn many others with him: 'If a thousand Jesuits had come to their own Catonsville and stood up to the law, what an effect we would have had, what horrors might have been averted!'

What Jesuits needed was not more money to equip schools and universities with bigger and better equipment, but the courage to put their lives where their words were. Berrigan's feelings about Arrupe's visit to him in jail were mixed. He appreciated that the General had ignored Vatican disapproval and would be attacked by patriotic American Catholics. But he resented the fact that Arrupe had taken little action on 'the questions I addressed to him some few years ago after my return from Latin America . . . they touch on the complicity of Jesuit institutions with the military establishment, in university research, chaplaincies with armed services, Society investments.' He saw the visit as a way of publicizing the Society's wonderful broad-mindedness and felt that 'to be a marginal Jesuit' was likely for him to be 'a permanent state of life . . . Certainly I cannot be a Jesuit because I discover moral clairvoyance in the leadership.'

Even Berrigan's shrewd and sometimes magnificent protestantism was subject to the law of diminishing returns, and the John Courtney Murray line still had plenty of followers. Fr Robert Drinan, elected to Congress as a liberal critic of the Vietnam war, refused in 1969 to accept draft cards turned in by Jesuit seminarians who had foregone clerical exemption in order to make this gesture. As a politician he could not, he said, allow his religious conviction or affiliation to affect his loyalty to the state. He also reasoned that he could work more effectively for peace from within the system. Nor was this the most glaring example of Jesuit 'pluralism'. By a grotesque coincidence, when Daniel Berrigan was released on parole Fr John J. McLaughlin SJ entered the White House as special adviser to Richard Nixon. Known as the President's 'hired collar', he continued to give aid and comfort to his employer in his hour of greatest need when the Watergate scandal broke. As late as June 1974 he referred to Nixon as 'the greatest moral leader of the last third of this century'.

As so often in the past, the courtier priest was treated more leniently by his superiors than the trouble-making missionary. McLaughlin was requested to move to a less ostentatious apartment and recommended to search his conscience in a week of earnest prayer. Berrigan went his way as a marginal Jesuit and his witness continued to reverberate, perhaps not always for the right reasons. Many a budding cleric, dazzled by the glamour of this poet-visionary, secretly yearned to be (in *Newsweek's* phrase) 'the sort of priest who causes the lights of the Vatican to burn through the night'; the sort of priest who, even in prison, could be accused by J. Edgar Hoover of conspiring to kidnap Henry Kissinger and blow up heating systems beneath government buildings in Washington. Two scholastics, Tony Meyer and Joe O'Rourke, angered their fellow-Jesuits by refusing the traditional 'kiss of peace' to Cardinal Cooke at their ordination ceremony because as chaplain to the American Air Force he was by implication at Vietnam 'hawk'. More draft files were burned, more demonstrations staged. And younger Jesuits not passionately concerned with Vietnam were still, like Berrigan, struggling to create their own values and uninclined to stay in the Society if it did not measure up to them.

Bart Rousseve, a black from New Orleans, aged thirty in 1970 when interviewed by George Riemer, and Ted Cunningham, a black from Omaha, then forty-two, were both convinced that white Jesuits – and indeed all white Christians – were deeply racist, as even their politeness showed ('I've never been called a "nigger" in the Society,' complained Rousseve). Cunningham rejected the Jesuit *corps d'élite* mentality. Both felt that whatever their family background Jesuits were turned into bourgeois by a training which equipped them to deal not with inner city but with prosperous suburban blacks. The Society, they thought, was not really hypocritical about its corporate wealth and its investments (for instance, in South African gold mines), but 'we don't act like Christ, more like a big institution that's very rich and that really doesn't care about doing more than baptizing a child and giving an education that whitens him. . . He's not allowed to be the person he is. He must be "culturally enriched" or "upgraded".'

Ken Feit, a thirty-year-old who was spending his three-year regency on trek felt that, in a good cause, Jesuits should be willing to regard jail as 'novitiate or at least one of the tests . . . I see many points of comparison between the novitiate and prison.' Earning his keep with odd jobs had, he thought, brought him closer to the real meaning of poverty. Many Jesuits might benefit from a hobo-like spell, and the Society would, in his view, never break through to poor blacks, Indians, chicanos or whites so long as it recruited mainly from its own high schools. But the paralyzing fear seemed to be that if it ceased to do so, vocations would dry up and the Society die. But would that be a bad thing? 'There is so much unconscious exclusivism in our training and that really bugs shit out of me. . . Why is it that practically every canonized Jesuit saint was an aristocrat of some sort? Berchmans was about the only exception and he was processing his papers to leave the order.' Paul Weber, of German-Irish extraction from Cascade, Iowa, agreed with many of Ken Feit's criticisms. Though himself a middle-

[293]

of-the-road Jesuit, working hard in an inner-city mission to make contact with slum-trapped blacks, he was acutely conscious of the class barriers. He hoped to stay on and be a 'stabilizer', but feared that the Society might lose its nerve and play too safe. John Culkin, a close friend of Marshall McLuhan, warned that the Society, once a leader in the communications business, had fallen way behind. 'My feeling is that the Jesuits are highly over-rated as a group . . . we're probably living on the perfume of a vase that's not that full any more . . . I may leave the Society, as I left Fordham, because both are suffering from the same kind of institutional malaise.'

Cunningham, Rousseve, Feit, Weber and Culkin have all been 'laicized' (i.e. have left the Society), so that of the radicals interviewed by Riemer in 1970 only Berrigan is still a Jesuit. Other interviewees, who have remained Jesuits, were all academic specialists who though by no means over-conformist had no reason, moral or intellectual, to leave. John Padberg, an historian, in 1970 teaching (and fund-raising) at St Louis University, was in 1979 President of the Weston School of Theology in Boston. The encyclopaedically erudite Walter Ong is still at St Louis University and was in 1979 President of the Modern Language Association of America. George Shoup, in 1970 the Kennedy Foundation's first Medical Ethics Scholar, was in 1979 a surgeon at Georgetown University hospital. R. J. Arenz, a scientist whose studies of hypervelocity impact helped to ensure the safety of aeronauts and who has worked on ballistic missile design for the Department of Defense, was in 1970 an assistant professor of mechanical engineering at Loyola University, Los Angeles, in 1979 Dean at Parker College, Cahokia, Illinois.

Berrigan's visits to Hungary, Russia and Czechoslovakia in 1964 had confirmed his feeling that ideally the Church should be a dissenting minority in tension with the state ('Under Marxism Christians have returned to their pre-Constantinian situation by being poor, pure and persecuted . . . what a great feeling, to be in a country where there's no head of state going to church every Sunday and corrupting it!'). His two-month 'exile' in South America had further radicalized him ('the scandal of this incessant misery of millions perpetuated by American investments to the tune of billions, the scandal of our missionary policy, which supports a reactionary Church standing in the way of human progress'). Though he doubted whether there could be any approximation to social justice in Latin America without bloodshed, he trusted that Christianity, not Marxism, would be 'the revolution within the revolution' that would upset the calculations of the US-sponsored Alliance for Progress.

The equally, but idiosyncratically, heterodox Ivan Illich shared these views (at eighteen he had been on the verge of joining the Society). In 1962 he had opened a 'de-Yankification' centre – officially the Centre of Intercultural Documentation (CIDOC) – near Cuernavaca in Mexico with the object of making at least some missionaries linguistically, historically and sociologically equipped for their job. He himself was influenced by the massive survey of a Jesuit sociologist, Émile Pin; and an Argentinian Jesuit compiled one of CIDOC's bulkiest publications, a twelve-volume work entitled *Guerrilla Violence in Peru, Bolivia, Colombia and Ecuador from 1960-1968,* complete with instructions for making napalm, blowing up bridges, and assembling machine-guns. Jesuits contributed substantially to a 'theology of liberation' which, though acknowledging the plausibility – and up to a point the viability – of Marxism, insisted that a Christian revolution could not be 'imprisoned in Marxist categories'. A five-volume *Theology for Artisans of a new Humanity* by Juan Luis Segundo, a Uruguayan Jesuit, was much used by the movement of Christians for Socialism in Chile which spread throughout Latin America and to Italy, Spain and France. Fr Gonzalo Arroyo, one of its founders, was deported from Chile after the military coup of September 1973 ('we aim,' he said, 'at a Church in solidarity with the interests and struggles of thè workers, but without breaking with the Church').

Aware that both capitalism and Marxism were trying to exploit the Church, Segundo, Arroyo, and other Latin American Jesuits knew that in a sub-continent where the Church had for so long been identified with the ruling classes it *had* to lean, or appear to lean, nearer to Marxism to have any chance of recapturing the masses. Roger Vekemans, a Belgian Jesuit and sociologist who had advised the reformist Frei government in Chile and later worked at the Institute of Social Action in Bogota, agreed that the 'marginal world' in Latin America resembled Marx's proletariat in an artificial degradation caused by economic exploitation which had isolated it from established society. Renato Poblete, editor of the Chilean Jesuit journal *Mensaje,* risked reprisals from the military junta by writing that though there was a danger that priests would again become over-politicized (this time as leftists), 'the examples of Cuba and Vietnam, the figures of Fidel Castro, Camilo Torres and Che Guevara inspired a new revolutionary spirit even among Christian groups.'

The Jesuit in fiction, though still mostly slippery and devious, was being gradually updated. Roger Peyrefitte's novels, *Special Friendships, The Keys of St Peter,* and *The Jews* contain in Fr de Trennes, a waspishly

[295]

witty Jesuit homosexual, probably the richest clerical rogue in recent literature. All three books are full of knowledgeable references to Jesuit history and offer a shrewd summary of the Society's great strength ('it never knows when it's beaten'). But they tend towards an ironical rehash of Zola's vindictive, resourceful Roman Jesuits, whereas Alan Gray, the American Jesuit villain of Piers Paul Read's *The Professor's Daughter*, published in 1971, is a fanatical militant who leads a group of university students in an attempted political assassination and dies gun in hand.

The image of the left-wing Jesuit intellectual gangster was not far removed from the fantasies of conservative Catholics, lay or clerical. And in Europe, though their activities were less headline-catching than those of Berrigan, Segundo or Poblete, the Jesuits' long-time reputation as the pope's janissaries threw into high relief any sign of insubordination. It seemed that Jesuits now wrote as they liked and that censorship was virtually non-existent. Piet Smulders, one of the theologians called in to draft a constitution for a National Pastoral Council in Holland, declared that 'all the Church is responsible for all the Church'. Fr Philip Land, formerly a professor at the Gregorian University, was dropped from the Catholic delegation to the World Population Conference in 1974 because he admitted to private reservations about *Humanae Vitae* (Paul VI's encyclical condemning artificial contraception). Angry bishops peppered Arrupe with complaints, and he himself was troubled by the statistics of membership. It began to look as if he had been elected to preside over the Society's disintegration.

By 1974 numbers had dwindled to 29,436, with less than half the number of scholastics. Most religious orders were having the same sort of experience: in 1973 the diocesan clergy had lost 8.8 per cent of its priests, whereas the average annual loss of Jesuit priests was running at 0.8 per cent. But the situation seemed to justify the summoning of an emergency General Congregation (GC 32) which would decide whether or not to renew Arrupe's mandate. It was even possible that for the first time in Jesuit history a General might be sacked. Preparations for the gathering were nothing if not thorough. In a long article in the *Guardian* on 21 January 1975 Peter Hebblethwaite, an English Jesuit who, with the scholar-poet Peter Levi, had recently been laicized, reported that Jean-Yves Calvez was the jet-age Nadal figure of the moment, selling GC 32 as zealously as the sixteenth-century Spaniard had sold the Constitutions and the *Ratio Studiorum*. 'A technocratic French Jesuit who picked up doctorates as other men buy suits, he travelled round the world in an attempt to stir up interest. In some places he was received with coolness if not actual hostility. Few could see the need for another congregation. . . Calvez's office produced thick wodges of indigestible material which was rapidly consigned to capacious Jesuit wastepaper baskets.' Computers processed the answers to massive questionnaires and over a thousand topics for discussion were framed.

Early in 1975 the Congregation issued three rather verbose decrees on Our Mission Today, Union of Minds and Hearts, and Poverty. Arrupe, now in his late sixties, tirelessly promoted these objectives. When he was not at his desk in Rome composing circular letters or weighty speeches he was flying hither and thither to visit his brethren or to address conferences. His addresses were for the most part variations on a theme already developed in a major speech to a German audience in 1972: 'For hundreds of millions of Catholics the real crisis of faith comes not from materialism or from unrestricted theological discussion but from the brutal misery of their existence.' Perhaps the most forceful restatement was made in Montreal on 21 November 1977 at the Third Inter-American Congress of Religious in his capacity as President of the Union of Superiors General. The witness of poverty, he said, was crucial in the Third World, but the danger of politicization had to be avoided. 'How will people be convinced that we believe what we preach if they see us enjoying a standard of living superior to many of our fellow citizens, if all we do smacks of privilege?' Surely the greatest service which religious could offer was 'to give irrefutable witness against consumerism by a life that is austere and frugal', the more so since 'austerity will have to prevail if the world wants to survive; and it will have to prevail either by force of a totalitarian state of whatever stripe . . . or by the way of evangelical love in virtue of which we all accept the sacrifice which the good of all demands.' It was important that as many religious as possible should show solidarity with the poor by 'working directly among them, often alone, in pastoral, auxiliary or social works . . . sharing their life, their needs, and their hopes.' 'Conscientization' was the chilling catchword for this process. But, said Arrupe, it must not be sullied by indulgence in 'guerrilla tactics or violence, urging rebellious radicalism, corrupting the work of conscientization with atheistic methodologies or ideologies.'

Despite the steep decline in membership, the proportion of Jesuits working in 'the newer churches' – the post-colonial term for missionary churches – had increased. Only eight months before the Montreal speech Arrupe had circulated a 'Letter on the Recent Killing of Some of

Our Brethren'. Five Jesuit missionaries had been murdered in the course of a few months: Fr Rutilio Grande in the Central American republic of El Salvador; Fr João Bosco Burnier in Brazil; Frs Martin Thomas and Christopher Shepherd-Smith and Brother John Conway in Rhodesia. These martyrs, wrote Arrupe, were 'men of average human gifts leading obscure lives in small villages, totally dedicated to the service of the poor and suffering. . . Their style of life was simple, austere, evangelical. . . These are Jesuits of the mould that the world and the Church need today. . . The essential thing, the Jesuit thing, is always to confess Christ before men. . . This will be the source of new vocations, for the blood of the martyrs is the seed of vocations.'

But numbers and vocations have continued to drop. At the beginning of 1978 there were 27,131 Jesuits, of whom about twenty thousand were priests, 3,400 scholastics (training for the priesthood), about four thousand brothers (lay coadjutors). The only encouraging growth areas, a general phenomenon not confined to the Society, were India and Indonesia, where the proportion of scholastics to priests was about one to two. The most serious decline was in parts of western Europe where the proportion was one to twenty or even worse. In the United States, Fr William C. McInnes commented in November 1978 that 'vocation statistics are grim. 112 Jesuits entered this Fall – a decline of 15 per cent from last year and the second year in a row for a decrease. . . Not only is the pipeline thin; the wellhead pressure has dropped.' Fr Robert F. Hoey, writing in *New England Province Newsnotes* in February 1979, thought he could detect 'a possible glimmer of light at the end of the long tunnel of declining Jesuit membership. . . Since 1972 the rate has lessened steadily so that 1978 showed only 289 fewer Jesuits than did 1977 . . . The Society reached its peak number of 10,741 scholastics at the start of 1955, ten years before the total membership peak (36,038) . . . after 1969 the rate of decline among scholastics slowed so that in 1977 there were only 127 fewer than in 1976, and in 1978 there were 10 *more* than in 1977.'

These comments followed a semi-crisis Congregation of Procurators held in Rome from 27 September to 5 October 1978. By an almost unanimous vote it decided not to call a General Congregation ('Father General is healthy and vigorous in his leadership, hence there is no need to consider a replacement for him in the foreseeable future'). In a long allocution, based on a study of reports from the provinces, discussions with his general and regional assistants, and, finally, private conversations with each of the delegates, Arrupe presented his views on the implementation of the decrees of GC 32. There were, he said, 'lights and shadows'. Solidarity with the poor had claimed the lives of eleven Jesuits in recent years. Yet he felt that the 'faith/justice thrust' was still seen as the specialized concern of the exceptional few rather than as 'a dimension of *all* our apostolic endeavours'; and he criticized 'the engagement of some Jesuits with Marxism and their public declarations of support for its ideology' as 'unacceptable, damaging our credibility and apostolic effectiveness, causing scandal and confusion'.

Several delegates living under right-wing Latin American dictatorships took exception to these remarks; others, from eastern Europe, told of their experience under Marxist régimes. One, who had been allowed out of 'the church of silence' for the first time in thirty years, said that he was not permitted to say Mass publicly or to preach or catechize, and had never given a retreat ('with all its evident trials, I'll take capitalism to communism any time'). A delegate who had spent eight years in mainland China stated that one hundred and thirty Jesuits were still in prison there. Startled by the sudden death of Pope John Paul I after a thirty-four day pontificate, the Congregation was at least as disturbed by the news that there being only forty-six novice brothers, there was a strong possibility that this grade would eventually vanish, causing an 'irreparable loss'. Summing up, Arrupe stressed the need for 'tough spirituality' combined with 'discerning fervour'; warned that though the Society was learning to live with 'a measure of internal pluralism' it should beware of 'superficial peace where deeper division does not come to the surface'; and set as a top priority for superiors in a time of shrinking vocations and ageing manpower 'a realistic rethinking of our activities, while avoiding the discouragement this can generate'. More hopefully, he suggested that 'the Society is in the process of leaving behind the fluctuations that have shaken it (equally with the Church itself), and of making its way along the new road with a step that is each time firmer.'

Arrupe had never (like Paul VI in reference to laicized diocesan priests) referred to leavers as 'defectors' or compared them with Judas. He was more inclined to look for faults in the structure or management of the Society. But after the great shake-out of the early 1970s there were signs that 'wild' radicalism, like the membership decline, was lessening. The movement for charismatic renewal, characterized by an openness to the power of the Holy Spirit which many Jesuits have found to illuminate the teaching of the *Spiritual Exercises*, has been smoothly assimilated, with due Ignatian care that it should not result in 'too much

[299]

detachment from the world': there were even weekly charismatic prayer sessions at the Gregorian University. A Jesuit Spiritual Centre in the United States was distributing cassettes for meditation-with-music retreats ('when Ignatius first developed his method of contemplation in the *Spiritual Exercises* he had available only his unsupported creative imagination to prepare his consciousness for the prayer experience'). In November 1976 Fr Robert Drinan was re-elected Congressman for the State of Massachusetts; and in June 1977 Dr Henry Kissinger, former US Secretary of State, was appointed a professor in Georgetown University's faculty of international affairs.

There were eighty Jesuits in Paraguay and the reductions were being gradually restored, partly as tourist attractions, a development of which President Stroessner approved while harrying Jesuit priests as subversive agitators – a predicament not unlike that faced by their predecessors two hundred years ago. In Ireland Fr Donal O'Sullivan, for long Director of the Irish National Arts Council, was remembered for his keen encouragement of living painters, and Fr Michael MacGreil won a prize for promoting peace and understanding with a weighty sociological study, *Prejudice and Tolerance in Ireland*. Fr Gotzon Garate, a Basque Jesuit, was loaded with literary honours for his Basque-language novels, short stories and essays. Fr Felix Sanchez Vallejo's suggestion for restoring a form of Latin as an European lingua franca was widely reported. In Tokyo, journalists marvelled at the achievement of Fr Hermann Heuvers, who after half a century in the city, mostly as a professor at the Sophia University, died aged eighty-seven with twenty plays in Japanese to his credit.

Jesuits were still busy and eminent as astronomers. Fifteen thousand feet up in the Andes Fr Antonio Foldi celebrated his fiftieth anniversary as a Jesuit and many years of work at San Calixto observatory in La Paz, Bolivia, by offering Mass in the open air. In December 1977 Fr Maurice Burgaud died at Tananarive, Madagascar, where he had for decades directed the work of the observatory (he was ninety-two, having joined the Society in 1902 and begun his career at the Zakawei observatory in Shanghai). Fr Patrick Treanor gained an international reputation as director of the Vatican Observatory.

Two Jesuits, probably the first resident priests to serve a Catholic community there, were ministering in the Shetland Islands among North Sea oil workers. In Croatia, the scene of the Ustase massacres, Jesuits were running a 'pro-family apostolate' that was estimated to have halved the number of abortions. 'Charismatic workshops' were humming in North America and in the Caribbean. American Jesuits worried over their conscientization to an extent which may help to explain the growth of 'workshops' on alcoholism. There were reminders that 'lay persons are not to be regarded as mere recipients of clerical ministrations. The laity *are* the Church along with (and not under) religious, priests and bishops'; words of advice about 'the primacy of *experience* as a learning tool' and the 'complementarity that holds between experiential and book learning – something very Thomistic, of course, but frequently not all that apparent in our highly academicized Jesuit environments'; heavy hints that 'we should learn to read the Gospels *desde los pobres*, as our Latin American confrères would put it', since 'the poor, the beloved of God . . . are his preferred locus of revelation.' The Centre for Applied Research in the Apostolate (CARA) was preparing to co-operate with the recently-launched Jesuits Interested in Business and Management (JIBAM). Fr Berrigan was still active. He replied to queries with a duplicated postcard regretting that 'due to preoccupation with wars, prisons, teaching, writing and applied Christianity, he cannot enter into correspondence, whether on his writings, beliefs, past performance or debatable future.' Late in 1978 he was speaking at Marquette University on 'The Palestinian Question and Peace in the Middle East: A Third Way', and sandalled Fr Richard McSorley was parading in Washington with a placard reading 'Should We Teach Life and Love or Death and Hate?'

Pope-watching was almost as keen as in the troubled years of Ignatius and Lainez. Soon after the election of John Paul II *National Jesuit News* commented that 'the new Pope seems to have had limited personal contacts with Jesuits. He is a graduate of the Angelicum, the Dominican institution in Rome'; but against that, 'we're told that John Paul used to visit our scholasticate in Cracow quite frequently.' Attempts were being made to tighten discipline. In 1976 one of the General's Letters drew attention to GC 32's resolution asking for full observance of 'the laws concerning thinking with the Church that are peculiar to the Society . . . the Congregation urges all of Ours who are engaged in scientific work or in publication to be faithful to such a tradition even today.' Superiors were recommended to 'paternally yet firmly apply the norms in force . . . so that while protecting a rational and much desired liberty, those instances are avoided which stain fidelity to the Magisterium.' Censors were to vet all texts, whether for books or articles, and to keep an eye or ear on records, films, videotapes and cassettes. Superiors were also to ensure that 'even when provoked by calumnies, Ours do not use a style more recriminatory than befits a religious', and that in all subsequent editions, 'if changes have been made, one copy of works written by Ours is sent to Father General.'

In August 1977 Fr W. F. Maher, the English provincial, wrote to All Houses on the subject of obedience, pointing out that 'two things seem clear in St Ignatius' outlook: first, that representation [criticism of an order] should be made as a result of prayer and thought which starts by seeking to defend the superior's decision; and secondly that it is made by personal approach to superiors without attempting to pressurize them . . . The procedure to be adopted is clearly described in GC 31 (D 17 n. 10) which ends with the phrase "but a man who, time after time, is unable to obey with a good conscience, should take thought regarding some other path of life in which he can serve God with greater tranquillity".'

Perhaps in the next ten years the Society's membership will increase and the Dutch joke – 'Would the last man to leave kindly switch off the electricity?' – be out of date. Perhaps the exciting jostle to rebuild from the base upwards has died down and the Society is now again more an institution than a movement. But that does not necessarily mean that a Jesuit's life is uneventful. Arrupe is fond of saying that 'the Lord has perhaps never been so close to us because never before have we been so insecure.' This is no exaggeration, particularly in El Salvador; in 1976 there were five bombings on the campus of the Jesuit-founded university, in 1977 three Jesuits were expelled and the remaining forty-seven ordered to leave by a certain date under threat of being shot on sight. In Rhodesia two more Jesuits were killed in 1978. André Gelinas, a Canadian Jesuit, emerged from Vietnam, where he had toiled for nineteen years, in mid-1976 to write one of the most vivid accounts of life under the Communist régime ('entire families killed themselves . . . Some Vietnamese asked me whether it was a mortal sin to commit suicide'). Yet he refused to be entirely pessimistic ('there is something to be said for the new spirit of solidarity, so alien to the frantic individuality which is one of the faults of our Western civilization'). The efforts of Fr Michael Hurley and his Irish School of Ecumenics at Milltown Park, Dublin, with conferences attended by Protestants, Russian Orthodox delegates and progressive lay people, roused the fury of the Rev. Ian Paisley, a Protestant demagogue who also objected to Fr Hurley teaching Protestant seminarians.

In spite of the trials and tribulations of recent years – the invitation, announced in March 1979, to return to China after thirty years of exile to open a medical school in Shanghai was a great fillip – Jesuit *esprit de corps* is still remarkably strong and most ex-Jesuits seem to remain well-disposed to the Society. Obituaries in Jesuit magazines are often stringently objective as well as moving. Of one martyred missionary a superior who had known him well wrote that 'all good qualities have their opposite defects . . . X was a deeply religious priest and dedicated to his work . . . but seemed to do little reading of a general nature and this made it difficult for him to join in lighter conversation. He had a sense of humour, but even that sometimes went a little awry.' Of another, an Irishman, a friend recalled that 'he must at times have found life with the Saxons of us very difficult. He never showed it. But perhaps a record of rebel songs of the IRA which we found in his room and which he had never revealed to us gives a glimpse of the sort of difficulty he had . . . His great question was: "What is your philosophy for a happy life?" This was simply the excuse to tell you his own, and needless to say we thought it a little quaint and medieval. "The secret of a happy life is to have a noble cause to fight for."'

Most Jesuits are struggling manfully to avoid the stagnation of which Fr Tyrrell complained, and it would be hard to disagree with the rest of his verdict: 'I do not see in the Society of Jesus a monstrous and deliberate conspiracy against liberty and progress . . . I see in it an institution good in its origin; beneficent in large tracts of its history; serviceable still in many of its ways; well-meaning to a great extent.' An English Jesuit who dropped dead at ninety while out on his daily walk had accepted a switch from thirty years of teaching to parish work and then to administration with the remark that 'if you are a Jesuit and you are given a job to do, you just get on with it. If you are obeying orders you presume that Divine Providence has something to do with it.' That kind of dogged resilience is still a notable Jesuit quality. A young American who had been accepted for 'regency' in India or Spanish Honduras, but found the way blocked by political emergencies, was sent instead to Tanzania. There he took charge of twenty orphan boys, taught religion in five government schools, and helped in a village settlement for old, destitute lepers. 'It is not merely out of a sense of their need but also of *our* need that I think a contemporary mission must spring,' he wrote. 'Perhaps we might better speak of the universal need of the Church for faith and justice. And,' he added, 'what agent is more universal, more international in its character, or more adaptable than our Society?'

Appendices

LIST OF THE GENERALS AND GENERAL CONGREGATIONS

1. Ignatius of Loyola, Apr 19, 1541 – July 31, 1556
2. Diego Lainez, July 2, 1558 – Jan 19, 1565
3. Francis Borgia, July 2, 1565 – Oct 1, 1572
4. Everard Mercurian, Apr 23, 1573 – Aug 1, 1580
5. Claudio Aquaviva, Feb 19, 1581 – Jan 31, 1615
6. Muzio Vitelleschi, Nov 15, 1615 – Feb 9, 1645
7. Vincenzo Carafa, Jan 7, 1646 – June 8, 1649
8. Francesco Piccolomini, Dec 21, 1649 – June 17, 1651
9. Luigi Gottifredi, Jan 21, 1652 – March 12, 1652
10. Goswin Nickel, Mar 17, 1652 – July 31, 1664
11. Giovanni Paolo Oliva, Vicar June 7, 1661
    General, July 31, 1664 – Nov 26, 1681
12. Charles de Noyelle, July 5, 1682 – Dec 12, 1686
13. Tirso González, July 6, 1687 – Oct 27, 1705
14. Michelangelo Tamburini, Jan 31, 1706 – Feb 28, 1730
15. Frantisek Retz, Nov 30, 1730 – Nov 19, 1750
16. Ignazio Visconti, July 4, 1751 – May 4, 1755
17. Luigi Centurione, Nov 30, 1755 – Oct 2, 1757
18. Lorenzo Ricci, May 21, 1758 – Aug 16, 1773
19. Tadeusz Brzozowski, Aug 7, 1814 – Feb 5, 1820
20. Luigi Fortis, Oct 18, 1820 – Jan 27, 1829
21. Jan Roothaan, July 9, 1829 – May 8, 1853
22. Pieter Beckx, July 2, 1853 – March 4, 1887
23. Anton Anderledy, Vicar Sept 24, 1883
    General March 4, 1887 – Jan 18, 1892
24. Luis Martín, Oct 2, 1892 – April 18, 1906
25. Franz Wernz, Sept 8, 1906 – Aug 19, 1914
26. Wlodmir Ledochowski, Feb 11, 1915 – Dec 13, 1942
27. John Baptist Janssens, Sept 15, 1946 – Oct 5, 1964
28. Pedro Arrupe, May 22, 1965

1. June 19-Sept 10, 1558
2. June 21 – Sept 3, 1565
3. Apr 12 – June 16, 1573
4. Feb 7 – Apr 22, 1581
5. Nov 3, 1593 – Jan 18, 1594

6. Feb 21 – March 29, 1608
7. Nov 5, 1615 – Jan 26, 1616
8. Nov 21, 1645 – Apr 14, 1646
9. Dec 13, 1649 – Feb 23, 1650
10. Jan 7 – Mar 20, 1652
11. May 9 – July 27, 1661
12. June 22 – Sept 6, 1682
13. June 22 – Sept 7, 1687
14. Nov 19, 1696 – Jan 16, 1697
15. Jan 20 – Apr 3, 1706
16. Nov. 19, 1730 – Feb 13, 1731
17. June 22 – Sept 5, 1751
18. Nov 18, 1755 – Jan 28, 1756
19. May 9 – June 18, 1758
20. Oct 9 – Dec 10, 1820
21. June 30 – Aug 17, 1829
22. June 22 – Aug 31, 1853
23. Sept 16 – Oct 23, 1883
24. Sept 24 – Dec 5, 1892
25. Sept 1 – Oct 18, 1906
26. Feb 2 – Mar 18, 1915
27. Sept 8 – Dec 21, 1923
28. Mar 12 – May 9, 1938
29. Sept 6 – Oct 23, 1946
30. Sept 6 – Nov 11, 1957
31. May 7 – July 15, 1965
    Sept 8 – Nov 17, 1966
32. Dec 2, 1974 – March 7, 1975

COMMON WORDS USED IN A PECULIAR SENSE WITH REFERENCE TO THE JESUITS

Annual Letters	A compilation made every year from reports sent in by local Superiors and together forming a general account of the work of a Province.
Assistancy	A grouping of Jesuit Provinces usually by national or geographical boundaries.
Assistant	Adviser to the Jesuit General on the affairs of the provinces making up an Assistancy.
Brother	A Jesuit not ordained, holding an administrative post or exercising a craft or peculiar skill, e.g. architect, infirmarian, military adviser.
Province	An administrative unit of the Jesuit Order determined normally by geographical or national factors.
Provincial	Priest appointed to take charge of a Province for a period of three to six years.
Consultation	A meeting of the Provincial with his advisers.
Consultor	One of four advisers of the Provincial who meet in conference once a month.

[305]

General	The head of the Society of Jesus elected for life by a General Congregation.
Novice	A candidate for admission to the Order.
Novitiate	House where the novices are trained.
Procurator	A delegate chosen by the Provincial Congregation to conduct the affairs of the Province in Europe or to represent its interests at a General Congregation.
Rector	Priest in charge of a larger Jesuit establishment.
Scholastic	A Jesuit student for the priesthood.
Visitation	Inspection carried out by a Provincial or a Visitor.
Visitor	A priest appointed to visit a Province and report on its affairs, always with specified terms of reference and authority.

LIST OF POPES

Clement VII, 1523-1534
Paul III, 1534-1549
Julius III, 1550-1555
Marcellus II, 1555
Paul IV, 1555-1559
Pius IV, 1559-1565
St Pius V, 1566-1572
Gregory XIII, 1572-1585
Sixtus V, 1585-1590
Urban VII, 1590
Gregory XIV, 1590-1591
Innocent IX, 1591
Clement VIII, 1592-1605
Leo XI, 1605
Paul V, 1605-1621
Gregory XV, 1621-1623
Urban VIII, 1623-1644
Innocent X, 1644-1655
Alexander VII, 1655-1667
Clement IX, 1667-1669
Clement X, 1670-1676
Blessed Innocent XI, 1676-1689
Alexander VIII, 1689-1691

Innocent XII, 1691-1700
Clement XI, 1700-1721
Innocent XIII, 1721-1724
Benedict XIII, 1724-1730
Clement XII, 1730-1740
Benedict XIV, 1740-1758
Clement XIII, 1758-1769
Clement XIV, 1769-1774
Pius VI, 1776-1799
Pius VII, 1800-1823
Leo XII, 1823-1829
Pius VIII, 1829-1830
Gregory XVI, 1831-1846
Pius IX, 1846-1878
Leo XIII, 1878-1903
St Pius X, 1903-1914
Benedict XV, 1914-1922
Pius XI, 1922-1939
Pius XII, 1939-1958
John XXIII, 1958-1963
Paul VI, 1963-1978
John Paul I, 1978
John Paul II, 1978-

Bibliography

note: unless otherwise indicated, all books were published in London

ARIES, Philippe, *Centuries of Childhood* (Jonathan Cape, 1962). Origins and development, to late 18th century, of the Jesuit educational system, set in a wide context.

ASHLEY, Maurice, *The Golden Century: Europe 1598-1715* (Weidenfeld and Nicolson, 1969).

ATKINSON, William C., *A History of Spain and Portugal* (Pelican, 1960).

ATTWATER, Donald, *The Penguin Dictionary of Saints* (1970).

AVELING, J. C. H., *The Handle and the Axe: Catholic Recusants in England from Reformation to Emancipation* (Blond and Briggs, 1976).

BANGERT, William V., SJ, *A History of the Society of Jesus* (Institute of Jesuit Sources, St Louis, 1972).

BARBER, Richard, *The Knight and Chivalry* (Longman, 1970).

BASSET, Bernard, SJ, *The English Jesuits from Campion to Martindale* (Burns and Oates, 1967).

BEA, Augustin, Cardinal, SJ, *The Church and the Jewish People* (Geoffrey Chapman, 1966). A commentary on the Second Vatican Council's Declaration on the Relation of the Church to Non-Christian Religions.

BEDANDA, René, *Les armes de l'Esprit: Témoignage Chrétien 1941-1944* (Paris, Editions Ouvrières, 1977).

BENSON, R. H., *The Light Invisible* (Hutchinson, n.d. c. 1912). For some of the mystic tales – especially 'The Green Robe' and 'In the Convent Chapel' – that influenced Teilhard de Chardin; *Come Rack! Come Rope!* (Hutchinson, 1912).

BERGONZI, Bernard, *Gerard Manley Hopkins* (Macmillan, 1977).

BERRIGAN, Daniel, SJ, *America Is Hard to Find* (SPCK, 1973). A selection of essays, poems and letters from the late 1960s and early 1970s.

BOXER, C. R., *The Christian Century in Japan, 1549-1640* (Cambridge University Press and University of California Press, 1951); *Race Relations in the Portuguese Empire, 1415-1825* (Oxford, 1963); *The Golden Age of Brazil, 1695-1750* (University of California, 1962); *The Portuguese Seaborne Empire, 1418-1825* (Pelican, 1973).

BOYD BARRETT, Edward, *The Jesuit Enigma* (Jonathan Cape, 1927); *Ex-Jesuit* (Geoffrey Bles, 1931).

BRAILSFORD, H. N., *Voltaire* (Thornton Butterworth, Home University Library, 1935).

BRENAN, Gerald, *The Spanish Labyrinth* (Cambridge University Press, 1943); *The Literature of the Spanish People* (Cambridge University Press, 1951); *St John of the Cross* (Cambridge University Press, 1973).

BRODRICK, James, SJ, *Blessed Robert Bellarmine* (Burns Oates and Washbourne, 1928); *St*

Peter Canisius (Sheed and Ward, 1935); *The Economic Morals of the Jesuits* (Oxford, 1934); *The Origin of the Jesuits* (Longmans Green, 1940); *The Progress of the Jesuits* (Longmans Green, 1946); *St Francis Xavier* (Burns Oates, 1962).

BURCKHARDT, Jacob, *The Civilization of the Renaissance in Italy* (Phaidon Press, 1944).

BURTON, Robert, *The Anatomy of Melancholy* (New York, Tudor Publishing Co., 1948).

CALDERON, Pedro de la Barca, *Six Plays* (J. M. Dent, Everyman series, 1948).

CAMPBELL, T. J., SJ, *The Jesuits, 1534-1921* (Encyclopaedia Press, 1921).

CARAMAN, Philip, SJ (transl.), *The Hunted Priest: Autobiography of John Gerard*, introduction by Graham Greene (Longmans Green, 1951); *Henry Garnet and the Gunpowder Plot* (Longmans, 1964); (ed.) *The Years of Siege: Catholic Life from James I to Cromwell* (Longmans, 1966), an anthology from contemporary sources; *C. C. Martindale: A Biography* (Longmans, 1967); *The Lost Paradise: an Account of the Jesuits in Paraguay, 1607-1768* (Sidgwick and Jackson, 1975).

CARR, Raymond, *Spain: 1808-1939* (Oxford, 1966).

CIANO, Count Galeazzo, *Diary, 1937-1938* (Methuen, 1952). For his dealings with Fr Tacchi-Venturi, SJ.

CISZEK, Walter, SJ, *With God in Russia* (Peter Davies, 1965). An account of the ordeal of a Jesuit, trained at the Russicum and sent to Poland as a parish priest in 1939, who was swept into Russia in 1940 and presumed dead – but emerged in 1963, one of two U.S. citizens exchanged for two Russian agents.

CLISSOLD, Stephen, *Spain* (Thames and Hudson, 1969); *Latin America* (Pall Mall Press, 1972).

COBBAN, Alfred, chapter 5 – The Enlightenment – in Vol. 7 of the *New Cambridge Modern History*.

COPLESTON, Frederick, SJ, *A History of Philosophy*, Vols. 3 and 4 (Burns Oates and Washbourne, 1953, 1958) and Vol. 9 (Search Press, 1975).

CORNEILLE, Pierre, *The Cid and Other Plays* (Penguin Classics, 1975). Introduction by John Cairncross.

CRONIN, Vincent, *The Wise Man from the West* (Rupert Hart-Davis, 1955), a biography of Matteo Ricci; *A Pearl to India: The Life of Robert de Nobili* (Hart-Davis, 1959).

DANIEL-ROPS, Henri, *A History of the Church of Christ*, Vols. 5-9 (J. M. Dent, 1962-66).

DELPECH, Jacques, *The Oppression of Protestants in Spain* (Boston, Beacon Press, 1955). Reports 'the conversion of the Jesuit scholar Don Luis Padrosa, director of the Loyola Institute in Barcelona. On 18 February, 1951 he announced his conversion to Protestantism and the next day left Spain for South America . . . His book *Why Did I Leave the Church of Rome?* is officially forbidden to circulate in Spain.'

DICKENS, Charles, *Pictures from Italy* (Chapman and Hall, 1907).

DICKINSON, Goldsworthy Lowes, *Letters from John Chinaman and Other Essays* (Allen and Unwin, 1946). Essay on 'Religion: a Criticism and a Forecast', written in 1903, for his comments on Jesuit education and on St Ignatius as 'the greatest ecclesiastical genius the world has ever seen'.

DOSTOYEVSKY, Fyodor, *The Brothers Karamazov* (Penguin Classics, 1976). In the Legend of the Grand (Jesuit) Inquisitor upbraiding a silent Christ for daring to return to earth and perhaps destroy the illusions of millions who are comforted by the gospel of St Ignatius, Ivan Karamazov argues that the Jesuits have taken upon themselves 'the curse of the knowledge of good and evil' so that many, instead of a minority of the elect, may at least *feel* that they are saved.

DOYLE, Sir Arthur Conan, *Memories and Adventures* (Hodder and Stoughton, 1924).

EVENNETT, H. Outram, *The Spirit of the Counter-Reformation*, (Cambridge University Press, 1958).

FALCONI, Carlo, *The Silence of Pius XII* (Faber and Faber, 1970).

FARRELL, Alan P., SJ, *The Jesuit Code of Liberal Education: the Development and Scope of the Ratio Studiorum* (Milwaukee, Bruce Publishing Co., 1938).

FISCHER, Louis, *The Soviets in World Affairs* (Cape, 1930). Vol. 2 for a section on Vatican-Kremlin negotiations in the 1920s, including the missions of Edmund Walsh and Michel d'Herbigny.

FOLEY, Henry, SJ, (ed.) *Records of the English Province of the Society of Jesus* (Burns and Oates, 1877-83).

FOSS, Michael, *The Founding of the Jesuits* (Hamish Hamilton, 1969).

FOSTER, John, *The First Advance* (Church History, Vol. I, A.D. 29-500: SPCK, 1972).

FREMANTLE, Anne, (ed.): *The Papal Encyclicals in Their Historical Context* (New York, Mentor Books, 1956); *The Social Teachings of the Church* (New York, Mentor Books, 1963).

FÜLÖP-MILLER, René, *The Power and Secret of the Jesuits* (Putnam, 1930).

GALLAHUE, John, *The Jesuit* (Heinemann, 1973).

GALLOP, Rodney, *A Book of the Basques* (Macmillan, 1930).

GANSS, George E., SJ (ed.), *The Constitutions of the Society of Jesus* (Institute of Jesuit Sources, St Louis, 1970). With introduction and detailed commentary.

GARDAVSKY, Vitezslav, *God is not yet Dead* (Penguin, 1973). A Czech philosopher who took part in the Christian-Marxist 'dialogues' of the 1960s, sets out his conclusions, with interesting comments on some Jesuit theologians (Teilhard de Chardin, Karl Rahner, Desqueyrat).

GOOCH, G. P., and Laski, H. J., *English Democratic Ideas in the 17th Century* (Cambridge University Press, 1967). The section on 'The Political Ideas of the Ultramontanes' comments on Lainez, Mariana and Jesuit theories of popular sovereignty ('the pages of the Ultramontanes were continually searched by those eager to discredit the positions of their Puritan opponents by exhibiting their similarity to the contentions of the hated Jesuits').

GOURMONT, Rémy de, *The Velvet Path* and *Dialogues of Amateurs*, two essays in a selection edited by Richard Aldington (Heinemann, 1944).

GRAHAM, R. B., Cunninghame, *Vanished Arcadia* (Heinemann, 1901).

GRAY, Francine du Plessix, *Divine Disobedience: Profiles in Catholic Radicalism* (Hamish Hamilton, 1970). Studies in depth of the Berrigan brothers and Ivan Illich.

GREAVES, R. W., ch. 6 – 'Religion' – in Vol. 7 of the *New Cambridge Modern History*.

GRIESINGER, Theodor, *The Jesuits* (W. H. Allen, 1885).

GUIBERT, Joseph de, SJ, *The Jesuits: their Spiritual Doctrine and Practice* (Institute of Jesuit Sources, St Louis/Loyola University Press, Chicago, 1964).

GUNTHER, John, *Inside Europe Today* (Hamish Hamilton, 1961). Comments on the Spanish Jesuits' 'enormous holdings of land and interlocking ownerships of mines, industries, shipping, utilities and transportation'.

HAPPOLD, F. C., *Mysticism: a Study and an Anthology* (Pelican, 1970).

HARING, C. H., *The Spanish Empire in America* (Oxford University Press, 1947).

HASTINGS, Macdonald, *Jesuit Child* (Michael Joseph, 1971).

HEARSEY, John, *Voltaire* (Constable, 1976).

HEBBLETHWAITE, Peter, *The Runaway Church* (Collins, 1975). A summary of Vatican II and its aftermath.

HEER, Friedrich, *The Medieval World, 1100-1350* (Weidenfeld and Nicolson, 1962).

HEMMING, John, *Red Gold: the Conquest of the Brazilian Indians* (Macmillan, 1978).

HERRING, Hubert, *A History of Latin America* (Cape, 1968).
HOBBES, Thomas, *Leviathan* (Oxford University Press, 1943). Published in 1651, Hobbes's great work identified Puritans and Jesuits as the main threats to political stability.
HOCHHUTH, Rolf, *The Representative* (Penguin, 1969). The 'Historical Sidelights' postscript comments in some detail on Pius XII's Jesuit entourage.
HOCHWÄLDER, Fritz, *The Strong Are Lonely* (Plays of the Year, 1956). A melodramatic version of the last days of the Jesuits in Paraguay.
HOENSBROECH, Count Paul von, *Fourteen Years a Jesuit: A Record of Personal Experience and a Criticism* (2 Vols., Cassell, 1911).
HOLLIS, Christopher, *St Ignatius* (Sheed and Ward, 1931); *Along the Road to Frome* (Harrap, 1958) – teaching at Stonyhurst, 1925-35, with some good anecdotes; *A History of the Jesuits* (Weidenfeld and Nicolson, 1968).
HOPKINS, Gerard Manley, *Poems and Prose* (ed. W. H. Gardner, Penguin, 1960).
HUGHES, Philip, *Rome and the Counter-Reformation in England* (Burns and Oates, 1944).
HUGHES, T., *A History of the Society of Jesus in North America, 1580-1773* (4 Vols., Longmans, 1907-17).
HUIZINGA, J., *The Waning of the Middle Ages* (Penguin, 1955).
HURN, David Abner, *Archbishop Roberts, SJ* (Darton, Longman and Todd, 1966).
HUXLEY, Aldous, essay 'Meditation on El Greco' in *Music at Night* (Chatto and Windus, 1931); *Grey Eminence: a Study in Religion and Politics* (Chatto and Windus, 1941); *The Devils of Loudon* (Chatto and Windus, 1952).
HYDE, Douglas, *I Believed: the Autobiography of a Former British Communist* (Heinemann, 1950). Tells how he was received into the Church by Fr Joseph Corr, SJ, in 1948, after attending a 'Sword of the Spirit' meeting at Wimbledon. 'On the platform were two Jesuits . . . I thought that all priests, nuns and monks were immoral, all Jesuits sinister and crooked . . . Fr Francis Devas . . . told me with a twinkle in his eye that if one could not be a good Catholic, one could at least be a bad one, the Church was not full of saints . . . the man who had seemed so unworldly on the platform was displaying a shrewd (Jesuitical if you like, in the best sense of the word) understanding of human types.' Later, Hyde became a regular contributor to *The Month*, the English Jesuit periodical.
JAMES, William, *The Varieties of Religious Experience* (Fontana Books, 1963).
JANSSEN, Johannes, *A History of the German People at the Close of the Middle Ages* (Kegan Paul, Trench and Trübner, 1896-1910).
JELLINEK, Frank, *The Civil War in Spain* (Gollancz, 1938).
JOHNSON, Paul, *A History of Christianity* (Weidenfeld and Nicolson, 1976). 'It was,' writes Johnson, 'characteristic of the American State, first to reject espionage on moral grounds, then to undertake it through the Central Intelligence Agency, a moralistic institution much more like the Society of Jesus than its Soviet equivalent.'
JOYCE, James, *A Portrait of the Artist as a Young Man* (Penguin Modern Classics, 1971).
KAMEN, Henry, *The Spanish Inquisition* (Weidenfeld and Nicolson, 1965).
KEMPIS, Thomas à, *The Imitation of Christ* (Fontana Books, 1974).
KENTON, Edna, (ed.), *Black Gown and Redskins: the Adventures and Travels of the Early Jesuit Missionaries in North America, 1610-1791* (Longmans Green, 1956).
KITCHEN, Paddy, *Gerard Manley Hopkins* (Hamish Hamilton, 1978).
LANDOR, Walter Savage, *Imaginary Conversations* (Walter Scott, 1886).
LASKI, H. J., *The Rise of European Liberalism* (Allen and Unwin, 1936).
LATOURETTE, Kenneth, *A History of the Expansion of Christianity*, Vol. 3, *Three Centuries of Advance, 1500-1800* (Eyre and Spottiswoode, 1940).

LESOURD, Paul, *Entre Rome et Moscou: Jésuite Clandestin, Mgr d'Herbigny* (Paris, Lethielleux, 1978).

LIPPERT, Peter, SJ, *The Jesuits* (New York, Herder and Herder, 1956). With preface by Fr Martindale.

LOYOLA, Ignatius, *The Spiritual Exercises*, translated and with intro. by Fr Thomas Corbishley, SJ (Anthony Clarke, 1973).

LUKE, Jemima, *The Female Jesuit: or the Spy in the Family. A True Narrative of Recent Intrigues in a Protestant Household* (Partridge and Oakey, 1851).

MACAULAY, Thomas Babington, review of Leopold Ranke's history of the Popes of Rome (1840) in Vol. 2 of *Critical and Historical Essays* (J. M. Dent/Everyman, 1931).

MACLAGAN, Sir Edward, *The Jesuits and the Great Mogul* (Burns, Oates and Washbourne, 1932).

MARTINDALE, C. C., SJ, *The Vocation of Aloysius Gonzaga* (Sheed and Ward, 1927).

MAUGHAM, W. Somerset, *Don Fernando* (Heinemann, 1935).

McCABE, S. J., *Twelve Years in a Monastery* (Smith, Elder, 1897); *A Candid History of the Jesuits* (Eveleigh Nash, 1913).

McKENDRICK, Melveena, *A Concise History of Spain* (Cassell, 1972).

MOLIERE, *Five Plays* (Penguin Classics, 1953), with intro. by John Wood.

MOORHOUSE, Geoffrey, *Against All Reason* (Weidenfeld and Nicolson, 1969).

MÖRNER, Magnus, (ed.), *The Expulsion of the Jesuits from Latin America* (New York, Knopf, Borzoi Books, 1965). A useful introduction sets the scene for extracts from a variety of authors.

NEALE, J. E., *Queen Elizabeth* (Cape, 1934).

NEILL, Bishop Stephen, *A History of Christian Missions* (1964, Vol. 6 of the Pelican History of the Church).

NEWMAN, John Henry, Cardinal, *Apologia Pro Vita Sua* (Sheed and Ward, 1946). Newman writes of 'the effect produced on me by studying the Exercises of St Ignatius . . . The command practically enforced was "My son, give Me thy heart."' He rates casuistry as 'a noble science'; reasons that moral theologians (notably St Alphonsus Liguori, following the Jesuits) are 'lax for the sake of others, not for themselves . . . knowing well that if they are as strict as they would wish to be, they shall be able to do nothing at all with the run of men.'

NICOLINI, G. B., *A History of the Jesuits: Their Origin, Progress, Doctrines and Designs* (Bohm, 1854).

ORWELL, George, *Collected Essays, Journalism and Letters*, Vol. I (Penguin, 1975). Reviewing Karl Adam's *The Spirit of Catholicism* (1932), Orwell remarked that 'if ever a word is raised against Rome, it is only some absurd tale of Jesuit intrigues or babies' skeletons dug up from the floors of nunneries'; and in 1938, reviewing Jellinek's *The Civil War in Spain*, he wrote that 'the world organization of the Jesuits only numbers about 22,000 people. For sheer efficiency they must surely have all the political parties beaten hollow!'

PADBERG, John W., SJ, Colleges in Controversy: *Jesuit Schools in France from Revival to Suppression, 1815-1880* (Harvard University Press, 1969).

PALLENBERG, Corrado, *The Vatican from Within* (Harrap, 1961), with a chapter on the Jesuits; *Vatican Finances* (Peter Owen, 1971).

PARKMAN, Francis, *The Jesuits in North America in the 17th Century* (Macmillan, 1899).

PASCAL, Blaise, *The Provincial Letters* (Penguin Classics, 1967).

PEARSON, Hesketh, *Conan Doyle* (Methuen, 1943). Summarizes Doyle's Jesuit schooling.

PEERS, E. Allison, *Spain, the Church and the Orders* (Burns, Oates, 1939). Some details of Jesuit trials and tribulations during the civil war.

PETRE, Maud D., *The Life of George Tyrrell* (2 Vols., Arnold, 1912).

PEYREFITTE, Roger, *The Keys of St Peter* (Secker and Warburg, 1957); *Special Friendships* (Secker and Warburg, 1958); *The Knights of Malta* (Secker and Warburg, 1960); *The Jews* (Secker and Warburg, 1967). In the latter, Peyrefitte claims that Ignatius Loyola, as well as Lainez, Polanco, Salmeron and Francis Borgia, was of Jewish descent.

PRADO, C., *The Colonial Background of Modern Brazil* (Columbia University Press, 1973).

PURDIE, Edna, article on Jesuit Drama in *The Oxford Companion to the Theatre* (Oxford University Press, 1967).

RACINE, Jean, *Andromache and Other Plays* (Penguin Classics, 1967). Introduction by John Cairncross.

RAHNER, Hugo, SJ, (with photographer Leonard von Matt), *St Ignatius of Loyola: a Pictorial Biography* (Longmans Green, 1956); *St Ignatius Loyola: Letters to Women, 1524-1556* (Herder/Nelson, 1960).

RAHNER, Karl, SJ, *Spiritual Exercises* (Sheed and Ward, 1963); 'The Exercises,' writes Rahner, 'are not a theological system, but essentially an election or choice . . . of the specific way in which Christianity can become a living reality in us.' (With Paul Imhof, SJ), *Ignatius of Loyola* (Collins, 1979).

RANKE, Leopold von, *A History of the Popes of Rome during the 16th and 17th Centuries* (John Murray, 1841).

READ, Herbert, *A Coat of Many Colours* (Routledge, 1945). Essay on Gerard Manley Hopkins.

RIDLEY, F. A., *The Jesuits* (Secker and Warburg, 1938).

RIEMER, George, *The New Jesuits* (Boston, Little, Brown, 1971).

ROBERTS, Archbishop, SJ, *Black Popes: The Use and Abuse of Authority* (Longmans Green, 1954).

ROBERTSON, Rev. Alexander, DD, *The Papal Conquest: Italy's Warning – Wake up, John Bull!* (Marshall, Morgan and Scott, 1909).

ROBERTSON, J. M., *A Short History of Christianity* (Watts and Co., 1931). Liberal M.P., free-thinker, and associate of Charles Bradlaugh, Robertson describes the Jesuits as 'striving by every available means, fair and foul, for the Church's supremacy . . . Jesuit education, where it became at all scientific, armed the born sceptics; and when it was limited to *belles lettres* it failed in the long run to make either earnest believers or able disputants.'

ROWSE, A. L., *The England of Elizabeth* (Macmillan, 1950); *The Elizabethan Renaissance* (Macmillan, 1972).

RUSSELL, P. E., (ed.) *A Companion to Spanish Studies* (Methuen, 1973).

SAINT-SIMON, Duc de, *Memoirs*, ed. W. H. Lewis (Batsford, 1964).

SARGANT, William, *Battle for the Mind: A Physiology of Conversion and Brain-Washing* (Heinemann, 1957). The Rev. George Salmon (1859) on Ignatius Loyola as 'the person, perhaps, who best understood the art of exciting religious emotion and reduced it to a regular system.'

SEDGWICK, Henry D., *Ignatius Loyola: an Attempt at an Impartial Biography* (Macmillan, 1923).

SERENY, Gitta, *Into That Darkness* (André Deutsch, 1974).

SEWARD, Desmond, *The Monks of War: the Military Religious Orders* (Eyre Methuen, 1974).

SMITH, Warren Sylvester, *The London Heretics, 1870-1914* (Constable, 1967). Chapter on George Tyrrell and Catholic Modernism.

STARK, Werner, SJ, *The Sociology of Religion*, Vol. 3, *The Universal Church* (Routledge and Kegan Paul, 1967).

STEENACKERS, F. F., *Histoire des Ordres de Chevalerie* (Paris, Lacroix, 1867). Suggests that the Knights Templars 'were the Jesuits of their time, who made up in military power what they lacked in subtlety'.

TAUNTON, Ethelred L., *A History of the Jesuits in England, 1580-1773* (Methuen, 1901).

TAYLOR, Isaac, *Loyola and Jesuitism in its Rudiments* (Longman, 1849).

TAYLOR, Jeremy, *Ductor Dubitantium* (Longman, 1852).

TEILHARD DE CHARDIN, Pierre, *The Prayer of the Universe*, a selection from *Writings in Time of War* (Fontana Books, 1973); *The Future of Man* (Fontana, 1974).

THOMAS, Hugh, *The Spanish Civil War* (Penguin, 1968).

THOMPSON, Francis, *St Ignatius Loyola* (Burns and Oates, paperback, 1962).

TOWERS, Bernard, *Teilhard de Chardin* (Lutterworth Press, 1972).

TREVOR-ROPER, H. R., *Religion, the Reformation and Social Change* (Macmillan, 1967); *Princes and Artists: Patronage and Ideology at Four Habsburg Courts, 1517-1633* (Thames and Hudson, 1976).

VAN DYKE, Paul, *Ignatius Loyola, the Founder of the Jesuits* (New York, Scribners, 1926).

VOLTAIRE, *Candide* (Penguin Classics, 1975).

WALL, Bernard, *Report on the Vatican* (Weidenfeld and Nicolson, 1956).

WAUGH, Evelyn, *Vile Bodies* (Chapman and Hall, 1930); *Edmund Campion* (Penguin, 1953); *Diaries*, ed. by Michael Davie (Weidenfeld and Nicolson, 1976).

WILLS, Garry, *Bare Ruined Choirs* (New York, Doubleday, 1972). Chapters on Teilhard and Daniel Berrigan.

WITTKOWER, R., and Jaffé, I., *Baroque Art: The Jesuit Contribution* (New York, Fordham University, 1972).

WOLFF, Robert Lee, *Gains and Losses: Novels of Faith and Doubt in Victorian England* (John Murray, 1977).

Index

[314]